EDUCATIONAL COMPUTING

Learning with Tomorrow's Technologies

CLEBORNE D. MADDUX

University of Nevada, Reno

D. LaMONT JOHNSON

University of Nevada, Reno

JERRY W. WILLIS

Iowa State University

Allyn and Bacon

Boston ▪ London ▪ Toronto ▪ Sydney ▪ Tokyo ▪ Singapore

Series Editor: *Arnis E. Burvikovs*
Editorial Assistant: *Matthew Forster*
Senior Marketing Manager: *Brad Parkins*
Production Editor: *Christopher H. Rawlings*
Editorial-Production Service: *Omegatype Typography, Inc.*
Composition and Prepress Buyer: *Linda Cox*
Manufacturing Buyer: *Julie McNeill*
Cover Administrator: *Kristina Mose-Libon*
Electronic Composition: *Omegatype Typography, Inc.*

Library of Congress Cataloging-in-Publication Data

Maddux, Cleborne D.
    Educational computing : learning with tomorrow's technologies / Cleborne D. Maddux,
  D. LaMont Johnson, Jerry W. Willis.—3rd ed,
        p.   cm.
  Includes bibliographical references and index.
  ISBN 0-205-31842-8 (alk. paper)
      1. Computer-assisted instruction—United States.   I. Johnson, D. LaMont (Dee LaMont)
II. Willis, Jerry   III. Title.

LB1028.5 .M136 2001
371.33'4—dc21   00-048474

CONTENTS

CHAPTER FOUR

The Internet and the Web in Society and Education   73

PART III   INFUSING TYPE II USES OF COMPUTERS INTO EDUCATION

CHAPTER EIGHT

Integrating Information Technology into the Curriculum   177

CHAPTER NINE

Applications Software in the Classroom: Word Processing, Databases, and Spreadsheets   192

CHAPTER TEN

The Internet and the Web in the School Curriculum   221

CHAPTER ELEVEN

Multimedia and Hypermedia in Education   251

PART IV   LOOKING AHEAD

PREFACE

Educational Computing is a book about an exciting experiment in education. The experiment involves making computers and related information technology available to teachers and students in schools, and it is based on the idea that information technology can be used to improve teaching and learning.

NEW TO THIS EDITION

In this edition you will find an expanded emphasis on the Internet and World Wide Web. Two new chapters are devoted to this topic. One discusses the Internet and the Web in terms of their effect on society and education from a global perspective, while the other chapter discusses the Internet and Web from a school curriculum perspective. In addition to this expanded coverage in terms of content, the Internet and Web are referenced throughout the book. Pertinent websites are listed for nearly every topic and concept discussed.

This edition also places a greater emphasis on integrating information technology into the curriculum. A new chapter addressing this topic has been added and many case studies summarizing successful integration projects have been woven into other chapters.

We are enthusiastic about the potential of improving teaching and learning with information technology. It is this potential that makes the discipline of educational computing so exciting. If we are successful in using information technology to make available new and better ways of teaching and learning, all of us will have been responsible for furthering a relatively new discipline in education. Few professionals are fortunate enough to be at that pivotal place in history in which their actions determine the success or failure of a new discipline.

Today's educators are at such a pivotal point. In fact, we believe the future of educational computing depends primarily on the actions of those who will be practicing their profession during the next ten years. Professionals in training, like you, are exploring the vast potential of microcomputer technology and will be called on to lead the way in integrating computing and teaching. This book is intended to help prepare you to assume a leadership role in the new discipline of educational computing.

HOW THIS BOOK IS ORGANIZED

This book is organized into four parts. Part I is an introduction to educational computing. Chapter 1 addresses the role of computers in society at large and in schools in particular. Chapter 2 considers some of the trends and issues relating to using information technology in education. Chapter 3 reviews the history of computing and provides a primer of computing equipment. Chapter 4 introduces the Internet and World Wide Web and discusses how they affect society in general and schools in particular.

Part II presents theories and concepts that form the foundation for integrating information technology into teaching and learning. Chapter 5 describes and discusses a paradigm for thinking about educational computing—Type I and Type II uses of computers. Chapter 6 introduces cognitive theories as guides to using technology in the classroom. Chapter 7 discusses uses of information technology in education based on a constructivist theoretical model.

Part III addresses Type II educational applications, or those that make available new and better ways of teaching. Respectively, Chapters 8 through 13 address integrating information technology into the curriculum, applications software in the classroom, the Internet and the Web in the school curriculum, multimedia and hypermedia, problem-solving software, and evaluating software.

Part IV provides a brief look at trends for the future. Chapter 14 considers what the future might hold for the use of information technology in education.

ACKNOWLEDGMENTS

We would like to thank the following reviewers: Elizabeth Buchanan, University of Wisconsin—Milwaukee; Stephen Gance, University of Wisconsin—Madison; and Melissa M. Groves, University of Tennessee, Knoxville.

CHAPTER ONE

COMPUTERS IN SOCIETY AND IN SCHOOLS

Goal: To become aware of some of the problems and possibilities in educational computing.

KEY TERMS

culture (p. 8)

cultural lag (p. 9)

cultural momentum (p. 4)

e-commerce (p. 6)

hacking (p. 5)

Internet (p. 1)

spamming (p. 5)

World Wide Web (p. 1)

This chapter is about the role of computers in society and in schools. It discusses the phenomenal recent growth of the **Internet** and the **World Wide Web,** and how these developments have greatly reduced the possibility that computers would not be accepted in U.S. schools. It discusses bringing about educational change and how and why this sometimes works the way we plan and sometimes does not. Information about change that has been gleaned from anthropology—the study of humans and how they live—is included to explain why such sweeping changes have been possible and how future educational innovators can bring about further positive changes in education. The chapter considers the ways in which computers are being used in schools and why such applications have become widespread. Recommendations for computer uses are also included.

Computers have the potential to revolutionize teaching and learning. This potential exists for the same reason that they have already revolutionized many other aspects of modern living—because they are uniquely effective tools whose power is so flexible that it can be applied to an almost unlimited variety of problems associated with many human endeavors. Furthermore, education can profit from computing without suffering any of the negative side effects about which critics have warned, such as a mechanistic approach to schooling, an erosion of human interaction and peer relations, neglect of the affective domain, or decline in the importance of the teacher as mentor.

Still, there is no such thing as a free lunch, and the great power and flexibility of computing presents a number of problems. After all, the computer, like any tool, can be poorly used or misused. This is true for whatever problem domain computers are used, including teaching and learning. We emphasize, however, that even though this book addresses the potential problems of information technology in education, the authors are basically quite optimistic about the future role of computing in education. The purpose of this book is to help teachers—present and future—make wise decisions about computers and their uses and to maximize this exciting teaching and learning tool.

THE INTERNET AND THE WORLD WIDE WEB

This is the third edition of this book, and much has changed since the last edition went to press. By far the most significant change has been the staggering growth in size and popularity of the Internet and the World Wide Web. Indeed, the evolution of the Internet and the Web has been so important—not only for education, but also for the entire culture and for much of the global community—that this phenomenon may be remembered as the single most influential development of the second half of the twentieth century.

Growth of the Internet and the Web

Be that as it may, it would be hard to argue that the speed of growth in size and popularity of the Internet and the Web is anything but unparalleled in recorded history. It is hard to believe, but true, that when President Clinton took office in 1992, there were only 50 pages on the Web. Although estimates vary widely, Lawrence and Giles (1999) suggested that as of February of 1999, there were at least 800 million web pages containing more than 6 trillion characters. Just a year later, a joint study published by Inktomi and NEC Research in February of 2000 estimated that the Web had grown to one billion indexable pages (Sullivan, 2000), with at least 67,000 new sites being added each day. At one point, the Web was doubling in size every 43 days, and by early 2000, with the number of web pages in the neighborhood of one billion, the doubling rate was still less than one year.

Access to the Internet and the Web

Growth has also been phenomenal, as measured by the number of people with access to the Internet and the Web. *The Computer Industry Almanac* (Juliussen & Petska-Juliussen, 2000) sets the 1999 worldwide figure at nearly 260 million users, with 110 million in the United States. *The Almanac* goes on to note that by 1999, more than 10 percent of the populations of 25 countries were Internet users. They project 490 million worldwide users by the year 2002 (79.4 per 1,000 people) and 765 million users by year-end 2005 (118 per 1,000 people world-wide). NUA Limited (2000), in a slightly more recent study, estimated that by February of 2000, there were at least 275.5 million Internet users in the world, with more than 136 million users located in the United States and Canada.

One of the more remarkable statistics about the popularity of the Web was revealed in a 1995 study in which researchers found that in one 3-month period that year, people in the United States and Canada spent as much time surfing the Web as the total playback time of all rented videotapes in the two countries (The Madison Avenue Group, 2000). These researchers concluded that the Web is beginning to compete successfully with more traditional entertainment media such as television and movies.

Importance of the Internet and the Web

We began this section by noting that the establishment and growth in size and popularity of the Internet and the Web may become known as the most signifi-cant development of the second half of the twentieth century. However, because of the unprecedented growth outlined above, a reasonable case could be made that the Internet and the Web already represent the most important development in human communication in modern times!

That honor has traditionally been assigned to the invention of the printing press. However, in the case of the printing press, centuries passed before books were affordable and widely available for common people to purchase. Even then, publishing was so complex, so expensive, and required such complicated machin-ery and skills that only the largest corporations and a few governmental agencies were able to actually produce and distribute books.

With regard to the World Wide Web, however, growth from 50 pages to one billion pages occurred in 8 short years! Even more importantly, the Web brought to ordinary citizens not only the ability to be consumers of information posted there, but also the ability to be publishers of their own information, with a poten-tial worldwide audience of millions. In fact, Web publication today is so quick and easy that it is available to almost any individual in any industrialized nation (and some emerging ones) who owns a modest computer and has some simple computing skills. Even children can and do publish their own pages on the Web.

THE INTERNET, THE WEB, AND THE SHIFTING OF POWER

What will be the ultimate result of the Web empowering common people with the means to usurp the formerly exclusive ability of corporate and governmental entities to disseminate information? Whatever the result, it will be profound. To control the dissemination of information is to wield power—perhaps even the greatest of power. The English poet, novelist, and statesman Edward George Bulwer-Lytton said, "The pen is mightier than the sword." If Bulwer-Lytton were alive today, he might say, "The keyboard is mightier than the sword."

In any case, as corporations and governments experience the rapid erosion of their monopoly on information distribution, they are scrambling to control, and sometimes to limit, the ability of ordinary citizens to use this new medium as they see fit. The traditional wielders of power are beginning to sense that their once-exclusive control of the means of information dissemination is slipping away, passing into the hands of millions of individual Internet and Web users around the globe. We should not expect this massive and unprecedented shift in power to take place without a struggle. Indeed, it is likely that the glut of proposed and enacted Internet- and web-related laws and regulations is at least partly a reaction of the traditional power barons in government and industry to the realization of what they are about to lose.

Fundamental changes have taken place in U.S. and worldwide culture. These changes have only just begun. We do not pretend to know what the final result of these revolutionary changes will be, but for those of us who enjoy using technology and observing its transforming effect on society and culture, the coming years may be the most interesting of all times to be alive.

THE INTERNET, THE WEB, AND THE FUTURE OF INFORMATION TECHNOLOGY IN SCHOOLS

The Internet and the Web have wrought such profound changes, that their effects, especially on teaching and learning in schools, are discussed extensively throughout this book. In addition to differences in the specific applications of computers in schools, the global success of the Internet and the Web has changed our fundamental attitude toward the future of computing in schools. When we wrote the last edition, we still feared that computers might not be accepted and integrated into school culture. The commitment involved in bringing computers into schools, both financial and in terms of human energy and enthusiasm, coupled with the poor ways that computers are often used in schools, was at the heart of our concerns. Simply put, we feared computers might end up gathering dust in school closets, as had many electronic innovations of earlier educational times. Sarah Heile (1996), in an article written at the height of our concerns, and before the rise of the Internet and the Web, rightly pointed out that the last new technologies to change education significantly were the blackboard and the textbook. No other new technology, she pointed out, really changed what happened in U.S. schools.

However, the Internet and the Web have changed all that. Indeed, the ubiquity of computers was spawned primarily by the fantastic growth and popularity of the Internet and the Web, as reflected in some of the astounding statistics on growth and popularity presented previously. Computers are now so firmly entrenched in the larger culture—embued with such **cultural momentum**—

that it would be impossible to prevent them from claiming a place in the schools of the future, even if educators or others tried to do so.

Educational computing is now established and computers will continue to find their way into schools in ever-increasing numbers. Andrew Glasner (1997), in a paper on computer graphics, asked rhetorically if we should continue to invest our time, effort, and enthusiasm in computers and information technology. His answer is yes, and his justification is that we really have no other choice:

> Why build? Because we can. To stop or even slow down powerful technologies in our culture is all but impossible; genetic engineering is only slightly affected by enormous widespread opposition. Nuclear technology was only scaled back after horrible disasters and near misses. Computers will continue to permeate our culture; we should be aware of this and try to reduce their negative effects.

This principle can also be applied to schools. Although schools have been slow to adopt computers, this technology has become incredibly powerful in cultures across the globe and is probably unstoppable in schools. Although we have been educational computing advocates since the 1980s, we must confess that we did not anticipate the speed with which computers and related information technology would achieve the global importance they enjoy today. However, between 1996 and the present, computers have achieved their greatest U.S. and worldwide gains in acceptance and importance.

Information Technology and the Quality of Schooling

Computers are revolutionizing the culture at large and promise to continue to do so for the foreseeable future. Therefore, it seems certain that education also will be transformed by computers. Whether the effect of computers in general, or the Internet and the Web in particular, on various aspects of our culture—inside and outside of schools—has been positive is, of course, a matter of opinion. There are certainly two sides to this issue, and throughout this book we attempt to present both the pros and cons of computer proliferation.

INFORMATION TECHNOLOGY: ADVANTAGES AND DISADVANTAGES

Suddenly the widespread use of information technology has directly resulted in entirely new ethical dilemmas ("cyberethics") and concerns. Issues of pornographic or otherwise inappropriate web sites, e-mail privacy, **spamming** (i.e., sending unsolicited e-mail aimed at selling a product), **hacking** (i.e., unauthorized use of computer networks), netiquette (etiquette on the Web), website vandalism, network security, sexual predators, computer viruses (destructive programs that erase or damage data on the computers of unsuspecting computer users), software piracy (illegal copying of copyrighted software), and a host of other concerns did not even exist until a few years ago. The seriousness of these problems is reflected by the results of a recent search of the Web using the *AltaVista* search engine (http://www.altavista.com/). More than 10,000 websites dealing with ethical issues related to information technology were found. There is even an academic journal entitled *Ethics and Information Technology,* and many colleges and universities now have courses dedicated exclusively to matters of ethics related to computing.

On the other hand, there is little doubt that computers have contributed materially to the increased business productivity of the last decade or so. Electronic spreadsheets, word processors, and databases were such a boon to business that they sparked much of the early enthusiasm of the business community toward computers. Today, the Internet and the Web have fueled the stock market to unprecedented heights, and **e-commerce** (buying and selling products on the Web) is being heralded as the wave of the business future. According to the White House (Office of the White House Press Secretary, 2000), since 1995 more than a third of all U.S. economic growth has resulted from information technology (IT) enterprises, more than 13 million people in the United States hold IT-related jobs, and the rate of IT employment growth is 6 times as fast as overall job growth.

Growth of Home Computing

As people across the globe have embraced computing, so too have school personnel and students. The number of computers in U.S. schools is growing rapidly, as is school connectivity to the Internet. One reason for the rapid increase in numbers of computers and in Internet connectivity in schools during the last few years is the huge increase in the number of private households with computers. The U.S. Census Bureau (1999) reported that by October of 1997 at least 40 percent of U.S. households had a computer, and 17 million households had access to the Internet and the Web. By the end of 1998, 26.2 percent of U.S. households had Internet access (National Telecommunications and Information Administration, 1999). By the year 2000, fully 50 percent of U.S. homes had a computer (UCLA Center for Communication Policy, 2000), almost 50 percent used the Internet, and 700 new households were being connected to the Internet each hour (Office of the White House Press Secretary, 2000). Home computer and Internet use has a profound effect on school computer and Internet use because parents, teachers, school administrators, and children who use computers and the Internet in their homes demand that computers and the Internet also be available in schools.

Growth of Computing, the Internet, and the Web in Schools

Because of the these profound changes, children are beginning to regard computers, the Internet, and the Web as necessary parts of their school and private lives, and, as just mentioned, they are more likely today than ever before to have access to them at school. At the time the last edition of this book was written, the ratio of students to computers in schools was approximately 20 to 1 (Okolo, Bahr, & Reith, 1993). In 1997, the number of computers in schools was growing at an annual rate of about 400,000 machines (Little, 1997). However, in 1999, more than 870,000 additional instructional computers were installed in U.S. schools (Market Data Retrieval, 1999). Today, the ratio of students to school computers has improved to at least 5.7 to 1; 90 percent of schools have Internet access; and of those, 71 percent have access within instructional classrooms (Market Data Retrieval, 1999). Furthermore, the U.S. Census Bureau (1999) reports that more than 14 million of the 57 million U.S. citizens who used the web in 1997 were public schoolchildren. Researchers at Market Data Retrieval (1999) found that, between 1998 and 1999, the percentage of schools reporting that the majority of their teachers used the Internet for instructional purposes jumped from 33 percent to 54 percent, while the percentage reporting that the majority of their teachers "use computers daily" increased from 47 percent to almost 70 percent. These researchers are so optimistic about school computers and school access to the Internet that they have said that the goal of providing Internet access to every U.S. classroom may be attainable during the year 2000.

From these statistics, it is apparent why we no longer fear that computers will not find their way into U.S. schools. Most U.S. schools already have computers and the number of computers in schools is increasing more rapidly than ever. As we have said, we believe the momentum is established, and school computers are here to stay.

Computers in the Culture at Large

How have such sweeping changes been possible in such a short time? Why have people throughout the world embraced this new technology? Why has there been such widespread adoption by schools, and why are so many educators and students so willing to invest their money, time, energy, and enthusiasm in learning these new skills? To understand the answers to these questions, it is necessary to look back at some of the recent history of computing.

Even a casual observer of events in the United States during the 1980s and early 1990s would have noticed the rapid proliferation of computers in almost every walk of life. In fact, by the mid-1990s, there were many more computers in the United States than there were people. Then, as now, most of this growth was in personal computers, which used to be called *microcomputers* (as opposed to mini- or *mainframe computers*). In fact, Gilder (1994) has pointed out that, from 1977 to 1987, the proportion of computing done with mainframes dropped from almost 100 percent to less than 1 percent. He estimated that by the early 1990s, more than 100 million personal computers would be in operation in the world, with at least half of them located in the United States. No one knows for sure how many more personal computers exist today, but many estimate that the total number of personal computers in the world is at least 1 billion (Promonet, 2000).

Although computers are common in homes and schools, the incredible growth of the computer presence in the United States occurred first and most dramatically in the business world. From video rental stores to fast-food restaurants to offices of all kinds, computers have become fixtures of U.S. business. In fact, when you compare the typical school environment to the typical business environment, it becomes apparent that schools have lagged far behind in implementing the use of computers.

EDUCATION AND CHANGE

Because many educators are vitally concerned with bringing about positive environmental and pedagogical change (such as integrating computers and schooling), it is essential that we understand how change occurs and how changes in our society and culture at large relate to change in our schools. The branch of social science that has intensively studied such changes is called *anthropology.*

What Anthropology Tells Us about Change

Educators in general and educators who are interested in information technology in particular can learn much from anthropology. We are especially indebted to a classic and timeless book by George F. Kneller entitled *Educational Anthropology* (1965), and we recommend it to readers who become interested in the points we discuss in this chapter.

The Role of Education in Cultural Change

Some anthropologists specialize in the study of **culture,** or the way of life shared by a given people, including both behaviors (beliefs, attitudes, and the like) and artifacts. Kneller points out that cultural anthropologists find that changes in the institutions of formal education, such as schools, typically follow changes in the culture at large. Kneller also suggests that such cultural lag makes it unlikely that schools can lead the way as agents of cultural change (Kneller, 1965).

Of the many reasons for this, the most interesting and powerful have to do with the purpose of formal education and who is chosen to control it. Kneller and many other anthropologists (e.g., Webb & Sherman, 1989) assert that the primary purpose of schooling is to help transmit the way of life (the culture) of a people to their offspring. Not surprisingly, individuals chosen to control formal education are invariably models of a specific way of life, having already attained a level of success and honor valued by society, and, therefore, well suited to fulfill this purpose of education.

Consider the type of people most likely to be elected to a school board in our country. They are almost always model citizens. They tend to be successful, affluent individuals who have frequently distinguished themselves in business, hold traditional values and attitudes, and lead conventional lifestyles. Boocock (1980) compares school board members to the general public: "By comparison with the general public, board members are disproportionately white, male, middle-aged, high in education, occupation, and income, and well established in their local communities" (p. 250). Underwood (1982) reported similar findings after conducting a national survey of school board members in the United States. A recent survey shows that little has changed in the demographic profile of the typical school board member. That study found that school boards tend to be made up of white, middle-aged, married males with advanced college degrees who are employed in professional positions earning more than $50,000 a year (Saks, 2000).

Such individuals are ideal choices to control the cultural institution (school) whose primary purpose is to pass on the cultural heritage. They are ideal because they have a vested interest in preserving the status quo (the current culture) and in resisting change. For such citizens, the existing culture has led to success and prosperity, and they are therefore conservative in the largest sense of the word. (The *American Heritage Dictionary of the English Language* defines the term *conservative* as "tending to favor the preservation of the existing order and to regard proposals for change with distrust.")

Education as a Weak Force for Cultural Change

There is yet another reason why formal education is incapable of initiating cultural change. Anthropologists have established that cultural change is not accomplished by any one cultural force, such as formal education, but by combinations of cultural forces exerted by institutions such as religion, mass media, the peer group, business, or various special-interest groups (Sarason, 1982). Formal education, by itself, is incapable of overcoming the momentum of these established and more powerful cultural forces. This explains why the integration of computers in schools began to receive strong public support only after computers proved successful in business, government, and the military, and in the manufacture of consumer goods, such as appliances, toys, and automobiles.

Anthropology, Schools, and Computers

Anthropology provides clues to why education was slow to bring computers into schools. In addition, and of more practical importance to computer-using educators, cultural anthropology provides clues that may be useful to those who plan the future advocacy of computers in education and to those who wish to maximize the effectiveness of their efforts.

Cultural Lag.   Those who advocate the use of new technology in education should understand the concept of **cultural lag.** This term refers to the tendency for some elements of culture to change less rapidly than others. Specifically, changes in technology in our culture commonly occur more rapidly than changes in values and attitudes.

One reason for this lag is that people in the United States resist changes in values more than changes in technology. It is revealing that individuals who dedicate themselves to changing technology are called *inventors,* a term with highly positive connotations, whereas those who specialize in changing values or attitudes are often called *revolutionaries* or *malcontents,* terms with definite negative undertones.

Computers and Values

It would be a mistake for any educational computer advocate to assume that because computers are a product of technology, they will be universally welcomed in schools by fellow teachers, school board members, or the general public. To understand why computers may be viewed with disfavor, we must understand that successful technological change is always linked to the values a society endorses. For example, Kneller (1965) pointed out that the automobile enjoyed nearly instant success because it was linked to the accepted values of social mobility, private ownership, and the love of speed.

Those who seek to convince other educators that computers should be used in schools and that more resources should be devoted to their use should give some thought to the values underlying computer technology. Some of these values are widely endorsed in our society. For example, in the business subculture, where computing has enjoyed widespread success and approval, the computer can be linked to powerful values about work. These include beliefs about the desirability of (1) work speed, (2) work efficiency, (3) work power, and (4) the removal of human error from work activities.

The first three of these underlying values are accepted almost without argument by the business subculture. So, too, is the fourth, although computing will likely be opposed by labor if computers are viewed as possible replacements for human workers. Even so, if computers are believed to be increasing profit, they will be linked to the most powerful and universally approved value in the business world, and labor is not likely to be successful in blocking their integration.

The Values Underlying Computing in Schools

Consider how the values of work speed, work efficiency, work power, and the removal of human error fare in education. The first three values are consistent with the values of most educators. Almost all teachers welcome the opportunity to increase the speed, efficiency, and power of teaching and learning, but the idea of removing human error from work activities may create an area of conflict. If teachers believe that computers will replace them, they may reject the new technology, just as labor frequently rejects technology that threatens jobs.

A difference is that opposition by educators has the potential to be far more effective than the opposition of labor in the business world. Unlike business, in education, no overriding profit motive exists to offset objections by teachers. Even more important, the education subculture strongly endorses the value of preserving human interaction and involvement for its own sake. Educators may view computers not only as possible displacements for teachers, but also as a dehumanizing influence on the educational enterprise that limits children's interactions with each other or with their teachers. If this attitude becomes widespread, strong opposition from within education will likely be encountered. Such fears contributed to the failure of teaching machines and programmed instruction, which were developed by B. F. Skinner and others during the 1950s and 1960s (Criswell, 1989).

Actually, fears that computers will replace teachers or that they will necessarily dehumanize education are unfounded. Computers are highly promising educational tools, but they do not have the ability or the potential to replace teachers. Like other tools, such as pencils or books, they may modify the way typical teachers teach, but they cannot eliminate human teachers. Research has shown that computers can be used to increase or to decrease human interaction in education, but the teacher is the critical factor in determining how much human interaction prevails. Thus, educational computing advocates should take care to point out to teachers that the intention is to use computers to empower, not supplant, humans and that research has shown that computers can be used to increase human interaction.

In addition to emphasizing the capacity of computing to increase the amount of human interaction in the classroom, it is equally important that we provide clear evidence that computing is accomplishing valuable educational goals. Those who control education (school administrators, school board members, and the general public) may be willing to ignore limited teacher opposition because such leaders value increasing the speed, efficiency, and power of teaching and learning. However, if they are not convinced that computing can lead to the achievement of these and other goals, as well as the consequent improvement of the school environment, they may not support the high cost of educational computing, especially if teachers initiate organized or widespread resistance. Thus, it is crucial that computer-using educators (1) make reasonable claims about what computers in education can accomplish and (2) provide evidence that computing benefits are being actualized.

Are computers a contemporary bandwagon in U.S. education? Are they just another fad? Given the increasing role of computers in U.S. work space, and in society in general, the answer must be a definite no. Although the general acceptance of computers in society is the main reason why educational computing is unlikely to suffer the same fate as teaching machines and educational television (disillusionment and eventual abandonment), we hasten to point out that computers differ from all previous electronic innovations in one important respect: they can be highly interactive. A group of students studying the ecology of deserts, for example, can explore the life cycles of common desert plants and animals at any of thousands of sites on the World Wide Web or with any one of several educational packages currently distributed on CD-ROM. (With regard to software and the Web, some people believe that the practice of purchasing software from stores or mail-order houses, installing that software on a specific machine, and running it on that machine, is doomed to obsolescence. Instead, they believe that all software will be available on the Web and will cost a small fee to run, not on our own machines, but on a web-connected computer. We will interact with the software only on the Web.)

They might, for example, "build" a desert environment and populate it with plants, animals, and selected resources. After creating the desert "microworld," the students would observe the life patterns and determine whether their mix of life forms and resources produced a sustainable world. This type of learning is much more interactive and engaging than reading a chapter in a textbook on desert ecology. Today, hundreds of computer programs (software) give students the opportunity to create, run, or build anything from urban environments and mathematical worlds to electronic machines. Other programs put students in the role of researchers and scientists who conduct experiments, explore unknown worlds, and study important problems. The World Wide Web, of course, is a vast storehouse of information for students to access.

The type of software or websites mentioned thus far, simulations and micro-worlds, is interactive in the sense that students—individually or in small groups—become involved in subject matter at many levels—as explorers, creators, problem solvers, scientists. Instead of reading a chapter and responding to questions, students make decisions, explore alternative formulations of the problem, and build a knowledge base for solving problems. As they do this, the computer (more accurately the software the computer is running) responds to students' decisions.

Another type of software supports collaborative interaction. Groupware, or collaborative writing software, and student writing and publishing programs all encourage students to write collaboratively and to share their writing with others. For example, students in a sixth-grade class might use collaborative writing software to produce a booklet on the history of their town or neighborhood. Software is available to support their work at every stage—from gathering information on the topic to producing a final version of their report with illustrations and photos as well as text. The final version can be proudly distributed to several audiences, including other students and parents.

Such software has been available for some time. It is now becoming available on the World Wide Web. As the Web continues to grow in importance, quality, and popularity, it will feature more and more educational software of increasing complexity and high quality.

INNOVATION, THEORY, AND RESEARCH

It is not difficult to find classrooms where computers are being used in innovative and interesting ways; however, it is easier to find classrooms where they are used in ineffective and boring ways. Why this happens is difficult to determine, but one reason may be the tendency on the part of practitioners and academics alike to divorce theory and research from practice.

Most teachers may not value research because teacher trainers have been unsuccessful in relating the theories they teach to practice in the classroom. In addition, most teachers, even after completing a master's degree, seem to categorize knowledge into that which is *practical* (useful in the real world of education) and that which is *theoretical* (useful only to write down as answers for tests in college education and psychology courses).

Such categorization represents a false dichotomy because theory and practice are actually inseparable. What is done in the classroom (practice) depends almost totally on how the teacher chooses to look at the world (theory). Therefore, a theory underlies and determines every action in every sphere of our lives. Consider the following analysis by Maddux (1988):

> If we attempt to operate without theory, how do we choose what might work in the beginning? And when it quits working, how will we know what to try next?... Without conscious theory, (a) we may rely on experts to tell us what to do, (b) we may use what is currently popular, (c) we may resort to trial and error, or (d) we may simply continue doing what we've always done in the past, whether it "works" or not. (p. 3)

Unfortunately, in many teacher-education courses theory is taught with little examination of its implications for practice, whereas practice is often approached with little understanding of the underlying theories that guide it. Our choice as teachers is not between theory and practice. We can, however, make an informed, conscious choice of theories or we can choose to practice according to theories of which we are unaware and uninformed. It is important that our choice of theories be a conscious one so that we can contemplate, evaluate, and revise it as new research and new experiences dictate.

Consciously using theory to guide practice may help us to avoid a common and debilitating aspect of educational practice—fads. Fads are educational practices that are adopted because they have high visibility in the popular press and in the culture. A fad may be educationally sound, or it may be unsound. We adopt them, not because growing evidence, from the experience of other teachers and from research, supports their use, but because they are the current bandwagon. The result is often a superficial adoption of the fad with little understanding of the whys and hows of it. Even valid educational innovations have little chance of success if they are adopted as fads. Another result is often unrealistically optimistic expectations about the benefits to be derived from the innovation, which can lead to a backlash that may result in abandoning the innovation even though it was moderately successful and highly promising. Teachers and teachers in training can take several positive measures to prevent or counter a backlash against computing in schools:

1. Avoid making unrealistic and unsubstantiated claims
2. Be suspicious of anyone who makes lavish claims for any computing application and demand evidence from software manufacturers and others who make such claims
3. Strive to maintain an open mind concerning the relationship of theory to practice and demand that professors and those who present in-service programs demonstrate how theory is related to practice

4. Recognize that useful theories are inspired and refined by research, read research reports, and encourage and participate in research projects in their own classrooms

School Computer Uses and the Computer Backlash

Unrealistic claims about computing in education can swing the pendulum toward an educational computing backlash. In addition, the poor way in which computers are sometimes used in schools can powerfully contribute to this backlash. Poor use of computers is partly due to difficulty in locating excellent educational software (the instructions that make computers perform specific tasks), a problem that we explore in depth in later chapters. Poor application is also due to uninformed decisions made at the classroom, school, or district level, a topic we now address.

How Computers Are Used in Schools

Research continues to show that drill-and-practice applications are overused whereas applications that teach higher-order thinking skills are underused. In addition, many teachers avoid integrating computers into the curriculum and instead use computing (primarily drill-and-practice) activities as rewards only. Such unimaginative computer implementation is unlikely to bring great educational benefits. Indeed, Arthur Leuhrmann (1994), in an article subtitled "Why Technology Has Had So Little Impact in Schools," suggested that the Information Revolution had profound effects in nearly all walks of life but bypassed our schools. He suggested that, if one's great-grandmother came back to visit earth, she would find the world much changed but classrooms essentially unchanged. Dyrli and Kinnaman (1994) agree and assert, "Technology has transformed almost every segment of American society—except education" (p. 92). Similarly, the President's Committee of Advisors on Science and Technology, in their *Report to the President on the Use of Technology to Strengthen K–12 Education in the United States* (1997), made the following observation:

> While a number of different approaches have been suggested for the improvement of K–12 education in the United States, one common element of many such plans has been the more extensive and more effective utilization of computer, networking, and other technologies in support of a broad program of systemic and curricular reform. During a period in which technology has fundamentally transformed America's offices, factories, and retail establishments, however, its impact within our nation's classrooms has generally been quite modest.

This is not to say that computers are *never* used effectively in schools. In fact, the literature is full of case studies and reports by teachers and others who are using computers to help bring about positive, basic changes in classroom organization and procedures and whose creative integration of computing into the curriculum illustrates the power and potential of educational technology. We authors of this text-book have seen many such classrooms during visits to schools across the nation.

The President's Committee of Advisors on Science and Technology (1997) are also optimistic about the potential of technology to improve schooling. Specifically, they identify the following educational improvements, which are consistent with a philosophy of education called *constructivism*. (Constructivism is addressed in depth in a later chapter in this book.) Furthermore, they assert that the use of computers and information technology in schools can greatly facilitate these desirable practices:

- Greater attention is given to the acquisition of higher-order thinking and problem-solving skills, with less emphasis on the assimilation of a large body of isolated facts.
- Basic skills are learned not in isolation, but in the course of undertaking (often on a collaborative basis) higher-level "real-world" tasks whose execution requires the integration of a number of such skills.
- Information resources are available to the student to be accessed at that point in time when they actually become useful in executing a particular task at hand.
- Fewer topics may be covered than is the case within the typical traditional curriculum, but these topics are often explored in greater depth.
- The student assumes a central role as the active architect of his or her own knowledge and skills, rather than passively absorbing information proffered by the teacher.

Forcier (1999) agrees and believes the following positive changes can already be attributed to the influence of computers and information technology in schools:

1. A change from whole-class to small-group instruction
2. A move from lecture to coaching
3. A move from working with better students to spending more time working with weaker students
4. A shift toward students becoming more engaged in their learning
5. A change to assessment based on products and outcomes
6. A shift from a competitive to a cooperative atmosphere in the classroom
7. A shift from all students attempting to learn the same thing at the same time to different students learning different things at their own rate
8. A move from an emphasis on verbal thinking to the integration of visual and verbal thinking (p. 8)

Why do not more teachers make wise use of computing? We have discussed some of the reasons in this chapter. Another powerful set of reasons has to do with the lack of modeling of effective use of information technology in preservice teacher training and the lack of excellent preservice and in-service training on the use of information technology in education. Many recent studies have identified the lack of good teacher preservice and in-service training as critical to the successful use of information technology in schools. The President's Committee of Advisors on Science and Technology (1997) included the need for teacher training among their six overall recommendations:

1. Focus on learning with technology, not about technology.
2. Emphasize content and pedagogy, and not just hardware.
3. Give special attention to professional development.
4. Engage in realistic budgeting.
5. Ensure equitable, universal access.
6. Initiate a major program of experimental research.

SUMMARY

Information technology in education is an exciting new discipline whose effectiveness depends on how today's teachers in training use technology in their own classrooms in the future. Although there was a time when it seemed possible that the public would not support the cost of bringing computers into schools, the vast growth in home and business computing, together with the popularity of the Internet and the World Wide Web, has practically eliminated that fear. The number of computers in schools in the United States has increased markedly since 1983 and continues to grow, especially in the years since the Internet and the World Wide Web became popular.

Computers were a success in business before they were introduced in education. This occurred because changes in education are always preceded by changes in the culture at large. Cultural anthropologists tell us that education cannot change culture, although the reverse is common. Changes occur first in the culture at large because in every culture formal education is controlled by leaders who are conservative. These leaders resist changes in formal education until the changes have become well accepted in other cultural institutions. Then, too, changes in the general culture are brought about, not by any one institution, but by the combined influence of several.

Anthropologists also tell us that changes in technology are accepted more readily than changes in values; however, all technological innovations are linked to values. For innovations to be successful, these underlying values must be endorsed by a society.

Computer advocates in education need to understand cultural change if their cause is to succeed. Teachers should be assured that computers cannot replace them but can empower them and their students. It should also be emphasized that computers can be used to increase, rather than decrease, human interaction in the classroom.

Educational computing advocates must also help establish and disseminate evidence that computers are helping to meet realistic goals. They can do this by making only reasonable claims about the value of computing, reading the research of others, participating in research studies, and telling parents and others about this research.

Research has revealed some problems in school computer use. Rote learning skills tend to be emphasized whereas the development of higher-order thinking skills tends to be neglected. Another set of problems is related to lack of competent, ongoing preservice and in-service education.

QUESTIONS TO CONSIDER

1. In your opinion, what is the most encouraging trend in computer use identified in the chapter? Why?
2. What is the most discouraging trend? Why?
3. What do you think would be the most important single step a teacher could take to help avoid the educational pendulum syndrome in educational computing?
4. Do you agree that people in the United States resist changes in the culture of values more than changes in the culture of technology? Give an example.

RELATED ACTIVITIES

1. Locate an article in a popular magazine about the use of computers in schools. Do you think the authors of this textbook would judge it to be extravagantly optimistic, realistic, or overly pessimistic? Why?
2. Interview a local teacher or administrator concerning his or her views on educational computing.
3. Interview a local businessperson concerning his or her attitudes about computers in business.

SUGGESTIONS FOR ADDITIONAL READING

Collis, B. (1988). *Computers, curriculum, and whole-class instruction: Issues and ideas.* Belmont, CA: Wadsworth.

Provenzo, E. F. (1999). *The Internet and the World Wide Web for preservice teachers.* Boston: Allyn & Bacon.

Roblyer, M. D., & Edwards, J. (2000). *Integrating educational technology into teaching* (2nd ed.). Upper Saddle River, NJ: Merrill.

Rothman, S., & Mosmann, C. (1985). *Computer uses and issues.* Chicago: Science Research Associates.

Weizenbaum, J. (1976). *Computer power and human reason.* New York: W. H. Freeman.

REFERENCES

Boocock, S. S. (1980). *Sociology of education: An introduction* (2nd ed.). Boston: Houghton Mifflin.

Criswell, E. L. (1989). *The design of computer-based instruction.* New York: Macmillan.

Dyrli, O. E., & Kinnaman, D. E. (1994). Preparing for the integration of emerging technologies. *Technology & Learning, 14*(8), 92–100.

Forcier, R. C. (1999). *The computer as an educational tool: Productivity and problem solving* (2nd ed.). Upper Saddle River, NJ: Merrill.

Gilder, G. (1994). The information revolution. In J. J. Hirschbuhl (Ed.), *Computers in education* (6th ed., pp. 32–35). Guilford, CT: Dushkin.

Glasner, A. (1997). *Computer graphics and cultural change.* Retrieved March 22, 2000, from the World Wide Web: http://www.research.microsoft.com/glassner/work/talks/GI97.htm

Heile, S. (1996). The virtual world. Retrieved March 20, 2000, from the World Wide Web: http://upaya.soc.neu.edu/archive/students/heile.html

Juliussen, E. & Petska-Juliussen, K. (2000). *U.S. tops 100 million Internet users according to Computer Industry Almanac.* Arlington Heights, IL: The Computer Industry Almanac. Retrieved March 20, 2000, from the World Wide Web: http://www.c-i-a.com/199911iu.htm

Kneller, G. F. (1965). *Educational anthropology: An introduction.* New York: Wiley.

Lawrence, S., & Giles, L. (1999). Accessibility and distribution of information on the Web. *Nature, 400,* 107–109.

Leuhrmann, A. (1994). Computers; more than latest in ed-tech: Why technology has had so little impact in schools. In J. J. Hirschbuhl (Ed.), *Computers in education* (6th ed., pp. 6–8). Guilford, CT: Dushkin.

Little, G. (1997). The world at our fingertips: Creative writers on the Web. *The CPSR Newsletter, 15*(1), 4.

Maddux, C. D. (1988). *Logo: Methods and curriculum for teachers.* New York: Haworth.

The Madison Avenue Group. (2000). *The CommerceNet/Nielsen Internet Demographics Survey: Executive Summary.* Retrieved March 21, 2000, from the World Wide Web: http://www.madisononline.com/resources/internet.html

Market Data Retrieval. (1999). *Technology in education 1999.* Shelton, CT: Author.

National Telecommunications and Information Administration. (1999). *Falling through the Net III: Defining the digital divide.* Washington, DC: U.S. Department of Commerce. Retrieved March 22, 2000, from the World Wide Web: http://www.ntia.doc.gov/ntiahome/fttn99/fttn.pdf

NUA Limited. (2000). *How many online?* Retrieved March 20, 2000, from the World Wide Web: http://www.nua.ie/surveys/how_many_online/index.html

Office of the White House Press Secretary. (2000, January). *Information technology research and development: Information technology for the 21st century.* Retrieved March 23, 2000, from the World Wide Web: http://www.whitehouse.gov/WH/New/html/20000121_2.html

Okolo, C. M., Bahr, C. M., & Reith, H. J. (1993). A retrospective view of computer-based instruction. *Journal of Special Education Technology, 12*(1), 1–27.

President's Committee of Advisors on Science and Technology. (1997). *Report to the President on the use of technology to strengthen K–12 education in the United States.* Retrieved March 23, 2000, from the World Wide Web: http://www.whitehouse.gov/WH/EOP/OSTP/NSTC/PCAST/k-12ed.html#2.1

Promonet. (2000). *Ask Dr. Internet.* Retrieved March 23, 2000, from the World Wide Web: http://promo.net/drnet/drnet17.htm

Saks, J. (2000). Local heroes: The people who run for school board. Boston: Family Education Network. Retrieved March 23, 2000, from the World Wide Web: http://www.familyeducation.com/article/0,1120,1-2629,00.html

Sarason, S. B. (1982). *The culture of the school and the problem of change* (2nd ed.). Boston: Allyn & Bacon.

Sullivan, D. (2000). *Search engine sizes.* Retrieved March 20, 2000, from the World Wide Web: http://searchenginewatch.internet.com/reports/sizes.html

UCLA Center for Communications Policy. (2000). *Landmark UCLA study will explore the evolution and impact of personal computers and the Internet.* Los Angeles: Author. Retrieved March 22, 2000, from the World Wide Web: http://www.ccp.ucla.edu/press_release.htm

Underwood, K. E. (1982). Your portrait: School boards have a brand-new look. *American School Board Journal, 69*(1), 17–20.

United States Census Bureau. (1999). *Computer use in the United States: October 1997.* Washington, DC: Author. Retrieved January 5, 2000, from the World Wide Web: http://www.census.gov/population/www/socdemo/computer.html

Webb, R. B., & Sherman, R. R. (1989). *Schooling and society.* New York: Macmillan.

CHAPTER TWO

TRENDS AND ISSUES IN INFORMATION TECHNOLOGY IN EDUCATION

Goal: To become aware of the issues and trends in using information technology in education, both from a historical and present-day perspective.

KEY TERMS

artificial intelligence (p. 25)
authoring systems (p. 41)
cognitive amplifier (p. 31)
computer-assisted instruction (CAI) (p. 22)
computer equity (p. 35)
computer ethics (p. 36)
computer literacy (p. 32)
computer-managed instruction
  (CMI) (p. 24)
digital divide (p. 35)
direct instruction (p. 22)
formal operational thinking (p. 29)
integrated learning systems (ILS) (p. 25)

just-in-time direct instruction (p. 24)
list processing (p. 31)
Logo (p. 27)
mail merge (p. 37)
metacognition (p. 30)
out-of-context direct instruction (p. 23)
portfolio assessment (p. 39)
preparatory direct instruction (p. 23)
presentation software (p. 39)
programmed instruction (p. 20)
student information systems (p. 38)
synthesized speech (p. 42)
turtle graphics (p. 29)

The decade of the 1980s was not the first period of interest in information technology in education. During the late 1950s through the early 1970s, a great deal of effort and enthusiasm was devoted to bringing computers and other machine instruction into schools. This early activity had its roots in the work of Sidney Pressey (1926, 1927). Pressey noted that objective tests were becoming common in schools. He believed that teachers would soon be unable to cope with the logistics of administering and scoring such tests. Therefore, in the 1920s he began experimenting with a machine to administer multiple-choice test items (Travers, 1967). At first, Pressey concentrated on developing the testing and scoring capability of his machine. However, he soon recognized its potential for teaching as well. He then began requiring students to work through the test a number of times, each time attempting to complete it with fewer errors.

Although Pressey's device generated some interest, it was never widely used. More than 30 years later, however, educators again became interested in the potential of teaching machines. B. F. Skinner, one of the founders of behaviorism, was responsible for this renewed interest. Skinner, a highly respected Harvard psychologist, developed his own machine and also created some of the early **programmed instruction.** By the mid-1960s, thousands of programmed instruction packages (often called *programs*) had been designed, some to be used in machines like the one Skinner developed and some to be used as programmed instruction books.

Skinner believed his machine had effects on students similar to the effects of a good private tutor. He believed the machines should (1) stimulate constant interaction between the program and the user because students were required to answer hundreds of questions in programmed instruction; (2) require students to master each concept or lesson before moving on to the next concept or lesson; (3) present material in small steps or frames; (4) prompt students when an error occurred; and (5) provide reinforcement for each successful step (Skinner, 1958). Although Skinner's work on teaching machines stimulated a great deal of interest and a large body of research, the devices were never widely adopted by educators. However, programmed instruction, which could be produced in book as well as machine formats, did enjoy widespread popularity in the 1960s and early 1970s.

An important point to keep in mind is that hundreds of research studies on the effectiveness of programmed instruction did show that, at least from a behavioral perspective, teaching machines and programmed instruction functioned as intended. Many studies as well as reviews of research concluded they were instructionally effective (Hilgard & Bower, 1966; Stolurow, 1961; Travers, 1968). Why, then, did they fail to gain wide and lasting acceptance? The reasons for the failure of this innovation may provide helpful information for those who are working toward the success of information technology in education. Certainly, it is vital for information technology in education advocates to realize that, historically, the touted effectiveness of an innovation such as programmed instruction has been no guarantee of acceptance (Slavin, 1987).

Later in his life, Skinner (1986) summarized some of the reasons for the failure of teaching machines and programmed instruction and offered an additional insight. He suggested that the Soviet Union contributed to the failure when it placed the first satellite in orbit in the late 1950s, sparking a rejection of behaviorism and fostering a resurgence of cognitivism (constructivism) in U.S. education:

> Americans were stunned. How could the Russians have beaten us into outer space? Something must be wrong with American education. Congress quickly passed the National Defense Education Act. Students were no longer to be told

things; they were to discover things for themselves. They were not to memorize, but to think, grasp concepts, explore, be creative. The cognitive movement that followed Sputnik I seemed to legitimize traditional theories of teaching and learning. (pp. 105–106)

By the mid-1960s, a strong and articulate backlash of professional opinion opposed the use of teaching machines and programmed learning. A widely quoted and influential article by Fitzgerald (1970) illustrates that backlash. The article began with a list of advantages claimed for teaching machines, including (1) saving money for teachers' salaries by making it possible for each teacher to supervise many more students, (2) reducing discipline problems and cheating by having each student work in a separate booth, (3) reducing aversive practices of teachers (because machines are patient and nonjudgmental), (4) providing an opportunity for home study, (5) increasing student attention by providing immediate feedback of results, (6) exposing students to the nation's best teachers through written programs, (7) providing uniformity of instruction and grading, and (8) providing a rationale for increasing teacher salaries by increasing productivity.

After listing these claimed advantages, Fitzgerald (1970) went on to assert that most of these claims were not valid. In addition, all advantages were overshadowed by an overriding disadvantage—rigidity. Behaviorists praised the individualization in programmed instruction, but in reality only the rate of completion was individualized. Everything else—content, sequence of instruction, type of assessment, method of presenting content—was prespecified. In Fitzgerald's words:

> Teaching machines are admittedly based on the theory of reinforcement, of rote learning, of stimulus–response, of a mechanical one question–one answer. This is an intrinsically undemocratic—worse, an anti-intellectual—theory of learning. We spend entirely too much time with machines these days. The most prominent example is watching television as a passive substitute for an active, emotional life with real people, but other examples come to mind. . . . I find the thought of millions of children spending hours each day with millions of machines in millions of separate cubicles an appalling prospect. (pp. 486–487)

These criticisms, which are framed with rhetoric that has much in common with political polemics today, are clear examples of conflicting theoretical perspectives. Whereas programmed instruction was based on behavioral theories, Fitzgerald's criticisms are based on constructivist theory. The two competing perspectives can be couched in different terms: teacher-centered versus student-centered, behavioral versus constructivist, discrete skills versus whole language, programmed learning versus discovery learning, and so on. Between the two extremes—all instruction should be behavioral and no instruction should be behavioral—is a middle ground that examines the purpose and context of instruction and finds appropriate uses for many different types.

The brief history and discussion of programmed instruction, teaching machines, and computer learning just presented provides a natural backdrop for a discussion of the development of information technology in education applications, beginning with the advent of the microcomputer and continuing today. All the applications discussed in the rest of this chapter are either direct descendents of or directly opposed to this early programmed instruction movement. In addition to presenting a foundation for understanding issues relating to information technology in education applications, this brief history and discussion illuminate the importance of computer education in general. Interestingly, B. F. Skinner suggested at one time that the microcomputer was the ideal medium for bringing programmed instruction into the public school. He even suggested that when computers are used in this fashion they should be referred to as teaching machines (Skinner, 1986). The link between programmed instruction and **computer-assisted instruction (CAI)** is particularly strong for two types of CAI: drill-and-practice programs and tutorial software.

DIFFERENT APPROACHES TO USING COMPUTERS IN EDUCATION

This section presents different approaches that represent views of how computers and related information technology can enhance teaching and learning. These approaches have been distinguished and identified on the basis of the type of software they employ and the theoretical underpinnings on which they rest. Classifying these approaches into distinct categories was an easier task in earlier stages of education computing than it is today, as the lines of distinction become less discrete. A discussion of these approaches will familiarize the reader with relevant ideas and terminology and provide the background necessary for fully understanding later chapters in this text.

Two Direct-Instruction Approaches

Direct instruction is a general term for an approach that is based on behaviorist theory. Both drill-and-practice and tutorial programs are types of direct instruction. Drill-and-practice programs are used to provide repetitive exercises for rote skills that have been taught some other way. Tutorial programs attempt to teach new material by direct-instruction methods.

Drill-and-practice software dominated early software production for two reasons: (1) it was quick and easy to produce and (2) it was a natural application of the first microcomputers to education based on prevailing thought about what computers could do and how they should be used in teaching. For example, almost anyone who could program in BASIC could turn out a drill-and-practice program that presented math facts, accepted student responses, provided feedback, kept a running score, and summarized error patterns. As Hannafin and Peck (1988) describe, "drill and practice designs provide practice for defined skills, immediate feedback to the student for each response given, and usually some form of correction or remediation for incorrect responses" (p. 144). Such programs were cheap; they required little expertise, and they seemed, on the surface, to represent the natural way to insert computer power into the teaching and learning process.

Tutorial software expands on drill-and-practice software by attempting to teach new concepts, ideas, and skills. Although tutorial software may include elements of drill-and-practice software, it is unique in that it presents new information and may be represented as providing an independent teaching environment. In its purest form, tutorial software is the embodiment of the teaching machine. Such software takes the learner through a sequence of steps that (1) present a new idea, concept, or task; (2) present a query designed to assess the student's grasp of the new idea, concept, or task; (3) provide feedback on the student's response; and (4) branch the learner to a different sequence based on his or her performance on the previous sequence. This description clearly reveals that the theoretical base for most drill-and-practice, as well as tutorial, software is behaviorism. Today, this type of software may incorporate sophisticated graphics, video, and sound, but the structure and design are based on behaviorist theory.

Appropriate Uses of Direct Instruction

Regardless of the name, direct instruction is the subject of considerable debate in virtually every subject area and at every level. Some argue that the problem with U.S. education today is that basic facts and skills are not being directly taught. Others argue that the focus on simple facts and basic skills is the problem. That debate will not be settled in this book, but a structure for thinking about the issues can be proposed. Computer-assisted direct instruction—both drill-and-practice and tutorial—can be divided into two types: skills-based direct instruction and just-in-time direct instruction.

Skills-Based Direct Instruction.   Skills-based direct instruction is a strategy to help students master basic or foundation skills. Skills-based direct instruction can be divided into two broad types of approaches: out-of-context direct instruction and preparatory direct instruction.

Out-of-context direct instruction is based on the assumption that the best way to teach a skill is to isolate it and master it through repeated practice. If you're teaching phonics skills, for example, this approach assumes the best way is to separate the phonics lessons from the act of reading. If you were using this approach, you would teach phonics skills in isolation until they became automatic and then help the student apply them to the process of reading. Many drill-and-practice as well as tutorial programs can be used for out-of-context direct instruction.

Preparatory direct instruction assumes that students need some direct instruction on fundamental skills but proposes that skill training is best accomplished within the framework of a meaningful activity. For example, as children are working on a math problem, it may become clear that they need some direct instruction on mastering a math skill. Drill-and-practice or tutorial programs can be used to provide that instruction.

Just-in-Time Direct Instruction.   The direct-instruction models discussed in the preceding section are all based on a skills or subskills approach: break down the content to be learned into subskills and teach those skills separately, then help children bring their newly developed skills to bear on the overall content or task to be taught. The subskills approach is widely used in education. In some methods it is the primary focus of instruction. Much, perhaps most, direct instruction uses this model. There are, however, other models. One is just-in-time direct instruction.

Just-in-time direct instruction is delivered at the point of need, usually determined by the student rather than the instructor. For example, a child writing a paragraph on a word processor might have a question about punctuation. She might press the HELP key, select PUNCTUATION from the menu that appears on the screen, and then select END OF SENTENCE because she is concerned about what punctuation should be used at the end of a particular sentence. The power of information technology such as computers is particularly suited to supporting just-in-time direct instruction.

Computer-Managed Instruction

Students taking courses in information technology in education at many universities find that the computer plays an important role in helping them master the concepts and skills that make up the course content. These courses are often patterned after an approach called the personalized system of instruction (PSI). They are self-paced and emphasize mastery learning. Such courses are divided into a series of modules that consist of a reading assignment from a text, a hands-on technology assignment, a computer-generated quiz, and some type of writing or production project relating to the theme of the module.

In such courses, the computer plays an important management role. Students take exams on the computer, and the computer scores the exams, displays results, provides study hints for improvement, records passing grades, and prints out reports of individual students' progress at any given point in the semester. The computer does not replace the instructor; instead, it is used as a tool to help the instructor manage the clerical and assessment work needed to make such a course run smoothly.

The preceding description of a modularized course is an example of **computer-managed instruction (CMI)**, a term that was coined to help distinguish certain computer applications that are management in nature from applications more closely involved in the teaching and learning process. In truth, CMI and CAI applications overlap in many ways, and some applications, discussed later in this chapter, incorporate both CMI and CAI.

Many variations of CMI are possible. It may mean an extensive computerized inventory of curriculum materials, using the computer to generate a variety of performance reports, or printing lists of students who have mastered specific instructional objectives. Any one or a combination of these and other management applications constitutes CMI.

CMI developed largely as an effort to introduce individualized instruction in schools. Many projects were difficult because of the massive amount of clerical work required. Once microcomputers became available, they were an obvious solution to this problem. In the late 1970s and 1980s, many efforts to individualize instruction for entire classes, or schools, used computers to keep track of student progress. Often, in direct-instruction settings, students were required to accomplish hundreds, even thousands, of objectives. Without computers it would be difficult, if not impossible, to keep up with recording student progress.

A natural part of any CMI approach is automated assessment. Computers are used for assessment in CMI systems by administering test items, calculating test scores, storing and retrieving test results, analyzing test items, and producing assessment reports. Some of these assessment facets, such as calculating, storing, and retrieving, are straightforward and simply take advantage of a computer's ability to handle data efficiently. These facets are included in most CMI efforts. Other applications, however, are somewhat controversial, because they represent demarcations from traditional assessment standards and procedures and are not standard CMI components. Educational psychometricians, experts in educational assessment, are always concerned about the reliability and validity of assessment procedures and believe that decisions in these areas cannot easily be automated without raising serious questions.

Although proponents of **artificial intelligence** and expert systems predict that many characteristics we consider human will be appropriated by computer programs, they have been promising this for many decades. Although technology has the potential to assist humans and even improve on their work, for now, computers are best used in the assessment process when restricted to mechanical aspects. Therefore, the assessment elements of any CMI system should be approached with caution.

Integrated Learning Systems

The most extreme case of CMI is a category called **integrated learning systems (ILS)**. At the beginning of the microcomputer age, companies that combined the work carried out by the pioneers of programmed instruction began springing up to produce products and services marketed to information technology in education. These companies constitute a multimillion-dollar industry.

Although the term *ILS* means different things to different people, it generally connotes the idea of a complex system that is marketed as an independent package for delivering all or a major portion of the school curriculum through technology. As one writer (Marshall, 1993) stated, "An ILS seems like a school executive's dream" (p. 14). Such a system includes hardware, software, training, and technical support. What better way to manage an organization than to have one system in which all the parts are consistent, organized, and controllable. In fact, some ILSs are referred to as *turnkey* approaches. This term is borrowed from the construction industry and refers to the process by which the contractor handles all aspects of a project and on completion hands the new owner a key that, when turned, renders everything operational. Maddux and Willis (1993) suggested that ILSs usually include the following features:

1. Assessment and diagnosis of student skills
2. Responsibility for delivering a substantial component of instruction in at least one subject area across several grade levels
3. Continuous monitoring of student performance and automatic adjustment of instruction where needed
4. Generation of student and class performance data in a variety of formats for use by teachers and administrators (Some ILSs can generate reports across school systems and provide comparative data.)

ILS usage tends to take place in very top-down educational environments, where rules and regulations covering many aspects of the teaching and learning process are passed from the school administration to the teachers and students in the classroom. Blaschke (1990) demonstrated this by conducting a study of current and projected use of ILSs. According to the study,

> districts that select ILSs tend to have one or more of the following characteristics: emphasis on centralized decision making where board members or superintendents exert great influence; and a policy which emphasizes quality control, accountability for student performance, and assurance that mandated curricula will be covered uniformly. (p. 20)

ILSs have become big business and will probably continue to grow. Many writers have discussed positive aspects of good ILSs, whereas others have waved an array of caution flags. In the final analysis, perhaps the success or failure of ILSs in improving U.S. education will be determined not by the ILSs themselves, but by the way in which they are used in the classroom. According to White (1992):

> Those who favor ILS adoption argue that ILS instruction (1) provides systematic exposure to the curriculum; (2) provides individualized pacing and review; (3) tracks errors, re-exposing the pupil to more instruction in order to reach the desired mastery level; (4) provides motivation through its interactivity and game format; (5) provides an accurate and comprehensive record of each pupil's progress; and (6) displays the real curriculum to observation, review, and potential revisions, so anyone can know exactly what a child has been taught. (p. 49)

It is clear that the ILS strategy for integrating information technology into the classroom would have some appeal to educators who favor a direct-instruction approach. For those who favor a more contructivist approach to education (see Chapter 7), however, such systems tend to be large teaching machines with little opportunity for either teachers or students to manipulate the system for personalized use. The best technology-enhanced teaching occurs when a teacher is able to control the small bits and pieces of available hardware and software to organize a technology-enhanced lesson. Such flexibility is severely limited in many ILSs. The best technology-enhanced learning occurs when students view available technology as a set of exploration and production tools. Technology must be flexible for students to be able to explore new meanings and then organize and present their conclusions. Students must be able to mix and match hardware and software in creative ways. They must be able to control the technology just as they can control other learning resources such as books, encyclopedias, paper, pencil, paint, scissors, and calculators.

The idea of automating schooling is not a new one, remember, nor one that has enjoyed even limited success. The teaching machine movement, which was begun by Pressey (1926, 1927) and continued by B. F. Skinner (1954, 1958), was an earlier attempt at automating teaching. The teaching machine movement failed, not because Pressey's and Skinner's devices did not work, but for a variety of social, psychological, and technical reasons. One reason for this failure was that the machines themselves became the focus and teaching came to be viewed as a mechanistic process that could be wholly converted to machine implementation.

LOGO: A UNIQUE COMPUTER LANGUAGE

One approach to harnessing the power of information technology to improve teaching and learning consisted of a unique software package that was designed and implemented to meet the requirements of an entire educational philosophy. This approach was called **Logo**, which is a computer language specifically geared toward children.

Historical Overview

Logo is a unique computer language that was developed by Seymour Papert, a computer scientist and mathematician at the Massachusetts Institute of Technology (MIT). In 1980, Papert presented his ideas about children, schools, computers, mathematics, learning, and Logo itself in a book entitled *Mindstorms: Children, Computers, and Powerful Ideas.* Papert's articulate and compelling writing style, coupled with his clear expertise in computing, mathematics, and learning theory, captured the imagination of many educators and sparked the beginning of the Logo movement.

While at MIT, Papert became interested in artificial intelligence. In the 1950s, Papert sensed that computers had potential as teaching and learning tools. However, before he could begin developing such tools, he believed he needed to know more about how children think and learn. Therefore, he spent 5 years (from 1958 to 1963) at the University of Geneva, studying with the eminent child psychologist, Jean Piaget. During this time, he became convinced that the computer could be turned into an object that could help children think. However, he believed that this would be possible only if communication between child and computer could be simplified. Furthermore, he believed that such communication should be interactive and natural. He envisioned a computer language that children could learn in the same way they learn to speak their native tongues. In other words, he wanted his language to be learned incidentally (through normal daily interaction and without the necessity of formal instruction). By 1963 Papert's work in this area had produced the Logo language.

As a boy, Papert (1980) was fascinated by automobiles. At an early age he played with two sets of automobile gears: one from a transmission, another from a differential (the part that transfers energy from the drive line to the rear wheels). At first, his pleasure derived merely from predicting the movement of the last gear in the chain based on the movement of the first gear. He then became fascinated with the functioning of the differential gear because it illustrated a nonlinear chain of causality. That is, it distributed motion from the transmission shaft differentially, depending on the resistance offered by the wheels. Papert said, "I remember quite vividly my excitement at discovering that a system could be lawful and completely comprehensible without being rigidly deterministic" (p. vi).

For Papert, gears became models for understanding a variety of difficult concepts:

> Gears, serving as models, carried many otherwise abstract ideas into my head. I clearly remember two examples from school math. I saw multiplication tables as gears, and my first brush with equations in two variables (e.g., $3x + 4y = 10$) immediately evoked the differential. By the time I had made a mental gear model of the relation between x and y, figuring how many teeth each gear needed, the equation had become a comfortable friend. (p. vii)

Thus, Papert's fascination with gears evolved into a versatile tool with which old knowledge was used to help acquire new understanding. Additionally, Papert suggests that his experiences with gears, which led to an understanding of mathematics, helped instill a positive attitude toward mathematics. Papert summed up his ideas about learning as follows:

> Slowly I began to formulate what I still consider the fundamental fact about learning: Anything is easy if you can assimilate it to your collection of models. If you can't, anything can be painfully difficult.... What an individual can learn, and how he learns it, depends on what models he has available. (p. vii)

Thus, Papert designed Logo as a thinking tool that provides children with powerful models that will assist them in understanding new concepts. Papert summed up his vision for Logo as follows:

> What the gears cannot do the computer might. The computer is the Proteus of machines. Its essence is its universality, its power to simulate. Because it can take on a thousand forms and serve a thousand functions, it can appeal to a thousand tastes. This book is the result of my own attempts over the past decade to turn computers into instruments flexible enough so that many children can each create for themselves something like what the gears were for me. (p. viii)

In *Mindstorms*, Papert made one of the most startling educational suggestions we have encountered. He suggests that using the discovery method of teaching children to program in Logo, coupled with sweeping changes in school policies and procedures, could result in narrowing the boundary between child and adult thinking. (Piagetian discovery learning involves the teacher serving as facilitator to help children discover things for themselves. This teaching role contrasts with traditional teaching in which the teacher serves as lecturer or disseminator of knowledge.)

In making this claim, Papert departs from traditional Piagetian thinking. As you may know, Piaget believed that children pass through four stages of cognitive development. He believed that the time spent in each stage varies from person to person, and he emphasized the importance of the environment in facilitating this progression. Although Piaget never maintained that other sequences were not possible, most Piagetian psychologists have concluded that the order of progression through the stages is part of human genetic heritage and is invariant.

Another way of expressing this is to say that Piagetian psychologists believe that the sequence in which people develop different intellectual abilities is part of the human condition and is relatively independent of cultural or environmental variables. In support of this contention, research has consistently shown that the sequence of stages through which children from various Western cultures pass as they mature does not vary (Wadsworth, 1989). Likewise, research on handicapped children has failed to find any other sequence of development (Brekke, Johnson, & Williams, 1975). Piaget suggested that **formal operational thinking** (adult thinking) is unavailable to children younger than about twelve years of age because (a) the logical structure of such tasks is too complex and (b) the necessary neurological structures are not sufficiently mature.

Papert agreed that these two variables play a role. On the other hand, he suggested that the order in which intellectual abilities are acquired is more responsive to the environment than Piaget suspected. Specifically, he suggested that some developmental differences may be the result of our culture's lack of materials that serve as the foundations of advanced intellectual structures. Papert's position, therefore, was that computers in general, and Logo in particular, could be used as tools and models to build ways of thinking in prepubescent children that Piaget thought were possible only from puberty onward. In other words, Papert suggested that Logo could make children capable of adult thinking!

After further refining his theories and field testing Logo, Papert suggested that school math is a corruption of true mathematics and made many suggestions for reforming education, including the suspension of grading, the adoption of Piagetian discovery learning, and the provision of a computer for every student. With respect to teaching mathematics, one of Papert's suggestions was that schoolchildren should be introduced to mathematics through geometry. In the meantime, Papert and his coworkers had integrated what they called *turtle graphics* into Logo. **Turtle graphics** involved a two-dimensional "turtle" (usually a small triangle or simple turtle shape) that could be moved around a computer screen, thus drawing designs (graphics) on the screen. The Logo turtle was a specific example of the general role Papert envisioned for computers in education.

He believed computers could be used to make difficult, abstract ideas more concrete and, therefore, more understandable to children. He referred to this general goal as using computers to concretize the abstract.

As it turned out, such exaggerated claims were somewhat detrimental to the field of educational computing, and to Logo, because they led inevitably to a backlash of public and professional opinion. A brief rhetorical battle developed between groups of ardent Logo disciples on the one hand and seasoned educators who scoffed at such drastic claims on the other hand. None of the many claims for Logo have proved as controversial as the claim that Logo can somehow improve cognitive functioning such as general problem solving. Although the issue is far from settled, much of the research on problem solving seems to show that such skills are more discipline specific than many teachers would hope. In other words, if a child learns to solve Logo programming problems, he will not necessarily be better at solving problems in other areas.

Although the question of whether programming cultivates transferable problem-solving skills is a relatively new one, the question of transfer itself is quite old. For example, it was once common for schools to teach Latin on the grounds that it improved general reasoning ability or resulted in increased mental rigor. When this contention could not be proved, Latin was dropped from many programs.

If skills learned in one domain carry over into some other domain, they are said to transfer. As just mentioned, skills learned in Logo do not necessarily transfer to other domains. At least such transfer does not occur automatically. There is some evidence, however, that transfer can occur, given the proper conditions. Black, Swan, and Schwartz (1989), for example, were able to document transferable problem-solving skills in a Logo project involving 133 subjects in fourth through eighth grades. This study was carefully controlled and well thought out, and the researchers included several features designed to minimize the shortcomings of other Logo research:

1. Due to the failure of nondirective discovery methods of teaching Logo, the researchers included well-structured activities.

2. Because other studies focused on children of all ages, the researchers used subjects in middle and junior high school, the ages at which formal operational thinking (abstract, or adult thinking) is thought to emerge.

3. Because many other researchers have not defined problem solving and have directed their studies merely at solutions rather than problem-solving strategies leading to solutions, Black, Swan, and Schwartz identified six problem-solving strategies judged useful in programming: (a) subgoal formation, (b) forward-chaining, (c) backward-chaining, (d) systematic trial and error, (e) alternative problem representation, and (f) analogical reasoning. Instruction and assessment were developed around these strategies.

4. Because other researchers have not emphasized the importance of **metacognition** (defined as the awareness of one's systematic thinking strategies, which are required for learning [Lerner, 1989]), Black, Swan, and Schwartz made efforts to model such metacognitive strategies and to help children develop metacognitive habits.

5. Most previous researchers have restricted the teaching of Logo to the turtle graphics capabilities of the language. Black, Swan, and Schwartz keyed in on this variable, instructing one subgroup in graphics only, one in graphics and **list processing,** and one in list processing only. More high-quality research such as this is obviously needed.

We feel compelled to mention a series of well-known research studies that are often called the *Bank Street Studies* (Kurland & Pea, 1983; Pea, 1983; Pea & Kurland, 1983a, 1983b, 1983c, 1984). These studies are popularly (and erroneously) believed to have proved that Logo does not improve transferable problem-solving skills. However, this research is so flawed that it defies interpretation. Among the many errors in this research, the fatal flaw, as Pea and Kurland themselves admitted, is that the children in the study did not master Logo programming skills. Therefore, the failure to find improved, transferable problem-solving skills among the so-called Logo group should not be interpreted as a reflection of Logo's lack of power to produce such results. The researchers should have tested their subjects on Logo programming skills and disqualified any who failed to show Logo mastery before testing for transfer.

Logo, however, is still being used by some teachers. A recent trend is for Logo and Logo-like programs to be made available on the World Wide Web. An example of such a web-based program can be found at http://www.atlantic.net/~caggiano/logo/logo.html. Although these programs differ from original forms of Logo, especially in that they operate without the actual Logo programming language, they do embody the thinking and teaching strategies of Papert and his disciples. Bull and Bull (1997) summarized the attitude of many regarding Logo as follows: "The most important heritage of Logo is not the dozens of different dialects of a family of programming languages, but the philosophy of education that can be applied to many different educational technologies" (p. 58).

We advocate the educational concepts and teaching strategies embodied in the Logo movement but oppose the unscientific discipleship that has formed around Logo. Research has yet to establish whether Logo has value as a **cognitive amplifier** or whether it can be used to narrow the boundary between child and adult thinking. However, other, less controversial reasons can explain why the educational concepts and teaching strategies put forth by the Logo movement are worth considering in planning strategies for integrating information technology into the classroom curriculum:

1. Logo-like strategies can provide an area of success for children, some of whom seldom have such an experience in a school setting.
2. Programming exercises of all types permit trial-and-error problem solving. Such exercises are somewhat self-correcting, which can be beneficial for children who have become highly sensitive to adult correction.

3. Simple Logo-like graphics provide practice in spatial relationships. This can be beneficial to students who have deficits in understanding spatial relations.
4. Many children are distractible. Distractibility interferes with academic tasks that require long periods of uninterrupted effort (long division, for example). However, Logo-like programming sessions can be interrupted and resumed later with little or no impairment in efficiency.
5. Peer tutoring and cooperative learning can be made part of Logo-like teaching strategies. These methods can facilitate social status and peer relations for children who experience difficulty in such areas.
6. Logo-like programming provides an interesting, relevant reason to use mathematics in a setting that is free of unpleasant associations. Thus, such strategies may prove useful in reversing the trend toward mathophobia.

OTHER TRENDS AND ISSUES

This section focuses on some of the trends that have shaped the field of information technology in education and some of the issues that have emerged along the way, specifically, issues and trends related to computer literacy, computer equity, computing ethics, laboratories versus integration of computers, and networking.

Computer Literacy

One of the most hotly debated issues in information technology in education has centered on the concept of **computer literacy**. The controversy involves several subissues: (1) how the term should be defined, (2) how important computer knowledge and skills are to learners now and in the future, and (3) what knowledge or skills should make up computer literacy. One of the first people to use the term was Andrew Molnar of the National Science Foundation. Molnar (1978) suggested that the next great crisis in education would be related to computer literacy.

Although it is difficult to separate cause from effect, two related phenomena occurred in the early 1980s that helped convince many people that computer literacy deserved a place in the school curriculum. The first of these events was the publication of formal reports of the findings of a number of commissions whose charge was to study and critique U.S. education. Most of these reports were highly critical of schools and recommended teaching computer knowledge and skills (computer literacy) in their list of educational reforms. One of the most highly publicized of these reports was *A Nation at Risk,* published in 1983 by the National Commission on Excellence in Education.

The second related event was the inclusion of this same recommendation in reports by numerous educational organizations, such as the National Council of Supervisors of Mathematics, the National Council of Teachers of Mathematics, and the National Council for Social Studies (Riedesel & Clements, 1985). Following these reports, professional journals fostered a debate about how to define computer literacy. This debate produced little, if any, agreement on definition.

Bramble and Mason (1985) made the excellent point that difficulty in defining computer literacy is to be expected because experts in language arts have failed to define literacy clearly even in the traditional sense.

By about 1984 most educators had accepted the idea that computers should have a place in the curriculum. The controversy then became whether literacy should mean learning about computers or learning how to use computers. From 1984 until the present time, the debate has narrowed somewhat. Advocates of each position argued among themselves about specific content or skills to be taught. This debate has been particularly keen among those who believe that computer literacy should mean teaching learners to use computers. Some such advocates asserted that all children should be taught to program computers, whereas others maintained that programming is a waste of time and that children should be taught to use programs written by others.

An excellent review and analysis of the early debate about computer literacy was written by Kelman (1984), who suggested that the two most common rationales for computer literacy are (1) computer literacy as prevocational necessity and (2) computer literacy as national economic necessity. According to Kelman, both are based on flawed assumptions. The assumption underlying the prevocational argument is that computers will continue to pervade the workplace and that, therefore, workers of the future will need to know progressively more about computers and how they work. However, Kelman maintains that, as computers become easier to operate, workers will need to know less about how they work. He points out that we are surrounded by electric motors but need to know little or nothing about them to use them.

The national economic necessity argument, according to Kelman, is that computer literacy skills should be taught to ensure that the United States does not lose its competitive economic edge among the nations of the world. According to this rationale, the United States suffers from a technology gap relative to other developed nations such as Japan and some Western European countries. Kelman denies that such a gap exists because new technological advances and inventions still come predominantly from the United States. Foreign countries sometimes do a better job of applying new discoveries, but Kelman suggests that their success is due to differences in (1) national economic policies, (2) industrial practices, and (3) the cost of labor. Kelman concludes by endorsing the suggestion by Watt (1981) that computer literacy should be viewed as analogous to literacy in one's native language. Specifically, says Kelman:

> Students should learn to use the computer for word, data, and number processing from their earliest possible years in school. They should also have the opportunity to use the graphics and sound capabilities of the computer to explore their creative urges. Moreover, teachers should provide opportunities for students to use computers in problem-solving and decision-making situations. At times, this may include programming a computer. At other times, it may not. (p. 16)

We tend to agree with those who emphasize that all students should be taught to use the computer as a tool. Common applications such as word processing, database management, spreadsheets, presentation software, and of course making use of the Internet are valuable tools to aid classroom learning. We also support the importance of literacy because computers now occupy an increasingly prevalent and important niche in our culture. Therefore, knowledge about computers, as well as basic computer skills, is part of the common intellectual heritage that educators are charged with transmitting.

In the early 1990s educators became concerned with the computer literacy of preservice and in-service teachers and university faculty, especially college of education faculty. This concern was the result of a widespread realization that teachers were not being properly trained in computer skills and, therefore, would not be able to train their students pro perly. Additionally, there was the realization that proper training of preservice teachers would first require mastery by teacher educators of some computer concepts and skills.

Teachers who lack adequate skills in using information technology continue to be a national concern as documented by the U.S. Department of Education in their grant initiative *Preparing Tomorrow's Teachers to Use Technology* (2000). According to this document:

> Federal, state and local agencies are investing billions of dollars to equip schools with computers and modern communications networks. Despite these investments, only 20 percent of the 2.5 million teachers currently working in our public schools feel comfortable using these technologies in their classrooms. (p. 1)

The direction set by the Department of Education with this major grant initiative really summarizes current thinking and direction regarding training teachers to use information technology in their classrooms. First, it strongly suggests that the federal government has taken the position that information technology is and must be an important element in U.S. public schools. Second, it takes the position that all teachers must be prepared to use information technology in their teaching. Third, it shifts the emphasis away from in-service training to preservice training.

The position taken by the Department of Education on this issue is that billions of dollars have been spent on getting hardware, software, and connectivity into the schools, and millions have been spent on in-service training. Now it is time to put money into ensuring that teachers who enter the teaching profession are prepared to integrate technology into the classroom. This, of course, makes good sense. Unless teachers are being prepared in their teacher training programs, the need for in-service training in this area will never end and in fact will continue to escalate.

Although debates flourished concerning what should be included in preservice information technology in education courses, Ehley (1992) argued that if preservice teachers are to understand the true value of computers in teaching, they must be exposed to excellent models of university teaching that employ integration of information technology. Therefore, she recommended that computer literacy courses for teachers include hands-on experiences, instruction in software evaluation, writing lesson plans, and research in information technology in education. In addition, however, she emphasized that this content must be taught with a heavy reliance on the computer as a teaching and learning tool so that students can experience actual curriculum integration in the computer course itself.

This position has become a national trend. Abate (2000) described a project in which classroom teachers who were proficient in integrating information technology into their curricula worked with university teacher-education faculty in a mentoring role. The faculty then modeled successful integration teaching practices in their teacher training courses. The unique concept of this project was that preservice teachers would encounter the same instructional methods they would be expected to use on entering the teaching force. Early in this program, Abate reported that "indications at this point are that both classroom teachers and university faculty are reacting favorably to the mentoring arrangement and more importantly that the university faculty are starting to integrate technology into their teaching" (p. 2093). The *Preparing Tomorrow's Teachers to Use Technology* grant initiative also addresses the problem of professors in teacher-education programs. This initiative places the emphasis squarely at the top by encouraging teacher training institutions to make sure the professors are modeling the integration of information technology and that preservice teachers experience the use of information technology throughout their teacher training programs.

Computer Equity

Computer equity has been an issue since computers were first brought into schools. Since the late 1970s and early 1980s, some educators have feared that having computers in schools might act to widen existing gaps between rich and poor, male and female, black and white, disabled and abled. In general, equity issues arise because (1) access to computers varies from school to school and (2) many people hold stereotypic attitudes about who should operate computers (Vockell & Schwartz, 1988).

Bohlin (1993), who reviewed the literature on computers and gender equity, cites many studies that identify the problem. This author begins by stating that whereas many female students are currently avoiding computer experiences, at the same time the federal government is estimating that 75 percent of all future jobs will require computer use. He goes on to assert that

> educators cannot afford to ignore this critical fact—that females perceive their competency to learn about computers to be significantly lower than their male counterparts. A significant long-term problem may be perpetuated by this "inferiority" perception—decreased participation can limit career choices, thus producing fewer female computer role models. This spiraling effect may continue to produce a substantial gap, resulting in a dramatic failure by our educational system. (pp. 155–156)

The technology equity issue has given rise to a new phrase, the **digital divide**, which, according to McConnaughey and Lader (1995), "has been applied to a phenomenon wherein the 'significant growth in computer ownership and usage overall...has occurred to a greater extent within some income levels, demographic groups, and geographic areas, than in others'" (p. 2). Snider (2000) takes the position that an important element in overcoming the digital divide is teacher training and says:

> An integral element of professional development includes a commitment in terms of exploration time and technical support. This commitment would allow teachers opportunities to build the skills and confidence necessary for weaving technology into the very fiber of the classroom. In this way, classroom technology becomes a transparent tool, and teachers and students use technology to support learning and express new knowledge. Thus, teacher preparation and common goals for implementation will have contributed to equitable access and opportunities for all learners to reach their highest potential as contributing members in the society of the information age. (p. 254)

Computer Ethics

As technology empowers human beings, new behaviors become possible, and ethical questions about these behaviors arise. **Computer ethics** has been a natural development. Many issues relate to computer ethics, but the one we consider most serious for educators is the violation of copyright law. This issue is straightforward: It is illegal to make unauthorized copies of a copyrighted computer program. Software is protected under U.S. copyright law. The law makes it a crime to copy without permission any program that has been copyrighted, except for the purpose of making one archival or backup copy for storage.

Unfortunately, teachers have a poor reputation for software honesty. It has been estimated that 10 to 50 percent of the programs used in schools are illegal copies (Mandell & Mandell, 1989). Some teachers have taken the position that violation of the copyright law is moral as long as the unauthorized copies are used for teaching children in schools. The law, of course, recognizes no such exemption for educators, and the courts do not accept such a defense. It is difficult to understand why some educators take this position. Most teachers would not suggest that stealing goods from a store is moral as long as they are passed on to a student! Just as the theft of a coat deprives the retailer of a fair return on their efforts, illegal copying of software (to avoid purchasing multiple copies) deprives the developer and distributors of a fair return on their efforts.

Laboratories versus Integration of Computers

Early efforts to infuse computers into schools resulted in placing all computers in one room, a computer laboratory. The "lab" was generally used in one of two ways. In the late 1970s and 1980s, one or two teachers were commonly assigned to the lab, where they taught children computing skills and concepts. As more and more teachers became aware of how computers could support instruction, another use of labs emerged. Teachers who normally taught in a regular classroom would bring their students to the lab for a few class periods to complete a particular project.

Computer labs are still popular, but the long-term success of computers in education depends on widespread use of computers as teaching and learning tools in individual classrooms, which fosters more curriculum integration. We agree with the observation that pencils would never have become essential educational tools if students had been allowed to use them only in "pencil labs."

OTHER APPLICATIONS

Most teachers choose teaching as an occupation because they enjoy interacting with students and watching them grow and learn. However, teachers are often required to perform many routine record-keeping tasks even when the tasks take time away from teaching. Preparing reports and records takes time; however, teaching itself involves a considerable amount of data processing and organization. Lessons must be planned, prepared, and organized; grades must be kept; student information must be organized and available to access; letters must be written to parents; and student organizations need support and maintenance. The burden of these tasks, which support teaching, can be alleviated by employing strategies for effective use of information technology. A discussion of some of these strategies constitutes the next section of this chapter.

Customized Letters and Reports

Teachers often must write the same general letter to more than one person, for example, invitations to parent nights, announcements of school events to which parents or other dignitaries are invited, reports on school progress, messages to colleagues who are also members of various organizations, and much more. Using a typewriter to create 30 personalized letters inviting parents to a school open house involves physically typing the same letter over and over to produce 30 copies, each differing in address and salutation only. However, using almost any word processor and a compatible database, you can apply a procedure called **mail merge** to create the letter once and then produce 30 different copies, each with a unique address and salutation.

A second relatively simple procedure that saves time is boilerplate paragraphs. Boilerplate is text material that you may want to use over and over again in different documents. Most word processors are capable of creating boilerplate paragraphs, which can be inserted in a document with a simple command. Some word processors use special commands, called *macros*, to insert boilerplate paragraphs. Others use the same mail merge procedure described earlier. You could, for example, create a database of common comments about student compositions, including a paragraph for subject–verb agreement, end-of-sentence punctuation, use of commas, and much more. You might be surprised by the number of hours mail merge and boilerplate paragraphs can save the average teacher each year.

Student Information Systems

Schools and school systems are constantly creating and updating a seemingly end-less list of records. Data overload has been a problem in schools for years; how-ever, computer technology can reduce the burden of record keeping that is placed on teachers. Today many teachers and principals spend much less time on all those records than they did only a few years ago. Most states now use **student information systems,** which are special computer programs that keep track of data needed by operational personnel, such as clerical staff, middle administra-tors, such as principals and department chairs, and top administrators, such as district and state superintendents.

Student information systems can automate many types of record-keeping procedures. One onerous task they help manage is daily attendance records. They provide the school and the school system with accurate and up-to-date records of attendance, excused and unexcused absences, and standard data such as average daily attendance (ADA). Required reports can be automatically generated for sub-mission to the district office. In addition, lists of students with excessive absences and of students with potential problems can be generated.

Electronic Grade Books

Most student information systems keep track of course grades; some even main-tain databases of 6-week grades. Few, however, can be used to record daily and weekly test grades, project grades, and other criteria for 6-week, semester, and yearly grades. Hundreds of electronic gradebook programs, however, have been created to do just that.

If you are responsible for keeping many types of student data, including grades, a gradebook program can be invaluable. The program can weight and average student scores to arrive at grades. This frees you of the tedious task of cal-culating grades and facilitates calculating grades with different weights so that the importance of a particular test, quiz, or activity can be better represented. In addi-tion, information about your students is easily accessible, so it is more useful.

Lesson Planners and Lesson Databases

Two other types of education software that are very useful are lesson planners and lesson databases. Lesson-planning software helps teachers create lessons they can use in the classroom, and lesson databases help teachers keep track of their col-lection of lessons.

A number of "stand-alone" programs do these tasks. A stand-alone program does one job, such as word processing. Lesson-related tasks can also be performed with several integrated programs. An integrated program can be used for several types of work, such as word processing, database management, and telecommunications. Good integrated programs of this type have both a lesson planner and a lesson database along with several other types of teacher utilities.

Portfolio Assessment Support

During the past 10 years the behavioral approach to education, which tends to be teacher-centered, has been increasingly challenged by educators who advocate a student-centered approach. One unique aspect of student-centered approaches is the demand they place on student assessment. If students have a major role in deciding what they study and explore and how they go about it, the assumption that a course will be based on a universal set of objectives all students must achieve is no longer valid. And, if that assumption is not valid, testing achievement by administering a standard multiple-choice test to every student in a class is no longer valid. If students are involved in many diverse and unique activities, assessment of their progress must address that diversity. One approach to this is **portfolio assessment.** Instead of administering multiple-choice tests, teachers help students collect and organize a selected portfolio of their work. Each student's portfolio is then evaluated. As students add compositions, artwork, test papers, and assignments to their portfolios, the portfolios can become quite bulky. Software has been developed to help teachers keep track of student portfolios. During the school year (or years) students and their teachers can add relevant samples of academic work as well as student and family data.

Presentation Software

Although a great deal of discussion today is about student-centered learning and collaborative group learning, the plain fact is that most of the time in most classrooms the lessons are teacher-centered. Lecture–discussion activities, demonstrations, and recitations are still commonplace, and new media can support traditional instruction in several ways. Supporting lectures and discussions with multimedia materials is possible virtually in any subject area and at any grade level. Several publishers distribute collections of photographs, drawings, and video on both CD-ROM and laser disk that instructors can use to create their own multimedia presentations. A new category of computer program, called **presentation software**, has emerged during the past few years as an alternative to the most common visual aid, the overhead projector, for presentations and lectures in both education and business.

The first generation of presentation software offered little more than an electronic way of creating a text-only overhead that could be displayed in color on a computer monitor or projected on a screen using an overhead projector and LCD panel. The current generation of presentation packages allows you to produce electronic presentations that contain color graphics, text in many sizes and shapes, sound, video that appears in a window on the screen, and animation. Figure 2.1 is a screen from a presentation created in Microsoft's *PowerPoint*, one of

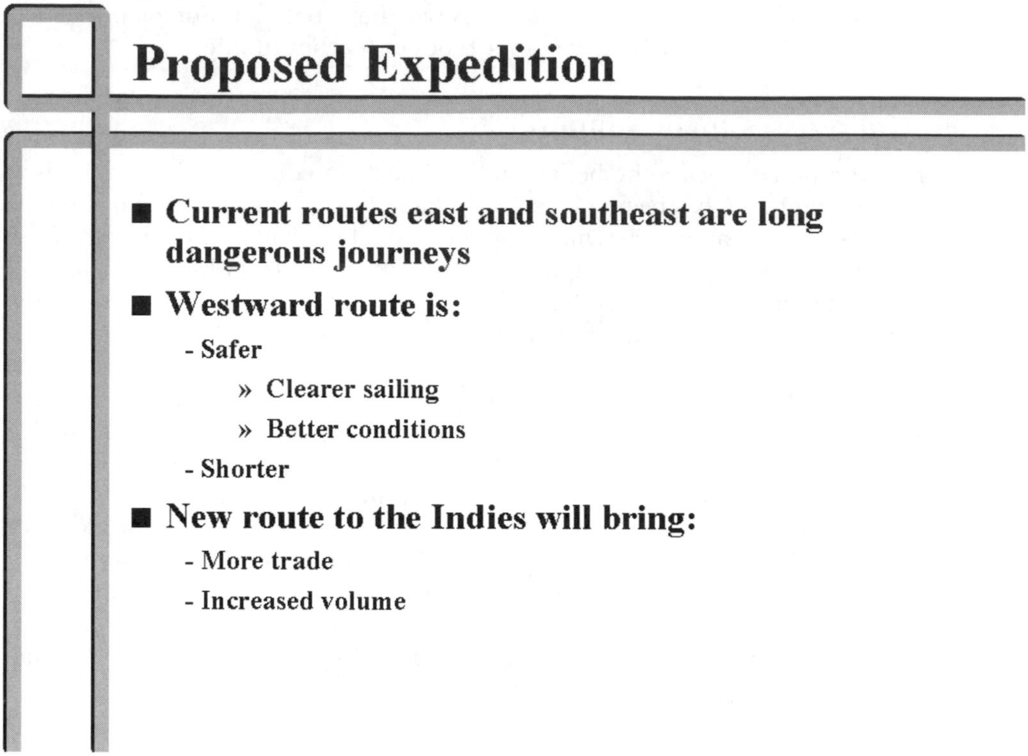

Proposed Expedition

- **Current routes east and southeast are long dangerous journeys**
- **Westward route is:**
  - Safer
    - » **Clearer sailing**
    - » **Better conditions**
  - Shorter
- **New route to the Indies will bring:**
  - More trade
  - Increased volume

FIGURE 2.1   *PowerPoint* is one of the more popular presentation software packages.

the more powerful presentation packages. *PowerPoint* is available in versions for both the Windows and Macintosh platforms.

PowerPoint is used widely in business as well as in education, and its strength is as a sophisticated electronic replacement for traditional overheads. It was originally designed for linear presentations: first comes slide 1, then slide 2, then slide 3. But today's version offers you the opportunity to create presentations that have hyperlinks. By inserting hyperlinks into your *PowerPoint* presentation you are able to respond to student questions, or to go off in one direction for your morning class and take another in the afternoon section.

A second popular presentation program is *Corel Presentation*, which is part of the *Corel Office* software suite. *Corel Presentation* is very similar to *PowerPoint*. You can use it to create high-quality slide shows and drawings for projects of all types, from proposals to multimedia presentations. It has a simple graphics editor that lets you modify images. Both *Corel Presentation* and *PowerPoint* make it possible to convert finished presentations to World Wide Web pages. An example of a useful *PowerPoint* presentation on the Web can be found at http://www.eiu.edu/~mediasrv/Staticimages/example/framesample.htm.

Authoring Systems for Teachers

The terms *authoring tool, authoring software, authoring language,* and *authoring system* have all been used to indicate computer software designed to facilitate the creation of instructional packages and multimedia materials. We use the term **authoring systems** to discuss this unique type of educational software. One of the popular authoring systems being used in education today is *Authorware*, produced by Macromedia. Although *Authorware*, like most authoring systems, can be used to create presentations, this type of software is probably best suited for creating interactive materials such as tutorials and simulations that use a range of visuals and require regular and varied responses from students. Other authoring systems include *HyperCard, Toolbook,* and *HyperMedia*.

Some teachers use authoring systems to create everything from presentations and tutorials for their students to interactive stories and electronic books. Authoring systems are also becoming popular for developing web-based versions of presentations and tutorials. The possibilities are considerable. For example, Higgins and Boone (1992) used an authoring system to create study guides for their history class. They replaced their traditional lectures with electronic study guides tied to the textbook for the course. Although authoring systems have great potential, in our experience most teachers are not willing to expend the time and effort necessary to learn such programs well enough to produce quality products.

Student Authoring Systems

Distinguishing between authoring systems for students and teachers is somewhat artificial. Teachers and students at all levels often use the same programs. *Authorware, HyperCard,* and *Toolbook,* for example, are used by students and teachers alike in some schools. Authoring systems such as *The Multimedia Workshop* are inexpensive and designed specifically for student use. Students can use *The Multimedia Workshop* to create traditional papers, newsletters, and presentations, as well as electronic and multimedia versions of these common student products.

COMPUTERS AS EFFECTIVE AIDS FOR INDIVIDUALS WITH DISABILITIES

The use of technology to aid individuals with disabilities is probably as old as the recognition of disabilities. Early technology for prosthetic devices consisted of wood and leather for constructing artificial limbs. As new materials, devices, and techniques have been developed to benefit the general population, attempts have been made to improve the quality of life for persons with disabilities. Electronic technology has brought about rapid and far-reaching changes in our society and has also contributed to the health and happiness of those who have disabilities. As stated by Lewis (1993), "In a few short years, technology has changed the way people with disabilities live, work, and learn" (p. 23).

Tyre (1988) suggested that computers are important in special education because students "are able to learn more, thus achieving a greater amount of their natural potential" (p. 14). Wiener (1990) attested to the potential of computer technology in special education:

> The potential for computers in special education is without limits. Computer technology can provide a voice for students with oral communication problems; serve as a writing medium for students who have difficulty manipulating a pencil; open the world for written communication for the blind; enable the deaf to communicate in a hearing classroom; and allow the physically disabled the opportunity to control their learning environment. (p. 18)

This section describes, in general terms, how technology can be used to assist persons with disabilities, particularly in terms of learning.

Speech Synthesis

Computer users (along with science fiction writers) have long been fascinated with **synthesized speech.** The idea of a machine being able to listen, understand, process, and talk makes for fascinating speculation. Whereas such machines exist only in the realm of science fiction, machines that can simulate human speech are real and serve as valuable aids to people with disabilities, especially those with visual and motor handicaps. Bronson (1987) pointed out that speech synthesis is the preferred method for the blind for getting information into and out of computers.

Although speech synthesis is certainly a boon to individuals with various types of disabilities, it is still not perfect. Most speech synthesis, though intelligible, is of fairly low quality and still sounds far too much like Darth Vader. However, the tremendous potential of speech synthesis is driving advanced research projects that have as their goal the development of a true voice substitute for those who cannot speak.

Special Input Devices

One type of technology that has helped many realize their potential is the special input device. We use the term to describe a variety of adaptations to traditional computer input. These adaptations allow people with motor impairments to control computers, which is essential if computers are expected to enhance their intellectual potential. For many individuals with disabilities, getting information into the computer with a standard keyboard, mouse, light pen, or a touch screen is impossible. Such devices require more motor control than some people can manage. Figure 2.2 shows a special light pen attached to the computer user's head so that the user can point the pen by moving his or her head.

FIGURE 2.2   Light pens can be attached to a hat to run a menu program. As the light remains on a letter or a number for a few seconds, the character is entered into the program.

The objective of a special input device is to provide a mechanism by which people with disabilities can use whatever degree of motor control they have to send signals to the computer. In some cases this might be a special keyboard with very large keys or a keyboardlike structure by which characters and words are pointed to with some object. In other cases, the computer user might control the computer by touching the computer screen with their hands or with some pointing aide to select menu items. For some individuals with disabilities, however, even devices such as special keyboards and touch-sensitive screens still demand too much motor control. For them, the computer can only be controlled by the slightest movement of one body part.

Switches are devices similar to a simple light switch. A light switch has only two positions, on and off. All the various switching devices used by individuals with disabilities to control computers act in a similar manner. They can be tailored to respond to almost any movement of the human body. They send one of two signals to the computer, on or off. What allows the disabled person to use the computer is a program that is controlled by the on–off signals sent to it through the switch. Examples of switches used by a disabled person are shown in Figure 2.3.

An example of the type of program that can be controlled by a switch is a special word processor. When using such a word processor, the disabled writer sees letters and numbers clustered in groups on the screen. A cursor slowly scans across the clusters until it arrives at the desired cluster. At this point, the writer activates the switch and the cursor pauses. It then scans the characters within the

FIGURE 2.3 Different types of computer switches.

cluster, and the writer again actuates the switch when the cursor points to the desired character. The selected character is then placed in a text area of the screen. In this way letters, numbers, and punctuation marks are linked together just as they would be by a writer using a standard keyboard. Obviously, this is a slow and tedious process compared to fluent typing. A person with a severe motor disability typically produces only about five words per minute using such a device; however, this process may open a new world to the person whose only previous form of communication has been a nod or a blink.

Aids for Individuals with Sensory Disabilities

When we speak of individuals with sensory disabilities, we are speaking of those who have visual or hearing impairments. A person with a visual or hearing impairment may be totally impaired, moderately impaired, or only slightly impaired. The technology that is used by such individuals is either designed to provide an alternative method of receiving sensory input or to enhance the partially functioning sensory mechanisms of the individual.

Concerning what technology is doing for individuals with visual impairments, Julia Anderson (1989), writing about computers and disabled persons in *Harvard Business Review*, said, "This technology revolution has forced corporations to rethink notions of the physical limitations on job performance in information processing" (p. 36). This is particularly true for individuals who are blind or visually impaired. Depending on the severity of the disability and the personal preference of the individual, the visually impaired person has a variety of electronic options from which to choose. Once information has been encoded into electronic signals, it can be decoded into speech, braille, or enlarged print on paper or a computer monitor. The signals can even be turned into vibrations that some blind people can interpret. A thorough listing of companies and organizations that provide special aides and resources for the blind and visually handicapped can be found at http://www.itpolicy.gsa.gov/cita/blind.htm.

Hardware and Software for Individuals with Disabilities

One of the first efforts to market hardware and software for individuals with disabilities involved the Adaptive Firmware Card, actually a circuit board that could be installed in the Apple II line of computers. It provided both the hardware and the software people with disabilities would need to access a computer. The Adaptive Firmware Card was originally marketed by Adaptive Peripheral but was later acquired by Don Johnston Developmental Equipment, a company that markets an array of adaptive hardware and software for individuals with disabilities. The Don Johnston company can be contacted on the Web at http://www.donjohnston.com/.

Today, many adaptive devices with accompanying software make it possible for individuals with disabilities to use computer and related technology. As with all technology, adaptive devices and software has improved markedly since the Adaptive Firmware Card. Many companies and organizations can be contacted on the Web. Some good starting points include

Assistive Technology in the Classroom—http://www.infinitec.org/assistechclass.html

Adaptive Device Vendors—http://www.brus-dso.odedodea.edu/special/softlist.html#anchor_Adaptive Device Vendors

Disabilities Resource Directory (DRI)—http://www.tfsksu.net/~cbaslock/olc_d1.html

Noel Brewer Adaptive Technology Aide—http://alamo.nmsu.edu/~nbrewer/index.html

Other Places to Go for Help

One of the first places to look for help for individuals with disabilities is your state's Vocational Rehabilitation Commission. In most states, these agencies are active in providing technical assistance and job support to individuals with disabilities. Most states have highly skilled specialists who can recommend hardware and software for people with special needs. Often, these agencies also offer training on how to use such hardware and software and may even loan certain products on a short-term basis.

An important resource for parents and teachers of students with disabilities is *Closing the Gap*, a bimonthly newspaper-style publication devoted to news and reviews regarding technology advances for individuals with disabilities. You can visit *Closing the Gap* on their website at http://closingthegap.com. Once each year, this publication features the Gap Resource Directory, a widely used guide to current hardware, software, producers, and organizations. *Closing the Gap* is one of the best resources for information about new developments in special education technology.

Another organization that can often provide advice on appropriate hardware and software for individuals with disabilities is Alliance for Technology Access, which can be contacted at http://trace.wisc.edu/gofr_web/ata.html. This organization defines itself as

> a growing movement of people across the country who are working to redefine human potential through the powerful and imaginative application of computer technology. It consists of a network of assistive technology resource centers whose members share a common vision and an uncommon commitment to improving the quality of life for children and adults with disabilities.

SUMMARY

This chapter presented the related origins of drill-and-practice and tutorial software. This software can be traced back to the programmed instruction movement in the 1950s and 1960s. In fact, much early educational software was based on the programmed instruction model, which itself was based on behavioral learning theory. Although traditional drill-and-practice software and tutorial programs are not as popular as they once were, they are still used in schools today. Now popular in schools today are CMI and ILSs. The merits of both CMI and ILSs will be determined, to some extent, by the theory of teaching and learning you prefer.

Some issues in educational computing were presented, specifically, computer literacy, equity, ethics, labs versus curriculum integration, networking, and teaching problem solving. We discussed the question of whether computer literacy skills should be taught to all students and whether these skills should include programming. We reviewed two frequently heard arguments for teaching literacy: the vocational argument and the national economic imperative argument. Both arguments seem to be flawed.

Computer equity concerns the lack of equal access to educational computing. Some educators fear that computing could actually increase social inqualities. The question of ethics arises naturally as a result of access to new behaviors through advances in technology. We have discussed ethical problems related to violation of copyright law and lack of equitable access to computing.

Although most teacher utility programs are a bit short on zip and eye appeal, they do offer teachers relief from some of the mind-numbing but required record-keeping chores that today grow like weeds in the educational garden. Using some of these programs can save hundreds of hours a year. Presentation software such as *PowerPoint* and authoring systems such as *HyperStudio* are increasingly used by teachers and students to create presentations, reports, and instructional material.

We have discussed the unique programming language Logo, along with the educational philosophy of Seymour Papert. Even though many of the claims made for Logo have not been realized, many of the concepts set forth by Papert, and championed by Logo disciples, are sound and worth considering when attempts are made to integrate information technology into the classroom.

We explained how the computer has become a valuable prosthetic device for students with varying disabilities, ranging from blindness and limited vision to lack of motor control. In keeping with the spirit and intent of this book, we have concluded by pointing out some cautions and concerns and by offering a challenge to educators.

QUESTIONS TO CONSIDER

1. Do you think computer literacy should be taught to all students? Why or why not? What do you think should be included?
2. What criticisms of teaching machines and programmed instruction have also been leveled at drill-and-practice as well as tutorial software?
3. How would you use presentation software and authoring systems in the content area you plan to teach? How might your students use them?
4. Should every teacher be aware of how technology can aid individuals with disabilities?
5. If Papert is correct about Logo narrowing the boundary between child and adult thinking, what would be the curriculum implications?

RELATED ACTIVITIES

1. Interview three people who work with a computer on their desk. Ask them questions designed to ascertain whether other people in their workplace tend to violate their privacy by reading what is displayed on their computer screens.
2. Find at least three reviews of integrated learning systems. At least one should be positive and at least one negative. Compare the reviews in terms of problems predicted, difficulties expected, and benefits anticipated. What theoretical framework does each reviewer use? How can you tell?
3. Select a small portion of a lesson you expect to teach or a topic in one of the college courses you are now completing. Use an authoring program or presentation software to create a brief presentation on the topic. Use at least two or three graphics in the presentation. One or more graphics should be scanned from another source. If the resources are available, use video from a laser disk or CD-ROM as well.
4. Locate at least three articles about Logo. Briefly summarize them and discuss whether any of these articles seem to be making unproved, unrealistically optimistic claims about the benefits of teaching Logo.

REFERENCES

Abate, R. J. (2000). Modeling instruction with modern information and communications technology: The Mimic Project. In D. A. Willis, J. D. Price, & J. Willis (Eds.), *Proceedings of the Society for Information Technology and Teacher Education 11th International Conference* (pp. 2090–2094). Charlottesville, VA: Association for the Advancement of Computing in Education.

Anderson, J. (1989). How technology brings blind people into the workplace. *Harvard Business Review, 67*(2), 36–40.

Black, J. B., Swan, K., & Schwartz, D. L. (1989). Developing thinking skills with computers. *Teachers College Record, 89*(3), 384–407.

Blaschke, C. L. (1990, November). Integrated learning systems/instructional networks: Current uses and trends. *Educational Technology, 30*(11), 20–23.

Bohlin, R. M. (1993). Computers and gender differences: Achieving equity. *Computers in the Schools, 9*(2/3), 155–166.

Bramble, W. J., & Mason, E. J. (1985). *Computers in schools.* New York: McGraw-Hill.

Brekke, B., Johnson, L., & Williams, J. D. (1975). Conservation of weight with the motorically handicapped. *The Journal of Special Education, 9*(4), 389–393.

Bronson, G. (1987, March). In the blink of an eye. *Forbes, 139*(6), 140–141.

Bull, G., & Bull, G. (1997). The evolution and future of Logo. *Computers in the Schools, 14*(1/2), 47–59.

Ehley, L. (1992). *Building a vision for teacher technology in education.* Washington, DC: National Library of Education. (ERIC Document Reproduction Service No. ED 350 278).

Fitzgerald, H. T. (1970). Teaching machines: A demurrer. In H. F. Clarizio, R. C. Craig, & W. A. Mehrens (Eds.), *Contemporary issues in educational psychology* (pp. 480–487). Boston: Allyn & Bacon.

Hannafin, M. J., & Peck, K. L. (1988). *The design, development, and evaluation of instructional software.* New York: Macmillan.

Higgins, K., & Boone, R. (1992). Hypermedia computer study guides for social studies: Adapting a Canadian history text. *Social Education, 56*(3), 154–159.

Hilgard, E. R., & Bower, G. H. (1966). *Theories of learning* (3rd ed.). New York: Appleton-Century-Crofts.

Kelman, P. (1984). Computer literacy: A critical reexamination. *Computers in the Schools, 1*(2), 3–18.

Kurland, D., & Pea, R. (1983, May). Children's mental models of recursive Logo programs. *Proceedings of the Fifth Annual Cognitive Science Society,* Rochester, NY: Cognitive Science Society.

Lerner, J. W. (1989). *Learning disabilities: Theories, diagnosis, and teaching strategies* (5th ed.). Boston: Houghton Mifflin.

Lewis, R. B. (1993). *Special education technology: Classroom applications.* Pacific Grove, CA: Brooks/Cole.

Maddux, C. D., & Willis, J. (1993, Spring/Summer). Integrated learning systems: What decision-makers need to know. *ED-TECH Review,* 3–11.

Mandell, C. J., & Mandell, S. L. (1989). *Computers in education today.* St. Paul, MN: West.

Marshall, G. (1993, December). Making the most of your ILS. *The Executive Educator,* 14–15.

McConnaughey, J. W., & Lader, W. (1995). *Falling through the net: A survey of the 'Have Nots' in rural and urban America.* Washington, DC: National Telecommunications and Information Administration. Retrieved May 25, 2000, from the World Wide Web: http://www.ntia.doc.gov/ntiahome/fallingthru.html

Molnar, A. R. (1978). The next great crisis in American education: Computer literacy. *AEDS Journal, 12,* 11–20.

Papert, S. (1980). *Mindstorms: Children, computers, and powerful ideas.* New York: Basic Books.

Pea, R. D. (1983). *Logo programming and problem solving* (Technical Report No. 12). New York: Bank Street College of Education, Center for Children and Technology.

Pea, R. D., & Kurland, D. M. (1983a). *On the cognitive effects of learning computer programming* (Technical Report No. 9). New York: Bank Street College of Education, Center for Children and Technology.

Pea, R. D., & Kurland, D. M. (1983b). *Children's mental models of recursive Logo programming* (Technical Report No. 10). New York: Bank Street College of Education, Center for Children and Technology.

Pea, R. D., & Kurland, D. M. (1983c). *On the cognitive prerequisites of learning computer programming* (Technical Report No. 18). New York: Bank Street College of Education, Center for Children and Technology.

Pea, R. D., & Kurland, D. M. (1984). *Logo programming and the development of planning skills* (Technical Report No. 16). New York: Bank

Street College of Education, Center for Children and Technology.

Pressey, S. L. (1926). A simple apparatus which gives tests and scores—and teaches. *School and Society, 23,* 373–376.

Pressey, S. L. (1927). A machine for automatic teaching of drill material. *School and Society, 25,* 549–552.

Riedesel, C. A., & Clements, D. H. (1985). *Coping with computers in the elementary and middle schools.* Englewood Cliffs, NJ: Prentice Hall.

Skinner, B. F. (1954). The science of learning and the art of teaching. *Harvard Educational Review, 24,* 86–97.

Skinner, B. F. (1958). Teaching machines. *Science, 128,* 969–977.

Skinner, B. F. (1986). Programmed instruction revisited. *Phi Delta Kappan, 68*(2), 103–110.

Slavin, R. E. (1987). Best-evidence synthesis: Why less is more. *Educational Researcher, 16*(4), 15–16.

Snider, S. L. (2000). "At-Risk" learners and the "Digital Divide": Exploring the equity in access issue. In D. A. Willis, J. D. Price, & J. Willis (Eds.), *Proceedings of the Society for Information Technology and Teacher Education 11th International Conference* (pp. 2049–2055). Charlottes-ville, VA: Association for the Advancement of Computing in Education.

Stolurow, L. W. (1961). Teaching by machine. *Cooperative Research Monograph No. 6.* Washington, DC: U.S. Department of Health, Education, and Welfare.

Travers, R. M. (1967). *Essentials of learning* (2nd ed.). New York: Macmillan.

Travers, R. M. (1968). *An introduction to educational research* (3rd ed.). New York: Macmillan.

Tyre, T. (1988). Technology gives kids with special needs the power to learn. *T.H.E. Journal, 15*(10), 14, 16.

Vockell, E., & Schwartz, E. (1988). *The computer in the classroom.* Santa Cruz, CA: Mitchell.

Wadsworth, B. J. (1989). *Piaget's theory of cognitive and affective development* (4th ed.). New York: Longman.

Watt, D. H. (1981). Computer literacy: What should schools be doing about it. In J. L. Thomas (Ed.), *Microcomputers in the schools.* Phoenix, AZ: Orax.

White, M. (1992, September). Are ILSs good education? *Educational Technology, 32*(9), 49–50.

Wiener, R. (1990). Computers for special education. *Tech Trends, 25*(4), 18–21.

CHAPTER THREE

HISTORY, HARDWARE, AND SOFTWARE

Goal: To understand the history of the development of computers, with particular emphasis on the conceptual and technical developments that brought us the modern personal computer.

KEY TERMS

Adobe PhotoShop (p. 60)
analytical engine (p. 51)
applications software (p. 61)
binary system (p. 51)
byte (p. 65)
CD-ROM (compact disk read-only
   memory) (p. 66)
CPU (central processing unit) (p. 65)
difference engine (p. 51)
disk drive (p. 66)
ENIAC (Electronic Numerical Integrator
   and Calculator) (p. 55)
integrated circuit (IC) (p. 57)
Iomega's zip and jaz drive (p. 66)
laser printer (p. 70)

local area network (LAN) (p. 67)
memory (p. 65)
microprocessor (p. 58)
Microsoft PowerPoint (p. 60)
mouse (p. 63)
operating systems (OS) (p. 60)
pixel (p. 67)
platforms (p. 59)
RAM (random-access memory) (p. 65)
ROM (read-only memory) (p. 65)
scanner (p. 64)
semiconductor (p. 57)
smart whiteboard (p. 68)
Windows-based computer (p. 60)

The history of computing is both long and short. It is short in the sense that modern electronic computers were not even invented until the 1940s. However, the field has a long history because many of the concepts that underlie modern computing have been around for centuries (Willis, Johnson, & Dixon, 1983). The first part of this chapter presents some of the concepts that underlie electronic computers.

A BIT OF HISTORY

One of the earliest ancestors of electronic computers is the music box. The sound from a music box is created by a slowly rotating drum with small metal pins protruding from it. As the drum revolves, the pins catch on extensions from the box's sound board and then flip back as the drum continues rotating. This relatively simple process can be used to create music boxes that play very complex, very beautiful compositions.

The important point to remember is that the music-box builder has only two options when placing pins on a drum: either put in a pin or don't put in a pin. Such a system that is based on only two possible choices is a **binary system.** The binary number system has only two digits, 1 and 0, and it uses these two digits to build larger numbers. The music-box builder converts binary 1s and 0s into pins on a drum (that is, 1 = pin, 0 = no pin). Today, computer designers convert binary numbers into electrical signals (1 = on, 0 = off). The basic principle is the same. The music-box builder and the modern computer designer both build complicated patterns from simple ones. Inside the computer everything is expressed in patterns of 1s and 0s.

Although the music box is one ancestor of the computer, it is not the only one. During the seventeenth, eighteenth, and nineteenth centuries, several scientists, including John Napier, Blaise Pascal, Gottfried Leibnitz, and Charles Babbage, invented mechanical aids for solving simple mathematical problems (Evans, 1981). The devices of Pascal, Leibnitz, and Babbage all used intermeshed gears to represent the basic mathematical operations of adding and subtracting. Adding numbers with these machines involved turning gears that in turn caused other gears to rotate. The answer to the problem was read from indicators attached to the gears. The most ambitious of these devices, the **difference engine** (Figure 3.1) of Charles Babbage, was so complex that it was never built successfully by Babbage.

The early, gear-driven calculating devices are most accurately considered direct ancestors of modern adding machines and calculators rather than computers because the machines performed one type of task, calculating, in a specific pattern. Computers, on the other hand, can be programmed or given instructions to perform many different types of tasks.

In spite of his difficulties in actually building the difference engine, the English mathematician Charles Babbage is generally considered the father of computing (Evans, 1981) because he also designed the **analytical engine,** a device that could be programmed or instructed to perform a variety of computational tasks. Babbage was assisted by Ada Lovelace, the daughter of the poet Lord Byron and a theoretical mathematician in her own right. Her contribution to the development of computing was acknowledged in the 1970s when a new computer language, Ada, was named after her.

Unfortunately, like the difference engine, the analytical engine was never successfully constructed by Babbage, although the concepts on which it was based were sound. Babbage intended to use cards with holes punched in them to tell the analytical engine what to do. He borrowed the idea from a French silk weaver,

FIGURE 3.1   Swedish industrialist George Scheutz built this version of Babbage's difference engine.

Joseph Jacquard, who had invented a weaving machine that created complex tapestries by following instructions on stiff cards with holes in them. Different patterns of holes produced different patterns on the tapestry. The cards with holes in them link back to our music boxes and to the punched cards that were used for many years to provide data to computers. These machines can all be programmed using a binary number system; the codes created by different binary patterns transmit instructions and data to the machine. Thus, the music box, loom, analytical engine, and desktop computer are all based on the same concept. Various results are produced with different instructions.

Computers are relatively young, therefore, not because of the complexity of the concepts used to create them, but because the problem of manufacturing them held back earlier efforts. Babbage's analytical engine was to be a huge assemblage of metal rods, wheels, and gears run by a steam engine. Charles Babbage died in 1871, but in 1876 a U.S. engineer named George Grant demonstrated a difference engine that worked. Grant, in fact, actually sold a number of machines, which he called *rack-and-pinion calculators.*

As the nineteenth century ended, the precision required to produce reliable mechanical calculators was available. It was also at this time that U.S. technology began to equal, and even to exceed, European technology. A U.S. citizen named Herman Hollerith developed a machine that greatly simplified the work on the 1890 census (Figure 3.2). Hollerith used a system whereby holes were punched in cards to represent different types of census information. Hollerith's Tabulating

FIGURE 3.2   The Hollerith tabulating machine.

Machine Company eventually became International Business Machines (Willis, 1987).

In the first half of the twentieth century, researchers continued to work on mechanical computers in the tradition of Babbage. For example, Vannevar Bush, a professor at MIT, built and demonstrated a differential analyzer in 1930 (Bitter, 1989). It was large, had many gears, and used electric motors. It could be reconfigured (reprogrammed) to perform many different types of calculating work. Bush's machine was the first to use electricity, not only to turn gears but also to store data. His machine could store numbers or quantities as electricity in one part of the system. The ability to store data for later use is called *memory*. Because memory is an important aspect of any electronic computer, Bush is considered by some to be the father of the electronic computer.

Bush's mechanical computer was a direct descendant of Babbage's analytical engine, but the day of the gear-driven computer was almost over. Other scientists decided to explore the possibilities of an electronic computer. (Much of the historical information in this section was taken from two excellent publications—T. R. Reid's [1985] book on the invention of the integrated circuit, *The Chip*, and Steven Levy's [1984] book on the development of the hacker ethic, *Hackers*—and from personal interviews.)

Konrad Zuse, a German engineer, and Howard Aiken, a Harvard math professor, both built hybrid (part mechanical and part electronic) machines in the period between 1930 and 1945. These hybrid computers were never widely used in Germany or the United States. The future belonged to fully electronic computers. Despite controversy over the name *Colossus,* many consider this still-secret British computer the first special-purpose, electronic digital computer. Because digital computers are based on the binary number system, they are essentially on/off devices. In computers, *on* and *off* are represented by 1 and 0, and all data inside digital computers consist of patterns of 1s and 0s. Colossus was developed by a secret team of scientists that included Alan Turing, a mathematician who made several contributions to the theoretical concepts of computing.

Turing was one of several pioneers who came to understand that binary math could be the basis of powerful computers (Hodges, 1983). He suggested that an on state in the computer be designated a 1 whereas an off state be designated a 0. Turing believed that machines could be designed to follow instructions and, by following those instructions, solve all sorts of problems. Turing's contributions to computing are somewhat surprising because few of the instructors who taught Turing thought he had much intellectual potential, and he twice failed the entrance exam to the college he wanted to attend. After earning a Ph.D. in mathematics from King's College of Cambridge University, Turing joined a team of scientists who developed Colossus. The team used Colossus to crack Enigma, the German military communication codes, during World War II.

Another major contributor to the intellectual and conceptual stew that led to the development of modern computers was John von Neumann, pictured in Figure 3.3 (Goldstine, 1972). Born in Budapest and educated at several major

FIGURE 3.3   John von Neumann is pictured here with one of the computers he helped develop.

European universities, he published a scholarly treatise at age 18. Both von Neumann and Turing believed that binary numbers should be the basis of computers.

At first glance it is difficult to see how a machine that can deal with only two states, on and off (or 1 and 0), could accomplish anything important. Fortunately, more than 100 years earlier another British mathematician, George Boole, had developed a complete algebraic system of logic that used only two digits, 1 and 0. Boole, who came from a poor family, never attended college (Boole, 1972). His love of mathematics led him to write a number of poems, including one called "Sonnet to the Number Three." Boole came to believe that human reasoning could be boiled down to sequences of decisions that had yes or no answers. His major book, published in 1854, was titled *The Laws of Thought, on Which Are Founded the Mathematical Theories of Logic and Probabilities.*

A complex system of logic that reduces everything to a series of yes or no decisions was not very appealing, although several contemporaries, including a mathematician named Charles Dodgson, did appreciate Boole's work. In books written under the pen name Lewis Carroll, Dodgson created many characters who viewed their world with yes–no, this-or-that logic. These books were titled *Alice in Wonderland* and *Through the Looking-Glass.* Early computer theorists, who needed a system of logic for a machine that could deal with only two states, on and off, found Boole's logic essential to their work. The offbeat logic system of a nineteenth-century shoemaker's son, who did not even graduate from high school, made electronic computers possible.

The leap from obtuse theory to electric circuits was made by George Shannon, a graduate student at MIT (Reid, 1985). He completed a master's thesis in 1937 that applied the yes–no, true–false Boolean logic to wire electrical switching circuits. Shannon expressed Boolean logic with electrically operated mechanical relays. Less than a decade later, others created a computer by expressing Boolean logic with vacuum tubes. Smaller and smarter computers were then built, first with transistors and then with integrated circuits. The medium of expression varies from one computer generation to another, but the fundamental logic in each generation of computers is George Boole's.

The first general-purpose, electronic digital computer was built in the United States (Evans, 1981). **ENIAC,** or **Electronic Numerical Integrator and Calculator,** was developed by J. P. Eckert and J. W. Mauchly at the University of Pennsylvania during World War II. It was a huge machine with thousands of vacuum tubes that were only moderately reliable, but ENIAC set the stage for greater things to come. The initial idea was to develop a device that could both determine artillery shell trajectories and predict the weather. Within a few years the machine was being used for a variety of business and government applications.

Because ENIAC was developed during a war, it was used for military applications such as calculating artillery shell trajectories. Before ENIAC, the tables used by artillery officers were hand calculated by teams of workers who might spend months or even years computing tables for just one type of armament. Although ENIAC generally operated for just a few minutes before one of its vacuum tubes burned out and had to be replaced, it reduced the time needed to calculate the tables to a few hours or minutes (Figure 3.4). That was a tremendous accomplishment. One member of the team of operators who kept ENIAC going was Grace Hopper, a young naval officer. One day, while trying to find the source of a problem, she found a bug caught between two electrical contacts. She removed the bug and ENIAC began operating again. Computer programmers today still use the term *debugging* when they look for errors in a computer program. Hopper, who later became Admiral Hopper, continued her naval career and was one of the U.S. pioneers of computer use.

ENIAC was the beginning of the age of computers. During the next two decades a number of developments transformed boxcar-sized computers like ENIAC to computers the size of a book. The first of these developments was the transistor, invented in 1947 (Evans, 1981), whose dependability, small size, and low-power requirements made modern computers practical. Transistors replaced vacuum tubes as the building blocks of computers. They were the first widely used solid-state, semiconductor components. The term *solid-state* refers to the state in

FIGURE 3.4 Tubes like this one were used in ENIAC.

which electrical activity takes place in a transistor (in the first transistor the solid was specially treated germanium; today silicon is used in most solid-state devices). The electrical activity in vacuum tubes occurred in a vacuum created inside a glass tube when certain metal elements were heated. The term **semiconductor** refers to elements that can be made to behave either as insulators or conductors.

Since 1947 several major advances in semiconductor technology have produced smaller and smaller components that perform more and more tasks. The most important of these advances is the development of the **integrated circuit** or **IC** (Figure 3.5). By 1958, transistors had revolutionized the electronics industry; however, each component in a transistorized electronic circuit had to be connected during manufacture to other components. In a large computer, this entailed millions of connections. These connections were generally made by hand, which meant they were expensive and prone to error.

In the summer of 1958, a young engineer who had been working for his new employer for only a few months developed a solution to the connection problem (Reid, 1985). Employees at the large Texas Instruments research center in Dallas, Texas, generally took their vacation at the same time each summer, but Jack Kilby was so new to the company that he did not have any vacation days. Kilby thus found himself working alone in the laboratory while everyone else was on vacation.

When his colleagues returned from their vacations, Kilby presented his design for the first crude integrated circuit. He had found a way to make different

FIGURE 3.5   Integrated circuits like these two make personal computing possible.

sections of the same small sliver of silicon (the element in semiconductors) work as resistors, capacitors, and transistors. An IC, often called a *chip*, thus contains many transistors, resistors, and capacitors in a circuit enclosed in a single small case. The production of chips can be automated, which means the interconnections between the different components inside the chip do not have to be made by hand. ICs solved the interconnection problem, and soon manufacturers all over the world were producing billions of chips each year.

Kilby, a tall Kansan who attended the University of Illinois after he failed the entrance examination for MIT, also invented one of the first new products that used ICs, the pocket calculator. He shares the credit for inventing the IC with Robert Noyce, a Ph.D. from MIT. (Kilby received the Nobel Prize in 2000.)

Large-scale integrated circuits (LSIs) soon followed ICs, with hundreds and then thousands of components packed into a single chip. Large-scale integration, followed by very large-scale integration (VLSI) and ultra large-scale integration (ULSI), enabled designers to put the equivalent of large rooms and then buildings full of 1950s-era vacuum-tube circuits on a sliver of silicon smaller than a penny. These LSI, VLSI, and ULSI circuits are the foundation of personal computers today. VLSI and ULSI technology made computers not only affordable and thus accessible to individuals, but also practical: it is the reason you can set a computer on your desk instead of building a large room to house it.

Another computer revolution occurred in 1971 when Intel Corporation produced the first **microprocessor** IC. These computers on a chip are what made personal computers possible. In 1974, the first microcomputer kit was advertised nationally. In 1977 and 1978, several companies, including Tandy/Radio Shack and Apple Computer, began selling assembled computers. These personal computers were designed so that the buyer could unpack the system, plug it in, and begin using it. Tandy/Radio Shack and Apple Computer still sell popular computers that are widely used in business and education.

Tandy/Radio Shack was a thriving corporation when it built its first computer, the TRS-80 Model One. Apple Computer, on the other hand, was the brainchild of Steven Jobs and Steve Wozniak (Figure 3.6), two California hippies who were friends in high school (Levy, 1984). Wozniak's homemade computer became the Apple computer, and the two Steves began Apple Computer in a garage. Jobs raised money by selling his Volkswagen van (a considerable sacrifice for a California boy living near the beach), and Wozniak sold his Hewlett-Packard programmable calculator. The original Apple computer could be purchased through the mail for $666.66. Soon after the first Apple computer was ready for sale, Wozniak began work on a new and better computer, the Apple II, which was demonstrated at a Homebrew Computer Club meeting in December 1976. Apple Computer is the only one of the original personal computer companies that is still a major force in the field.

Personal computers today are a far cry from the ENIAC computer, which occupied 3,000 cubic feet of space, used 140,000 watts of power, weighed 30 tons, and contained 18,000 tubes, 70,000 resistors, and 10,000 capacitors.

FIGURE 3.6   Apple Computer cofounders Steve Wozniak and Steven Jobs are pictured on the left. Both left the company several years ago although Jobs returned to Apple in 1997. Pictured on the right is John Scully, former president of Pepsico, who led Apple for several years.

COMPUTER HARDWARE TODAY

Although many companies manufacture personal computers, only two general types of computers are in widespread use in schools. These two types, often referred to as **platforms,** are distinguished by the operating system they use. The two platforms are Macintosh and Windows. Although most school computers are based on one of these two platforms, the old Apple II series is still around. Unfortunately some schools have not been able to replace these 1980 vintage computers, but some schools that have been able to purchase newer computers prefer to keep the old Apple II computers because they still have some use for students.

Apple II, Macintosh, and Windows machines use different systems. Software written for one platform, such as an Apple II, cannot run on the other platforms. The major reason for the differences among these platforms is the central processing unit or CPU. You may hear, however, that software designed for Windows systems can run on certain Macintosh computers. To some extent this is true, and computability between the Macintosh and the Windows platforms is improving. However, full compatibility does not yet exist. The Macintosh platform has taken the lead in this area by building into their operating system conversion programs that convert Windows files to Macintosh files and Macintosh files to Windows files. This can also be done on Windows machines, but additional software must be used. Of course, converting files is different than running software, and only pertains to using the same stored data, such as a word-processing file, on either platform. For example, you can create a document using *Microsoft Word* on a **Windows-based computer** and read it into *Microsoft Word* on a Macintosh computer.

Progress is being made in compatibility between the Windows and Macintosh platforms. Although you cannot purchase one generic software package that runs on both platforms, you can purchase the same type of software for either platform, and in some cases the software looks almost identical on either platform. Two examples are **Microsoft PowerPoint** and **Adobe PhotoShop.** You must purchase the version of these software packages that is suitable for the platform you are using (i.e., Windows or Macintosh). However, if you observed the Windows version and the Macintosh version of one of these programs running side by side, you would notice only slight differences.

Operating Systems

All the hardware power in the world won't matter if you are having trouble interacting with your computer. This is when the computer's **operating system (OS)** comes into play. In a nutshell, an OS is a computer program that translates the work you are doing on your computer into a language the computer can understand. It also enables all the different pieces of hardware in your computer to communicate with each other. For example, when you click your mouse on the print icon while using a word-processing program, it is the OS that tells the computer to send your document to the printer in a code that the computer can understand. A good analogy for an OS is a traffic cop who stands at an intersection and directs traffic. Three major operating systems are in use today: Macintosh OS, Windows, and UNIX. Both Macintosh and Windows operating systems are now object-oriented. Many routine actions can be performed by manipulating objects on the screen. For example, to delete a file using Macintosh OS, you would point the mouse cursor at the file, hold down a button on the mouse, and drag the image of the file over to the trash can icon. When you release the mouse button, the trash can "fattens up" to show it has something in it.

Early IBM desktop computers used an operating system called *MS-DOS*, which is short for *Microsoft disk-operating system.* MS-DOS, or *DOS* for short, is a command-line operating system. Originally, computers were referred to as *IBM compatible* if they used this operating system. When this system is in operation, you may see nothing more than C:\> on the screen. This operating system requires you to type commands, rather than click on icons, to instruct the computer what you want it to do. For example, you would type the command FORMAT A: to format a new diskette for use in an MS-DOS computer. The command to delete a file could be as lengthy as DELETE:\WPDOCS\MYLETTER.WP5. Compare that to dragging the image of the file over to a trash can on the screen. Learning MS-DOS is often not easy for occasional users who have difficulty remembering the commands to run programs. MS-DOS is still used by those who prefer to control their computer more directly or when system problems arise that require direct manipulation.

Although Windows and Macintosh are the two operating systems most common in schools, a third operating system, UNIX, is found primarily on larger computer systems connected to networks. UNIX is powerful but complex, and difficult to learn. About the only people who prefer UNIX are "power users" who enjoy or require fast, powerful, networked computers. Some UNIX-based computers are used in schools as file servers for networking, but are usually operated by a technology professional.

SOFTWARE

Another name for software is *program*—a computer can do nothing without a program. Computers use different types of programs. One type of program is the OS we just discussed. The OS is usually already stored in a computer when it is purchased and seldom changed other than to be upgraded when new versions are released.

Applications Software

Many of the uses of computers in schools do not call for specialized educational software. A word-processing program, for example, might be used in a third-grade reading class, a middle-grade science class, or a high-school economics class. The same word-processing program might also be used on a home or business computer. Programs like word processors are often referred to as **applications software.** An English literature class might use the database management features of a program such as *Microsoft Works* or *Apple Works* to create a file of information on the social and political conditions that existed when various poets or novelists wrote their best works. A drafting class can use computer-aided design (CAD) software, and an accounting class can use electronic spreadsheets such as *Microsoft Excel.* A third-grade class project on local history might use scanning software to create electronic versions of old photographs, or presentation software to create a class presentation, or telecommunications software to send a copy of the report to students in another school.

Specialized Educational Software

Tens of thousands of educational programs are available today that teach everything from basic reading readiness skills to college-level physics. Many of these programs are outstanding examples of quality software, but a great many are poorly conceived and are of little value for teaching and learning. In addition, the design of educational software can be based on any of several popular theories of teaching and learning. Software considered good by proponents of one theory might be considered poor by proponents of another educational theory. The issue of theories and their role in educational computing is discussed in more detail in later chapters. Chapter 13 of this book covers software quality and software evaluation extensively.

THE HARDWARE ASPECTS OF A COMPUTER SYSTEM

Software is one aspect of a computer system. The other aspect is the hardware, the physical components of a computer. The final section of this chapter deals with the features that are most important when the computer is used for educational applications.

Keyboards

The primary method of transmitting information and instructions into the computer is the keyboard. Keyboards, like wines and steaks, are subject to personal preference. However, some generally agreed-on points can differentiate a good keyboard from a bad one. Keyboards are fairly well standardized today. Those purchased from one company look about the same as those purchased from another company. However, some keyboards are specialized, and two trends have emerged in this area.

The first trend is the ergonomics keyboard. This trend came about as a reaction to carpal tunnel syndrome, a cumulative trauma disorder. These disorders are often caused by extensive computer use. Carpal tunnel syndrome affects the hands and wrists. This condition has become the focus of much attention because so many people spend so much time using computers. The condition is believed to be linked to repetitive use of the hands, a consequence of keyboarding. As a result, companies that market computer peripherals have produced keyboards of various shapes and styles in an effort to prevent this condition from developing. One example of such a keyboard is the i-Surfboard (see Figure 3.7) marketed by MarkNet Enterprises (http://www.mandmw.com/ergonomics.html). According to MarkNet:

> Our keyboard and mouse platforms help you to conform to OSHA's new Ergonomic Standard to provide unrivaled comfort while operating a computer. Not only do our systems minimize stress and repetitive motion in the arms, wrists, and hands, they even reduce eye strain by allowing you to move farther away from your computer's monitor. Our i-Surfboard and Mouseboard allow you to swivel, recline, or rock while keeping your keyboard and mouse where you need it.

A second trend in keyboard design is the wireless keyboard. Logitech (http://www.logitech.com) has developed a line of keyboards that use digital radio technology. This technology allows a person to move about freely with their keyboard and mouse and have full control over their computer. With radio technology you do not need to be in direct line of sight with your computer.

FIGURE 3.7   MarkNet Enterprises' i-Surfboard keyboard.
Photo courtesy of MarkNet Enterprises, www.mandmw.com.

Alternative Input Devices

Some specialized educational programs work best with input devices other than the keyboard. When school computers are purchased, this should be taken into consideration because some computers have no provisions for connecting input devices such as joysticks, whereas others provide connections for several types of input devices.

Joysticks and game paddles, required to play many computer video games, are one type of alternative input device. Several companies manufacture large oversized keyboards with specially labeled templates that make some programs much easier for young children to use. Also growing in popularity are graphics tablets, which allow you to create color graphics on the computer screen by drawing with a stylus on the surface of a special tablet that can sense when and where the stylus is moved. Graphics tablets are important for art classes and for classes in which students are learning drafting programs such as *AutoCad.* A company that specializes in good quality and reasonably priced graphics tablets is Acecad (http://www.acecad.com).

The Mouse.   Although the mouse is a relative newcomer to the microcomputer era, it is now ubiquitous. The **mouse,** of course, controls the movement of the cursor and is also used to give the computer commands. Macintosh first incorporated the mouse as a standard part of their computer systems. It is now almost as standard as a keyboard when it comes to purchasing a computer. The mouse, and Macintosh's mouse-oriented software, was one reason the Macintosh earned the reputation of being the computer that was easy to learn. Mice, like keyboards, are now becoming specialized. Just as with keyboards, mice are becoming more ergonomically sensitive and can be used remotely via radio control.

Trackballs.   Another type of pointing device is the trackball (Figure 3.8). Although not as popular as the mouse, a trackball functions the same as a mouse. A trackball is like an upside-down mouse—inside a stationary housing is a ball that you move with your finger to manipulate the cursor on the screen. Trackballs are more popular with those who play computer games and are often used with laptop computers. The trackball is built into many laptop computers, thus eliminating the need to be at a work area with a flat surface, necessary for the proper functioning of a mouse.

Scanners and Card Readers

Few computer peripherals have grown in popularity in recent years more than the **scanner.** An optical scanner is a device that scans a sheet of paper and converts what it sees into signals that are sent to a computer. Scanners are used for a variety of purposes in schools. Multiple-choice tests can be scored with a scanner if students enter their answers on a special sheet of paper. Attendance data, the daily lunch count, semester grades, and many other types of data can also be entered into the computer using a scanner if teachers use special sheets of paper to collect the data. Several companies also sell card readers that can be connected to personal computers. Card readers can also be used to score tests and input routine information such as attendance data.

The primary use of scanners by students is for photo scanning, a process whereby they digitize their hard-copy photographs. These digitized images can

FIGURE 3.8   A trackball keyboard.
Reprinted by permission from Key Tronic.

then be used in *PowerPoint* presentations, combined with text for written reports and school newspaper articles, and entered into class and school websites. With the right software, scanners can also be used as optical character readers (OCRs). OCRs can read the text printed on a page and convert it to computer data.

Scanners are now so popular that they have become both better and cheaper over the past few years. Zdnet (http://www.zdnet.com) is a website that categorizes and reviews scanners. Scanners are now of a quality and price that any school with computers can easily make one available for student use.

The Central Processing Unit

The **CPU,** or **central processing unit,** is the heart of a computer system. Although most CPU integrated circuits are smaller than an Oreo cookie, they have as much electronic capability as components manufactured a few decades ago, which would have filled a large building. Using advanced microelectronic techniques, manufacturers can cram millions of circuits into tiny silicon chips that work independently and use less power than an electric razor. There are several manufacturers of CPU chips. Intel makes most of the CPU chips used in Windows-based computers and Motorola makes most of the chips used in Macintosh computers. CPU chips are primarily responsible for the steady progress in speed and capacity of computers. Companies that manufacture CPU chips are constantly conducting research to find ways to cram more power into a smaller unit. Within just a few years, starting in the mid-1990s and ending in the year 2000, computer users saw CPU chips move from speeds of less than 100 megahertz to a speed of 1,000 megahertz. It would be a waste of time to speculate on how much progress will be made in CPU chips. The rule has been that they double in speed and power every eighteen months. Nobody knows when this will end.

Memory

The CPU is the brain of the computer, but it cannot do much all by itself. It must have the support of several other types of integrated circuits that perform special functions. One very important type of specialized IC is **memory.** You need memory in your computer for three reasons. First, the computer must have some instructions built in so that it can start itself when you switch on the power. Manufacturers generally put the instructions the computer needs to get started in integrated circuits called **ROM,** or **read-only memory.** The data in ROM cannot be changed by the user. They are permanent.

All computers also have another type of memory, **random-access memory (RAM).** When you want the computer to run a program that is stored on a disk, you must load that program into the computer's memory (RAM). In addition, programs such as word processors and student record-management software need memory to store data, such as daily attendance or that report you are writing. Programs and data are stored in RAM. Computer memory is divided into **bytes.** One byte can hold the code for one character. The memory capacity of computers is usually expressed in *K* or *meg* (for megabyte), which is equal to 1,048,576 bytes. Like all other aspects of computers, the amount of RAM commonly available is ever increasing. In just a few years the amounts of RAM recommended between the mid-1990s and the year 2000 changed from 16 megabytes to 128 megabytes. This rapidly increasing need for RAM is largely the result of the ever-increasing use of graphics on ordinary home and school computers.

Mass Storage

When you turn the computer off, anything stored in general-purpose memory (RAM) is erased. It exists only as long as the power is on. You thus need some means of storing programs and data outside the memory of the computer. The first personal computers in schools used a cassette recorder to store data and programs. Cassettes were cheap, but slow and generally unreliable. Fortunately, most computers in schools today use disk drives for storage.

Disk drives became the next means of mass storage. They were fast and reliable, and even the least expensive models stored more than 700 K of data on a flexible round platter of Mylar called a *floppy disk.* Early disks were 5¼-inches in size and stored in a flexible paper or plastic sheath. The next advancement in disk drives used 3.5-inch disks that were housed in a sturdy, rigid plastic case. These disk drives are still in use in many computers, offering a convenient, inexpensive way to stores and transport data. Another mass storage device is the hard-disk drive, which works much faster than floppy disks, stores hundreds of times more data than floppy disks, and has become a standard device on nearly all computers. Storage capacity of hard-disk drives is now measured in gigabytes, which is one billion bytes or approximately 1,000 megabytes.

Another type of mass storage device is the **CD-ROM** disk, short for **compact disk read-only memory,** which is the same small disk used in compact disk players for music. With current technology, it is possible to store billions of bytes of data, both text and graphics, on one compact disk. Several publishers of encyclopedias, for example, provide their entire set of encyclopedias on one or more CD-ROM disks. The electronic versions of these encyclopedias can be searched by entering keywords into the computer. The computer then searches the CD-ROM for relevant information, and the pages of the encyclopedia appear on the computer screen.

CD-ROM is also used to store graphic images, databases of information, video, sound, and much more. When you search a computer for information at your college or university library, you are probably using a computer with a CD-ROM drive attached to it. A new trend in this type of storage device is the digital versatile disk (DVD). The disks used in these drives look just like the CD-ROM disks but allow more speed and capacity, and now have read/write capability (CD-RW), which means they can be used both to read data from the CD and to write data to the CD. They can be used over and over just like floppy disks.

Another practical mass storage device that has become very popular is **Iomega's zip and jaz drives.** These drives have become almost ubiquitous. They are popular because they are inexpensive and resemble the familiar 3.5 floppy drives, yet they hold from 100 megabytes to more than 1 gigabyte of data.

Networking

Many schools with Macintosh or Windows-based equipment have connected their computers through a **local area network (LAN).** LANs make it possible for teachers, administrators, and students to communicate with other users through electronic mail systems. They also make it possible to share data between computers (including computers located thousands of miles away) if the LAN is also connected to the Internet. A great advantage of having a school connected by a LAN is that all the computers in the school can share expensive peripherals such as printers, high-capacity disk drives, and scanners. A very recent trend is to eliminate mass storage devices from individual computers and store all data on the high-capacity disk drive on the LAN server. This trend could cut the price of school computers significantly. Some speculate that we are moving toward a day when all computers are connected in one way or another. Small groups of computers will be connected by a LAN server; LANs will be connected as wide area networks (WANs); and WANs will be connected to the Internet. Some people speculate that all software and data will eventually be shared through these networks, and personal computers will be small, inexpensive, and have lots of RAM.

OUTPUT DEVICES

Video Monitors

The most common input device for a personal computer is a keyboard, and the most common output device is some sort of video display. The terms *video display, monitor,* and *CRT* (for cathode-ray tube) all refer to the same thing. Transmitting signals from the computer to a video screen involves two major components: the video circuit in the computer and the display itself. Both are critical to high-quality video. For a significant time period, not much about computer monitors changed other than providing higher and higher resolution. Starting in the late 1990s, however, companies began offering a lot of variety. One significant trend was size. Although the 13-inch monitor had become standard, larger sizes caught on. Monitors now commonly range in size from 13 inches to 21 inches.

A less obvious feature of a monitor is resolution. You may read advertisements that describe the graphics capability of your computer in terms of pixels. **Pixel** is short for *picture element*. A computer, for example, might have a graphics mode that is 280 by 192 pixels. This means the computer can divide the screen into 280 rows and 192 columns. Each point where a row and column intersect is a pixel. A pixel is like one tiny square on a sheet of graph paper. The computer is capable of controlling whether a tiny rectangle of light is displayed at a particular point. A computer whose best graphics display mode is 280 by 192 pixels is rather crude today. The larger the number of pixels a computer can control, the finer is the resolution of the graphics the computer can display. A display with 280 by 192 resolution would have to create images from no more than 53,760 (280 × 192) pixels. When you see images on a computer screen that look like a color photograph, you are looking at an image made up of hundreds of thousands of tiny pixels.

Another factor that determines how good an image looks is the number of colors that can be displayed on the screen. In a crude 280 by 192 display, if each pixel is either on or off, you need only 53,760 spots in the video memory of the computer to keep track of what should be displayed. However, if the on pixels can be red, blue, or green, the memory required to store the image is tripled. Today some computers support millions of colors on the screen.

Another trend in monitors has been the advent of the liquid crystal display (LCD) monitor. The main advantage of this type of monitor over the traditional CTR monitor is physical space savings. These LCD monitors can be manufactured to be 2 to 3 inches thick with very high resolution. Visit Samsung at http://www.samsung.com for more information. These monitors range in size and have extremely high resolution (e.g., 1,280 by 1,024 pixels), but they are expensive. It is predictable, however, that in time they will become the standard.

Projection Devices

As computer graphics, video, and sound have become easier to create and use, schools have looked for devices that can effectively project graphical images and video clips onto a screen or large monitor so they can be viewed by a group. *Microsoft PowerPoint* has become very popular in schools where students create multimedia presentations. Showing these presentations, however, can sometimes be a problem. One product that has been used to project computer images and video is the LCD panel, which fits on top of an overhead projector. You connect the LCD to your computer, switch on the overhead, and whatever is on the computer screen is projected onto the viewing screen as well.

Early LCD panels provided poor resolution and tended to fade as the overhead projector warmed up. These LCD panels have improved but are rapidly being replaced by multimedia projectors. 3M (http://3M.com) makes a variety of these projectors, and some are geared specifically for school use. The multimedia projector seems to be what all presenters have been looking for. It is small, light, and produces very high resolution. A laptop computer and a multimedia projector allow ultimate portability from classroom to classroom, school to school, or state to state. The presenter walks into a room with the laptop in one hand and the projector in the other, connects the two, finds a screen or white wall, and the show begins.

Another output device that will probably become common in schools in the future is the **smart whiteboard.** This device represents a marriage between classroom whiteboards and computer display screens. They can be as large as regular whiteboards and can be written on with marker and erased—this is the whiteboard side of the marriage. The computer display-screen side of the marriage allows you to present any file you have in your computer on the board—word processing, spreadsheet, database, or graphics. The synergetic benefit that comes from this marriage is that you can also incorporate what is written on the board into a computer file; you can modify and manipulate the information on the board and save the modified version in the computer. It is expected that as distance learning becomes more prevalent, this device will become a classroom necessity. One example of a smart whiteboard is the TeamBoard by TeamBoard (http://www.teamboard.com).

Printers

After the video monitor, the most popular output device for a computer is a printer. Ironically, despite our ability to create, store, and transfer information electronically, one of the first things we want to do is print so that we can see the results of our creative efforts on paper. When the very first microcomputers were developed, there was no practical way to print. When, finally, small, reasonably priced printers became available in the early 1980s, they were greeted with huge enthusiasm.

We remember being in San Francisco at a large computer trade show in 1983 where Epson unveiled its new dot-matrix printer. This was the first printer that was inexpensive enough for the home, school, or small office to afford, and small enough that it could be carried under one arm. Almost every person at that show, where there were thousands of people, left with at least one Epson printer, and many left with two. The dot-matrix printer produced characters by knocking the ribbon against the paper with a series of wires in the print head. Dot-matrix printers totally dominated the printer market for nearly 15 years. They produced a type of print whereby characters were composed of tiny dots of ink on paper.

Another printing method that was once quite popular in situations for which a higher quality print was desired was the solid character impact printers. One type of solid character impact printer was the daisy-wheel model. Some daisy-wheel models produced output as good as that of an office typewriter. These printers, however, were expensive and prone to break down because they incorporated many moving parts.

Two main types of printers dominate the market today, but there are hundreds of different models. Today's printers work at speeds that range from 6 pages per minute (ppm) to 20 ppm. Choices have to be made between print quality and print speed if you want to stay with a low-cost printer. To gain increased speed and quality at the same time, you have to pay. For a computer lab where students complete and print assignments, a fast printer that produces readable but not necessarily high-quality output is preferred over a high-quality printer that is slow. It can be frustrating to realize, 5 minutes before class ends, that the printing your students just began will take 15 minutes to finish. On the other hand, you want a high-quality printer to produce correspondence for parents and the class newsletter. If you have only enough funds to buy quality or speed, the way the printer will be used will determine which feature is most desirable.

An important characteristic to consider when purchasing printers for the classroom or school computer lab is print quality. Print quality is determined by resolution, and resolution is measured by dots per inch (dpi). Printers with higher resolution are able to print more lifelike images with fewer jagged edges and finer detail. The standard for most printers today ranges from 600 × 600 dpi to 1,200 × 1,200 dpi.

Far and away the most common printers in schools are ink-jet printers. These small printers can produce fairly high-resolution print at reasonably fast rates. Almost all models print in color, and they are so inexpensive that many computer dealers include them as a bonus when a computer is purchased. Ink-jet printers produce characters on paper by spewing out minute droplets of ink that hit the paper in the pattern of the characters you want to print. The Hewlett-Packard (http://hp.com) DeskJet models, for example, are very popular in schools today, and thousands of college students have these printers in their dorm rooms. Ink-jet printers are capable, when special paper is used, of producing color images that have been scanned that are satisfactory for most school uses.

A final printing method is laser technology. Several companies, including Apple, Epson, OkiData, and Hewlett-Packard, produce **laser printers.** They combine the technology of a copy machine, which uses dry ink powder (toner), with a laser beam that draws an image of the page on a photosensitive drum in the printer. Laser printer output approaches the quality of a typesetting machine. Laser printers can produce text in a wide range of sizes and styles, as well as high-quality graphics, even photographs that have been scanned. Laser printers are the foundation of a new use of computers, desktop publishing. Many books, newsletters, magazines, brochures, and reports today are published using desktop publishing programs, such as *PageMaker,* and laser printers. Laser printers combine high-quality output with speed. The only drawback to laser printers involves initial cost. Although the cost of laser printers is constantly decreasing, they still cost about two to three times what an ink-jet printer costs.

Laser printers are beginning to appear in school computer labs and administrative offices. When the extra cost of purchasing a laser printer can be justified, they are desirable. High-school journalism programs, for example, are beginning to use laser printers because they allow students to produce a high-quality student newspaper. In fact, compared to the cost of paying a printer to typeset a student newspaper, desktop publishing with a laser printer can reduce the cost of publishing by as much as 50 percent. Typesetting costs, so high in many areas, can be completely eliminated, and students receive better training because they are involved in more steps of the process. The same laser printer can be used for student and teacher handbooks and other school documents.

SUMMARY

The concept of a computer, a device designed for computing, was started as a mechanical machine developed through the work of Pascal, Leibnitz, Babbage, and Hollerith. Babbage and Hollerith designed mechanical computers, but the technology of the nineteenth century was not sufficiently advanced to make their production possible. What nineteenth-century minds envisioned, twentieth-century technology produced. The impetus of World War II led Alan Turing and others to develop Colossus, a computer designed to crack German codes. The computers of the 1940s were huge because their major components were vacuum tubes. The development of the transistor in the late 1940s revolutionized the electronics industry, but it was the invention of the integrated circuit in 1958 that permitted the development of the microcomputer. This led to the production of computers that could be purchased and used by individuals and schools.

Today, educators are most likely to encounter two computer platforms in schools: Macintosh and Windows. The software available may be classified into two categories: educational and applications software. The hardware of computing is the machine itself and its peripherals. These usually consist of input devices such as keyboards and computer mice; the CPU, which is the heart of the computer; the memory that supports the CPU; mass storage devices such as floppy and hard-disk drives; network hardware; and output devices such as monitors and printers.

QUESTIONS TO CONSIDER

1. Compare the application of basic research, such as George Boole's system of logic, to the development of computer technology with the application of basic research, in fields such as psychology and education. Are there parallels in the way basic research finds its way into practice?

2. If the transistor and integrated circuit had not been invented, what role would computer technology play in education today?

3. If CD-ROM and laser-disk technology were as widely available and inexpensive as overhead projectors, how might they be used to support instruction in K–12 schools? In colleges and universities?

RELATED ACTIVITIES

1. Check the library at your school for books on the history of computing. The lives of pioneers such as George Boole, Charles Babbage, Ada Lovelace, Alan Turing, Steve Wozniak, and many others provide very interesting reading.

2. Check recent issues of general-interest computer magazines such as *PC World, PC Magazine,* and *MacWorld.* What hardware topics are "hot" today? Are some aspects of computer hardware about to change drastically?

REFERENCES

Bitter, G. (1989). *Microcomputers in education today.* Watsonville, CA: Mitchell.

Boole, M. (1972). *A Boolean anthology.* New York: Association of Teachers of Mathematics.

Evans, C. (1981). *The making of the micro: A history of the computer.* New York: Van Nostrand Reinhold.

Goldstine, H. (1972). *The computer from Pascal to von Neumann.* Princeton, NJ: Princeton University.

Hodges, A. (1983). *Alan Turing, the enigma.* New York: Simon & Schuster.

Levy, S. (1984). *Hackers: Heroes of the computer revolution.* Garden City, NY: Doubleday.

Reid, T. R. (1985). *The chip.* New York: Simon & Schuster.

Willis, J. (1987). *Educational computing: A guide to practical applications.* Scottsdale, AZ: Gorsuch/Scarisbrich.

Willis, J., Johnson, L., & Dixon, P. (1983). *Computers, teaching, and learning.* Beaverton, OR: Dilithium.

CHAPTER FOUR

THE INTERNET AND THE WEB IN SOCIETY AND EDUCATION

Goal: To introduce the concepts of the Internet and the World Wide Web, to discuss the hardware and software that make up the Internet, and to explore the impact the Internet has on society, including education.

KEY TERMS

America Online (AOL) (p. 93)
antivirus software (p. 91)
attachment (p. 91)
browser (p. 85)
cracker (p. 92)
cyberporn (p. 87)
download (p. 80)
e-commerce (p. 75)
e-mail (p. 77)
file transfer (p. 80)
forum (p. 80)
hacker (p. 91)
home page (p. 83)
hypertext markup language (HTML)
　(p. 83)
Internet (p. 80)
Internet Explorer (p. 86)
Internet protocol (IP) (p. 85)

Internet service provider (ISP) (p. 92)
JAVA (p. 84)
modem (p. 79)
Netscape (p. 86)
newsgroup (p. 80)
online addiction (p. 89)
plug-in (p. 84)
search engine (p. 86)
server (p. 84)
special interest groups (SIGs) (p. 78)
universal resource locators (URLs)
　(p. 85)
upload (p. 80)
virus (p. 90)
web address (p. 84)
World Wide Web, or Web (WWW)
　(p. 83)

This month I (JW) received a call from a colleague in another department here at Iowa State University who was trying to bring a well-known scholar to Iowa to deliver a keynote speech at a conference. The speaker was from England and, though he had accepted the invitation, he insisted that he fly business class or better. At first, that did not appear to be a problem. It was possible, by buying a ticket during one of the inevitable sales, to travel between Chicago and London, the nearest European portal, for less than $700 (and even less when you purchased the ticket from one of the consolidators or "bucket shops" that advertise on the Internet). So, how much more could a business-class ticket cost? Perhaps it was double, but $1,400 was within the budget. As it turned out, a business-class ticket for October, when the conference was to be held, wasn't $1,400—it was $7,000! That presented a problem because it was well beyond the budget. My colleague had heard that bargain airfares could be found on the Internet, and he asked for my help. After searching several databases on the Web (http://www.tiss.com; http://www.travelsecrets.com; http://www.cheapflights.com), I was able to find a ticket for about $3,000 (Figure 4.1).

This experience illustrates one way the Internet is influencing the way we buy and sell everything, from antiques to airline tickets. In the last year I have purchased many items over the Internet, including

Tickets to Warsaw, London, Istanbul, and Kiev, Ukraine

Hotel rooms in Warsaw, Istanbul, Antalya (Turkey), San Diego, and San Francisco

A multisystem VCR that plays tapes from all over the world

Scholarly books

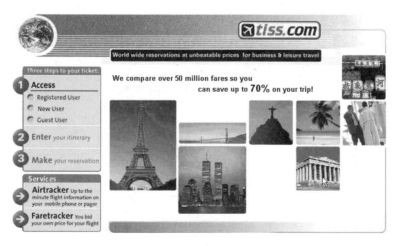

FIGURE 4.1   TISS.com (http://www.tiss.com) is Europe's leading e-travel site specializing in discount airline tickets. The search of its database for cheap airline tickets is free to all users.

Reprinted by permission of TISS GmbH.

The World Wide Web, which is explained later in this chapter, has become a critical component of U.S. society and is rapidly becoming a major tool of commerce and collaboration all over the world. This chapter introduces you to the many ways in which the Internet is influencing society today. In general, that influence can be classified into four categories: commerce, information, collaboration, and education.

THE INTERNET AND COMMERCE

The World Wide Web has become a means of selling everything from exotic teas and coffees to surplus airplanes. The term for this is **e-commerce** or *electronic commerce*. I regularly use Amazon (http://www.amazon.com) to buy all sorts of books. Amazon has a database of more than a million books, and the site lets me search for books on everything from instructional design to Greek philosophy. Amazon is always available; it remembers who I am when I access the site; and it dependably ships the books I order and notifies me via e-mail about the status of my order.

Several studies on the growth of e-commerce suggest that the Internet will have a major impact on the way people buy and sell goods during the next 10 years. Buying and selling goods via websites is, however, only one way the Internet is influencing commerce.

Auction Sites

Priceline (http://www.priceline.com) is one of the best-known sites for individuals and companies to list items for sale and accept bids (Figure 4.2). An amazing variety of items are auctioned on the Web every day, and the auctions take on a range of formats. For example, Priceline allows you to indicate when and where you want to travel by air and then state the price you are willing to pay. Within an hour this site will send an e-mail message indicating whether an airline accepted your bid.

Investments

Several hundred companies now allow customers to buy and sell stocks, commodities, and bonds over the Internet. Of the many online brokers one of the better-known is Charles Schwab (http://www.Schwab.com). Investment sites range from the barebones, no-frills sites, which do no more than help you buy and sell stocks, to sites with all sorts of investment advice and information. Stock brokers and other professional investors and advisors could not survive today without their computers, and computers are increasingly important for individual investors as well.

THE INTERNET AND INFORMATION

Recently, my wife, who is Ukranian, mentioned the U.S. artist Rockwell Kent, who is a favorite of hers. I had never heard of this artist. Having been raised in

FIGURE 4.2 Priceline.com (http://www.priceline.com) offers a new type of e-commerce: name-your-own-price.

Reprinted by permission of priceline.com.

the United States, I smugly felt that if I had not heard of the artist, he was probably not a prominent one. Perhaps she was mistaken. Could he be British, or had she gotten the name wrong? I searched the Internet using Infoseek (http://www.infoseek.com), one of the specialized programs that searches the Internet for sites relevant to the topic you enter. I typed "Rockwell Kent" and up popped a page indicating there were 602 different sites on the Internet with information about this artist. I discovered, for example, that the Adirondack Museum in Blue Mountain Lake, New York, was mounting an exhibit of his work for the summer of 2000. I learned that "also on loan to the exhibition are paintings donated to the Soviet Union in 1960 by Rockwell Kent, and not seen in the United States since that time when Kent was the subject of scrutiny by federal agencies" (Ferris, 2000).

Reading further I found this explanation of the popularity of Rockwell Kent and his subsequent disappearance from the U.S. art scene at about the time I was becoming interested in art:

> Once considered a perennial favorite in the exhibition halls of New York, Chicago, Pittsburgh, San Francisco, et al., Rockwell Kent, by choice and by turn-of-the-cards, virtually vanished from the museum and gallery circuits by the late 1940s. For generations, art aficionados had heaped praise upon Kent's trademark, austere canvases, rich-black wood engravings and his equally commanding ink drawings.
>
> Between 1928 and 1938 alone, Kent was either the feature artist or an individual participant in no less than 40 exhibitions. His book illustrations, writings and lectures dramatizing his global adventures, designs in metalware and ceramics, murals and advertising commissions for such diverse clientele as Steinway, Westinghouse and American Car and Foundry made his work practically inescap-

able. His notability was such that the *New Yorker* magazine published the ditty, "That day will mark a precedent, which brings no news of Rockwell Kent."

Yet by the early 1950s, American society had, in the midst of the "red scare," displaced Kent as their cultural icon. Senator Joseph McCarthy and his troubadours of trepidation had hurled enough mud at Kent that those less firm in their stance than the artist himself, readjusted their aesthetic appreciation for fear of guilt by association. The crowning blow to Kent's popularity came when the fashionable swing away from realism turned toward abstract expressionism. Kent was relegated to obscurity by denial—his name and his work stricken from society and fine arts literature. His life-long friend and noted art historian, Carl Zigrosser, considered this fluctuation from "extravagant praise to fanatic denunciation" a phenomenon "based on nonaesthetic considerations or a misunderstanding of the real import of his work." (Ferris, 2000)

Now I understood why Nina, who grew up in Russia, was familiar with Rockwell Kent and I was not. Although he was a U.S. artist, he had been pushed out of the artistic limelight in the United States during the McCarthy era in the fifties and, perhaps for the same reasons, brought into the limelight in the Soviet Union.

This story illustrates one of the basic characteristics of the Internet: the unbelievable amount of information available. Today the Internet is used by professionals in all fields, and by parents, teachers, and children to locate information about a topic. In earlier periods access to a good library was an important source of information. Today, a person living on an isolated ranch in rural Wyoming can, with Internet access, comb through websites around the world for information on a topic. The same Internet access is available to the person in Wyoming and the person living in New York City.

However, the increased availability of information brings with it various problems. A student in a rural school with a small library might find three or four sources of information about a topic such as the role of insects in the pollination of vegetable crops. That same student might find hundreds, even thousands, of websites about that same topic. In the first case, the student's task is to find as much information as possible or at least enough information to write a paper or prepare a report. In the second case, the student's task is to filter out many sites and pick the best ones for further exploration. The skills of selecting information sources that have appropriate content and suitable access have not been taught to previous generations of students. They will become essential skills as the Internet becomes a primary source of information.

THE INTERNET AND COMMUNICATION AND COLLABORATION

Most people today are familiar with **e-mail**—a method of sending messages to individuals who also have accounts on computers connected to the Internet. What is less widely known is that several other ways of communicating and collaborating exist via the Internet. For example, thousands of interest groups—forums and

SIGs (special interest groups)—operate on the Internet. Are you interested in adult education? Using simulations in the middle grades? Setting up international networks of students who work on a common project? Groups on these and many other topics share ideas, problems, and information, and often constitute a virtual, or online, community. You could probably list any 10 topics that interest you and be able to find a forum or SIG on the Internet about each of those topics. Some groups are open and you join simply by sending a message to an Internet address; others are closed (membership is by invitation only) or restricted (you must apply for membership). Some are local (i.e., for teachers in a particular school district); some are national or international. Some are very active, sending 20 or more messages a day, and some are relatively quiet, sending no more than 2 or 3 messages a month.

In addition to forums and SIGS, there are also special tools for collaborating over the Internet. Colleagues may exchange drafts of articles and proposals, hold meetings online, and collaboratively write documents with each person having a chance to revise drafts and share ideas. All this is commonplace today and likely to become essential in many professions in the near future.

THE INTERNET AND EDUCATION

Educational uses of the Internet are discussed in detail in Chapter 10. It is important to note that the Internet has become a staple in schools. Students use it to communicate with others, to search for information, and to disseminate the work they do.

Summary

The Internet is rapidly changing the way business operates. It has become an important source of information for adults and children alike. It is increasingly used to support many different forms of communication and collaboration, and it has already taken its place in schools. It has, in less than 20 years, had a profound impact on many aspects of contemporary life, and it is likely to have even more impact in the future. That future, however, depends on the hardware and software that supports the Internet. The following section introduces these aspects of the Internet.

THE TECHNICAL SIDE OF THE INTERNET

The electronic computer was invented in the 1940s; by the middle of the 1950s, computers were a novel but useful tool for U.S. business and government. By the mid-1960s computers had become not only useful but also essential for many large businesses. The ability of these businesses to exchange data among computers in different locations became a necessity. Perhaps an insurance company with a branch office in California needs to send data on new policies to the home office computer in Des Moines, Iowa. Perhaps a wholesale grocery company with warehouses all over the country needs to send data each night from the regional warehouses to the central computer in Chicago where a combined inventory is kept. For all sorts of reasons, computers need to be able to exchange data.

To satisfy this need, computer scientists and telephone engineers developed a way of sending data over telephone lines from one computer to another. At first, when computers were multimillion-dollar behemoths, the process required special telephone lines. Computer technicians attached special devices called **modems,** or *modulator/demodulators,* to the computers. Modems converted computer data to tones (modulated) that could be easily transmitted over phone lines. On the other end, a modem attached to the receiving computer converted the tones back into computer data (demodulated).

As data-transfer technology developed, and computers became smaller and less expensive, both home and small-business computers began to be set up to send and receive data. At that time, telephone companies charged expensive fees to companies that used "dedicated" phone lines to connect computers. Telephone companies resisted the idea of a small business or family using their inexpensive ordinary phone line to connect two computers. At first, phone companies tried to outlaw any use of ordinary telephone lines for computer use. Some even tried to make families with computers pay the same price they charged large businesses for computer access. When that failed, they tried to prevent anyone from connecting a "foreign device" to the telephone line. Such devices, they said, could damage the phone lines and cause all sorts of problems. Connecting modems to regular phone lines was declared illegal, and individuals as well as small businesses who did so were threatened with the loss of their phone service.

Then, in 1968, a historic ruling changed the future of computers and telephone service. The small Dallas, Texas, company CarterPhone, which produced modems, filed a complaint with the Federal Communications Commission that protested the rules against connecting customer-provided equipment to their phone lines. CarterPhone's lawyers argued that the phone network was a public network, operated as a regulated monopoly by the telephone companies, and as such should be open to many sorts of uses. The FCC ruled against the Bell System, which at that time controlled most of the local and long-distance telephone service in the country. The FCC rejected Bell's argument that connecting modems and similar devices to the phone system would be dangerous. After the ruling, some phone companies continued to try to place restrictions on modems, but it quickly became general practice to allow modems to be connected to any phone line as long as they did not interfere with the operation of the phone network. This small victory by CarterPhone is the foundation today for what some have called the *Internet Revolution.*

After the 1968 decision, inexpensive modems became a popular option for small computers. When the personal-computer revolution began in earnest in the 1970s, modems, which cost only a few hundred dollars, were popular accessories. Communicating via computer over phone lines did not become immediately or wildly popular, however. The system of using computers to communicate was rudimentary: programs were complicated, difficult to use, and limited. The equipment was unreliable and often very slow. However, intrepid personal-computer users explored and expanded the frontiers of modem use, connecting to computers in the neighborhood, the city, and the world.

The Arrival of the Internet

Early uses of telecommunications—communications between computers over phone lines—were very limited. Individuals or computer clubs, for example, might set up a computer with a modem that others could access from their computers. These were generally small-scale efforts that tended to appear and disappear quickly. Telecommunications, however, took a giant step forward with the arrival of the **Internet.**

Accurately defining or describing the Internet is a difficult task. One way to begin is to say that the Internet is a network of networks. It connects many regional, company, and national networks in a vast supernetwork that links together millions of computers. In fact, it is now the world's largest computer network (NetLingo, 2000). (Actually, it is more accurate to say it is the world's largest network of networks.) Computers linked by this network can communicate with each other, and individual users of any of these computers can exchange electronic mail, share research data, discuss hobbies (complete with pictures and sound), or communicate for any reason whatsoever. Marine, Kirkpatrick, Neou, and Ward (1993) suggested that "the Internet exists to facilitate the sharing of resources among participating organizations, which include government agencies, educational institutions, and private corporations; to promote collaboration among researchers; and to provide a testbed for new developments in networking" (p. 1). Today, the role of the Internet has expanded to serve the needs of individuals as well as organizations.

Today's Internet can be traced to a U.S. Department of Defense network called *ARPAnet* (NetLingo, 2000). ARPAnet was developed by (and the name was derived from) the Department's Advanced Research Project Agency and was commissioned in 1969. ARPAnet was an experimental computer network designed to survive a nuclear war. It supported four different types of computer activity (NetLingo, 2000):

1. *Remote Access.* Individuals could connect to a computer from a distance and use the computer as if they were sitting at the keyboard of that computer.
2. *File Transfer.* Anyone with access to a computer could perform a **file transfer:** send, or **upload,** a file to a computer, or retrieve, or **download,** a file from the remote computer to their computer.
3. *Electronic Mail.* Individuals could send messages to other users on the same network.
4. *Newsgroups.* Individuals could join **newsgroups** or **forums** in which individuals with similar interests discussed relevant topics. Interests might relate to nuclear physics, the genetics of corn plants, or anything else.

ARPAnet gradually became available to many outside the military, but the basic concept behind this network of networks was still to provide support to specialists. That was about to change, however. In 1986, the National Science Foundation (NSF) developed a new network. As Krol (1992) points out, NSF's contribution to the Internet was its philosophy that the more computers connected to the network, the better:

> Up to that point, Internet access had been available only to researchers in computer science, government employees, and government contractors. The NSF promoted universal access by funding campus connections only if the campus had a plan to spread the access around. So everyone attending a four-year college could become an Internet user. The demand keeps growing. Now that most four-year colleges are connected, people are trying to get secondary and primary schools connected.... All this activity points to continued growth, networking problems to solve, evolving technologies, and job security for networkers. (p. 13)

Although NSFNET was a major step in the evolution of the Internet, it is not synonymous with it. The Internet emerged from NSFNET and included that network plus many others. The NSFNET began as a linking of five supercomputers in the United States. The primary purpose was to allow scientists across the country to have access to these powerful computers. Many other networks were developed after NSFNET; however, the developers of these networks knew about NSFNET and wanted users of their network to have access to it. Therefore, they made sure that their networks were compatible with NSFNET and could communicate with any of the computers linked by NSF.

In this way, the Internet grew at an almost unbelievable rate. Today, the Internet consists of NSFNET and many other networks, large and small, as well as individual users of these various networks who can now communicate with each other. Today, no one knows for sure how many people have Internet access, but the number is in the tens of millions, if not hundreds of millions, and the rate of growth is both rapid and increasing.

THE OTHER SIDE: THE WORLD WIDE WEB

The Internet makes it possible to connect, over phone lines, to other computers all over the world. That, in itself, is not very exciting to most people. There is a story, perhaps an urban myth, that one of the founders of the first successful personal computer company was fascinated by how black boxes worked. A *black box* is the name for a device that allows access to long-distance telephone circuits without paying for the service. The story goes that as a teenager, the future founder would sit in a dorm room and dial a number in Asia using his black box. Then he would connect from that number to another number further west. He would again connect that number to a number somewhere in Europe and from there to a number on the East Coast of the United States. From the East Coast he would connect to the phone in the adjacent dorm room. When his friends heard that phone ringing, they knew he had connected a circuit that circled the globe.

Fascinating as that feat was to some, most people are interested in using the phone to communicate with someone (or something). They want the process to be as simple as possible and the experience to be as rich as possible. When phoning a friend, for example, we are limited to voice communication, but there is a long history of work on phones that transmit video as well as audio.

The Internet made telecommunications possible, but it did not make the process easy nor the experience rich. Early users of the Internet had to use software that was so complex and so poorly designed that it discouraged all but the most technically proficient and doggedly dedicated. Moreover, for all its complexity, that early software was very limited. For example, e-mail programs limited the user to sending simple text messages only. By contrast, an e-mail message today may contain all of the following:

1. Simple text
2. Formatted text such as that produced by a word processor or desktop publishing program
3. Images such as photographs, drawings, and illustrations
4. Video
5. Audio including voice and music
6. Links such as the electronic address of a location on the Internet
7. Multimedia material containing all six types of data mentioned above

The capability for sending sophisticated e-mail, among other transmissions, resides in what we call the *World Wide Web* (*WWW*). In 1990, Tim Berners-Lee was a physicist in Geneva, Switzerland. He worked at CERN, the Counseil Européen pour la Recherche Nucléaire, which is now known as the European Particle Physics Laboratory. He recognized the potential of the Internet to facilitate communication among physicists all over the world. He was also frustrated with how difficult and limited then-current telecommunications programs were. He set out to create a new way of communicating. The result was the World Wide Web (Hanrahan, 1995).

Berners-Lee felt that physicists should be able to send hypertext documents to colleagues. Hypertext is discussed in a later chapter, but, in essence, hypertext documents can be read in many different ways. They contain hyperlinks that allow you to click on a word or image and "jump" to another part of the document. Berners-Lee also wanted the documents to support multimedia. That is, they should handle many different forms of text as well as a variety of images, video, and audio. Although many of these capabilities could not be supported in the beginning, the format Berners-Lee developed for exchanging documents was quickly accepted by physicists as well as several million other Internet users around the world. (Ironically, before the World Wide Web was accepted, the developer tried to present a paper about it at a conference on the Internet that was held in Texas. His proposal for the paper was rejected, which just goes to show that revolutionary ideas are not always immediately recognized as such, even by experts! The conference organizers did, however, allow a poster session on the idea.)

The **World Wide Web,** or **Web (WWW),** is the means by which most of the information on the Internet is communicated today. The Web is a complex and ever-changing entity as well as a process. However, if we think about it in a general way, it is really composed of only six different parts: a programming language called *HTML,* supporting software, server software, the addressing protocol, browser software, and search software.

The Programming Language: Hypertext Markup Language.   Today you can go to websites all over the Internet and get information on everything from the price of eggs in Hong Kong to reviews of the latest Hollywood movie. An increasing number of individuals, families, and schools even have their own **home page,** or website, where you may find everything from a picture of the latest grandchild to the story of a sixth-grade class study of bay pollution in Houston, Texas. Regardless of what you call them, websites, sites, or home pages, they have been written in **hypertext markup language (HTML).** This language is a coding system that tells your computer how to display material on your screen.

In the early days of the Web, people who wanted to develop web pages had to learn HTML to code the pages. For example, to display a simple line of text such as *Chapter 1* in a web page in large, bold type and the color violet, you might code in this way:

```
<B><font size=+4 color=#FF66FF>Chapter 1</font></B>
```

Unless you're interested in programming, writing HTML code to create a web page is boring, frustrating, and time consuming. Fortunately, just as word processors help you write text documents, web-processor programs exist that can help you create web pages. Many of these programs use the point-and-click method of formatting. If you want a line of text to appear red, for example, you point to the text, then pull down a menu, and click on the color red. That's it! No trying to remember the code number for red or how you write the command. Today first-graders are creating perfectly acceptable web pages for their school projects, and teenagers have created sophisticated websites that draw hundreds of thousands of visitors each year. Some popular web-creation programs that are in widespread use today:

FrontPage (from Microsoft)
PageMill (from Adobe)
HomePage (from Claris)

Many other programs exist that are geared toward knowledgeable web-page designers. You may graduate from one of the relatively easy programs listed above to one such as *Dreamweaver,* which is powerful but more difficult to learn.

Support, or Helper, Software.   Almost as soon as HTML became popular, people began to talk about what it could not do. For example, there is no built-in capability in HTML for listening to music. New versions of HTML added features regularly, but not fast enough to satisfy some. Consequently, helper programs that could be used with HTML and web-creation software were developed to support many types of data:

1. *RealAudio* is a program you use to play audio. I (JW), for example, often listen to a rock-and-roll radio station in Hong Kong on my office computer in Ames, Iowa.
2. *Quicktime VR* is a program you can use to display virtual reality video on your computer.
3. *Shockwave* is a program you can use to display many types of animation.

Many other programs allow you to do everything from watch music video clips to explore a 3-dimensional simulation of the human heart. The term **plug-in** is sometimes used to describe helper programs that assist your browser to display or play files. **JAVA** is one helper program that is actually another programming language, which someday may replace HTML. JAVA "applets" are programs written in JAVA that expand the power and capability of HTML. Some sites today are created almost entirely with JAVA instead of HTML.

Server Software.   Once a web page has been developed, it must be published on a server. A **server** is a computer connected to the Internet that hosts websites. Your college or university probably has several servers where websites can be published. Many elementary and secondary schools today also have servers where classes, teachers, and even individual students publish their websites. These computers need a connection to the Internet plus special server software. They are usually maintained by specialists and are not the responsibility of users. In fact, people are increasingly renting space on servers maintained by a team of specialists. For as little as $15 a month, you can buy enough space on a professionally maintained server to store a relatively large website.

The Addressing Protocol.   When cities emerged from small villages, formal addresses became necessary. You could no longer simply address a letter to "Old Tim who lives beside the sheep pasture." Now that there are millions of sites, it is necessary for each site to have a unique **web address.** (The same is true of e-mail addresses. One of the e-mail addresses I (JW) use is jwillis@aol.com. Because more than a thousand addresses are similar to mine, such as jrwillis@aol.com and jwillis27@aol.com, I often receive other peoples' e-mail. I have received, in error, the plan for a religious service to be held several thousand miles away, as well as the picture of a naked woman whose boyfriend was the intended recipient!)

Two levels of Internet addresses exist: one for humans and one for computers. A typical website address resembles the following:

http://www.netlingo.com

HTTP is short for *hypertext transfer protocol.* When it appears at the beginning of an address, it indicates the location is a website. Other addresses begin with different initials. *FTP,* for example, which is short for *file transfer protocol,* appears at the beginning of addresses for sites where files are stored that can be downloaded to your computer.

The colon and slashes (://) are used to separate one part of the address from the next. The *www* also indicates the location of a site. Some sites no longer include *www* in the address because it is not absolutely necessary. The next part of the address, *netlingo* in our example, identifies the specific site. The NetLingo site is the location of a dictionary of Internet terms you can access to look up meanings of terms associated with the Internet. The final component of an address, *.com* in our case, indicates the type of organization publishing the site: *com* indicates a commercial site; *gov* is the ending for government sites; and *edu* is used by educational institutions. The address of Iowa State University's website, for example, is http://www.iastate.edu. Addresses ending in *edu, com,* and *gov* generally denote U.S. sites. For non-U.S. sites, the ending of the address indicates the country where the site is located: *ca* is short for Canada, *uk* is short for United Kingdom, and *ru* is short for Russia.

Web addresses made up primarily of text can be easy for people to remember. For example, I (JW) often check the price of plane tickets on the Southwest Airlines website. The address is http://www.iflysw.com. Addresses like this are called **URLs,** or **universal resource locators.** When you type an address like the one for Southwest Airlines, your computer sends that address to a special server that converts it to one the computer can read. The converted address is composed of numbers and is called an **Internet protocol (IP)** address.

http://www.truserve.com   —the URL for an Internet service provider in Iowa

http://208.142.211.10   —the IP address the computer needs for the provider

You don't generally have to concern yourself with IP addresses; they are designed for computers to read. However, when you see a long number listed as an address, you will know it is the IP version that the computer uses to take you to the website.

Browser Software.   Before you can access all those great websites, you need a special type of software on your computer, called a **browser.** Browsers are programs that enable you to access websites. One reason why the Web became so popular so quickly is that a browser called Mosaic was created at the supercomputer center at the University of Illinois that facilitated users' ability to view all sorts of data on websites, including color graphics. Mosaic, developed by Marc Andreessen while he was working as a student programmer at the University of Illinois, was the first sophisticated browser, but soon afterward at least 50 browsers were competing for attention.

Today a number of browsers are still available, but only two are widely used. Marc Andreessen graduated and became one of the founders of Netscape Corporation. The **Netscape** browser was, in the mid-1990s, the undisputed champion of browsers. Today, it faces heavy competition from Microsoft's **Internet Explorer,** and debates about which is best can become heated. In addition, whether Microsoft used unfair and illegal tactics to corner this segment of the computer market was a core issue in the antitrust suit against Microsoft in 1999 and 2000. Microsoft lost that suit, and the government had proposed that Microsoft be broken into two separate companies to keep Microsoft from illegally damaging competitors like Netscape. (Netscape, by the way, was purchased by America Online in 1999.)

Our advice is to try out both browsers—Netscape and Internet Explorer (both are given away free to users)—and decide which one best suits you.

Search Software.   In the early years of the Internet, very few information resources were available on the Net. Those that were available tended to be specialized papers and reports that appealed to small, tightly knit groups of scholars who shared an interest in one form of specialized research or another. Today the Internet faces the opposite problem. Instead of finding a lack of topics that interest you, you are likely to find that the billions of documents on the web hamper your ability to find exactly what you're looking for. This embarrassment of riches led to the creation of a special form of software—search engines. A **search engine** is a system composed of two parts: (1) a specially constructed database of the content of documents available on the Internet. (Some search engines only have websites in the database; others include Internet resources such as discussion groups.) (2) A user interface that lets you specify terms you want to look for on the Internet.

Search engines vary in the number of sites in the database and in the form and sophistication of the user interface. Three popular search engines are:

AltaVista—http://www.altavista.com
Infoseek—http://www.infoseek.com
Snap—http://www.snap.com

Many other search engines are available, but for most searches those listed should do the job. They all work in approximately the same way. Go to the search engine website; type a word, phrase, or set of words; and click the Search button. The engine will then return a list of "hits." You can click on the name or title of a hit and go to that website.

If you would like to explore the more than 100 search engines that are operating on the web today, you can go to the Search Engine Watch website (http://searchenginewatch.com/) and read comparative reviews as well as use links to go to search engine sites. Most browsers (like Netscape Communicator and Internet Explorer) also provide a list of search engines. Most sophisticated search engines support complex searches that make use of Boolean logic and special characters to help you formulate a precise search. Following are some examples that work with Infoseek, but other search engines have similar features.

■ *+social_class +employment.* This search has two terms in it: *social class* and *employment.* Putting a + in front of a term means a hit must contain that term. Because both terms have a +, this search will only report hits that contain both the terms *social class* and *employment.* The underline character (_) between *social* and *class* is a connector. It indicates you want *social class* treated as one term instead of two different words. If you leave out the underline and instead insert a space between *social* and *class,* the search engine would look for hits with the words *social* or *employment.*

■ *"International Business Machines."* Without quotes, this search would locate websites that have any one of the three words *international, business,* and *machines.* However, they would not necessarily be in the order listed in the search. Put quotes around the three terms and the search will only select sites that contain the term *International Business Machines.* A site with *international* in one paragraph, *business* in another, and *machines* in yet another would not be considered a hit.

Using search engines has become an essential skill of web surfing today because of the quantity of sites with information. Search engines allow you to look for sites with specific types of information that interest you.

THE DARK SIDE OF THE WEB

The Internet is truly changing society, but the direction of that change is not always positive. Anyone who argues that the Internet has brought only benefit to society simply has not looked carefully at the matter. This section considers six ways the Internet has had a negative impact on society.

Easy Access to Pornography

Some societies severely restrict access to information, but the United States has traditionally supported an open society that encourages a free flow of information. Diverse opinions are allowed to be expressed and disseminated but some types of content are also distributed that many people feel are harmful. A case in point is pornography. Although traditional access has always been possible, it has typically not been easy. Today anyone with Internet access and the ability to use a search engine can find thousands of sites on the Web that contain pornography. The content of these sites is called **cyberporn.**

Much of the pornography, as well as nonpornographic erotica, on the web is legal. The right of adults to have access to this material is fairly well established at this point. Pornography involving children and access by children are other matters, however. Both are illegal. Many schools, for example, have had to contend with the fact that the same computer and Internet connection that give eighth-grade students access to 50 or 60 sites about volcanoes can also be used by an enterprising student to view hundreds of sites with pornography and erotica. How should society deal with this?

The answers are quite diverse—from banning Internet use in schools to allowing completely open access. Most educators come down somewhere in the middle: allow Internet use but develop ways of monitoring and supervising access. Most schools now have acceptable use policies that prohibit using school computers to access pornographic or erotic sites. A number of software programs can be installed on a computer to prevent children from accessing inappropriate sites. Currently, programs such as *NetNanny, CyberPatrol,* and *SurfWatch* are the most popular, but new programs appear regularly. To find the latest information on this type of software, you can use a search engine to look for sites.

As a general set of guidelines for dealing with this issue, Barbara Feldman's (2000) suggestions to parents are also applicable to teachers. They are summarized as follows:

1. Know what your kids are doing online. Supervise your children's computer activities, just as you do their television time.
2. Never give out personal information online, such as a home phone number, address, last name, name of school, passwords, or credit card information. Your kids would not give their address to a stranger on the phone, nor should they divulge it online.
3. Be cautious of online chat rooms. I allow them only with my supervision. Chat rooms are the cyber equivalent of CB radio. Users can "type" to each other in real time, and messages are viewed by everyone in the chat room. Private chat rooms are also available. The problem is, as a famous *New Yorker* cartoon (which showed a dog sitting at a computer) put it, "on the Internet no one knows you're a dog" (or a child or an adult masquerading as a child).
4. Teach your children to come to you if anything ever makes them feel uncomfortable, such as inappropriate questions or an invitation to a private chat room. Do not respond to offensive e-mail.
5. Never allow your children to meet "face-to-face" someone they've "met" online.
6. Limit online time as you would television viewing.
7. Use parental control software as appropriate. Parents routinely lock up household chemicals to protect their toddlers, and the Internet can also be selectively locked. Today there are several software products to keep kids out of adult Internet sites.

Several of the guidelines address the possibility that children may come into contact with adults, or other children, who entice them into unsavory relationships. More than one female teenager, for example, has been lured into a sexual liaison by much older adults.

Fraud and Deception

Another common problem on the Web is fraud and outright deception. This is nothing new, but the Internet has become a popular method for crooks to separate people from their money. Deals that sound too good to be true on the Internet are just as likely to be fraudulent as similar deals pitched to you by mail or over the phone.

Addiction?

Can someone become addicted to the Internet? Many articles have appeared in the popular press, and even more cartoons, about this possibility. The Center for On-Line Addiction (Figure 4.3) at http://www.netaddiction.com/ defines five forms of **online addiction:**

1. Cybersexual addiction (addictions to adult chat rooms or cyberporn)
2. Cyber-relationship addiction (online friendships, including cyber affairs, conducted in chat rooms, MUDs, or newsgroups that replace real-life family and friends
3. Net compulsions (compulsive online gambling, online auction addiction, and obsessive online trading)
4. Information overload (compulsive web surfing or database searches)
5. Computer addiction (obsessive computer game playing or programming, mostly a problem among men, children, and teenagers)

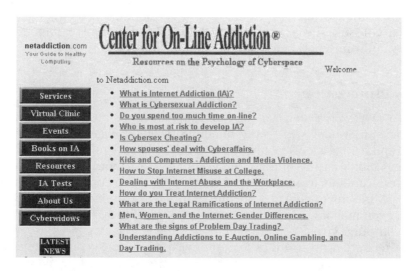

FIGURE 4.3   The Center for On-Line Addiction (http://www.netaddiction.com) is a consultation firm and resource network that specializes in e-behavior and Internet-related conditions.

Reprinted by permission of the Center for On-Line Addiction.

Although only a small percentage of Internet users have any of these addictions, they are real and can cause significant problems for individuals and families. The Center for On-Line Addiction has a test you can take to determine whether you are addicted. The test includes the following questions:

> Do you feel preoccupied with the Internet (think about previous online activity or anticipate the next online session)?
>
> Do you feel restless, moody, depressed, or irritable when attempting to cut down or stop Internet use?
>
> Have you jeopardized or risked the loss of a significant relationship, job, or educational or career opportunity because of Internet use?

The website for the Center for On-Line Addiction has a number of resources to help addicts and their friends and families deal with the problem.

Hate Groups

One of the prices of an open society is the dissemination of ideas and beliefs that are abhorrent to many members of the society. Hate groups are based on beliefs that another group—racial, religious, ethnic, or political—is inferior, too powerful, or inherently evil. Many hate groups have established websites. The presence of such groups presents a particular problem to parents and teachers who send children to the Internet to search for information. An Internet search on the Holocaust may well turn up sites that dispute it happened. Several Internet sites are devoted to monitoring hate groups and to developing ways of reducing their influence. One such site is HateWatch: An Educational Resource Combatting Online Bigotry, at http://www.hatewatch.org/index1.html (Figure 4.4).

Virus Propagation

When I (JW) was a teenager the most popular forms of vandalism were throwing rocks at windows in empty buildings, stealing watermelons from farmers' fields, and baiting a local deputy into chasing your car with his slower vehicle. (Of course, I didn't do any of these things, but I heard about them.) Although these acts were certainly frustrating to at least one or two people, they were generally localized and minor. Today, someone with talent can, if they want, cause thousands, even millions, of people a great deal of trouble by creating and disseminating a computer **virus.**

There are many forms of computer viruses, but the general intent is to cause something to happen in a computer that was not intended by the user. This can be as innocuous as displaying a message on the screen and as destructive as erasing all the files on your hard disk. This type of electronic vandalism has, unfortunately, become widespread. And, because the Internet is worldwide, it means

FIGURE 4.4   HateWatch(http://www.hatewatch.org/index1.html) is a web-based educational resource and organization that actively monitors hate groups on the Internet.

Reprinted by permission of HateWatch.

someone halfway around the world can reach out and touch your computer in very destructive ways. While this chapter was being written, the ILOVEYOU virus, which originated in the Philippines, was damaging computers all over the world.

Although computer viruses can be transmitted to computers in many ways, an increasingly popular method is via e-mail messages. Generally, these viruses take the form of an **attachment** to an e-mail message. An attachment is a file that is sent with an e-mail message. When you download that attachment and open it, the damage is done. Some viruses even locate the addresses of people you have e-mailed recently and send themselves to your friends! To protect yourself from e-mailed viruses and others, you should, at a minimum,

1. Install a current version of **antivirus software** on your computer. Companies such as MacAfee and Norton make programs that check your computer for many types of computer viruses and destroy them or give you a warning.
2. Suspect and *not* download e-mail attachments from people you don't know. Also don't download an attachment from someone you *do* know if you believe the message may be bogus.

Organized Anarchy

Although the term **hacker** originally referred to someone who was in favor of free and open access to computers, the meaning has gradually evolved over the years. Today the term *hacker* can be used to refer to people who commit the following acts:

1. Someone who tries to break into other people's computers without permission. Sometimes the purpose is to show that it can be done, and sometimes, either inadvertently or on purpose, the hacker damages the files on the computer. One recent example involved a teenager who broke into the data files of a cancer research study at a leading medical center and destroyed some of the data.

2. Someone who develops ways of illegally gaining access to commercial software and distributes that information on the Web. Some sites simply place commercial programs such as *Microsoft Word* on the Web to allow people to download the program. Other sites put digital copies of current music on the Web and invite downloads. **Cracker** sites are more sophisticated. Many commercial programs today are distributed in a demo version. You can try out the demo of the program and, if you like it, purchase the rights to use the full version. This generally involves entering a serial number provided by the company. At cracker sites people describe how to "crack" the demos to make them fully functional without paying the software company for the program.

3. Finally, some hackers are outright terrorists. One recent example involved a Russian hacker who found a way to break into the computers of a company that sold products over the Internet. He was able to download to his computer the names, addresses, and credit card numbers of thousands of customers. He then sent the company a ransom note demanding several hundred thousand dollars. He threatened to post the credit card information on the Web if he was not paid. He was not paid and posted the information. Thousands of people were forced to cancel their cards and apply for new ones with new numbers.

There have always been people who wish to disrupt the system and cause problems, but the Internet presents these people with a powerful tool to do just that. Society has not yet found effective ways of dealing with the computer-based anarchists who can mount attacks on busy sites to shut them down, distribute credit card numbers to the world, as well as a host of other destructive acts.

A FINAL POINT: ALTERNATIVES TO THE WEB

Surfing the Web has become a pastime of millions of computer users today. Generally, this means you have a computer with a modem at home (or have some other type of connection that is even faster than a modem), and you have subscribed to an **Internet service provider (ISP).** Several companies such as AT&T, Earthlink, Microsoft, Prodigy, and Sprint have a national network with local numbers in most areas. Other ISPs serve only a limited geographic area. All ISPs are services that provide Internet access. Once you are connected to the Internet via your ISP, you can surf the Web using a browser such as Internet Explorer.

An alternative to this approach is very popular today. **America Online (AOL)** provides two services. With America Online you can connect to the Internet in much the same way you do with an ordinary ISP. In addition, AOL contains a great deal of content on its own servers and provides subscribers with special software that makes it much easier to use than a standard browser. The fact that AOL has more than 20 million subscribers suggests that the easy-to-use, colorful interface and the many services supported by AOL itself have considerable appeal. Moreover, you can assign children their own accounts on AOL and specify how much access they have. You can, for example, restrict children's use to child-friendly sections of AOL. This is a plus for many parents and teachers.

QUESTIONS TO CONSIDER

1. Think of the jobs your grandparents had, and those of your parents. Are those jobs different today because of computers and the World Wide Web? How? Are all the changes positive?

2. How should society respond to the dark side of the Internet? Does the Internet challenge some of the cherished ideals of a democratic society? Or are the problems created by open access less significant than the benefits?

RELATED ACTIVITIES

1. What sort of Internet/World Wide Web access is provided by your college or university? Can you find out whether you are permitted to have your own e-mail address, access to the Internet from home, and space for your personal web page?

2. Remember the four ways the Internet is changing our society: commerce, information, collaboration, and education. Select an aspect of each of these applications that interests you, and use a search engine to find out more about that aspect.

3. Select an aspect of the World Wide Web—HTML or JAVA, supporting software, server software, the addressing protocol, browser software, or search software—and prepare a briefing paper on that topic for other students. Concentrate on the information a novice user of the Web would find most useful.

REFERENCES

Feldman, B. (2000). Protecting our kids on the Internet. Retrieved April 16, 2000, from the World Wide Web: http://www.surfnetkids.com/safety.htm.

Ferris, S. (2000). Rockwell Kent exhibition. Retrieved April 16, 2000, from the World Wide Web: http://www.northeastjournal.com/PastStories/rockwellkent0699.htm.

Hanrahan, M. (1995). *A research report.* Master's thesis, Asia Pacific International University, San Francisco. Retrieved April 16, 2000, from the World Wide Web: http://www.wayoutthere.com/Thesis/title.html

Krol, E. (1992). *The whole Internet. User's guide & catalog.* Sebastopol, CA: O'Reilly.

Marine, A., Kirkpatrick, S., Neou, V., & Ward, C. (1993). *Internet: Getting started.* Englewood Cliffs, NJ: Prentice Hall.

NetLingo. (2000). The Internet language dictionary. Retrieved April 16, 2000, from the World Wide Web: http://www.netlingo.com.

CHAPTER FIVE

TYPE I AND TYPE II USES FOR COMPUTERS

Goal: To understand the differences between Type I and Type II educational computer applications and how these categorizations can be helpful in designing and implementing appropriate educational programs.

KEY TERMS

administrative software (p. 108)
assessment software (p. 106)
backlash (p. 96)
computer-managed instruction (CMI) (p. 108)
computer simulations (p. 112)
database management (p. 111)
drill-and-practice software (p. 103)
electronic spreadsheets (p. 110)
expert systems (p. 107)
graphics software (p. 119)
higher-order thinking skills (p. 97)
Internet (p. 115)

Logo (p. 103)
meta-analysis (p. 109)
presentation software (p. 119)
problem-solving software (p. 114)
programming language (p. 112)
prosthetic aids (p. 115)
telecommunications software (p. 115)
tutorial software (p. 105)
Type I (p. 96)
Type II (p. 96)
word processing (p. 108)
World Wide Web (p. 115)

Computers have the potential to become education's single most useful teaching and learning tool. Today's small computers are amazing technological achievements; however, the value of any tool does not depend solely on the qualities of the tool itself. If the tool is to be useful, a necessary (but not sufficient) requirement is that users must choose to apply the tool to important tasks. Equally crucial is the requirement that the problem to be solved be consistent with the particular solution on which the tool's design is based. A third requirement is that the cost of the tool be proportionate in relation to the seriousness of the problem it addresses.

The hammer, for example, is an extremely successful tool. It is used primarily for the important task of driving nails into wood, a necessary step in achieving larger goals, such as building houses and other expensive structures. The hammer is so successful a tool that almost everyone owns or has access to one. But the hammer would probably not have succeeded if it had first been used merely to prop open doors. Although the hammer could function as a doorstop, it is not well suited to this purpose, and its cost is excessive compared to the minor problem it would solve.

Although we doubt that anyone is employing a computer as a doorstop, some educators may not be devoting enough careful thought to the kinds of teaching and learning tasks to which this tool can best be applied. These educators do not gain the full educational value of computing, and they contribute to the **backlash** (negative reaction) against educational computing.

The success or failure of educational computing is closely tied to value judgments about educational practices and computer applications. In a sense, the primary purpose of this book is to help provide educators with a sound rationale for making such value judgments. All other goals and objectives are subordinate to this end.

In the course of making value judgments about educational computing, it is helpful to categorize computing as Type I or Type II applications. These terms are defined and discussed in the following section. The rest of the chapter is devoted to a discussion of characteristics of typical Type I and Type II software, followed by examples of each.

CHARACTERISTICS OF TYPE I AND TYPE II EDUCATIONAL COMPUTING APPLICATIONS

Some educational applications of computing are designed to make it easier, quicker, or otherwise more efficient to continue teaching the same topics in the same ways we have always taught them. These are called **Type I** applications. **Type II** applications make available new and better ways of teaching.

It is obvious from these definitions that a higher value is placed on Type II applications than on Type I applications; however, Type I applications should not be completely avoided. There is certainly nothing wrong with making traditional teaching easier, faster, or otherwise more efficient. In fact, good Type I computer applications are useful and convenient, and can and should play an important educational role. (They are best used to release the teacher from a variety of mundane and repetitive teaching tasks so that time and effort can be devoted to more important, more complex, and more creative teaching.)

However, Type I applications by themselves, no matter how well applied, cannot justify educational computing to media critics, other educators, school board members, legislators, or the public at large. Type I uses are insufficient because educational computing is too expensive to devote entirely to relatively trivial problems.

Although dollar costs continue to decline, computer hardware and software still require substantial financial investment. The less obvious, and probably more significant, expense is in terms of the time, effort, and enthusiasm of teachers and students. Teachers and students have a limited supply of these ingredients to invest in teaching and learning. If the time, effort, and enthusiasm of either group are devoted to materials and methods that are inefficient or that can achieve goals of relatively limited importance only, such materials and methods are not likely to receive lasting support. Therefore, although excellent Type I applications are to be supported and encouraged, a balanced, successful educational computing program requires the development and use of both Type I and Type II applications.

Unfortunately, Type II applications are very difficult to develop and test, and thus Type I educational applications have been more common. Many observers have pointed out that Type I software, such as drill-and-practice materials, far outnumbers other applications (Collis, 1988; Higgins & Boone, 1993; Jonassen, 2000; Roblyer & Edwards, 2000; Woodward & Carnine, 1993). Research findings have supported this observation. Jonassen (2000) reports that numerous surveys in various countries have shown that fully 85 percent of available educational software falls into this category. In fact, Pelgrum and Plomp (1991), in their survey of educational computing in school districts in 19 countries, found that drill and practice was the most frequently mentioned use of computers. Morrison, Lowther, and DeMeulle (1999) point out that during the 1970s and 1980s, most educational software fell into the drill-and-practice category, and suggest that much of it merely "mimicked flashcards" (p. 2).

In 1988, the Office of Technology Assessment completed an important study that revealed that more than 10,000 commercial programs were available and that most of this software provided rote drill (15 percent), skills practice (51 percent), or tutorials (33 percent). The report concluded that software aimed at developing **higher-order thinking skills** (problem solving, critical thinking, and the like) was scarce and more expensive as well as more difficult to produce. The report also speculated that software producers emphasized Type I software because they were less sure that Type II software would be a commercial success.

There have been many vocal critics of the use of drill-and-practice software in schools. Many of these critics, including the authors of this book, continue to suggest that drill-and-practice applications are often not the best use of computer resources in schools. Others, however, have stridently condemned the use of drill and practice, and suggested that it has no place in schools. However, a recent trend in the literature is somewhat less critical of this extremely common application. The following is representative of the approach often found in the literature in the first half of the 1990s to drill-and-practice software in schools:

> In the rush of enthusiasm to place computers in schools, we have witnessed the introduction of programs which make little use of the technology's potential interactive qualities and flexibility. Programs have been developed that critics claim have emphasized an educational philosophy more in tune with Victorian schools than with those of the late twentieth century. (Sewell, 1990, p. 13)

O'Brien (1994) agreed and suggested that overreliance on Type I software could result in "mind-killing drill and practice" (p. 13). In fact, drill-and-practice software has been called "drill-and-kill" software by some critics. The following paragraph, written almost 10 years later, is representative of the more recent trend to differentiate between good and poor drill-and-practice applications, and to take a more balanced view of this application:

> Criticism leveled in the past at drill and practice software was really aimed at poorly designed software that was boring, that treated all users the same regardless of ability, and that employed undesirable feedback. Teachers tell of students deliberately giving incorrect responses in order to see flashy animated graphics on the screen. The reward offered by that software for making correct responses was the presentation of another boring problem. (Forcier, 1999, p. 71)

Similarly, Roblyer and Edwards (2000) acknowledge that drill-and-practice software is common in schools, but suggest that the often virulent criticism of the past was due primarily to overuse of this type of software by teachers, and to the desire of critics to make a target of behaviorism—an approach to teaching that they perceived as outdated. Roblyer and Edwards (2000) go on to suggest that drill-and-practice software, if well designed and wisely used, has several benefits, including the ability to provide immediate feedback, stimulate good motivation, provide nonjudgmental correction, and save teachers time. They suggest that teachers should use effective drill-and-practice software but limit the time to 10 to 15 minutes per day, make assignments based on the individual needs of students, and incorporate the software into learning stations.

Why did drill-and-practice software dominate education for so long? Cohen and Spenciner (1993) suggest that the dominance of drill and practice was partially the result of the lack of availability of other types of educational software at the beginning of the computer education movement. Software houses, in their rush to furnish schools with software, chose drill and practice as their entry into the market simply because it was quickest and easiest to develop.

What has been responsible for the trend toward a less negative evaluation of drill-and-practice software? One factor is probably that much of the original criticism was excessive to begin with, and the current trend is simply a movement back toward a more reasonable and moderate evaluation. Another is a recent, obvious improvement in the technical and pedagogical quality of much of the available drill-and-practice software. Drill-and-practice software has improved considerably in the last few years. Another possible explanation is that former critics, who now have much more choice in selecting different types of educational software, no longer feel trapped into using drill-and-practice software.

The growth in size and popularity of the Internet and the World Wide Web, and their growing implementation in schools, is another possible reason for a less critical approach to drill-and-practice software. This development has resulted in teachers making much less use of drill-and-practice software, and much more use of the Internet and the Web for more valuable teaching tasks. Jonassen, Peck, and Wilson (1999) agree and suggest that "the interconnection of communities of learners" (p. 14) via the Internet and the Web, is the fastest-growing use of information technology in education. They go on to note that the wide availability of inexpensive, multimedia computers and the evolution and acceptance of the Internet in the mid-1990s dramatically changed the way teachers make use of information technology and computers.

We do not want to imply that drill-and-practice software is no longer criticized. Many critics continue to condemn this type of application. Many of the most vocal and negative critics are those who adhere to a constructivist philosophy of teaching and learning. A later chapter explores constructivism and its role in information technology in education at length. The following quotation, found on an ETS (Educational Testing Services, 1999) website, is illustrative of such criticism, which often assumes that drill-and-practice software emphasizes lower-order thinking skills, whereas teachers and schools should be concentrating on higher-order skills, such as problem solving and creativity: "Finally, using computers for drill and practice, the lower-order skills, is negatively related to academic achievement" (Educational Testing Service, 1999).

Although such criticism is still common, the field seems to be moving toward a less hostile attitude toward drill-and-practice software, provided it is not overused and is individually prescribed. A recent search of the World Wide Web, using the AltaVista search engine (http://www.altavista.com/) and the search string +*"drill-and-practice"*, produced almost 8,000 hits.

If you are interested in sampling the differing opinions about this controversial application, replicate the search and visit some of these sites. (The plus sign and the quotation marks in the search string are necessary to limit hits to those sites containing only the entire phrase, and to eliminate sites containing either the words *drill* or *practice*.)

The following section presents the characteristics of Type I and Type II computer applications. As you read about these characteristics, you may wonder why creating yet another categorization system was necessary, when categories such as drill and practice, simulations, and applications already exist. The Type I/Type II system, however, differs from these other systems in that it embodies an educational value judgment, whereas traditional categorizations are merely descriptive. The Type I/Type II categorization system is based on a commitment to finding new and better ways of teaching, instead of simply facilitating existing methods. In addition, the Type I/Type II system can be applied to educational software yet to be developed, whereas traditional categories may not be appropriate for future applications. Finally, many teachers have told us that the Type I/Type II categorization provides a useful way of thinking about possible computer applications in education.

We have talked about this system and published articles about it for a number of years. An educational computing journal even featured the system on its cover (*The Computing Teacher*, February 1987).

Type I Applications

Although Type I applications vary considerably, the following list details some characteristics they usually share.

1. *Type I applications generally stimulate relatively passive involvement on the part of the user.* Type I applications generally do not require a high degree of intellectually active involvement. Although users are usually required to respond in some way, the responses generally do not involve higher-order, complex cognition.

Intellectual passivity has played a major role in past failures of electronic innovations in education. Educational television is an interesting case in point. Although nothing about educational television itself encourages or requires only passive user involvement, network and most cable television fare conditions children to be intellectually passive viewers. We have noted that our own children are frequently unable to recall what they have just viewed on network television. It is not surprising that children who have become accustomed to modern viewing fare tend to adopt the same passive viewing style even when presented with more intellectually stimulating material.

Fortunately, the nature of computers and computing encourages more active user involvement than do other electronic media. Very little software has been written that allows children to turn on the computer and simply sit back while the machine does all the work. Virtually all educational software, even the poorest Type I software, requires some user involvement. Children must hit the space bar, type *yes*, answer questions, or otherwise make choices at various points in the program. However, Type I applications require less active intellectual involvement relative to that required by Type II applications.

A good example of Type I software is any one of the many programs designed to drill children on math facts. Typically, problems are generated at random and displayed on the computer screen. The user types the answer, and the computer checks the user's response and provides some feedback about correctness. Most programs keep a record of the number of correct and incorrect responses and provide that record on demand or at the conclusion of the program.

Although such drill-and-practice programs (often called *CAI*, or *computer-assisted instruction*) can be very useful and have a valuable role in educational computing, they are not by themselves important enough to justify the time, effort, and money required to implement computers in schools. It is important that children learn their math facts, and the computer is an efficient way to provide math-fact drill and practice, but other noncomputer activities are less expensive and almost as efficient as a computer application.

2. *With Type I applications, the software developer predetermines almost everything that happens on the screen.* The user may vary his or her answers or even make choices about difficulty level or speed of presentation, but the majority of what happens on the screen is predetermined by those who plan and develop the software. In the math example cited above, the programmer decided where the problems would be placed, how the machine would respond to correct and incorrect answers, and all other aspects of program execution. Virtually the only time that control is passed to the user is when the program pauses and waits for an answer to be entered from the keyboard.

3. *In Type I applications, the type of interaction between user and machine is predetermined by the developers of the software, and the contribution of the user must conform to a very limited repertoire of acceptable responses.* With math drill-and-practice software, for example, the only time the user plays a role is when the machine stops and waits for an answer. At that point, the only acceptable response is a single number.

4. *Type I applications are usually aimed at the acquisition of facts by rote memory.* Once again we emphasize that using drill and practice to develop rote memory skill can be very important. We find fault with such applications when they are the only educational computing applications used.

5. *With Type I applications, everything the software is capable of doing can usually be observed in a very short period of time, frequently in 10 minutes or less.* The math drill-and-practice software just described may be capable of generating problems at several difficulty levels using more than one computational process; however, the student can usually sample everything this software is capable of doing in 5 minutes or so.

Type II Applications

Type II applications of computing support new and better ways of teaching and learning. If computer use improves teaching or learning or is essential to teaching or learning (i.e., teaching or learning would be impossible or extremely difficult without the use of a computer), then the application in question is most likely a Type II application. Type II applications, like Type I applications, vary considerably; however, some characteristics are shared by most Type II applications. Generally, these characteristics contrast those listed for Type I applications.

1. *Type II applications generally stimulate relatively active intellectual involvement on the part of the user.* A good example of a Type II application is a fourth-grade class using a children's writing and publishing program to create a class newspaper. Compare the range and depth of intellectual involvement needed for a group of students—who take on roles such as reporter, graphic artist, editor, fact checker, layout artist, and printer—with the involvement needed to respond to a Type I drill-and-practice program, such as the math-facts software described previously.

2. *With Type II applications, the user, rather than the software developer, is in charge of almost everything that happens.* In fact, with many (but not all) Type II applications the focus shifts away from the computer screen, where most of the action in Type I applications takes place. In many Type II applications, students determine when and how to use the computer to support their efforts to solve problems, present information, persuade others, and collect data. A good example of this shift in focus and approach between Type I and Type II applications is the creation of a class newspaper (mentioned previously).

3. *In Type II applications, the user has a great deal of control over the interaction between user and machine, and the repertoire of acceptable user input is extensive.* For example, when students are creating a composition using word processing, they determine when (or whether) to invoke the spelling checker, the thesaurus, and various editing aids such as global searches, replacements, and block moves. They also decide when to use collaborative writing tools, which allow more than one student to contribute to the creation and editing of a piece. By contrast, a Type I math-fact drill-and-practice program controls both the schedule and the type of user interaction allowed.

4. *Type II applications are usually aimed at accomplishing more creative tasks than are Type I applications.* Designing an urban environment with city services and utilities as well as manufacturing sectors, residential areas, schools, and parks and then watching it evolve and grow (or disintegrate) is obviously a more creative task than learning multiplication facts. Thousands of drill-and-practice programs are on the market today, but a growing number of programs, such as *SimCity, SimCity3000, SimTower, SimIsle, SimMars, SimFarm, SimAnt, Sim Theme Park, SimEarth* and others, all distributed by Electronic Arts or the subsidiary Maxis, Inc., enable students to create and manage environments that behave according to realistic models. The newest of these simulations, designed by Will Wright, is *The Sims*. This game allows you to create and control an entire simulated family and other simulated characters. You control every aspect of how they live their lives, including building their homes and buying their possessions. An excellent website, Sim Gateway (http://sim.gamestats.com/), addresses all aspects of these complex simulations.

5. *With Type II applications, many hours of use are generally necessary for a user to discover everything a specific program is capable of doing.* SimCity, for example, is so complex that the producers created *SimTown,* a simpler and less demanding educational simulation for younger children. Because Type II applications require more time and effort to master and understand, finding useful and reliable published reviews of Type II software is difficult. On the other hand, good reviews of Type I software are relatively easy to find. Unfortunately, staff writers and others who prepare software reviews for computer magazines are frequently not regular users of the software they review. In fact, they are often totally unfamiliar with the software when they begin their review; instead they rely on what they learn while using the software for a few minutes before beginning to write. This may work well with Type I software, but days, weeks, or even months of use in a classroom may be needed before a teacher or student can thoughtfully critique a Type II application.

EXAMPLES OF TYPE I AND TYPE II APPLICATIONS

Type I applications make it easier, quicker, or otherwise more efficient to continue teaching the same topics in the same ways they have always been taught whereas Type II applications make available new and better ways of teaching. When classifying a specific piece of software, the characteristics given for each type in the preceding discussion should be used only as aids. Final determination about the category depends on adherence to one or the other of these definitions. Another aid to classification is the fact that certain kinds of educational software tend to fall consistently into one category or the other.

Typical Type I Software

Drill-and-Practice Software.   Software designed to allow the user to practice a skill that has already been acquired is called **drill-and-practice software.** This software may drill the student on math facts, sight vocabulary, parts of speech, names of the 50 states, or any other skill dependent primarily on rote memory. Figure 5.1 depicts an example of drill-and-practice software.

One of the authors once wrote a drill-and-practice computer program for an adult with learning disabilities who had obtained a job as a management trainee in a supermarket. The job required the trainee to learn a code number for every vegetable sold in the produce department. The program, written in the **Logo** computer language, randomly chose the name of one of the 75 vegetables, displayed the name on the screen, and required the trainee to type in the code number. Alternatively, the trainee could elect for the computer to display the code number. The trainee's role then was to type in the name of the vegetable that corresponded to the code number. The program kept track of right and wrong answers and then provided a summary of performance. This program represents a Type I application.

The most important indicator of category is that the software makes it more efficient to practice the number–name associations in a highly traditional manner. In support of Type I classification, note that the program has all five of the common characteristics of Type I software discussed previously: (1) relatively passive user intellectual involvement, (2) predetermined control of most of what happens on the screen, (3) predetermined interaction between the user and computer and a highly limited repertoire of acceptable user responses, (4) a goal of

```
              47
           +  35
           ------
              82

    Correct:  You got 5
              problems right!
              You missed 1.
```

FIGURE 5.1   Example of drill-and-practice software.

acquisition by rote memory, and (5) familiarity with all capabilities of the software after only a few minutes of operation.

The vegetable drill software (1) required only that the trainee associate a vegetable name with a number or a number with a vegetable name; (2) employed a predetermined scheme for problem and answer placement, reinforcement, and the like; (3) limited acceptable user responses to either a vegetable name or a number typed in at strictly defined, restricted, and predetermined points in program execution; (4) focused entirely on the acquisition of the rote association of specific numbers with specific vegetable names; and (5) revealed the limited capability of everything it was programmed to do (displaying numbers and accepting vegetable names or vice versa) in only a few minutes.

Once again, it should be noted that even though Type I software in general and drill-and-practice software in particular do not represent the most advanced educational computer use, this does not mean that such software should not be used. At times drill and practice is the method of choice for a particular learning objective. As Roblyer and Edwards (2000) suggest, although recent interest in software designed to teach problem solving rather than rote skills is increasing, drill-and-software programs will probably continue to be useful in many classrooms for some time to come. Therefore, they recommend that instead of ignoring this application, teachers concentrate on selecting and using high-quality drill-and-practice software to help achieve realistic goals.

Because drill-and-practice software is so commonplace, Vockell and Schwartz (1992) provide an excellent list of five guidelines to avoid misuse:

1. Use unsupervised drills only during the practice stage and never during the learning stage. This is necessary to ensure that students respond with the correct answer 90 to 95 percent of the time.
2. Before using drill-and-practice software, check to be sure that students thoroughly understand the material.
3. Do not overdo drill-and-practice software. Our rule of thumb is that such software should not be used for more than a maximum of 15 minutes with elementary students and half an hour with secondary students.
4. Select drill-and-practice software only to reinforce material that has been introduced in some other way.
5. Limit the use of drill-and-practice software so that students do not erroneously conclude that a topic or a concept is difficult or boring, that understanding the material is not necessary, or that mastery can be attained through memorization or by applying some rote routine.

Vockell and Schwartz (1992) conclude with the following excellent summary of the strengths and weaknesses of drill-and-practice software:

At their best, drills help students develop automaticity—important skills and concepts become so familiar that students can automatically use them when pursuing higher-level activities. At their worst, drills trivialize the subject matter by making students focus on lower-level activities to the exclusion of applying these skills and concepts to the higher-level activities that the subject matter is really about. (p. 44)

Bitter and Pierson (1999) agree and add that drill-and-practice software is ideal for students who need to practice discrete skills. They suggest that drill-and-practice software is more motivating than the same kinds of activities that make use of paper and pencil, and have the added benefits of providing immediate feedback to the learner, making repeated use possible without taking time away from teachers for grading, as well as keeping track of individual progress.

Pensacola Junior College maintains an excellent website (http://www.it.pjc. cc.fl.us/itech/cai/drill.htm) that is actually a tutorial program on drill-and-practice software and on how to build such programs for placement on the World Wide Web. Joseph Howell (1998), the author of this site, includes the following general comment about drill-and-practice programs:

Drill and practice is one of the most widely used, and widely misused, tools of computer-assisted instruction. Poorly designed drill exercises are ineffective and boring. But well-designed drill-and-practice—built on the foundation of random generation, quality feedback, and controlled navigation—can effectively reinforce learning and motivate learners.

Literally thousands of examples of drill-and-practice programs exist on the Web. For example, Scott Van Bramer (1998) at Widener University maintains an extensive page of links to chemistry drill-and-practice programs (http://science. widener.edu/svb/tutorial/index.html). Dozens of examples can be accessed from this page of links. To find other drill-and-practice programs on the Web, go to any search engines, such as AltaVista (http://www.altavista.com/), and follow the instructions for searching drill-and-practice sites outlined earlier in this chapter.

Tutorial Software.   Whereas drill-and-practice software is designed to provide a way to practice a skill that has already been learned, **tutorial software** is designed to teach the skill in the first place. Figure 5.2 shows a tutorial program are designed to teach keyboarding skills. Thousands of tutorial programs are available for free on the Web.

Most available tutorial software falls into the Type I category, although there is really no reason why Type II tutorial software could not be written. (It would be Type II if it used new and better methods of teaching the material, methods that would not be possible without the computer.) Other examples of Type I tutorial programs include any of the commercial programs available to tutor students in preparation for taking the Scholastic Aptitude Test and those intended to orient beginners to the use of a specific computer or specific software. These tutorial programs, like most such programs, take the user through a series of steps by emulating traditional methods of lecture, demonstration, and student trial activities, and most could be easily transformed into a workbook format without

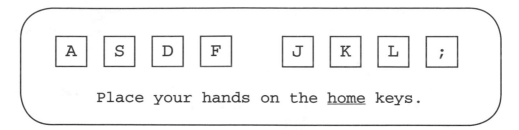

FIGURE 5.2   Example of a tutorial program designed to teach keyboarding skills.

significantly changing the overall methodology or diminishing the effectiveness of the instruction.

Tutorial software is probably the most common kind of educational software on the Web. Thousands of such programs can be found there. A good way to begin looking for such software is with a search engine such as AltaVista (http://www.altavista.com). Type in the search string + *"tutorial software"* or + *"tutorial program"*. (Include plus sign and quotation marks.)

The latter of these two search strings produced more than 10,000 hits, including links to specific turorial software as well as articles about tutorial programs. One excellent site, Math Tutorial Software, is maintained by LF Software (2000) at http://www.mathshareware.com/. This site has links to many shareware tutorial programs for mathematics. You can download and install on your computer any of the math tutorial programs listed at this site.

Assessment Uses.   Assessment software seems to be growing in popularity. There are two broad types of this software.

1. One type is designed to administer, score, summarize, and interpret the results of *standardized tests.* The first three of these functions represent by definition Type I applications because they intend to make tests that were originally developed for noncomputer implementation more convenient, more accurate, or less time-consuming to administer.

2. Another similar type is designed to create, administer, score, summarize, and interpret the results of *teacher-made tests.* Many such programs are available on the Web. Some are designed to aid in creating paper-and-pencil tests; some are for use with tests to be administered on a stand-alone computer; and others are for use with tests that are administered on the Web itself.

One example is a site by Question Mark Computing Ltd. at http://www.questionmark.com/home.htm—Testing, Survey, and Assessment Software. The site offers free trials of commercial software for handling tests and surveys. The software can be downloaded for a free 30-day trial and consists of two packages—QM Perception, and QM for Windows. The former is intended for tests or surveys to be administered on NT web servers whereas the latter is for administration via floppy diskette, CD, stand-alone PCs, or file servers.

Another example of assessment software is *WebCT: Web Course Tools* (WebCT, 1999), a complex package that has become popular for use in classes in higher education and in some secondary schools. The company claims to have more than 6 million student accounts at more than 1,350 institutions located in 55 countries. WebCT maintains an extensive website at http://webct.com/ and an excellent tutorial on how to use the software itself at http://about.webct.com/v2/ tutorial.html. WebCT is commercial software that can be used to create entire, web-based, online courses or to publish materials that supplement a classroom-based course. The WebCT site lists the following description of WebCT software:

> WebCT is a tool that facilitates the creation of sophisticated World Wide Web–based educational environments. It does this in three ways:
> 1. It provides an interface allowing the design of the presentation of the course (color schemes, page layout, etc.).
> 2. It provides a set of educational tools to facilitate learning, communication, and collaboration.
> 3. It provides a set of administrative tools to assist the instructor in the process of management and continuous improvement of the course.

WebCT also offers a free, instant trial course with the ability to accommodate up to 50 student users for 6 months. One excellent feature is that the software is always free to download and to use to create a course. A license must be purchased only if the user decides to offer the course to students. Although the licenses are not free, they are quite affordable. A complex pricing scheme is based on the number of student users. The minimum cost for a license includes up to 50 students, and the fees for 4, 6, 8, or 12 months are $100, $140, $180, or $250, respectively. Fees for licenses then range upward based on the number of student users. Fees for licenses for an unlimited number of students (more than 51,200) are $1,200, $1,680, $2,160, and $3,000, respectively.

Some characteristics of Type I or Type II applications are difficult to apply to this class of software because such characteristics were developed for use with educational software designed for direct teaching. As always, the final determination of category depends on adherence to the definitions of Type I or Type II applications.

Some of the software designed to *interpret* the results of standardized testing is in a class by itself. This type of software is intended to be Type II software. If successful, this software would be classified Type II because it is intended to make judgments of the most knowledgeable experts in a field available to anyone who has access to a computer and the software.

Software intended to perform this function falls into a category known as **expert systems.** Expert systems have not yet fulfilled our initial high expectations. Most authorities agree that no expert systems have yet been developed that acceptably emulate the judgment of educational or psychological experts.

```
What kind of test do you want to make?
   a. multiple choice
   b. matching
   c. short answer
Type a, b, or c and press Return.
```

FIGURE 5.3   An example of administrative software designed to help teachers create different tests.

Administrative Uses.   Administrative applications include software for producing, calculating, coordinating, or compiling registration information; attendance records; graphics; student grades; room, teacher, or school schedules; mailing labels; budgets; filing; or other secretarial tasks to aid administrative activity. Figure 5.3 depicts one screen from a piece of **administrative software** designed to help teachers create tests in several different formats.

It should be obvious from this discussion that the way in which software is used can determine whether the application falls into the Type I or Type II category. For example, although using word processing to teach composition skills is a Type II application, using word processing as a secretarial substitute for typewriting is a Type I application.

Computer-Managed Instruction.   Computer-managed instruction (CMI) is a mixed bag of applications designed to perform tasks or combinations of tasks such as organizing student data, monitoring student progress, testing student mastery and prescribing further instruction or remediation, recording student progress, and selecting the order of instructional modules to be completed.

The term *computer-managed instruction* is not appropriate because only people, not computers, can be managers and because no direct instruction takes place. Regardless of terminology, CMI should probably be considered a Type I application, for it is generally used to teach something more efficiently than the way in which it has always been taught.

Typical Type II Software

Word Processing.   Using **word processing** to teach written composition is a Type II application because it makes possible the teaching of composition in a way that is not possible without the computer. The ease of revision made possible by word processing cannot be duplicated with noncomputer activities. Although researchers continue to find contradictory results and are still attempting to determine exactly which student writing achievement outcomes are most favorably influenced by instruction implementing word processing, there is little doubt that word processing results in some more positive achievement gains than traditional instruction.

Some of the contradictory research findings in this area are probably the result of the great variety of word-processing programs, types of teaching, and other variables studied. However, almost all researchers have found that student attitudes toward writing improve following instruction using word processing and that students write more and revise more. In addition, it seems clear that improvements, when they are found, depend on whether the word processing took place in concert with excellent writing instruction and on whether students are given enough time to learn to use the word-processing program efficiently (Roblyer & Edwards, 2000).

Roblyer, Castine, and King (1988) have made the excellent point that because word processing takes the drudgery out of the composing and revising process, favorably influencing both student achievement and attitude, effects on student achievement need only be equal, not superior, to traditional instruction to support sufficient justification for its use. Roblyer (1988) subjected word-processing research to **meta-analysis,** a statistical technique that permits analyzing the collective results of a number of individual research findings. She concluded that word processing is one of the most potentially powerful uses of microcomputers for instruction. The qualifier *potentially* is very important because the computer and software components of Type II applications are only part of the instructional approach that determines their success, or lack of success, in the classroom. Although word processing, including the many programs designed specifically for use by children, has considerable potential to support innovative and interesting educational experiences, the same programs can be used to support boring, ineffective instruction.

The lesson to be learned from the most recent research on word processing is that the manner in which word processing is used in instruction is the most important consideration in determining whether it is beneficial to students. Of course, the same can probably be said for all educational applications of information technology.

When the use of word-processing software meets the criteria for Type II applications, the educational experience possesses all the characteristics common to applications in this category:

1. Relatively active intellectual involvement
2. User control of almost everything that happens on the screen
3. User control of interaction with the machine and an extensive repertoire of acceptable user input
4. Focus on creative instead of rote tasks
5. Many capabilities that require hours, days, or even weeks to fully understand and use

Spreadsheets and Databases. Two other types of application software that can be part of Type II instruction in education are spreadsheets and databases. **Electronic spreadsheets** let students organize numerical data and automate calculations and comparisons of various pieces of data that have been collected. Electronic spreadsheets greatly simplify common accounting tasks involving complex formulas that virtually all businesses must perform. Many business calculations are highly interdependent. Because of this interdependence, changing a few numbers in a calculation might require the revision of thousands of other entries in an accounting ledger because the numbers that are changed may be used in formulas to calculate other entries. For example, if one entry represents the wholesale cost of a raw material used in the manufacture of a certain product, a change in this number requires changing many other numbers, such as tax paid on each item, percentage of profit, and commissions to be paid to salespeople. Spreadsheets automate this process: once you enter the new numbers, the spreadsheet program automatically recalculates the entire electronic spreadsheet (i.e., the ledger is now in your computer's memory instead of in printed ledger books).

The versatility with which electronic spreadsheets handle tasks that involve comparing and combining numbers as well as computing complex formulas has, however, also been put to use in education. In addition to obvious uses of spreadsheets, such as keeping track of grades, they can be used in many ways in the classroom.

Many websites discuss the use of spreadsheets for educational purposes. One such site is Spreadsheets, Mathematics, Science, and Statistics Education, located at http://sunsite.univie.ac.at/Spreadsite/#spreadexed. This site contains links to dozens of sites pertaining to the use of spreadsheets to assist in teaching mathematics, science, and statistics. The Center for Environmental and Conservation Education maintains a page of links to dozens of other sites containing ideas for the use of spreadsheets and actual, downloadable spreadsheets (http://cesme.utm.edu/resources/other/SS/Spreadsheets.html). Examples at this site include spreadsheets for finding the value of a combination of coins, for studying and calculating area and perimeter, for learning about the behavior of batteries wired in series, and many others. The Center for Technology and Teacher Education also maintains a site containing ideas for using spreadsheets at all levels of education and provides downloads of *Excel* spreadsheets (http://curry.edschool.virginia.edu/teacherlink/math/interactiveexcel.html). The North Carolina Department of Public Instruction maintains spreadsheet lesson plans and free spreadsheets to download at http://www.dpi.state.nc.us/Curriculum/computer.skills/lssnplns/sstoc.html.

Spreadsheets can be used to help teach virtually any subject at almost all levels. For example, Ramondetta (1992) described the use of electronic spreadsheets to help elementary students evaluate the amount of trash they create by analyzing lunchroom trash. Students count and categorize data on trash thrown away in the lunchroom and then consider alternative approaches to reduce the amount of trash generated. Other problem-solving and brainstorming lessons based on electronic spreadsheets include playing a simulation of the stock market

(Crisci, 1992); studying probability using coin tosses (Chesebrough, 1991); studying conservation of energy using rolling and sliding spheres (Krieger & Stith, 1990); and evaluating the quality of life or "livability" of different cities by gathering data and analyzing them with a spreadsheet (Hannah, 1986).

To locate other ideas and to find hundreds of pre-prepared spreadsheets to download, use to a search engine such as AltaVista (http://www.altavista.com) with the search string +*"spreadsheets"* +*"education"*, including the plus signs and all quotation marks. The last time we performed this search, we found almost 50,000 hits.

Although electronic spreadsheets manipulate numerical data, the results of the manipulation need not always be rows and columns of numbers. Some of the websites just mentioned include ways in which the graphical output of spreadsheets such as *Microsoft Excel* can be used in mathematics classrooms to represent complex mathematical relationships.

Database management software, which is somewhat similar to word processing and electronic spreadsheets, is another Type II application. Database management software makes it possible to create an electronic filing system. Once data are correctly entered, the user can search the data for all cases conforming to some predetermined criterion or combination of criteria. For example, a social studies class might collect data about tropical rain forests. Students can then search the file for all cases of tropical rain forests that conform to some criterion (such as all rain forests between certain latitudes, with a given range of annual rainfall, or with certain flora or fauna).

The Berrien County Michigan Instructional Technology Team (Berrien County Intermediate School District, 1998) has a web page (http://www.remc11. k12.mi.us/bcisd/classres/intideas.htm) that presents many excellent ideas for the use of database software in each subject area. Ideas for social studies include using a database to compare information such as literacy rates, mortality rates, per capita incomes, or other information about a region. Students are then asked to create and answer questions about the information gathered. Similarly, New Hampshire Public Television (2000) maintains a site featuring dozens of science lesson plans (http://www.nhptv.org/kn/vs/scilab5g.htm), many of which make use of database management software. In one example of an astronomy lesson, children use database software to enter data about planets and then use the search capabilities of the software to compare and contrast various planetary features.

Databases can be used in the classroom in two general ways. First, students can use database programs to organize and sort data *they have collected*. The previous examples are of this type. The second approach involves using a database *prepared by someone else* to find and organize information and to draw conclusions. Many databases available today were created specifically for classroom use.

Perseus, for example, is a database of material related to ancient Greece, with many illustrations and photographs. Originally, the Perseus Project resided on CD-ROM and various print media. However, the Perseus Project can now be found on the World Wide Web at http://www.perseus.tufts.edu/, where it currently consists of more than 225 gigabytes of data. The Perseus web database includes a sophisticated search feature to help users find the information they are looking for. A description of the project as found on the Perseus information page (http://www.perseus.tufts.edu/PerseusInfo.html) follows:

> The Perseus Project is an evolving digital library of resources for the study of the ancient world and beyond. Collaborators initially formed the project to construct a large, heterogeneous collection of materials, textual and visual, on the Archaic and Classical Greek world. Planning for Perseus began in 1985; the project was formally established in July, 1987. Since then, the Perseus Project has published two CD-ROMs and created the on-line Perseus Digital Library. Recent expansion into Latin texts and tools and Renaissance materials has served to add more coverage within Perseus and has prompted the project to explore new ways of presenting complex resources for electronic publication. (Crane, 2000)

Programming Languages.   Several programming languages, including Logo, have been created specifically for use in schools. However, controversy continues concerning the issue of whether cognitive benefits can be gained by teaching a **programming language** to children and, if so, what these benefits are.

Although final determination of category would require resolution of this controversy, computer programming should be considered a Type II activity for two reasons. First, learning to program involves definite benefits despite the fact that these benefits have been exaggerated by some advocates. Second, these benefits are unique to computer programming and are not easily derived through noncomputer activities. In addition, all the characteristics unique to Type II applications have the potential to be present in the experience of learning to program:

1. Programming requires a high level of intellectual involvement as the user attempts to supply the code to accomplish some task.
2. Programming, just like word processing, engages the user in determining what happens on a blank screen, thus allowing complete user control and providing a powerful method for entering and revising whatever codes the user chooses to create a program.
3. The user controls interaction with the computer, and the flexibility and range of acceptable user input is extensive.
4. Programming is a highly creative problem-solving exercise.
5. The full capabilities of a programming language cannot be learned in only a few minutes.

Simulations.   **Computer simulations** make available experiences that are too expensive, too dangerous, or otherwise unavailable to students. Thus, simulations are Type II applications by definition.

Some of the most sophisticated and complex simulations have been developed for use by the military. Examples of these simulations are any of the complex computer flight simulators in use today. Cost and safety are obvious advantages of flight simulators over actual flight. A single actual flight in a modern jet fighter is dangerous and costs thousands of dollars for the fuel alone. The same flight in a jet simulator is completely safe and involves only the cost of the computer and software, which can be used again and again for years. In addition, flight simulators make it possible for trainers systematically to confront trainees with a wide variety of flight conditions, such as severe weather, equipment malfunctions, and attack by enemy planes or ground weapons.

Generally, educational simulations are not as well developed as are highly complex and sophisticated simulations like flight simulators. Nevertheless, simulations present one of the most exciting potentials for educational computing. Although not as common as drill-and-practice or other educational applications, many excellent educational simulations are available. A recent search using the AltaVista search engine and the search string +*"educational simulations"* produced more than 2,000 hits.

Examples of simulations include taking a field trip to a rain forest or botanical gardens, controlling the ecosystem of a deserted island, constructing a new planet and controlling its ecosystem, designing a machine for a factory, leading a wagon train across the Oregon Trail, managing a farm, and operating a hotdog concession at high-school football games for a year.

In the planet simulation, users choose land configurations, bodies of water, climate zones, types of animals and plants, and a host of other variables. Once these choices are made, the simulation of life on the planet begins, and students can see the results of their choices on the entire ecosystem as some species become extinct while others flourish.

The Internet and the World Wide Web have made possible an entirely new set of *interactive* simulations. For example, Simulations, Inc. provides *The Electronic United Nations*, a free simulation available at http://www.simulations.com/eun/index.htm. A teacher can download the software and use it with the class to create a "classroom country." The class then participates in a simulated United Nations by interacting on the Web with other classroom countries around the world.

Most characteristics of typical Type II software are present in simulations. In the simulation of life on a hypothetical planet, (1) active intellectual involvement is required for the user to avoid altering conditions in such a way that life forms cannot survive; (2) the activity requires creative manipulation of the characteristics of different species so that survival is possible; and (3) the simulation is so complex that a user could never experience all possible combinations of planetary conditions and life forms.

Two characteristics of most Type II software may not be applicable to some simulations. For example, in many simulations, most of what happens on the screen is predetermined by the software developer instead of the user (even though it could be argued that the manipulation of the variables in our example is completely controlled by the user). In addition, the developer of the simulation predetermines the nature of the interaction as well as acceptable responses. (Again, it could be argued that the user-chosen variables in the planet simulation have almost unlimited possible combinations. Still, the user is limited to changing variables determined in advance by the software developer, and they must fall within the predetermined acceptable ranges.) Therefore, these two common qualities of Type II software do not seem to apply to educational simulations. Nevertheless, simulations are one of the most exciting and promising applications in educational computing.

Problem-Solving Software. **Problem-solving software** is a relatively new educational application. At least two types of software could fall into this category. The first is based on the assumption that universal or generic problem-solving skills can be learned in one domain and then transferred to other domains. Educators who accept this assumption might use a piece of software by Sunburst Communications called *The Incredible Laboratory,* which depicts a list of imaginary chemicals the user can choose to add to a beaker. Each ingredient produces a specific feature in a monster that is supposedly produced by the chemical mixing. In addition, the chemicals can be combined to form other results. The user is required to use trial and error and the process of elimination to deduce the effect of each chemical as well as the effects of combining chemicals.

Another software package, also from Sunburst, falls into the category of problem-solving software. This package, called *Memory Building Blocks,* includes six concentration-type games. Teachers can change the gameboard and speed in order to match the difficulty level to the ability of the student. Sunburst maintains these games "build visual and auditory memory skills" (Sunburst, 2000).

The underlying assumption of those who advocate the use of these and other similar software is that trial-and-error strategies, process-of-elimination skills, and visual and auditory memory are teachable and are generic problem-solving strategies. Advocates also believe such skills, learned while using *The Incredible Laboratory,* can transfer to other situations, such as those found in mathematics, social studies, and daily living. The assumption of transferability of generic problem-solving skills is open to question, and more is said about this kind of software in a later chapter.

Another type of problem-solving software is designed as a problem-solving tool in the same way that a calculator is a tool for solving calculation problems. The software is designed to focus attention on or to clarify specific skills or concepts needed for problem solving within a single domain. (Remember that the first type of problem-solving software described was aimed at teaching generic problem-solving skills that would transfer to other domains.)

An example of this second type of problem-solving software is Judah Schwartz and Michal Yershalmy's *Function Supposer* (marketed by Sunburst Communications). This software includes three applications: the Function Grapher, which plots functions, uses zoom, builds tables of values, and finds roots; the Function Transformer, which assists symbolic and graphical understanding of concepts such as factor, expand, and simplify; and the Function Comparator, which helps explain the nature of equations, inequalities, and identities. In addition, the software permits addition, subtraction, multiplication, and division of functions. The aim of the software is to encourage students to discover generalizations about functions by making it practicable for them to graph a function quickly and easily, thus enabling movement back and forth between equation and graph. The software is a vast improvement over plotting functions by hand, or even with a graphing calculator, because these traditional methods are often clumsy and time consuming.

The jury is still out on the efficacy of software such as *The Incredible Laboratory*. Many psychologists doubt there is a set of generic problem-solving skills, the mastery of which automatically transfers to other subject domains. However, there is some indication that problem-solving skills may be similar, in which case teaching strategies can be used to facilitate transfer from one domain to another.

The *Function Supposer* can be classified as Type II software because it makes possible teaching functions in a way that is not possible without the use of a computer. In addition, the software has all the characteristics of Type II software, in the same way that word processing does.

Computers as Prosthetic Aids.   One of the least controversial applications of computers in schools is the use of **prosthetic aids.** One example is computer-generated synthetic speech, used for a variety of purposes. Text-to-speech synthesizers can accept text entered at the keyboard and convert it to speech. This application can be invaluable for individuals who have communication disabilities. A more sophisticated application for use with hearing-impaired or aphasic children can convert unintelligible speech to synthetic speech, or to print, or both.

Other applications in this category include special input devices that allow individuals with physical disabilities to use a computer. For example, devices for individuals with limited movement capabilities permit computer input through head, chin, tongue, or eyebrow movement. Large-print word processors and Braille word processors are available for individuals with visual impairments. Such applications are obvious Type II applications because they make learning possible for persons who could not participate without the use of a computer.

Telecommunications Software.   **Telecommunications software** enables a computer to communicate with another computer, often across great distances. We have always recognized the great educational potential of telecommunications, but, until recently, a number of vexing problems have prevented this potential from being realized. In fact, in the past, these problems reduced telecommunications to little more than a toy for computer hobbyists and rendered telecommunications impractical for most teachers and students in schools.

Historically, the primary problems that limited the educational effectiveness of telecommunications were expense and lack of a wide variety of educationally relevant activities accessible through telecommunications. Both these problems have disappeared as a result of the development of the **Internet** and the **World Wide Web**.

Accurately defining or describing the Internet is a difficult task. One way to begin is to state that the Internet is a complex network of other computer networks and individual users. In fact, today it is the world's largest computer network.

What kinds of activities can schools and teachers do with the Internet? Chapter 4 of this book discusses this topic in depth. However, no summary of available resources is complete for long because new activities and resources become available almost from moment to moment. LaQuey and Ryer (1993) provide a brief summary of what is currently available on the Internet:

> Whether you want to find the latest financial news, browse through library catalogs, trace your genealogy, exchange information with your colleagues, or join in lively political debate, the Internet is the tool that will take you beyond phones, faxes, and isolated computers to the real electronic information frontier. The Internet can shrink the world and bring knowledge, experience, and information on nearly every subject imaginable straight to your computer. It can give you the power and speed of a supercomputer, even if you have only a microcomputer and a modem. (p. vii)

Provenzo (1999) agrees, and adds:

> The Internet and the World Wide Web are important to a field like education for many reasons. I believe the most significant reason is that the Internet brings a massive set of information resources into the classroom that have never been available before. Students can easily visit web sites around the World. No matter how isolated or poor, a child with a connection to the Internet and the World Wide Web can have access to the great museums and libraries of the world. The Louvre Museum in Paris, the Library of Congress in Washington, DC, or the Victoria and Albert Museum in London is literally just a computer with browser program and modem, a telephone connection, and a mouse-click or two away. Even the surface of the planet Mars and the outer reaches of the Solar System can be explored by a student with an internet connection, a modem and fairly inexpensive computer. (p. 3)

These two quotations effectively summarize the two great educational features of the Internet and the Web—the vast storehouse of information that can be tapped by students and the fantastic interactive and communication capabilities enjoyed by users.

In one sense, the accurate answer to the question of what kinds of tasks teachers and students can accomplish with the Internet is any task that involves information. Because almost any educational task requires information in some form, educational uses of the Internet are limited only by the imagination and creativity of students and teachers.

We stated at the beginning of this section that the two major problems that must be solved for telecommunications to qualify as Type II application are (1) limited availability of a variety of educationally useful tasks and (2) excessive expense. The reader can appreciate how the Internet solves the first problem by providing an almost unlimited variety of information. Marketplace competition is the solution to the second problem by driving down the cost of using commercial telecommunications services.

The Internet is certainly not the first computer network that has been available to the general public or to teachers and students; however, in the past, widely available commercial networks such as CompuServe and The Source, while offering much useful information, were excessively expensive. Monthly subscription fees and expensive charges for each minute of use (particularly during school hours) made even cursory use of such networks impractical in most schools. Then, too, when users of these commercial networks were located in rural areas or areas in which the network did not maintain a local network telephone number, long-distance charges made use even more prohibitively expensive.

Recently, with the arrival of many new competitors, including Prodigy, America Online (AOL), and the Microsoft Network (MSN), the cost of using commercial telecommunications services has decreased significantly. These Internet service providers (ISPs) commonly charge a monthly fee for unlimited access. Although thousands of local ISPs exist, most function only as on-ramps to the Internet and the Web. A few others, such as AOL, additionally provide their own databases for customers of their service.

Although the Internet is not free, most schools gain access by first logging on to a university computer network or a computer network operated by some state agency. When this is the case, charges are paid by the agency or university and the school is not charged. Another recent trend is school districts establishing their own local area networks connected to the Internet. Schools then log on to the network and thus have Internet and Web access. The effect of these recent developments has been to make Internet access available to many public schools without direct charges to the school or its students and teachers.

Although we are very enthusiastic about telecommunications, particularly about the educational potential of the Internet, as with any educational innovation, some problems must be addressed. One of the authors of this textbook has published an article that outlines some of the problems and suggests possible solutions (Maddux, 1994). Although this article was written in 1994, the problems identified are still current today. A summary of these problems and suggested solutions follows:

1. *Schools tend to concentrate on technical aspects of obtaining access to the Internet or other networks while neglecting the issue of how telecommunications can be used to improve teaching and learning.* Educators should continue to work to obtain wide access to the Internet but also should concentrate on finding and disseminating excellent educational uses.

2. *Many schools have antiquated computer hardware and software.* Principals and other decision makers should be persuaded that replacement and maintenance costs should be built into school budgets. Up-to-date computers that run sophisticated telecommunications software are needed, and these computers should be equipped with modems. Classrooms also need telephone lines that can be used for telecommunications. Some school districts are already installing high-speed "direct connect" data communication lines to bypass slower and less reliable telephone lines to provide fast, dependable access to the Internet.

3. *Few schools provide sufficient support for teachers who wish to incorporate telecommunications.* Both technical and curriculum support are needed. Teachers need help establishing and maintaining connectivity, and they need help in producing teaching materials and in generating ideas for the intelligent integration of telecommunications into existing curricula.

4. *Schools lack coherent structure, stability, and documentation for Internet use.* The Internet changes rapidly, and someone in the school must provide in-service training and accurate, current documentation on how to use various features.

5. *A current trend is schools censoring use of the Internet or completely prohibiting its use on the grounds that some inappropriate material is available.* Schools should avoid censorship because it is morally repugnant to many people and because it does not work. There are so many different routes to any given information on the Internet and the Web that it is probably impossible to block every path to objectionable material. Then, too, almost *everything* is objectionable to *someone,* and deciding what to censor and what not to censor is a problem without a good solution.

Educators should discuss this problem with school boards and school administrators and should consider having children and parents subscribe to a code of behavior. All parents should be made aware that inappropriate material is available via any given medium, including television, print, radio, and the telephone, and that responsible network use is an individual responsibility.

Some schools have responded to this problem by installing special software called *filtering software* to act as a censor. Such software is intended to block access to pornographic, excessively violent, or otherwise objectionable material. There are many problems with this strategy, in addition to the moral objections just mentioned. For example, critics have charged that some of this software has blocked access to legitimate sites, such as those dealing with breast cancer (because of the word *breast*). There have even been charges that the developers of some of this software have built-in blocks to sites that present political views in opposition to the developers' views.

In any case, this is a growing industry, and many companies and software packages are involved. Some better-known packages and related websites are *CyberPatrol* (http://www.cyberpatrol.com/dyn_hm.htm), *NetNanny* (http://www.netnanny.com/), *CYBERsitter* (http://www.cybersitter.com/), and *Cyber Sentinel* (http://www.securitysoft.com/). Literally dozens of such packages and a wealth of information and opinions, both pro and con, are available on the Web. An AltaVista (http://www.altavista.com/) search using the search string *"filtering software"* (including the quotation marks) produced almost 20,000 hits.

6. It is difficult for students, teachers, or any other users to determine whether information on a web page is accurate, authoritative, up to date, unbiased, or otherwise reliable. Educators should lobby their professional organizations to start electronic journals and other network entities that have undergone peer review and field testing.

Graphics Software, Presentation Software, and Other Software.   Graphics software is designed to enable users to draw or manipulate pictures (graphics) on the computer screen. **Presentation software** can be used to help teachers and others make presentations using a variety of media. These types of software, as well as other types yet to be developed, have the potential to be Type II software when they are used in such a way that users are able to learn in new and better ways.

Summary

Computers and information technology have the potential to revolutionize teaching and learning. However, if the computer is to be successful in education, it must be used to solve important educational problems.

We have found it helpful to classify educational computing applications as either Type I or Type II. Type I applications make it easier, quicker, or otherwise more efficient or more convenient to continue teaching the same topics in the same ways as they have always been taught. Type II applications make available new and better ways of teaching.

Type I applications are much more common than Type II applications, probably because Type I applications are much easier to develop. Both Type I and Type II educational applications are useful, but Type I applications alone will not convince lawmakers, school board members, taxpayers, and others that educational computing benefits are worth their cost. Type I and Type II applications have very different characteristics. Type I applications

1. Call for relatively passive user intellectual involvement
2. Employ screen events that are largely predetermined by the software developer
3. Call for developer-determined interaction between user and machine
4. Are aimed at rote memory
5. Can usually be completely reviewed in a short period of time

Type II applications usually share all or most of the following characteristics:

1. They require relatively active user intellectual involvement.
2. They place much of the control of what happens on the screen in the hands of the user.
3. They give the user control of the interaction between user and machine.
4. The goal of the application is the accomplishment of relatively creative tasks.

5. Many hours of use are required before the user experiences everything the software is capable of doing.

Examples of Type I applications include drill-and-practice applications, tutorial uses, assessment software, administrative uses, and CMI. Examples of Type II software include word processing, spreadsheet and database management software, programming languages, simulations, problem-solving software, computers as prosthetic aids, and telecommunications software.

LOOKING AHEAD

You should now be gaining an appreciation for the wide variety of educational software available and for the issues and controversies that surround some of these applications. The next chapter is devoted to technology and theories of learning and contains material that is critical for teachers to make wise use of computers and information technology.

QUESTIONS TO CONSIDER

1. Why do you think some tools in education are successful whereas others never catch on?
2. Which Type I educational application do you think is the most potentially useful to you? Why?
3. Which Type II educational application do you think is the most potentially useful to you? Why?
4. Do you think Type II applications will ever completely replace Type I applications? Why or why not?

RELATED ACTIVITIES

1. Go to your College of Education computer laboratory or a retail store that sells computer software and ask someone who works there to demonstrate a piece of educational software.
2. After viewing the software, decide whether you think it is Type I or Type II software, and tell why you think so.

REFERENCES

Berrien County Intermediate School District. (1998). *Classroom resources: Technology curriculum integration ideas!* Berrien Springs, MI: Author. Retrieved April 5, 2000, from the World Wide Web: http://www.remc11.k12.mi.us/bcisd/classres/intideas.htm

Bitter, G. C., & Pierson, M. E. (1999). *Using technology in the classroom* (4th ed.). Boston: Allyn & Bacon.
Chesebrough, D. (1991, May–June). Using computers: Chances are.... *Learning, 19*(9), 56.
Cohen, L. G., & Spenciner, L. J. (1993). Reading and writing: Integrating software into the curric-

ulum. *Rural Special Education Quarterly, 12*(4), 44–51.

Collis, B. (1988). *Computers, curriculum, and whole-class instruction: Issues and ideas.* Belmont, CA: Wadsworth.

Conner-Sax, K., & Krol, E. (1999). *The whole Internet: The next generation.* Sebastopol, CA: O'Reilly.

Crane, G. R. (Ed.). (2000). *The Perseus Project.* Medford, MA: Tufts University. Retrieved April 6, 2000, from the World Wide Web: http://www.perseus.tufts.edu/

Crisci, G. (1992, January). Play the market. Curriculum connection. *Instructor, 101*(5), 68–69.

Educational Testing Service. (1999). *Does it compute? The relationship between educational technology and student achievement in mathematics.* Princeton, NJ: Author. Retrieved April 3, 2000, from the World Wide Web: http://www.ets.org/research/textonly/pic/dic/dicthree.html

Forcier, R. C. (1999). *The computer as an educational tool* (2nd ed.). Upper Saddle River, NJ: Merrill.

Hannah, L. (1986, December–January). Social studies, spreadsheets and the quality of life. *The Computing Teacher, 13*(4), 13–16.

Higgins, K., & Boone, R. (1993). Technology as a tutor, tool, and agent for reading. *Journal of Special Education Technology, 12*(1), 28–37.

Howell, J. H. (1998). *Building online drill and practice.* Pensacola, FL: Pensacola Junior College. Retrieved April 4, 2000, from the World Wide Web: http://www.it.pjc.cc.fl.us/itech/cai/drill.htm

Jonassen, D. H. (2000). *Computers as mindtools for schools* (2nd ed.). Upper Saddle River, NJ: Merrill.

Jonassen, D. H., Peck, K. L., & Wilson, B. G. (1999). *Learning with technology: A constructivist perspective.* Upper Saddle River, NJ: Merrill.

Krieger, M., & Stith, J. (1990, September). Spreadsheets in the physics laboratory. *Physics Teacher, 28*(6), 378–384.

LaQuey, T., & Ryer, J. C. (1993). *The Internet companion: A beginner's guide to global networking.* Reading, MA: Addison-Wesley.

LF Software. (2000). Math tutorial software. Emerald Isle, NC: Author. Retrieved April 4, 2000, from the World Wide Web: http://www.mathshareware.com/

Maddux, C. D. (1994). The Internet: Educational prospects—and problems. *Educational Technology, 34*(7), 37–42.

Market Data Retrieval. (1999). *Technology in education 1999.* Shelton, CT: Author.

Morrison, G. R., Lowther, D. L., & DeMeulle, L. (1999). *Integrating computer technology into the classroom.* Upper Saddle River, NJ: Prentice Hall.

O'Brien, T. C. (1994). Computers in education: A Piagetian perspective. In J. J. Hirschbuhl (Ed.), *Computers in education* (pp. 12–14). Guilford, CT: Dushkin.

Office of Technology Assessment. (1988). *Power on! New tools for teaching and learning* (Publication No. 052-003-01125-5). Washington, DC: U.S. Government Printing Office.

Pelgrum, W. J., & Plomp, T. (1991). *The use of computers in education worldwide.* Oxford, England: Pergamon.

Provenzo, E. F. (1999). *The Internet and the World Wide Web for preservice teachers.* Boston: Allyn & Bacon.

Ramondetta, J. (1992, April–May). Using computers. Learning from lunchroom trash. *Learning, 20*(8), 59.

Roblyer, M. D. (1988, September). The effectiveness of microcomputers in education: A review of the research from 1980–1987. *T.H.E. Journal,* 85–89.

Roblyer, M. D., Castine, W., & King, F. (1988). *Assessing the impact of computer-based instruction.* New York: Haworth.

Roblyer, M. D., & Edwards, J. (2000). *Integrating educational technology into teaching* (2nd ed.). Upper Saddle River, NJ: Merrill.

Sewell, D. F. (1990). *New tools for new minds: A cognitive perspective on the use of computers with young children.* New York: St. Martin's.

Sunburst Communications. (2000). Memory building blocks. Pleasantville, NY: Author. Retrieved April 7, 2000, from the World Wide Web: http://sunburstdirect.sunburst.com/cgi-bin/SunburstDirect.storefront/1556259465/Product/View/11338

United States Census Bureau. (1999). *Computer use in the United States: October 1997.* Washington, DC: Author. Retrieved January 5, 2000, from the World Wide Web: http://www.census.gov/population/www/socdemo/computer.html

Van Bramer, S. (1998). *Chemistry drill and practice tutorials.* Chester, PA: Widener University. Retrieved April 4, 2000, from the World Wide Web: http://science.widener.edu/svb/tutorial/index.html

Vockell, E. L., & Schwartz, E. M. (1992). *The computer in the classroom* (2nd ed.). New York: Mitchell McGraw-Hill.

WebCT. (1999). *WebCT: Web course tools*. Peabody, MA: Author. Retrieved April 4, 2000, from the World Wide Web: http://www.webct.com/

Woodward, J., & Carnine, D. (1993). Uses of technology for mathematics assessment and instruc-tion: Reflections on a decade of innovations. *Journal of Special Education Technology, 12*(1), 38–48.

CHAPTER SIX

TECHNOLOGY AND THEORIES
OF LEARNING

Goal: To relate the major theories of teaching and learning to ways of using information technologies such as computers in education.

KEY TERMS

anchored instruction (p. 127)

behaviorism (p. 128)

clean learning (p. 134)

cognitive apprenticeship (p. 137)

cognitive constructivism (p. 133)

collaborative problem solving (p. 136)

constructivism (p. 133)

critical theory (p. 140)

dirty learning (p. 134)

drill-and-practice software (p. 126)

factory model (p. 132)

frames (p. 129)

indiscriminate view of technology (p. 124)

inert learning (p. 143)

integrated learning system (ILS) (p. 131)

linear instruction (p. 133)

nonlinear instruction (p. 133)

problem-based instruction (p. 127)

programmed instruction (PI) (p. 129)

situated learning (p. 136)

social constructivism (p. 135)

tutorials (p. 132)

zone of proximal development (ZPD) (p. 136)

Throughout the 1980s and 1990s, articles in professional publications and the popular press touted the importance of computers and other information technologies in education. As information technologies, particularly computers, took on larger and more critical roles in business and industry, the demand for the same technologies in education increased. In popular magazines, professional journals, newspapers, television programs, commission reports, and the position papers of national organizations, computers were often proposed as the "solution" to nearly all the ills of education.

Most of the clamor in the 1980s to use more computers in schools was indiscriminate. That is, the effort was not to increase any particular way computers were used or to increase the use of technology to teach any particular type of information or subject matter. Much of the enthusiasm for computers in schools was, in fact, based on a naive assumption that simply placing computers in classrooms would be beneficial. We know now that the unbounded confidence in the ability of machinery alone to improve education is unfounded. That applies to computers as well as any other type of equipment. Many teachers today can report that they tried to use computers once or twice and did not find them useful. Today thousands of computers are in classroom closets because teachers have not been trained to use them or the software provided was inappropriate. Tens of millions of dollars of software sit unused in cabinets because of poor quality or lack of suitability to the teacher's instructional objectives. These problems—inadequate or nonexistent training for teachers and poor or inappropriate software—are only two of the many problems that can block effective use of technology.

One other problem not often discussed is the **indiscriminate view of technology.** Although the indiscriminate view is not often explicitly stated, it is implicit in many of the decisions school leaders make concerning the purchase and use of technology in schools. The indiscriminate view of technology is the perspective of many who advocate greater use of technology as well as many who are critical of technology in the classroom. Here are a few assumptions inherent in the indiscriminate view of technology:

1. Virtually any use of technology in the classroom is useful (or harmful).
2. All levels of education, and all types of instructional objectives, are enhanced (or are hindered) when technology is used.
3. Teachers who resist using technology are generally resistant to change of any type, are often incompetent, and often have computer anxiety that makes them afraid to use technology in the classroom (or are valiant defenders of professional integrity).
4. Research has shown that educational computing can be powerfully effective (or ineffective) in the classroom.

Each of these assumptions can be stated in a positive way (e.g., research shows educational computing is effective) or a negative way (e.g., research shows educational computing is not effective). For example, the 1991 literature review by Kulik and Kulik is one of many that concludes that the use of computer-based instruction is generally effective in the classroom. On the other hand, Clark (1985) analyzed many of the same studies and questioned whether computers contribute anything to the effectiveness of classroom instruction. More recently, Thomas Reeves (1998), in his thoughtful review of the role of media and technology in education, quoted several sources to highlight the diversity of opinion about computers in schools. The following quote represents the negative camp:

> There is no good evidence that most uses of computers significantly improve teaching and learning, yet school districts are cutting programs—music, art, physical education—that enrich children's lives to make room for this dubious nostrum, and the Clinton administration has embraced the goal of "computers in every classroom" with credulous and costly enthusiasm. (Oppenheimer, 1997, p. 45)

Reeves quotes others who are much more positive, but he is concerned about why opinions about technology are so diverse. One possible explanation is that different scholars use different theoretical frameworks to evaluate the role of computers in schools. Different theories point to different conclusions even when the same data are analyzed. Maddux and Willis (1993) made a similar point about teachers. Many teachers may oppose a particular type of computer-based instruction, the integrated learning system (ILS), because it is built on models of teaching and learning that conflict with their theoretical views. Thus, teachers who do not use technology in the classroom may be anxious about computers, may simply lack the knowledge of how to use technology, or may be opposed to the type of computer instruction advocated and supported by their computer coordinator or school district.

It is this third possibility—opposition to (or support for) the type of computer instruction advocated by experts such as school-district computer coordinators—that is the focus of this chapter. This chapter emphasizes that no such monolithic entity called *educational computing* or *educational technology* can be evaluated, supported, and promoted as a universal cure to educational ills. No organizations advocate greater use of pencils, pens, or student tablets because these items can all be used in many different ways. Computers and related information technologies can be used in even more diverse ways than pencils or tablets.

To illustrate this point, consider the two programs described in the following sections. Both require students to use computers; however, as you read the descriptions of these two pieces of software, ask yourself whether these programs are alike or different. Would a teacher who likes and uses one of them be expected to like and use the other? Would an educational psychologist who explains the underlying learning theory of one program conclude that the same theory underlies the other? Would a researcher studying the effectiveness of one program generalize the conclusions to the other program?

Example 1: *Word Gallery 3.0*

Word Gallery is actually a suite of programs for elementary schoolchildren. The programs make extensive use of color graphics, music and sound effects, and synthesized speech. One of the programs concentrates on sight-word vocabulary. A picture is displayed in the middle of the screen. One of the words in the boxes that surround the picture is the correct one for that picture. Figure 6.1 is a screen

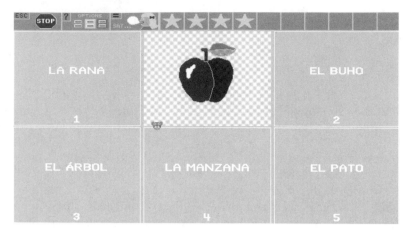

FIGURE 6.1   A screen from the Spanish version of *Word Gallery.*
Screen shot reprinted with permission from Kinderware, Inc.

from the Spanish version of the vocabulary game. (*Word Gallery* works in several languages, including English, French, German, and Spanish.) To respond to this item correctly, the child must move the mouse cursor (shaped like a bee) over the square with *la manzana* in it and click the mouse button.

The *Word Gallery* spelling program uses a similar format. As shown in Figure 6.2, a picture is displayed in the middle of the screen. To respond to this item correctly, the child must use the mouse to click on letters at the bottom of the screen. *Word Gallery* is typical of thousands of programs generally referred to as **drill-and-practice software.** They are available for virtually every subject area and grade level—from shape recognition for preschoolers to details of the periodic table for college chemistry.

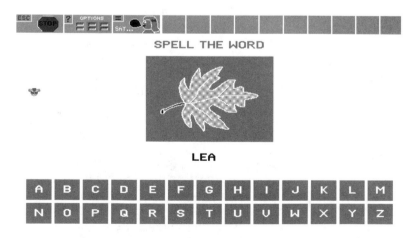

FIGURE 6.2   A screen from the spelling exercise in *Word Gallery.*
Screen shot reprinted with permission from Kinderware, Inc.

Example 2: The *Jasper Woodbury* Series

The *Jasper Woodbury* series is much more difficult to explain briefly than is *Word Gallery*. To say that *Jasper Woodbury* is designed for use in upper elementary through high-school math classes is correct, but it does not really convey what it is all about. It is based on two important principles of teaching: **anchored instruction** and **problem-based instruction.**

> The major goal of anchored instruction is to overcome the inert knowledge problem. We attempt to do so by creating environments that permit sustained exploration by students and teachers and enable them to understand the kinds of problems and opportunities that experts in various areas encounter and the knowledge that these experts use as tools. We also attempt to help students experience the value of exploring the same setting from multiple perspectives (e.g., as scientist or historian). (Cognition and Technology Group at Vanderbilt, 1990, p. 3)

All the lessons in *Jasper Woodbury* are derived from simulations of real situations with problems that students must solve. With videoclips from a videodisc, readings, and teacher-supported discussions, students become familiar with the situations in which Jasper Woodbury finds himself. He may, for example, propose to his school principal that a dunking booth be part of the next school fair (a teacher falls into a tank of water if a student hits a target with a ball). Jasper must use several types of math to complete a proposal for the dunking booth. Jasper Woodbury's effort to set up a dunking booth at the school fair is the "anchor" by which the coherence of the math lesson is secured (Figure 6.3).

Williams (1994) described the anchored simulations in the *Jasper* series as an effort to situate learning in a context of individual problems that students can work on over an extended period of time. Each unit in the *Jasper* series challenges students to solve a number of simulated mathematics problems. Before playing a simulation, students view video from a laser disk that presents a complex mathematics problem as a story they can solve by working collaboratively with classmates and the teacher. The *Jasper* series provides a sequence of anchored problems within the simulation, and students work on both the original problem and variations on it. As they problem solve they learn fundamental concepts and procedures in math. Williams (1994) describes one of the problems in a *Jasper* lesson:

> The prototype simulation is anchored in a trip planning problem in which the main character purchases a boat and must decide if he has sufficient daylight and gas to drive the boat home. The student learns to solve this 16-step problem in class before using the simulation. Within the simulation, the student is challenged to a race by the main character and must make a single modification to an otherwise identical boat in order to win the race. The student then makes qualitative predictions about the race and confirms them quantitatively. When the [computer] simulation is run, the two boats race against each other giving the student feedback on the predictions and calculations. The student is encouraged

Complex Trip Planning
Journey to Cedar Creek
Rescue at Boone's Meadow
Get Out the Vote

Statistics and Business Plans
The Big Splash
Bridging the Gap
A Capital Idea

Geometry
Blueprint for Success
The Right Angle
The Great Circle Race

Algebra
Working Smart
Kim's Komet
The General is Missing

FIGURE 6.3   The *Adventures of Jasper Woodbury* (see http://peabody.vanderbilt.edu/projects/funded/jasper/preview/AdvJW.html) consists of 12 videodisc-based adventures that are designed like good detective novels. You can find a description of each episode at http://peabody.vanderbilt.edu/projects/funded/jasper/.
Reprinted by permission from the Learning Technology Center, Vanderbilt University.

to undertake a systematic series of changes to the parameters affecting the boat's performance. Through this process, the student acquires a general model of trip-planning problems. (p. 692)

Word Gallery and *Jasper Woodbury* differ considerably. Some differences are unimportant or happenstance, but other differences reflect fundamental disagreements about how students learn and how teachers teach. The assumption that computer use is a monolithic, unitary activity that has much in common from one classroom to another is incorrect. The saying "a rose is a rose is a rose" just does not hold when referring to computers in the classroom. Technology can be used in significantly, critically different ways in the classroom. Many of those differences can be traced to theories of learning and teaching that were the foundation for the design and development of educational software and lessons involving technology. In the remainder of this chapter, four of the best-known learning theory "families" are explored with an emphasis on the implications of those theories for educational uses of technology. The four theoretical families are behavioral, cognitive constructivist, social constructivist, and critical theory.

BEHAVIORAL THEORIES

Behaviorism, broadly defined to include variants such as information-processing theory, has been the dominant theory of learning in North America for most of the twentieth century. During much of the 1970s and 1980s, when computers were being placed in the classrooms of many schools for the first time, behavioral theories were very popular. An earlier innovation, **programmed instruction (PI),** was also based on behavioral theories. Programmed instruction involved breaking down content into small pieces of information called **frames.** Several frames from a book on behavioral psychology by Holland and Skinner (1961, pp. 41–43) illustrate this type of instruction:

> A technical term for "reward" is reinforcement. To "reward" an organism with food is to _____ it with food.
> [The answer "reinforce" is provided on the next page.]
>
> Reinforcement and behavior occur in the temporal order: (1) _____;
> (2) _____.
> [The answer "(1) behavior, (2) reinforcement" is provided on the next page.]
>
> A reinforcement does not elicit a response; it simply makes it more _____ that an animal will respond in the same way again.
> [The answer "probable" or "likely" is provided on the next page.]

A programmed-instruction textbook might contain several thousand frames of information. Students would read a frame and answer a question about the frame. Then they would check their answer (get *feedback*) and proceed to the next frame. When PI was administered by a "teaching machine," the possibilities for effective teaching seemed unlimited to many. Here is how B. F. Skinner, the father of PI, described the operation of a teaching machine in 1961:

> A frame of textual material appearing in the square opening is incomplete: in place of certain letters or figures there are holes. Letters or figures can be made to appear in these holes by moving sliders (a keyboard would be an obvious improvement). When the material has been completed, the student checks his response by turning a crank. The machine senses the settings of the sliders and, if they are correct, moves a new frame of material into place, the sliders returning to their home position. (p. 384)

Skinner felt this simple system would work best in the elementary grades but that a more complex system would be necessary in "junior high school, high school, and college, and in industrial and professional education" (p. 385). With a more powerful teaching machine,

> the student sees printed material in the large window at the left. This may be a sentence to be completed, a question to be answered, or a problem to be solved. He [or she] writes his [or her] response in an uncovered portion of a paper strip at the right. He [or she] then moves a slider that covers the response he [or she] has written with a transparent mask and uncovers additional material in the larger opening. (p. 85)

Skinner goes on to describe how the machine could explain common errors when the student makes a mistake. At each error the student would punch a hole in the paper beside the error so the teacher could review progress. He concluded that "exploratory research in schools and colleges indicates that what is now taught by teacher, textbook, lecture, or film can be taught in half the time with half the effort by a machine of this general type" (p. 85).

Skinner argued that PI was more effective than traditional teaching methods for several reasons:

1. *Immediate knowledge of results.* Because students answered questions almost continuously they were frequently reinforced by positive feedback. Also, feedback was immediate.
2. *Individualized learning.* Students can progress through PI material at their own rate without being either held back or left behind by teacher-centered group instruction.
3. *Expert instruction.* Students follow a "coherent sequence" of instruction; that is, they follow a sequence of instruction designed by experts.

PI faded into obscurity in the 1970s for several reasons:

1. Many PI packages were very boring.
2. PI did individualize the *pace* of learning, but both the *content* and the *sequence* of content were essentially identical for all students. The only common variation on content was "branching" for remedial work when a student did not correctly answer a question. Many topics call for much more individualization of content and sequence than is possible with PI.
3. Breaking down subject matter into small digestible bits of information did not work well for many types of material.
4. Learning in isolation was not always the most effective approach. PI tends to isolate students, but collaborative group work may be more effective in some situations.
5. PI tends to isolate factual information from its context. Some theories of learning argue that learning occurs best when it is situated within a context that has meaning for the student.

PI was essentially dead by 1972 but rose, like the phoenix, from its ashes a few years later. When schools began installing inexpensive personal computers in classrooms in the mid-1970s, programmed instruction was a handy model for developing educational software. Computers became the new teaching machines; they even had the keyboards Skinner had wished for in 1961. PI-style programs represent a logical extension of the programmed-learning movement of the sixties. As color graphics, multimedia, sound, and voice synthesis first became possible and then affordable on personal computers, developers incorporated those features into K–12 software products. Today tens of thousands of educational software products, such as *Word Gallery*, are based on behavioral models of instruction. Recent software such as *Word Gallery* takes advantage of technological advances that were not even dreamed of in 1961, but the underlying theory of learning is the same.

Today the most successful expression of the behavioral approach to educational technology is the **integrated learning system (ILS).** Although ILSs vary considerably, most have these characteristics in common (Maddux & Willis, 1993):

1. Computer-based assessment and diagnosis of student skills
2. Delivery of instruction via a group of computers that are interconnected or "networked"
3. Continuous monitoring of student performance and automatic adjustment of instruction when needed
4. Generation of student and class performance data in a variety of formats for use by teachers and administrators

ILSs generally begin with a computer-administered diagnostic–prescriptive evaluation of the student's current achievement level. Then the software breaks down the content to be taught into small units, teaches a unit, assesses progress, and then moves on to the next unit or provides remedial instruction as indicated. The most popular ILSs cover core content areas such as reading, language arts, and mathematics, but many also include instruction in science and social studies. ILSs are offered by a number of companies and, because they often include both the software and hardware, can cost $100,000 to $700,000 per school if every student in the school regularly uses the system for at least some instruction.

Although expensive, they are often touted as the total solution to low-achieving schools, something that can be very appealing to a school board, superintendent, and principal. In fact, they have so much appeal that Bailey (1992) wondered, "Why do they [ILSs] continue to dominate the school technology market?" when many new forms of technology-supported teaching and learning are available. Using figures from 1989, he concluded that sales of ILSs account for half the money schools spend on educational software. In their analysis of ILSs, Shore and Johnson (1992) concluded that their strengths are in three areas:

1. *Lab-based ILSs are less threatening.* ILSs can be set up in a separate computer lab and maintained by a lab manager. Teachers who use the lab do not have to know as much about technology as they would if computers were put in their classrooms.
2. *ILSs offer a total curriculum solution to technology.* It can be difficult to select and set up hundreds of individual pieces of educational software. ILSs, on the other hand, involve making one decision rather than many and are the only systems that "have the power to deliver a total curriculum sequence across all grade levels."
3. *ILSs monitor the progress of all students.* "The entire student population of a school can be monitored across all grade levels and multiple subjects. Students are automatically channeled to the appropriate lessons..."

Proponents of some of the theories discussed later in this chapter would probably consider many of Shore and Johnson's ILS strengths as weaknesses because they express a **factory model** of instruction by which students are treated as products that, with quality control, are shipped from the factory with exactly the same basic knowledge. Critics would, however, generally agree with Shore and Johnson's list of ILS weaknesses:

1. *Some ILSs are difficult to use.* ILSs are an outgrowth of old, large computer systems that were designed to be used primarily by computer specialists. Some ILSs reflect that ancestry and are very difficult for teachers (or anyone else) to use without an extensive background in computer science.
2. *Teachers and students may have limited access.* ILSs are expensive, and it is easy to underestimate how much equipment is needed for all students in a school to receive instruction in several subject areas via an ILS. The result can be scheduling and access problems.
3. *Some ILSs lack flexibility.* Many ILSs come with predefined curricula. You use the curricula built into the system or you don't use it.
4. *ILS is only one type of educational technology.* One reason programmed instruction died out is that most of it was relatively boring. Much of the instructional material on ILS is also relatively boring. Many other types of educational technology are available—multimedia, hypermedia, telecommunications, satellite-based distance education, cooperative problem-solving programs— and many of these appear to be much more interesting to students. Some of those other types are advocated by supporters of learning theories that oppose behaviorism.

The role of the three most common behavioral methods of using the computer in the classroom—drill-and-practice programs, **tutorials,** and integrated learning systems—is hotly debated today. Some, particularly those who advocate some of the theories that are discussed later, argue that very little, if any, of what students need to study is best learned through these methods. On the other hand, the more positive opinion of many educators is reflected in this quote about using drills in teaching technical knowledge:

> Some educational experts do not hold drill and practice CAI programs in high esteem. However, in subjects, such as electricity and electronics, that require students to learn many mathematical analysis procedures, drill and practice CAI programs can be highly effective. The ability of a computed program to compose many variants of a circuit or problem can be used to expose students to more variety than is possible using textbooks alone. The immediate correction and grading is without question highly motivational to students. When carefully constructed, drill and practice programs can present students with challenges rather than chores. The motivational and learning value of immediately seeing "CORRECT!" appear on the computer screen after working a complex problem is enormous. Drill and practice CAI programs can be used to good advantage to reinforce procedures and processes taught in the classroom/textbook or through a computer based tutorial. Good drill and practice CAI should use a random generator to create a variety of variations of each problem/situation presented to learners to make re-

peating a lesson worthwhile. To the extent possible, good drill and practice material should measure not only on a correct/incorrect basis but time on task or other meaningful measures of accomplishment. (Datasync, 1999)

This generally positive view of behavioral methods of teaching with computers comes primarily from professional experience. That view is, however, supported by a recent review of the research literature. Reeves (1998) points out that many new approaches to using computers in schools are based on other theories: "the good news is that even with the primarily behavioral pedagogy, computers as tutors have positive effects on learning as measured by standardized achievement tests, are more motivating for students, are accepted by more teachers than other technologies, and are widely supported by administrators, parents, politicians, and the public in general" (p. 12). Another major evaluation of the research on effectiveness was conducted by Educational Testing Service. That study concluded that computer-supported instruction

can individualize instruction and give instant feedback to students, even explaining the correct answer. The computer is infinitely patient and non-judgemental. This motivates students.... Students usually learn more in classes in which they receive computer-based instruction. Students learn their lessons in less time with computer-based instruction. Students also like their classes more when they receive computer help in them. (Cooley, Cradler, & Engel, 1997, p. 35).

COGNITIVE CONSTRUCTIVIST THEORIES

Many new pieces of educational software based on behavioral theories of teaching and learning are announced each year. However, by the end of the 1980s a significant percentage of the more innovative educational computer programs were based on **constructivism.** The face of educational software changed dramatically. PI-style software is linear. Students begin at the starting point of a lesson and progress, step by step, to the end. In the late 1980s **linear instruction**—with branches to correct errors, frames that divided information into hundreds of small bits, tell-and-test sequences, and long lists of behavioral objectives—lost some of its luster. Many innovative programs today are geared toward **nonlinear instruction.** Students make many choices about what they explore and in what sequence different aspects of a topic are studied. These new programs, such as the *Jasper Woodbury* series discussed earlier, are based on constructivist learning theory.

Constructivist models have emerged from the work of developmental theorists such as Jerome Bruner, Jean Piaget, and Lev Vygotsky. There are, however, two major strands of the constructivist perspective. One strand might be called **cognitive constructivism;** it adopts the epistemology of Piaget as a foundation for practice. The emphasis is on how children build their knowledge of the world. In this theory, children construct their own knowledge of the world through assimilation and accommodation.

Within the field of educational computing, the best-known cognitive constructivist theoretician is Seymour Papert (1993), who characterizes behavioral approaches as "clean" teaching whereas constructivist approaches are "dirty" teaching. The contrast emphasizes the difference between **clean learning** approaches, which isolate and break down knowledge, versus **dirty learning** approaches, which are wholistic and integrative. Papert illustrated the differences between behavioral and constructivist teaching by contrasting the traditional method of teaching dancing with the way Baby learned to dance in the movie *Dirty Dancing:*

> Clean learning reduces dance to formulas describing steps, and clean learning reduces math to formulas describing procedures to manipulate symbols. The formula for the fox-trot box step is strictly analogous to the formula for adding fractions or solving equations. (Papert, 1993, p. 135)

Dirty learning, by contrast, is emotional, complex, and intertwined with the learner's social, cultural, and cognitive context. Papert's idea of clean and dirty learning gives us a somewhat fuzzy feel for the differences between behavioral and constructivist visions for teaching and learning.

Copley's (1992) contrast of two approaches to instruction—didactic (behavioral) and constructivist—provides a bit more detail:

> The didactic approach, one of information transmission, views teachers as masters of particular knowledge domains, whose job is to transmit expertise to students primarily by lectures and recitation. In the didactic class, students memorize facts and concepts of the domain, practice skills until they have mastered them, and demonstrate mastery on appropriate tests. (p. 617)

Copley's description of a constructivist approach is quite different:

> The constructivist model, one of facilitating learning, views teachers as facilitators whose main function is to help students become active participants in their learning and make meaningful connections between prior knowledge, new knowledge and the processes involved in learning. The role of students from this perspective is to construct their own understandings and capabilities in carrying out challenging tasks. (p. 681)

Constructivist approaches to technology in the classroom are not yet commonplace. However, a number of promising approaches exist within this theoretical framework. You will learn about a few of them in this chapter, and others are presented in later chapters. As a point of departure for your study of constructivist learning, consider the eight characteristics (Jonassen, 1994) that differentiate constructivist learning environments (CLEs):

1. CLEs provide multiple representations of reality.
2. Multiple representations avoid oversimplification and represent the complexity of the real world.

3. CLEs emphasize knowledge construction instead of knowledge reproduction.
4. CLEs emphasize authentic tasks in a meaningful context rather than abstract instruction out of context.
5. CLEs provide learning environments such as real-world settings or case-based learning instead of predetermined sequences of instruction.
6. CLEs encourage thoughtful reflection on experience.
7. CLEs "enable context- and content-dependent knowledge construction" (p. 35).
8. CLEs support "collaborative construction of knowledge through social negotiation, not competition among learners for recognition" (p. 35).

Some of these characteristics apply especially to the other strand of constructivism, *social constructivism*, which is discussed in the next section. Others apply to virtually all constructivist approaches. For example, because children must construct or build their own reality, they need multiple representations, or views, of a concept or issue. A computer simulation of life in a particular culture, for example, might provide multiple representations by allowing players to take different roles such as worker, aristocrat, and ruler. A study of meteorology might involve trying to predict the weather as a meteorologist and playing roles, such as farmer, of people who use weather predictions.

SOCIAL CONSTRUCTIVIST THEORIES

Another cognitive psychologist, Lev Vygotsky, shared many of Piaget's assumptions about how children learn, but he placed more emphasis on the social context of learning. Piaget's cognitive theories have been used as the foundation for discovery learning models in which the teacher plays a limited role. The cognitive constructivism discussed in the previous section and Vygotsky's theory overlap a great deal. However, Vygotsky's constructivist theory, which can be called **social constructivism,** has much more room for an active, involved teacher. "Psychologists such as Piaget...have emphasized biological maturity as an inevitable condition for learning. Vygotsky disagreed, holding that the developmental process was towed by the learning process and any pedagogy that did not respect this fact was sterile" (Blanck, 1992, p. 50).

For Vygotsky the culture gives the child the cognitive tools needed for development. The type and quality of those tools determine, to a much greater extent than they do in Piaget's theory, the pattern and rate of development. Adults such as parents and teachers are conduits for the tools of the culture, including language, cultural history, and social context. Today they also include electronic forms of information access.

We call Vygotsky's brand of constructivism *social constructivism* because he emphasized the critical importance of interaction with people—other children, parents, teachers—in cognitive development. If Vygotsky is correct and children develop in social or group settings, the use of technology to connect rather than separate students from one another would be a more appropriate use within this theory. Much of the **collaborative problem solving** that is at the center of the *Jasper Woodbury* programs is an example of applied social constructivism. This series also builds on the best known of Vygotsky's theoretical concepts, the **zone of proximal development (ZPD).**

Vygotsky's ZPD emphasizes his belief that learning is, fundamentally, a socially mediated activity. Thinking and problem-solving skills can, according to Vygotsky, be placed in three categories. Some can be performed independently by the child. Others cannot be performed even with help. Between these two extremes are skills the child can perform with help from others. Those skills are in the ZPD. If a child uses these cognitive processes with help from others, such as teachers, parents, or fellow students, the cognitive processes can soon be practiced independently. As Vygotsky (1987) put it, "What the child is able to do in collaboration today he will be able to do independently tomorrow" (p. 121). Whereas an extreme interpretation of Piaget can lead to the conclusion that teachers teach best who get out of the way and let a naturally unfolding development take its course, Vygotsky's theory requires an involved teacher who is an active participant, and guide, for students.

Although Vygotsky died at the age of 38 in 1934, most of his publications did not appear in English until after 1960. Some did not even appear in Russian until the 1950s because of Stalinist repression of intellectuals. There are, however, a growing number of applications of social constructivism in the area of educational technology. One such use was described by Martin (1992). She worked with elementary teachers who taught a science lesson developed by the researcher that linked the everyday questions of children to scientific or systematic thinking, an important concept in Vygotsky's theory. The teachers used a segment of *Voyage of the Mimi,* a multimedia simulation that uses laser-disk video. In essence, students become the crew of a ship that travels to different parts of the world on scientific expeditions. The video stored on a laser disk helps set the scenes for the simulated world cruise and provides information needed to solve some of the problems presented to the crew members.

Martin's data showed that one critical factor in the way the lesson was taught was the teacher's own working assumptions about *everyday,* versus *scientific,* problems. One teacher separated the two completely and led the class in separate explorations of the two, even though the goal of the lesson was to bring them together cognitively. That is a decidedly non-Vygotskian approach because it does not draw on the cultural and social experiences of the children. Another teacher used the everyday experiences and knowledge of students as a starting point and helped them think through and analyze the scientific problems they faced in *Voyage of the Mimi.*

Vygotsky's theories, and those of other developmental psychologists, were the foundation for the concept of **situated learning,** which was proposed by Seely, Brown, Collins, and Duguid (1989). In her review of situated learning, McLellan (1994) explained that Seely and his colleagues believed that "many teaching practices implicitly assume that conceptual knowledge can be abstracted from the situations in which it is learned and used" (p. 5). Situated-learning proponents, however, argue that "knowledge is situated and is partly a product of the activity, context, and culture in which it is used" (p. 5). Thus, it cannot be taught in the abstract. It must be taught in context. Brown, Collins, and Duguid (1989) suggested one form of situated learning, **cognitive apprenticeship,** that has the goal of helping students construct their own understanding of the topic. Activities that support this goal include coaching and mentoring, providing cognitive "scaffolding" to help learners make sense of a topic, and helping students relate the topic to both personal experiences and the context in which that knowledge is applied.

Situated-learning proponents also support both collaborative problem solving and anchored instruction as instructional strategies. For the teacher considering adopting this approach to the classroom, "the challenge of situated learning theory becomes one of developing methodologies and course content that support cooperative activity and reflect the complex interaction between what individuals already know and what they are expected to learn, recognizing that ultimately meaning can only be established *by* and not *for* the learner" (Harley, 1994, p. 47). Seen from this perspective, the design and delivery of instruction is not the creation and use of detailed lesson plans that specify exactly what the teacher and students should be doing at various points in the lesson. As Harley (1994) put it, "Prespecified, step-by-step instruction can no longer be developed on the assumption that the process can control the specifics of meaning constructed by the learner" (p. 49). Instead, it is the creation of an environment where groups of students can, and do, explore and analyze, think and reflect, propose and act. Technology can support such environments in many ways—from supplying sources of information such as CD-ROM databases to providing tools of expression that students can use (Figure 6.4). Another way is creating interesting environments in which to study a topic.

One such environment was developed by John Bransford and his colleagues at Vanderbilt University (Cognition and Technology Group at Vanderbilt, 1993). The Cognition and Technology Group at Vanderbilt (CTGV) designed situated-learning environments around the movies *Young Sherlock Holmes* and *Oliver.*

> Students first watched these videos [from videodisk because they had much more control over viewing] and then explored them from the perspective of a filmmaker who might be checking each one for quality and authenticity. How interesting and causally connected were the major plot and subplots? How authentic were the settings and the actions of the characters in the settings? By tracing causal connections, character motives, and goal-oriented behaviors, students were able to learn a great deal about the structure of stories, about the nature of life in turn-of-the-century Victorian England, and about general guidelines for exploring the quality and authenticity of a wide variety of stories and settings. (p. 54)

In commenting on the challenges they faced using anchored instruction and situated-learning environments, CTGV commented:

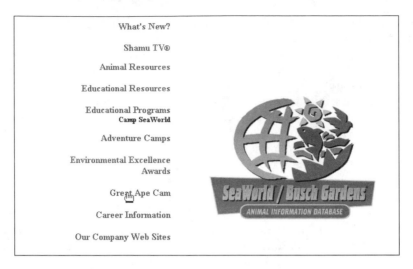

What's New?

Shamu TV®

Animal Resources

Educational Resources

Educational Programs
Camp SeaWorld

Adventure Camps

Environmental Excellence
Awards

Great Ape Cam

Career Information

Our Company Web Sites

FIGURE 6.4   SeaWorld/Busch Gardens (http://www.seaworld.org/) is one of many free information databases on the World Wide Web that can provide support to situated learning.

One of the greatest challenges that anchored curricula pose for teachers derives from the need to change their role from a "provider of information" to a coach and often a fellow learner.... In the Sherlock program, different students might choose to explore a variety of issues relevant to the Young Sherlock and Oliver anchors—issues such as the Egyptian culture that is mentioned in the movie, the nature of schooling in Victorian England, and so forth.... In order to encourage and support student generated learning, teachers must be flexible; they cannot follow a fully scripted lesson plan. In addition, teachers cannot be experts in each topic that students choose to pursue, so they must often become learners along with their students. This can be difficult for many teachers, especially when children are accustomed to classroom cultures in which the teacher normally functions as "expert" rather than as "guide" and "learner." (p. 54)

The Vanderbilt group describes other problems teachers face when using situated-learning environments. For example, teachers report it is sometimes difficult to decide when "students really need guidance versus when students are struggling in a constructive way with a problem or issue" (p. 64). Situated learning is not raw "discovery" learning: students are not compelled to rely on their own devices without guidance and support from the teacher. In good Vygotskian style, teachers take on active roles in the classroom and provide some direct instruction. Direct-instruction provider is only one of many roles the teacher plays, however, and it is not the most important.

All classrooms in which instructional strategies compatible with Vygotsky's social constructivist approach are used don't necessarily look alike. The activities and the format can vary considerably. However, four principles are applied in any Vygotskian classroom:

1. *Learning and development is a social, collaborative activity.* The interaction children have with adults and other children is critical. This suggests that using technology to enhance communication, contact, and interaction would be beneficial. The interaction should not, however, be one of information delivery. According to constructivist theory, you cannot really teach anyone anything. Students must construct understanding and knowledge in their own minds. That process is facilitated by collaboration. Programs that support collaborative problem solving and interactive decision making enrich the learning environment.

2. *The ZPD can serve as a guide for curricular and lesson planning.* Children don't simply know something or not know it. They may arrive at a particular learning experience without knowing something but be ready to master the task if they have appropriate support. Appropriate support may include everything from thoughtful guidance from the teacher and productive discussion sessions with fellow students to electronic information resources such as encyclopedias on CD-ROM, software such as grammar checkers that help students identify potential writing weaknesses, and electronic brainstorming software that supports group problem analysis. In addition, the teacher may help students puzzle through a complex concept by simplifying it so it can be accommodated by their ZPD. Then, as they develop understanding and the ZPD expands, the concept can be made more complex.

3. *School learning should occur in a meaningful context.* Several movements in education, including authentic instruction, situated learning, anchored instruction, and Papert's dirty teaching, emphasize the need to provide learning experiences within a meaningful context—often that context in which what is learned will be applied. Again, technology can facilitate this in many ways. Students in an economics class, for example, can take on the roles of national leaders in a computer simulation of economic decisions. A geography class studying Scotland can take a simulated trip around the country and use desktop publishing software to create a newsletter complete with scanned photographs and charts about the country.

4. *Relate out-of-school experiences to the child's school experiences.* Movements such as whole language instruction emphasize the need to organize school learning around the culture and experiences the child already knows and understands. Technology can help accomplish that in several ways. A fifth-grade class studying history, for example, could create a multimedia presentation, complete with scanned photographs, old maps, and excerpts from newspaper files, about the history of the town where they live. A middle-grade science class could use telecommunications to share data on water quality with students in other parts of the country or the world.

The last two summary points—that learning should occur in meaningful contexts and should relate to the child's own experiences—are nicely illustrated in an article by Polin (1991) that introduced Vygotsky to computer-using teachers. In the article, she described the work of several Russian computer-using educators. They were disappointed when students did not seem to learn much from an educational simulation. The goal of the simulation was to help children understand a complex concept that frequently confused children of that age. The researchers used the computer simulation in a typical manner that provided quick feedback on conceptual mistakes that would take the students in the wrong direction. The children were not allowed to follow up on their own hunches, which naturally would have come from their own experiences. (This scenario is similar to that discussed earlier where the teacher did not try to connect the way we solve everyday problems with ways of solving scientific problems.) When that approach did not work, the Russian researchers allowed the students to develop their own models of the concept and use them to try to solve problems presented in the simulation. The children were allowed to do that even if their theories were completely incorrect. Most of the children, when allowed to develop their own theories and then apply them in the simulation, were able to analyze the errors in their understanding of the concept and correct them. Thus, although they could not be *taught* the concept, even by the computer simulation, they were able to *construct* it when the instructional approach to using the simulation was changed.

Critical Theory

In some books, Vygotsky's theory, which puts more emphasis on the social and cultural foundations of teaching and learning, is presented as an alternative to Piaget (e.g., Moll, 1992). Thus Vygotsky is associated with social constructivism whereas Piaget is the foundation for cognitive constructivism. This is the conceptualization we have followed in this chapter.

In other publications, Vygotsky is treated as another supporter of the political and economic theories of Marxism. In fact, a third alternative to behaviorism is based on one of the most widely adopted forms of modern Marxism. **Critical theory,** also known as the *Frankfurt School* or *neo-Marxism,* has been used by a number of scholars to analyze the way information technology is used in education. Some critical theorists who write about technology cite Vygotsky as a foundation for their work, along with philosophers such as Habermas and other members of the Frankfurt School. Critical theory, like Marxism, focuses on political and power relationships in a culture and the interaction of different groups in a society. Critical theory also argues that information technology, or technology in general, is not value free. "I see IT [information technology] as another means of production and as such it has to be viewed in the context of the political, ideological and cultural assumptions of the society that has given rise to it" (Cooley, 1992, p. 96).

Technology, when incorporated into education, brings with it a set of values and assumptions that, however implicit, are nevertheless influential. Over the past few years a number of papers have been published that analyze educational computing from the critical theory perspective. A paper by Scott, Cole, and Engle (1992) is a good example. Although much in this article is inaccurate and the authors are sometimes very selective in their literature review (perhaps to make a cherished point), it does provide a good overview of the way a critical theorist views educational computing. The authors argue that any approach to educational computing must consider the historical and social context of educational computing as well as the cultural implications of what is taught.

The critical theory perspective of Scott, Cole, and Engle has solid connections to Marxist and neo-Marxist scholarship in curriculum theory and educational philosophy (Apple, 1991; Friere, 1985). It interprets the use of technology in the schools through a filter of concern about the purpose and function of all social institutions, with a particular emphasis on social class issues, worker–capitalist relations, and questions of control and power. Scott, Cole, and Engle (1992), for example, introduce their history of educational computing in the United States by asserting that the use of electronic computers began in the military establishment and that the military remains the most important organization promoting research in computer-based education. They conclude, "Our own view is that one needs to be suspicious of educational technology that embodies presupposed fixed tasks and goals and a restricted range of social arrangements of a top-down, authoritarian nature" (p. 191). In their review the authors also address many questions about scholars who work from other theoretical perspectives: equity issues, gender issues, the definition of computer literacy, differences in the type of computer experiences offered to poor and well-to-do children, overblown promises that cannot possibly be fulfilled, and the undue influence of commercial vendors on school curriculum through sales of ILSs.

Other critical theory critiques of technology and education generally echo the perspective of Scott, Cole, and Engle. They are critical of behavioral models of instruction because they are based on capitalist "efficiency" models of factory work that demean the laborer (the student) and produce undesirable outcomes. For example, Streibel (1991) is critical of computers in education. He limits his analysis to three ways computers can be used in education: "the drill-and-practice approach, the tutorial approach, and the simulation and programming approach" (p. 287). Then he concludes that a common framework "runs throughout the three approaches" (p. 287). The common framework is based on behavioral learning theory.

All Streibel's arguments against using computers in education relate to the three uses he selected. Drill-and-practice programs "represent a very one-dimensional form of education because they restrict the goal structures, reward structures, and meaning structures of educational events to the domain of educational productivity...[and] therefore constitute a deterministic form of behavioral technology" (p. 287). Computer-based tutorial programs "are biased against experiential learning (outside of the technological framework), quantum leaps in learning, and reflective thinking. Their value in education is therefore very limited" (p. 287). In commenting on programming and simulations Streibel believes:

> Computers tend to *legitimize* those types of knowledge that fit into their framework and delegitimize other types of knowledge.... Hence, computers tend to legitimize the following characteristics of knowledge...: rule-governed order, objective systematicity, explicit clarity, non-ambiguity, non-redundancy, internal consistency, non-contradiction (i.e., logic of the excluded middle), and quantitative aspects.

They also tend to legitimize deduction and induction as the only acceptable epistemological methods.

By way of contrast, computers tend to *delegitimize* the following characteristics of knowledge…: emergent goals, self-constructed order, organic systematicity, connotation and tacitness, ambiguity, redundancy, dialetical rationality, simultaneity of multiple logics, and qualitative aspects. And finally, they tend to delegitimize the following epistemological methods: abduction, interpretation, intuition, introspection, and dialectical synthesis of multiple and contradictory realities. (p. 317)

Apple (1991) makes a similar argument when he concludes that

currently, considerable pressure is building to have teaching and school curricula be totally prespecified and tightly controlled for the purposes of "efficiency," "cost effectiveness," and "accountability." …Given these pressures, what will happen to teachers if the new technology is accepted uncritically? One of the major effects of the current (over) emphasis on computers in the classroom may be the deskilling and depowering of a considerable number of teachers. (p. 67)

Critical theorists have been much more active as critics of what has been done than as creators and developers of models of what can be done. Most innovations in educational technology in recent years have come from cognitive constructivists and social constructivists. However, critical theorists do make some important points, particularly concerning equity issues, such as equal access to technology resources in rich and poor schools, and in regard to cultural and gender bias in some educational software. You need not adopt critical theory as your only foundation for practice to understand the importance of these issues. And although critical theorists have not been very active in developing instructional approaches that include technology, they often recommend approaches developed by cognitive and social constructivists (Scott, Cole, & Engle, 1992).

SUMMARY

Four major theories of learning and teaching currently guide both the development of educational technology and its use in schools. The behavioral model has been dominant for most of this century but is currently being challenged by two constructivist approaches, cognitive constructivism, based on the work of Jean Piaget, and social constructivism, based on the work of Lev Vygotsky. Considerable overlap exists between these two constructivist approaches, and they are sometimes lumped together and simply called *constructivism*. In addition, critical theory serves as a framework for many critics of current practices. All four theories have a great deal to say about how technology should be used in schools. At the practical level, important implications can be drawn from each of the four theories, and in many cases the theories lead us to different approaches of instruction.

Some of the differences relate to emphasis. Social constructivism, for example, puts more emphasis on interaction between teacher and student (and between students) than does cognitive constructivism. Other differences relate to assumptions about how humans learn. Behavioral approaches, for example, tend to emphasize the need to break down complex subject matter into smaller bits that are taught one by one. Later they are recombined to bring the student to an understanding of the larger, more complex concept. Drill-and-practice software and tutorial software are two examples of this approach. Constructivist approaches, on the other hand, argue that breaking down the content into separate bits destroys the meaning and removes the material to be taught from its natural context. They believe that this leads to **inert learning,** learning that is isolated from its context and therefore not useful except for answering multiple-choice tests. The constructivists believe the best learning happens within a meaningful context. Constructivists prefer situated-instruction approaches such as problem-based learning, anchored instruction, and cognitive apprenticeships.

Although a few teacher-education students graduate as confirmed behaviorists, constructivists, or critical theorists, the great majority take an eclectic approach to teaching. They may be behavioral in some lessons and constructivist in others. As you read the remaining chapters in this book, you may want to think about how the approaches fit into the four theories discussed in this chapter. Is an approach behavioral, constructivist, or mixed? Is a criticism of a particular way of using technology based on behavioral, constructivist, or critical theory?

As a final point, as you evaluate software and instructional strategies, they need not be discarded if they do not fit a theoretical framework you prefer. In many cases the way you use the material in your classroom can be adapted to better fit your theory of teaching and learning.

QUESTIONS TO CONSIDER

1. After reading this chapter, do you have one theory of learning you prefer? Why? Should aspects of several theories be considered when planning instruction? Which aspects? Which aspects of classroom computing technology would they influence?

2. Would aspects of the content you plan to teach be better taught from a behavioral or constructivist approach? Why?

3. If you adopted a critical theory perspective, how would you critique the use of technology in the school district you know best? Would there be equity issues? Gender issues?

RELATED ACTIVITIES

1. Locate four reviews of educational software of interest to you in magazines, journals, an electronic resource, or the ERIC microfiche collection of documents. What theory of learning underlies the software reviewed? How can you tell? What theory of learning does the reviewer advocate? How can you tell?

2. Find software relevant to a subject and grade level you plan to teach. Select at least one piece of software that can be used for behavioral instruction and one that can be used for constructivist instruction (either social or cognitive). Explain why the software fits the theory.

3. Locate at least three lesson plans on a subject and grade level you plan to teach.

Analyze them in terms of activities and instructional strategies that reflect the perspective of a particular learning theory. One plan should be primarily behavioral, another primarily cognitive constructivist, and another primarily social constructivist. Many lesson plans are available from the Internet and in the ERIC microfiche collection.

REFERENCES

Apple, M. (1991). The new technology: Is it part of the solution or part of the problem in education? *Computers in the Schools, 8*(1/2/3), 59–81.

Bailey, G. (1992, September). Wanted: A road map for understanding integrated learning systems. *Educational Technology, 32*(9), 3–5.

Blanck, G. (1992). Vygotsky: The man and his cause. In L. Moll (Ed.), *Vygotsky and education* (pp. 31–58). Cambridge, UK: Cambridge University.

Brown, J., Collins, A., & Duguid, S. (1989). Situated cognition and the culture of learning. *Educational Researcher, 18*(1), 32–42.

Clark, R. (1985, Winter). Evidence for confounding in computer-based instruction studies: Analyzing the meta-analysis. *Educational Communication and Technology, 33*(4), 249–262.

Cognition and Technology Group at Vanderbilt. (1990). Anchored instruction and its relationship to situated cognition. *Educational Researcher, 19*(6), 2–10.

Cognition and Technology Group at Vanderbilt. (1993). Anchored instruction and situated cognition revisited. *Educational Technology, 33*(3), 52–70.

Cooley, M. (1992). Human-centered education. In C. Bigum & B. Green (Eds.), *Understanding the new information technologies in education.* (pp. 87–98). Geelong, Australia: Deakin University, Centre for Studies in Information Technologies and Education.

Cooley, R., Cradler, J., & Engel, P. (1997). *Computers and classrooms: The status of technology in U.S. schools.* Princeton, NJ: Educational Testing Service.

Copley, J. (1992). The integration of teacher education and technology: A constructivist model. In D. Carey, R. Carey, D. Willis, & J. Willis (Eds.), *Technology and teacher education annual—1992* (pp. 617–622). Charlottesville, VA: Association for the Advancement of Computing in Education.

DataSync. (1999). Resources for electronics training. Retrieved April 16, 2000, from the World Wide Web: http://www.datasync.com/~etcai/

Friere, P. (1985). *The politics of education: Culture, power and liberation* (D. Macedo, Trans.). South Hadley, MA: Bergin and Garvey.

Harley, S. (1994). Situated learning and classroom instruction. *Educational Technology, 33*(3), 46–51.

Holland, J., & Skinner, B. (1961). *The analysis of behavior.* New York: McGraw-Hill.

Jonassen, D. (1994, April). Thinking technology: Toward a constructivist design model. *Educational Technology, 34*(4), 35–36.

Kulik, C., & Kulik, J. (1991). Effectiveness of computer-based instruction: An updated analysis. *Computers in Human Behavior, 7*(1), 75–94.

Maddux, C., & Willis, J. (1993). Integrated learning systems and their alternatives: Problems and cautions. In G. Bailey (Ed.), *Computer-based integrated learning systems* (pp. 121–136). Englewood Cliffs, NJ: Educational Technology.

Martin, L. (1992). Detecting and defining science problems: A study of video-mediated lessons. In L. Moll (Ed.), *Vygotsky and education: Instructional implications and applications of sociohistorical psychology* (pp. 372–402). Cambridge, UK: Cambridge University.

McLellan, H. (1993, March). Situated learning in focus. *Educational Technology, 33*(3), 5–9.

Moll, L. (Ed.). (1992). *Vygotsky and education: Instructional implications and applications of sociohistorical psychology.* Cambridge, UK: Cambridge University.

Oppenheimer, T. (1997, July). The computer delusion. *Atlantic Monthly,* 45–62.

Papert, S. (1993). *The children's machine: Rethinking school in the age of the computer.* New York: Basic Books.

Polin, L. (1991, August–September). Vygotsky at the computer: A Soviet view of "tools" for learning. (Research Windows). *The Computing Teacher, 19*(1), 25–27.

Reeves, T. (1998). *The impact of media and technology in schools: A research report prepared for The Bertelsmann Foundation.* Athens, GA: The University of Georgia.

Scott, T., Cole, M., & Engle, M. (1992). Computers and education: A cultural constructivist perspective. In G. Grant (Ed.), *Review of research in education* (Vol. 18, pp. 191–251). Washington, DC: American Educational Research Association.

Seely, J., Brown, J., Collins, A., & Duguid, S. (1989, January–February). Situated cognition and the future of learning. *Educational Researcher, 18*(1),32–42.

Shore, A., & Johnson, M. (1992, September). Integrated learning systems: A vision for the future. *Educational Technology, 32*(9),36–39.

Skinner, B. (1961). Why we need teaching machines. *Harvard Educational Review, 31,* 377–398.

Streibel, M. (1991). A critical analysis of the use of computers in education. In D. Hlynka & J. Belland (Eds.), *Paradigms regained* (pp. 283–334). Englewood Cliffs, NJ: Educational Technology.

Vygotsky, L. (1978). Thinking and speech. In R. Rieber & A. Carton (Eds.), *L. S. Vygotsky. Collected works* (Vol. 1, pp. 39–285). New York: Plenum.

Williams, S. (1994). Improving qualitative reasoning with an anchored computer simulation. In T. Ottmann & I. Tomek (Eds.), *Educational multimedia and hypermedia, 1994* (p. 692). Charlottesville, VA: Association for the Advancement of Computing in Education.

SOFTWARE DISCUSSED IN THIS CHAPTER

Word Gallery. Available from Kinderware, Inc., P.O. Box 1068, North Bend, OH 45052-1068.

Jasper Woodbury materials are available from Optical Data Corporation, 30 Technology Drive, Warren, NJ 07059. Phone (800) 524-2481.

CHAPTER SEVEN

CONSTRUCTIVIST USES OF EDUCATIONAL TECHNOLOGY

This chapter was coauthored by Valentyna Kolomiyets.

Goal: To explore uses of technology in the classroom that are based on constructivist theories of teaching and learning.

KEY TERMS

anchored instruction (p. 155)

cognitive apprenticeship (p. 155)

cognitive flexibility hypertext (CFH) (p. 156)

cognitive flexibility theory (p. 157)

collaborative construction of knowledge (p. 149)

collaborative learning (p. 150)

constructivism (p. 147)

constructivist learning environment (CLE) (p. 147)

context dependent (p. 149)

cooperative learning (p. 150)

formal education (p. 165)

ill-structured subject matter (p. 156)

inert knowledge (p. 148)

informal education (p. 165)

knowledge construction (p. 148)

models (p. 160)

problem-based learning (PBL) (p. 155)

simulation (p. 159)

situated learning (p. 154)

socially constructed knowledge (p. 149)

virtual reality (VR) (p. 159)

well-structured subject matter (p. 156)

Many teachers, and parents, today are familiar with computer programs that drill students on two-digit multiplication or sentence punctuation. These are typical Type I applications of computers, and as such they are relatively easy to explain and understand. It takes only a few minutes to see how a typical drill program works:

- Present a problem
- Ask the child to respond
- Evaluate the answer
- Present another problem

Today most graduates of U.S. schools who used a school computer outside their computer literacy class probably used drill or tutorial programs. However, one emerging type of instructional application is not so easy to explain or understand. Thomas Reeves (1998), a professor at the University of Georgia, has pointed out that over the last 25 years

> few people outside the research community acknowledge that the nature of computer-based learning has also undergone enormous change.... The earliest forms of computer-based instruction were heavily influenced by the behavioral psychology of B. F. Skinner (1968). These programs were essentially automated forms of programmed instruction. They presented information to the student in small segments, required the student to make overt responses to the information as stimulus, and provided feedback to the student along with differential branching to other segments of instruction or to drill-and-practice routines. (p. 12)

Although Reeves acknowledges that "this basic behavioral model continues to dominate mainstream educational application of computers such as integrated learning systems" (p. 12), he also points out that newer forms of computer-supported instruction are now appearing. Many of these new approaches are based on constructivist theories of teaching and learning.

WHAT ARE CONSTRUCTIVIST LEARNING ENVIRONMENTS?

Constructivist teaching is complex and sometimes frustrating. Constructivist learning can be the same: complex and frustrating. Fortunately, teaching and learning from a constructivist perspective can also be wonderfully fulfilling. The constructivist context in which students learn and teachers teach is sometimes called the **constructivist learning environment (CLE).** CLEs are so diverse it is difficult to specify anything that can be found all the time in every CLE. However, Jonassen (1994) has encapsulated the ideas of CLEs in the few guiding principles that follow.

"Provide multiple representations of reality" (p. 35).   Constructivism is based on the idea that reality is socially constructed—groups of people decide what they think reality is, and thus different groups have different views of what reality is. By helping students explore different versions or representations of reality, teachers help them explore the natural complexity of the world without oversimplification.

"Focus on knowledge construction, not reproduction" (p. 35).   As Jonassen (1994) puts it, "Constructivists emphasize the design of learning environments rather than instructional sequences. These environments...do not seek to predetermine a sequence of instruction or a prescribed set of activities and thought processes by the learner. Rather they seek to provide a supportive environment in which the learner can interpret at least a simulated reality in order to better understand that reality" (p. 35). Jonassen makes the point, however, that a CLE is not the same as an "anything-goes" setting where students get no guidance and no support. "Constructivist environments are not the unregulated, unsupported, anarchic, sink-or-swim, open-discovery learning cesspools that many fear" (p. 35). Focusing on **knowledge construction** is one way of avoiding the problem of inert knowledge, which is discussed next.

"Present authentic tasks (contextualizing rather than abstracting instruction)" (p. 35).   This guideline and the previous one are important ways of addressing one problem—**inert knowledge.** Trying to deliver prepackaged content that students memorize or learn, so they can answer questions about it on an objective test, often leads to what some have called *inert knowledge*—knowledge that cannot be applied or used outside the school setting (Crews, Biswas, Goldman, & Bransford, 1997). As this quote from David Berliner (1999) illustrates, inert knowledge has been a concern since the early part of the twentieth century:

> The work of the Cognition and Technology Group at Vanderbilt (1990), deriving some of their ideas from Whitehead's (1929) discussion of inert knowledge, is compatible with the ideas expressed here. Inert knowledge, said Whitehead, is school knowledge, recalled when people are explicitly asked to do so, but of no particular use in daily life. Everyday life is not filled with propositions of the type that educational psychology and the other sciences are good at deducing; rather, it is comprised of cases, episodes, and emotional relationships, and it is filled with personal meaning. In short, life is lived and recalled in a narrative form, as a story, not as propositions. There is even evidence that the brain stores propositions and episodes in different ways (Squire, 1987).
>
> The Vanderbilt group, for example, embedded instruction in videodisc adventures, to anchor it, to give it meaning, and with much apparent success. People who acquire their knowledge in context learn that knowledge is a tool, a means to achieve something, not an end in itself—a point made by Dewey (1933) almost 60 years ago. If what we learn is out of context—like so much of mathematics and language as learned in school—it becomes inert. The whole-language movement in contemporary elementary education appears to be a much-needed reaction to forms of instruction leading to the retention of inert knowledge. I have come to believe that most of what we teach in educational psychology is taught like phonics and vocabulary in reading, or like logarithms and geometry in mathematics; that is, it is taught in a decontextualized manner. Perhaps much of our research lies fallow because we often fail to give it the quality of a tool. We fail to embed it in meaningful contexts; we fail to embed it in stories that teachers and policymakers can use. (Berliner, 1999)

Many of the constructivist learning environments discussed later in this chapter are designed to help students construct knowledge that can be useful outside the classroom.

**"Enable context- and content-dependent knowledge construction"
(p. 36).**   If multiple versions of reality exist, much of what we "know" must
be dependent on the context in which that knowledge is situated. No content
is universal and independent of the context in which it is learned. Consider, for
example, mathematics. A few years ago I (JW) was giving a talk to a group of science professors in which I argued that even mathematics is **context dependent.**
A chemistry professor in the audience took issue, maintaining that the number
3 exists independent of any context and independent of the human mind. I suggested that the number 3, and everything else in mathematics, *is* socially constructed. The meaning of *three,* or *3,* or *III,* has been constructed by humans
through social interaction and discussion. This debate continues in scientific and
scholarly literature (e.g., Steffe, 1998). The point is that some educators consider
even a fundamental subject such as mathematics to be **socially constructed
knowledge.** If knowledge is socially constructed, mathematics as well as other
topics should be learned in context, rather than in the abstract, because part of
the meaning is in the context. In addition, learning in context is another way to
avoid the inert-knowledge problem.

**Support "collaborative construction of knowledge through social nego-
tiation, not competition among learners for recognition" (p. 37).**   If individuals construct knowledge through social interaction, it makes sense to situate
schooling in an interactive context. As Jonassen (1994) put it, teachers should
encourage "collaboration among learners and with the teacher, who is more of a
coach or mentor and not a purveyor of knowledge" (p. 37).

Jonassen also proposed three other elements or attributes of CLEs, which he
described as "general attributes": context, construction, and collaboration. CLEs
can be structured in many different ways, but most of the popular ways support
all three of Jonassen's general attributes. Many, however, more strongly support
one attribute over another. The following list organizes some types of CLEs by the
attributes they emphasize:

CONTEXT

Authentic instruction	Anchored instruction
Modeling	Cognitive flexibility hypertext
Simulation	Apprenticeships
Situated learning	Cases

CONSTRUCTION

Problem-based learning	Reflective learning
Whole-language learning	Reading and writing workshops
Mentoring	Coaching
Project-based learning	

COLLABORATION

Collaborative learning
Cooperative learning
Learning communities

There is considerable overlap among the CLEs listed above. Situated learning, for example, is a general term that includes anchored instruction as well as apprenticeships. Moreover, this list is not exhaustive; other CLEs have not been included. Unfortunately, we are restricted by space from exploring all the CLEs in the list. Instead, we focus on four approaches that are commonly supported with technology. They are cooperative learning, problem-based learning (including anchored instruction), cognitive flexibility hypertext, and simulations, which is explored in even more detail. This chapter ends with a discussion of the strengths and weaknesses of constructivist uses of technology.

COLLABORATIVE AND COOPERATIVE LEARNING ENVIRONMENTS

Most U.S. adults today did most of their schoolwork individually. They received assignments from the teacher, completed those assignments, and were graded on the quality of their individual work. The most common form of interaction between students in a classroom was "class discussion," which often involved individual students answering questions posed by the teacher.

This relatively accurate description of past U.S. education is becoming less accurate as a description of current and future scenarios. **Collaborative learning,** which involves students working together on projects or problems, is becoming increasingly popular at all levels—from kindergarten to graduate school. Bruffee (1993) succinctly describes one form of collaborative learning:

> In collaborative learning students work on focused but open-ended tasks. They discuss issues in small consensus groups, plan and carry out long-term projects in research teams, tutor one another, analyze and work problems together, puzzle out difficult lab instructions together, read aloud to one another what they have written, and help one another edit and revise research reports and term papers. (p. 1)

Put more succinctly, collaborative learning involves two or more peers working together on a learning activity that requires them eventually to arrive at a shared solution. The learning activity may be organized around three tasks:

1. Answering a question (developed by the teacher, the students, or both) that generally should be broad and fuzzy rather than narrow and precise (e.g., not, "What is the gross national product of Peru?" but instead, "Could aspects of the current national policy of Peru that facilitate big business but inhibit microbusinesses be changed to encourage both big and microbusinesses?")
2. Solving a problem that is broad and defies a specific solution that is easily identified
3. Addressing a controversial issue that cannot be resolved easily if at all

Cooperative learning involves more than occasionally posing a question and dividing students into small groups for part of a class period. As the *Teaching Assistant's Handbook* at the University of California Santa Barbara states:

Cooperative Learning is a Strategy that involves students in established, sustained learning groups or teams. The group work is an integral part of, not an adjunct to, the achievement of the learning goals of the class. Cooperative learning fosters individual accountability in a context of group interdependence in which students discover information and teach that material to their group and, perhaps, to the class as a whole. The teacher's role changes as Alison King (1993) says "from sage on the stage to guide on the side." Although they learn in groups, students are evaluated individually on the learning they have achieved.

Cooperative Learning Is Structured and focused to make sure that learning is taking place. The teacher chooses the groups to reflect a diversity of viewpoints, abilities, gender, race, and other characteristics. Letting students choose their own groups can result in a homogeneity that reduces the acquisition of social skills and increases the possibility of a lack of focus on the learning task (Cooper, 1990).

The Groups Contain Fewer Than Six Students—Most Likely Four. Four is a good number; more than that, and individuals may not have equal opportunity to contribute. Four students can work in pairs (each student having three potential partners) or together. The group is large enough to contain a diversity of perspectives, yet small enough to facilitate useful interaction (Millis, 1993).

Cooperative Learning Creates a Classroom Community that involves students in a kind of interdependence whereby all are working toward a common goal, often with group members responsible for different aspects of the content and teaching it to other members of the group. The group's work is not complete until all its members have mastered the content. Furthermore, individual learning is reinforced as a result of explaining the content to others. Once established, the groups can stay together for the entire semester or can be reformed to concentrate or disseminate their acquired knowledge at various stages throughout the semester.

Cooperative Learning is a Sustained Approach that lasts longer than a 15–20-minute small-group discussion. An entire course or module may be taught using the cooperative learning method. Because they are in the same group for a longer period of time, students experience greater continuity than in occasional small-group situations. The cooperative method enables the groups to identify areas that they need to study further. Groups can recognize connections between what they have learned and what they are discovering, thereby integrating their knowledge. It is important to note that this method encourages students to seek information actively; they are no longer only passive recipients of information.

Cooperative Learning Requires and Enhances Students' Communication Skills. The success of the group depends upon the interaction of its members. Before cooperative learning can begin, students will learn some of the skills required for successful group interaction:

> paraphrasing other's words to ensure and verify comprehension;
> giving and receiving feedback;
> allowing everyone to contribute ideas; and
> refraining from taking over the group or allowing another to do so. (UCSB, 1999)

When is cooperative learning used? And what topics are amenable to cooperative learning activities? Cooperative learning is most popular today in professional schools, especially medical schools, and in universities. However, it is regularly used in undergraduate and graduate education at colleges and universities all over the world. Topics studied using cooperative learning cover the waterfront—from physics to literature. We discuss a few examples that illustrate the diversity of settings in which cooperative learning is used.

Algebra has always been a difficult subject for students who are not mathematically inclined. Coston (1994) used cooperative learning to make algebra both more understandable and more appealing to students. The college algebra curriculum used an innovative combination of cooperative groups, who worked on problems and concepts in algebra, and graphing calculators. This combination of technology and cooperative learning involved the use of one specific type of technology. Other reports describe the use of several forms of technology.

For example, the GLOBE website (http://www.globe.gov/) describes ways to integrate several types of technology into cooperative learning projects. GLOBE stands for Global Learning and Observations to Benefit the Environment (Figure 7.1). Lessons and projects on this site incorporate material in science, social studies, and math. Many of the projects are cooperative learning activities that involve students in many schools located all around the world. For example, students can use the Internet to communicate with team members at schools around the world and to share data they have collected. They can also create their own websites to report the outcomes of their environmental studies. They can learn to use many types of computer-based data collection instruments as well as digital cameras and geopositioning satellite devices. A quick trip to the site can give you an idea of the many current projects supported by GLOBE.

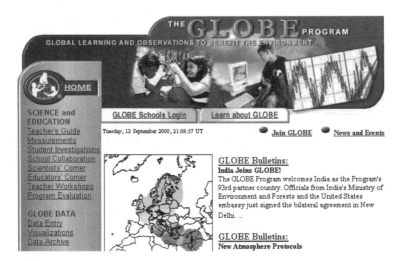

FIGURE 7.1   GLOBE (http://www.globe.gov/fsl/GSI/NAV/MAP/Init.pl ?lang=en&nav=1) enables students and teachers from 8,500 schools to engage in cooperative, inquiry-based learning activities. You can find the participating schools by clicking on the map. The schools are located in the countries that are colored green.

Reprinted with permission of The GLOBE Program, which invites all teachers and their schools to join GLOBE. To learn more about GLOBE or to sign up for training, visit the website at www.globe.gov.

Another source of ideas and concepts about collaborative learning and technology is the WebQuest site (http://www.lfelem.lfc.edu/tech/DuBose/webquest/wq.html). The idea of webquests was developed by Dr. Bernie Dodge. A webquest is a learning activity in which some of the information needed is on the Internet. The WebQuest site has information about many different projects, and many of them include collaborative learning activities. A sample of the lessons you can read about on that site follows:

- The incubation and hatching of baby chicks from eggs
- An exploration of the impact of water pollution that begins as follows:

Splish Splash you were taking a bath.... Uh-Oh! Where's the water? You live in a small town on the coast of sunny California and there is a serious problem. You have no more running water. You call the water plant and the news is not good. Due to high bacteria levels in the water supply, the Pacific Ocean, the plant had to temporarily shut down. You now begin to think about all the damage that has probably been done to this huge body of water to cause such a predicament. Even though you just missed a shower, you wonder about the thousands of species of life that actually have to live in that dirty mess! You decide that something must be done. But what? In this three day activity, you are going to make a difference!

This learning activity, which was created by Yolanda Toni, is an innovative way to get students to begin thinking about the impact of pollution.

- Fai Anderson's art webquest begins with the following introduction:

Janice Preston, principal of Ryder School, wants to improve the physical look of Ryder School. She LOVES classic pieces of art, but she doesn't have a favorite artist. She is looking for ideas and MURAL designs for the walls of Ryder. The school's motto is, "It takes an entire village to raise a child." Your group is bidding for the job. If she likes your mural, she will assign your group to a wall to decorate. You could be IMMORTALIZED on the walls of Ryder!

- Diane Rzaza's social studies webquest assigns students the role of a staff member for a senator who must decide how to vote on the question of trade with China:

Congratulations! You have just landed your first job as a staff member to the new senator from Illinois, Senator Jones. Just in time for her, she needs your research expertise (while she is busy fundraising). Here is your first project. In a few weeks, she will be joining other senators at a breakfast with the President, hoping to influence him on his decision. She will also have to vote on the renewal of most favored nation status for China. At issue are several concerns she has: workers and businesses in the United States; the history of a variety of human rights abuses in China. During the next three class sessions, you will have the opportunity to research the subject, arrive at an informed decision, and construct a position paper for your senator to use to convince the President of her ideas and also for debate on the senate floor. For the next three sessions, working in groups of four, you will search several web sites and investigate other sources to become familiar with the topic. After you have compiled all the data, divide yourselves into two groups. Two of you will be opposed to most favored nation status, while two of you will be for it. After each pair lists their reasons, come to a consensus. Finally prepare a position paper. In it make sure that you list NOT ONLY the reasons for your decision, but include arguments to refute the opposing viewpoints.

The uses of cooperative learning mentioned here are only a tiny sample of those found in printed literature and on the World Wide Web. In spite of the many examples you can read about, however, Bruffee describes collaborative learning as "underdeveloped, underused, and frequently misunderstood" (p. 1). Cooperative learning is still uncommon in U.S. classrooms despite many outstanding examples. Although it requires additional skills on the part of the student (e.g., the ability to work in groups) and extra roles for the teacher (mentoring and guiding groups without "taking over"), cooperative learning has much to offer.

To conclude, a word about collaborative versus cooperative learning is appropriate. Some professionals distinguish between the terms *collaborative* and *cooperative learning.* Both involve group activities that emphasize cooperation rather than competition among students. However, some authors use the term *cooperative learning* for situations in which the teacher takes most or all of the responsibility for deciding what is to be studied and how the groups are to operate. When cooperative learning means this, the term *collaborative learning* is used to mean noncompetitive group activities that engage students in making decisions about what is learned and how. In actual practice and in much of the literature, the terms are used interchangeably. We have used the term *cooperative learning* to indicate learning activities in which students make many of the decisions about what is to be learned and how, as well as activities in which the teacher sets some boundaries in terms of topic or method.

SITUATED LEARNING: PROBLEM-BASED LEARNING AND ANCHORED INSTRUCTION

In a paper that is now a classic in the field, John Seely Brown, Allan Collins, and Paul Duguid (1989) introduced and explained in some detail the idea of **situated learning.** They began by pointing out that the "breach between learning and use, which is captured by the folk categories 'know what' and 'know how,' may well be a product of the structure and practices of our education system" (p. 32). They go on to argue that separating the learning context (school) from the context in which the knowledge is supposed to be used may be detrimental. The result is often "abstract, decontextualized formal concepts" (p. 32). They suggest that "by ignoring the situated nature of cognition, education defeats its own goal of providing usable, robust knowledge. And conversely, we argue that approaches... that embed learning in activity and make deliberate use of the social and physical context are more in line with the understanding of learning and cognition that is emerging from research" (p. 33). Thus, if you want students to learn something they can later use, embed the content to be learned in meaningful contexts; don't teach it as an abstract, isolated fact. Brown, Collins, and Duguid eloquently express this idea with a metaphor:

Old-fashioned pocket knives...have a device for removing stones from horses' hooves. People with this device may know its use and be able to talk wisely about horses, hooves, and stones. But they may never betray—or even recognize—that they would not begin to know how to use this implement on a horse. Similarly, students can often manipulate algorithms, routines, and definitions they have acquired with apparent competence and yet not reveal, to their teachers or themselves, that they would have no idea what to do if they came upon the domain equivalent of a limping horse. (p. 33)

Brown, Collins, and Duguid (1989) suggested several types of situated learning. One is **cognitive apprenticeship.** In this process students take on the role of an apprentice who is working with a master. Traditional craft apprenticeships involved novices learning trade skills from master shoemakers, boat builders, and so on. Cognitive apprenticeships take the same approach but focus on cognitive knowledge. As students learn math, or history, or science, they approach the problems of the field under the watchful eye of a master who serves as a mentor, guide, and advisor. The master (teacher) often models appropriate ways of thinking about the problems and issues under study and then helps students work on those problems and issues by themselves. All this happens with authentic learning contexts in which the content of the study is addressed in a meaningful context. If math is the content, for example, address problems that require an understanding of math.

Situated learning has become a major focus of development since 1989. One form of situated learning that has become very popular in medical education is **problem-based learning (PBL).** PBL is being used to teach everything from emergency room diagnosis to knowledge of pharmaceuticals. Several examples discussed in the section on cooperative learning are also forms of PBL. Students are either given or themselves pose a problem and then set out to solve the problem. More information on problem-based learning can be found on many websites devoted to PBL. Two books that may also be of interest are *The Challenge of Problem-Based Learning* (Boud & Feletti, 1998) and *Problems as Possibilities: Problem-Based Learning for K–12 Education* (Torp & Sage, 1998).

One person and one institution that have contributed the most to the current high level of interest in situated learning are Dr. John Bransford and the Peabody College of Education at Vanderbilt University. Bransford and his colleagues at Vanderbilt have spent more than two decades conducting research and developing innovative teaching strategies in the tradition of situated learning. The Vanderbilt researchers have been developing a particular form of situated learning (and problem-based learning) called **anchored instruction.**

Anchored instruction is problem-based and situated in a meaningful context. The context in this case is established by an anchor. "The purpose of an anchor is to establish a common core of knowledge for all class members. A well-crafted video or rich informational book is [often] selected as the anchor" (Cena & Mitchell, 1998, p. 560). The Vanderbilt group's use of a commercial movie, *Young Sherlock Holmes,* to anchor social studies and literature instruction is discussed in Chapter 6. *The Adventures of Jasper Woodbury,* a series of anchored-instruction experiences supported by laser disks are also covered in Chapter 6. Cena and Mitchell (1998) described how they selected an anchor for a language arts lesson.

> For our unit on Life in the Middle Ages, we chose David Macaulay's 1973 award-winning book *Cathedral* (Houghton Mifflin). This book explores the construction of a mythical gothic cathedral. The Public Broadcasting System (PBS) has made two television programs based on the book—a half-hour animated version and a full-hour version combining animation with actual footage of Chartres cathedral in France. Although either the text or video could be used as anchors, we found that the video provides a particularly excellent introduction to Macaulay's work and gives students a feel and understanding of what life was like in a medieval town. (p. 560)

Anchored instruction has also been used with videodisc technology to teach comprehension to preschool children at risk (Johnson, 1987), to enhance science instruction (Marsh & Kumar, 1992), to support high-school biology, science, and art (The Sandalwood High School Team, 1999, at http://www.sandalwood.duval.k12.fl.us/uswgr.htm), and to improve the writing skills of elementary school students (Kinzer & Risko, 1988).

COGNITIVE FLEXIBILITY HYPERTEXT

Cognitive flexibility hypertext (CFH) is barely out of the instructional technology laboratory at the University of Illinois (Spiro & Jehng, 1990), but the idea has considerable potential, and new media instructional packages may be available in a few years that use this instructional model. The originator, Rand Spiro, distinguishes between simple, **well-structured subject matter** and complex, **ill-structured subject matter.** The rules of subtraction are an example of well-structured content, whereas urban planning is an ill-structured knowledge domain. Much of social studies and multicultural education is ill-structured, as is the practice of most professions, including teaching. Much of the basic factual information in science is well-structured, but deciding how to respond to industrial pollution in an ocean bay is ill-structured. In fact, much of the advanced content in many fields is ill-structured.

Spiro believes traditional, linear forms of instruction, such as textbooks (or drill-and-practice and tutorial software), are probably effective at teaching simple, well-structured information. He argues, however, that "as content increases in complexity and ill structuredness, increasingly greater amounts of important information are lost with linear approaches" (Spiro & Jehng, 1990). This happens for two reasons. One relates to a change in the nature of the subject matter, and one relates to a change in instructional objectives.

> Two important things happen as you move beyond the initial introduction to a content area to more advanced stages of knowledge acquisition in that area: First, the conceptual content tends to become more complex and the basis of its application more ill structured; and, second, the goals of learning and the criteria

by which learning is assessed shift (or should shift): (a) from superficial or introductory level familiarity with concepts to the mastery of *important* aspects of complexity (despite their difficulty); and (b) from accurate reproductive memory and imitative rule following...to the ability to apply what was taught in new and greatly varying contexts...knowledge transfer.... Learning and instruction for mastery of complexity and applications in a complex and ill structured domain *cannot* be compartmentalized, linear, uniperspectival, neatly hierarchical, simply analogical, or rigidly prepackaged. (pp. 167–168)

The linear nature of traditional instruction, and the tendency for that instruction to look at the subject matter from one perspective, limit its effectiveness with complex, ill-structured content. Spiro's **cognitive flexibility theory** suggests that an instructional approach called cognitive flexibility hypertexts would be more effective with complex, ill-structured subject matter. Using new media allows developers to create a new type of learning environment that has the following characteristics:

1. Students have random access. They can enter the nonlinear instructional environment at many different points.
2. A major learning activity is guided, nonlinear exploration of the learning environment.
3. Multiple representations, explanations, dimensions, and viewpoints of the content are provided.
4. Learning is organized around individual cases, but each case is divided into minicases, encouraging cognitive flexibility, which is

   the ability to adaptively reassemble diverse elements of knowledge to fit the particular needs of a given understanding or problem-solving situation. In an ill-structured domain, one cannot fit the wide variety of real world cases of a given type that will be encountered to the same 'plaster case' knowledge structure (although a common failing of advanced learners is that they will try very hard to do this). (p. 184)

5. The conceptual landscape of the case is "crisscrossed" many times in the course of study. The concept of crisscrossed landscapes is derived from the work of Ludwig Wittgenstein (1953), an Austrian philosopher. Because covering a complex, ill-structured topic from one viewpoint or direction tends to oversimplify, a desirable alternative is to cross the same cognitive landscape many times

   so that the region would be revisited from a variety of vantage points, each perspective highlighting aspects of the region in a somewhat different way than the other perspectives. A synoptic view of the complexity of the conceptual landscape would cumulatively emerge over a number of traversals.... By crisscrossing a conceptual landscape in many directions, knowledge that will have to be *used in many ways* is *taught in many ways*. (p. 185)

This type of learning environment involves more than text. In the best-known prototype of cognitive flexibility hypertext, a laser disk of the classic movie

Citizen Kane was combined with computer software to allow students to explore several different themes in the movie. The goal was to help students develop skills in literary comprehension and interpretation, a decidedly complex and ill-structured knowledge domain, judging by the work of high-school students in English class. Ten themes can be explored, each of which has been proposed as a means for understanding the film. For example, one theme concerns a hollow man and focuses on the main character's soullessness. One is that wealth corrupts, and one pertains to outsized ambition. Students have access to material supporting each theme, and they can play segments of the movie that relate to each theme. The themes thus provide multiple representations of the subject matter.

In addition to the theme exploration supported by the software/laser disk package, the package also supports 25 minicases. These short (30- to 90-second) video segments were selected because they relate to more than one of the 10 themes. For example, a 45-second clip of Kane working with associates all night at a newspaper he has just purchased is relevant to the themes of outsized ambition and power. As students use cognitive flexibility hypertext, they have access to many types of support, including expert commentaries, and have the option of creating their own paths through the content. They could, for example, create a new set of minicases or videoclips that all relate to a combination of two or three themes.

As noted earlier, cognitive flexibility theory has only recently emerged from the development laboratory, but it may well become a popular format for designing instructional materials for complex, ill-structured content. You can read more about cognitive flexibility in the paper *Cognitive Flexibility Theory* by Spiro and Coulson. It is available at http://www.gwu.edu/~tip/spiro.html. If you access this website, you can download a short audioclip of Rand Spiro explaining his theory.

Do situated learning, problem-based learning, and anchored instruction refer to the same approach? Situated learning is generally considered the broad theory that covers approaches to learning such as PBL and anchored instruction. Brown, Collins, and Duguid's theory of situated cognition (another name for situated learning) provides the foundation for a number of approaches to teaching and learning. PBL and anchored instruction are not completely different approaches to creating CLEs. Instead these terms are usually used interchangeably. One major difference, however, is that PBLs can be created that do not have specific anchors, other than the problem itself. Therefore, PBL is the broad term, and anchored instruction is a specific type of PBL.

SIMULATIONS

> "A picture may be worth a thousand words, but a computer simulation is worth a thousand pictures."
>
> —Quoted from the user's guide for the *SimHealth* computer simulation

When a teenager drops a quarter into an arcade game and takes control of an interstellar fighter, the teenager is spending money on a computer adventure game, or, more precisely, a computer simulation. Many of the more successful arcade games are, in fact, adventure games or simulations that allow you to play a role in a computer-simulated environment. **Simulations** are models or descriptions of events and conditions. Players take a role in the simulation and help determine what happens next by the decisions they make (Figure 7.2). Computer-supported simulations today have three major functions: recreation, decision support, and instruction. The first function, recreation, was very popular in the 1980s.

Although video games are not as popular as they once were, many individuals of all ages still spend their quarters on arcade games that simulate everything from galactic warfare to the Los Angeles freeway. In addition, millions of homes also have video game systems made by Nintendo, Sega, Sony, and others. The newest innovation in this field is **virtual reality (VR)** (Andolsek, 1995). Using advanced technology, virtual reality games (or VR games) have added a new dimension to this type of entertainment. In VR games, players put on special helmets and gloves. Then, instead of watching the game develop on the video screen, they have the feeling of being "in" the game environment. If they are walking through a forest, they "see" the forest around them through special video

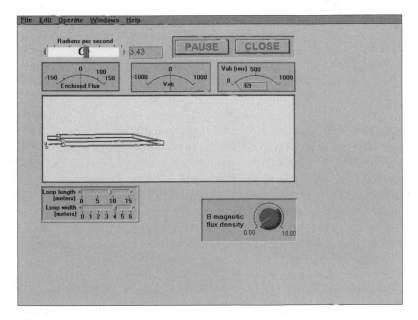

FIGURE 7.2 This wire loop simulation (http://ourworld.compuserve.com/homepages/ b_whaley/overview.htm) allows students to adjust the magnetic field, loop length, loop height, and loop angular velocity and see changes in the amount of voltage generated. You can download this and other free science simulations from http://ourworld. compuserve.com/homepages/b_whaley/.

Reprinted by permission from Brad Whaley.

devices in the helmet. If they move an arm or hand, sensors in the gloves transmit data to the computer, and the image of the player makes corresponding moves in the virtual environment. Virtual reality is too expensive and too experimental for routine use in education today, but that will likely change in this decade.

At the same time your younger brother or sister is playing the latest video or VR game, thousands of specialists in multinational corporations, intelligence agencies, and the military are also putting computer simulations to work. Today, computers are used to simulate different world and national conditions in efforts to make better decisions. On a less grandiose level, a corporation can simulate the effects of marketing a product under several different advertising strategies (for example, upscale ads that emphasize snob appeal to justify a higher price versus "it's for everybody" ads that aim for high volume and emphasize a lower price). Simulations of this sort are often called **models.** Essentially, models are aids to making important decisions.

Although both recreational and decision support simulations are fascinating in their own right, we concentrate on instructional simulations. Simulations designed primarily for instructional purposes are called *games* in some of the literature. The terms *game* and *simulation* sometimes refer to programs that recreate aspects of a real or semireal environment. The terms *adventure simulation* and *adventure game* often refer to recreations of imaginary or fantasy environments; however, the four terms are used inconsistently in the research and professional literature. In this section, the general term *simulation* is used to refer to games and simulations that represent both real and imaginary or fantasy environments.

A Bit of History

Constructivist instructional strategies such as anchored instruction and cognitive flexibility hypertext are relatively recent innovations even though the theories on which they are based have been around for many years. This is not the case for simulations. Although computer simulations are relatively new and educational applications are even more recent, the method has a long history. The instructional applications of simulations can be traced back at least to the seventeenth century, when war games were used to simulate battles between opposing forces. Chess, in fact, is a somewhat abstract extension of a war game that is hundreds of years old. The modern war game derives from a simulation called *Kriegspiel* (German for *war game*) developed by Von Reisswitz for the Prussian army. It used maps and wooden blocks that represented troops. By World War I, versions of Kriegspiel were played by officers in virtually every modern army in the world.

In the mid-1950s simulations were introduced in business training programs. *Top Management Decision Simulation,* a computerized simulation published by the American Management Association in 1956, divided participants into teams that operated two competing one-product companies. Today hundreds of business-oriented simulations deal with virtually every aspect of enterprise. Most colleges of business include some simulation experiences in their undergraduate and graduate programs. Some simulations are uncomplicated and contain relatively simple activities that allow players to make only a few decisions. Others take hours or even days to play and require players to make hundreds, or even thousands, of decisions. In some business schools, students complete a capstone course that is really a semester-long simulation.

In the 1970s two popular simulations on operating a business, *Sell Bicycles* and *Sell Lemonade,* were developed and distributed to schools by the Minnesota Educational Computing Corporation (MECC). Both were for elementary or middle-school students and ran on Apple II computers. They were created to teach concepts of supply and demand. Players make decisions about production, retail costs, price structure, and advertising. In *Sell Bicycles,* two teams start with $5,000 in their accounts and 200 bicycles in their warehouses. The objectives of the lemonade simulation are similar. Students run a simulated lemonade stand and must make decisions about the amount of lemonade to make each day, the price of a glass of lemonade, and how much to spend on advertising.

From 1975 to 1985, educational simulations were relatively specialized products. Most teachers who used them in the classroom acquired the software by ordering it from specialized educational distributors. Today, in a city like Houston, a teacher can go to any of four or five large software stores in the area and buy any of more than a hundred educational simulations off the shelf. Thousands of parents also buy these programs for their children. Perhaps the best-known educational simulations are the *Sim* series (Figure 7.3). *SimCity* puts you in charge of managing the growth and development of a city; *SimEarth* takes a similar approach to running the planet; *SimLife* lets you create new life forms for ecological niches and see if they survive; and *SimHealth* simulates the process of developing consensus in a democracy for a national health care policy.

SimHealth players take the role of a politician who must design a national health care system and experience the consequences of that design. The program begins with four general options:

1. Patch up the current system.
2. Combine two or more proposed systems.
3. Build a new system from scratch.
4. Evaluate several of the current proposals.

To succeed you must consider the power and interests of diverse groups, including health care providers, patients, insurance companies, big business, small business, and more. The task is daunting but possible. As the *SimHealth* manual states, "In this political world of give, take, and compromise, your biggest challenge will be to design and enact a national health care system without betraying your personal values." *SimHealth* does not, however, have a preprogrammed solution to the health care crisis that students can select to play the simulation successfully. The program starts with a series of questions that help you define your values and the balance between them with regard to liberty, equality, community, and efficiency. "Success" is related to how well you uphold the values you have

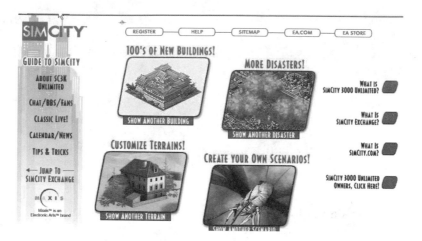

FIGURE 7.3   A screen from the website for *SimCity3000* (http://sc3000.gamestates.com/images/screens/ss-msc4.jpg).

Reprinted by permission from Electronic Arts/Maxis.

espoused. *SimHealth*, like all the simulations in this series, is a complex program that helps students grapple with difficult issues that are often very confusing even to adults.

SimFarm is advertised as *SimCity*'s country cousin, which is an accurate description. *SimCity*, which is available in several versions including *SimCity3000*, has been used in classrooms from the middle grades through graduate school to help students understand the complexities of planning and decision making in urban contexts. *SimFarm* uses the same format for rural living. You start the simulation owning a good farm. You then decide what type of farming you will do (family farm, agribusiness, and so on), the type of crops you will grow, what markets you will try to serve (nearby town, organic foods specialty market, world agriculture market), and how you will grow and market your produce (use chemical fertilizers and pesticides or grow organic produce; buy more land or sell some you own; borrow more money from the bank; take advice from experts or not). Like *SimHealth*, the *SimFarm* program is complex, but it gives students an excellent feel for the types of decisions a farmer must make in the twenty-first century (Figure 7.4). The *Sim* series of simulations are so popular that a very active website (http://www.simcity.com/us/guide/) operated by the publisher supplies players with all sorts of information.

Why Do Students Find Simulations Appealing?

Simulating is not the same as being a new research scientist in an environmental laboratory or a city planner trying to channel growth and development in healthy and beneficial directions. Simulations are, however, one of several types of instructional strategies that closely approximate real experience. Like the other con-

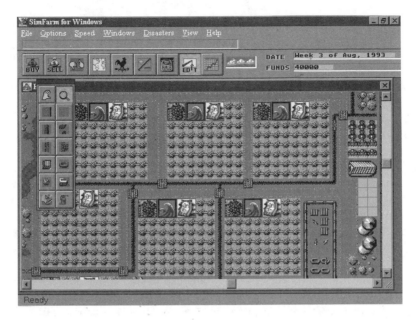

FIGURE 7.4   A screen from *SimFarm* (http://www.maxis.com/games/simfarm/screens.html).

Reprinted by permission from Electronic Arts/Maxis.

structivist methods discussed in this chapter, simulations allow the student to play an active role in an environment with a set of rules. The environment may be realistic or fantasy. For example, *GAS* is one of eight programs in the third volume of *Modern Physics,* a series of physics simulations developed at Stanford University. *GAS* simulates the thermal motion of gas molecules in a box. Students can adjust several variables, such as pressure, temperature, and the ratio of spectral to diffuse wall reflections. Students then observe what effect changes have on the behavior of the molecules. Although the environment simulated in *GAS* is realistic, it does not take into consideration all factors that affect the behavior of real gas atoms in an enclosed space. *GAS* is not a complete recreation of reality, but it does simulate real events and relationships.

GAS deals with aspects of the real world, but many simulations do not. For example, *Winnie the Pooh and the Hundred Acre Wood,* a simulation for young children, takes place in British author A. A. Milne's Hundred Acre Wood, where Christopher Robin's friend Pooh Bear lives. The skills learned playing this simulation—map coordinate skills and logical thinking skills—can be used in the real world, but the simulation's environment is fantasy.

Simulated environments may also be concrete or abstract. *Santa Fe Trail* is a concrete simulation set in the period between 1820 and 1829. Players try to freight goods from Franklin, Missouri, through desolate and dangerous territory to Santa Fe, a trip of about 800 miles. The first part of the trip requires freighting on the Mississippi River. *Santa Fe Trail* helps students understand an interesting and important aspect of U.S. history. Another program, *The Would-Be Gentleman,* is a simulation of social mobility during the reign of Louis XIV of France (Figure 7.5). The model underlying the simulation reflects the economic and social conditions of the time, and players who lack considerable knowledge of the period can find it difficult to succeed. *The Would-Be Gentleman* begins in 1638 and ends in 1715. The simulation comes with a short manual, but the program is intended for use in classes that cover this period of French history through readings and presentations. The simulation allows students to play a role in that society but requires students to use knowledge gained from class instruction to succeed.

The context of *The Would-Be Gentleman* is complex but still concrete. *Tarski's World,* on the other hand, simulates an abstract environment (Figure 7.6). This Macintosh program was named after a famous Polish logician, Alfred Tarski. *Tarski's World* is an introduction to first-order logic, a subject many introductory philosophy students have difficulty grasping. In *Tarski's World* students apply first-order logic in an abstract, artificial world populated by geometric figures (cubes, tetrahedrons, and dodecahedrons) of varying sizes. Students can write sentences in first-order logic using a set of symbols that have specific meanings and then test the validity of their sentences in *Tarski's World*. The simulation checks the sentences for semantic and syntactic correctness to determine whether they are logically correct in the world currently displayed on the screen. The program also allows students to create their own worlds.

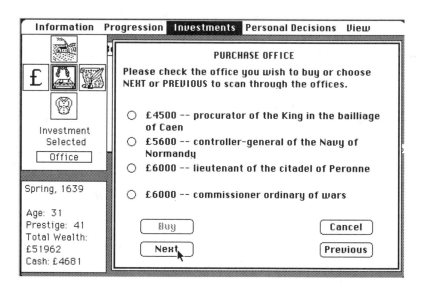

FIGURE 7.5   This screen from *The Would-Be Gentleman* displays information on potential investments. Other screens report on progress over several generations and list personal decisions players can make.

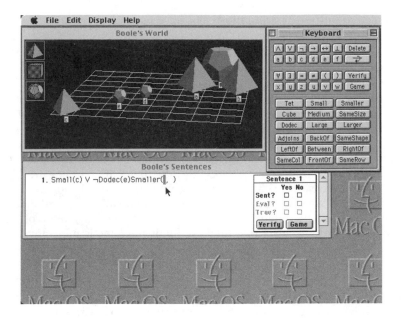

FIGURE 7.6 This screen illustrates items in a world named Boole that was created with the *Tarski's World* software. A keyboard has been displayed on the right by the player to create sentences in the dialog box at the bottom of the screen. Those sentences are written in first-order logic. The program will check the sentences to determine if they are "correct" according to the rules of the current "world."
Reprinted by permission from Dikran Karagueuzian.

Tarski's World does not simulate a real world. It is not, as many simulations are, a program you use only once or twice before moving on. It is much like a test bench by which you test a newly manufactured product or a succession of products to see whether they work correctly. What you are testing in this simulation, however, is your own ideas and understanding.

Regardless of whether simulated environments are realistic or fantasy, concrete or abstract—all simulations are active. They call for students to become participants in the simulation, a major factor contributing to their effectiveness. A simulation is difficult to experience passively. You must process input, plan actions, analyze problems, make decisions, monitor progress, and coordinate your efforts to accomplish a goal. This participatory element has been championed by proponents of many different theoretical perspectives. John Dewey, Jean Piaget, Jerome Bruner, and Lev Vygotsky have all argued that involvement in the learning process is crucial to success. Sociologists use the terms **formal education** and **informal education** to distinguish between the type of learning that goes on in a typical U.S. high-school history class (formal) and the way a child on an undeveloped Pacific island learns to fish by going out in a boat with an elder who is an expert (informal learning). Simulations are one way of bringing some aspects of informal learning into the classroom.

The active nature of simulations is one reason for their appeal. Another is the aspect of play. Simulations are games in which we can play roles we know are not real. Through simulations computers can become electronic playgrounds as well as tools for learning:

> Some researchers believe play may well have been an important factor in the development of our species: Skills for producing workable adjustments may well have propelled [hu]manlike primates over the evolutionary threshold to *Homo sapiens.* Anthropologists have hypothesized that [hu]mans' great evolutionary leaps began in play with tools, with language, or with social roles. To recreate the physical and social features of one's world by wrestling with, chasing around, leaping on, and otherwise physically interacting with them is a biological core of play. Even humans seem to make these sallies…. When current-day adolescents chase and fight imaginary intergalactic foes in the electronic playground of a computer arcade, we may speculate that they are following genetic imperatives to experience and to create. (Fagen, 1983, p. 73)

Chris Crawford, a well-known programmer who designed a number of educational simulations, including an international relations program called *Balance of Power,* also has strong views on the importance of play (Crawford, 1983):

> A teenager stands transfixed before a video machine. His pockets bulge with quarters, and his dinner—a room-temperature slice of pizza—sits forgotten on a paper plate. Asked what he is doing, he responds, "Nothing, just playing." His mother feels differently. "He's wasting his time," she says. "That's what he's doing."
>
> They're both wrong. The teenager is learning—and learning well. Games are one of the most ancient and time-honored methods of educating. They are the ideal learning technology, for they have received the seal of approval of natural selection. (p. 78)

Crawford and other proponents of simulations and games offer many reasons why they are powerful learning tools. For Crawford, play is a primary reason for their success. Play is the "original means of educating children, and formal education, with classrooms, certified teachers, curricula, and all the other trappings, are 'the newfangled notion,' the untested fad, the violators of tradition" (p. 79).

Another scientist interested in both play and learning is psychologist Thomas Malone (1980). His dissertation at Stanford University was a study of what makes computer games fun. One of his major conclusions was that the three factors that make games fun would also make educational programs more fun for students:

1. *Challenge.* A challenging activity must have a goal whose outcome is uncertain. Children don't enjoy games they can beat every time nor games that are impossible to win.
2. *Fantasy.* Children seem to enjoy and prefer activities that involve fantasy. For example, learning Boolean logic in a computer simulation that involves working with a fantasy character named Rocky who has magic boots is

much preferred by most children to lectures on Boolean logic followed by worksheets and an end-of-the-week test.
3. *Curiosity.* In Malone's words, learning situations "should be neither too complicated nor too simple with respect to the learner's existing knowledge" (p. 89). The optimal learning environment is one where "the learner knows enough to have expectations about what will happen, but where these expectations are sometimes unmet" (p. 89).

Many of the best simulations are excellent examples of how Malone's three elements can be expressed in educational software. Crawford (1983) hopes someday, when technology is fully integrated into the educational system, that "students may frolic through multiplication tables and algebra, through adverbs and prepositions, as gaily as lion cubs wrestling with each other on the plains of the Serengeti" (p. 79).

All three of Malone's factors are found in *Scotland 100 Years Ago*, a simulation–database package of software designed for use with a class of 9- to 13-year-olds who are divided into several groups (Martin, 1984). Each group takes on the identity of a fictional but realistic character living in Scotland one hundred years ago. The task of each character is to complete a journey across Scotland, making many decisions as well as overcoming obstacles encountered along the way. Students access the computer database as they play the simulation. It provides information on the regions the character is passing through and describes other sources of information the group can consult, such as books and maps.

The computer manages the journey and can even provide printed copies of maps and descriptions of regions. Much of the work and the learning occur away from the computer, as students gather information and work in groups to decide what to do next. In a typical classroom application, students may engage in a variety of activities, such as interpreting maps, writing diaries about the character's journey, presenting progress reports, and solving problems. Simulations such as *Scotland 100 Years Ago* can be the anchor for a wide range of learning activities.

Malone's three characteristics are also found in the simulations supported by the Educational Simulations of Space Project (ESSP). ESSP maintains a website (http://www.riceinfo.rice.edu/armadillo/Simulations/) at Rice University in Houston, Texas, where teachers interested in engaging students in simulations of space can find all sorts of information and resources.

If you would like to explore the use of simulations in education, you may want to explore the Simulations and Games in Education website at (http://www.insead.fr/Encyclopedia/Education/Advances/games.html. In addition, a May 2000 search of the website for Amazon, the online bookstore, identified 153 books on this subject using the search term *simulation education*. To conduct your own search, go to http://www.amazon.com and enter your search terms. For example, if you are looking for simulations for mathematics education, you might use the terms *simulation, education,* and *mathematics.*

ADVANTAGES OF CONSTRUCTIVIST SOFTWARE

Because students find constructivist approaches inherently appealing, they are potentially useful for instruction. Do they have other advantages over alternative instructional strategies? Simulations have seven potential advantages, most of which are shared with the other types of constructivist software discussed earlier in this chapter.

Fun

Simulations, cognitive flexibility hypertext, and anchored instruction are probably easier to make attractive and interesting than most other instructional strategies.

Low Expense

Simulations and other constructivist approaches are almost always less expensive than real-world learning situations. As Balajthy (1984) put it, "Simulations are an inexpensive way to provide background experience. An actual visit to a forest lake to observe the food chain may be optimal but not feasible" (p. 592). In simulations such as *Odell Lake,* students can explore the food chain of a freshwater lake from the keyboard of their classroom computer.

Safety

Constructivist instruction can provide experiences in the authentic, realistic contexts that such instruction emphasizes for learning situations in which allowing students to experiment freely could be dangerous. Many simulations, for example, allow students to perform experiments or practice skills in ways that would not be possible in the real world because of safety issues.

Better Transfer

Students who learn by playing a simulation, using a cognitive flexibility hypertext, or participating in anchored-instruction experiences may find it easier to transfer what they have learned to the real world. Pilots, for example, spend hours in flight simulators instead of in lecture halls because the complex skills they learn in the flight simulator are more easily transferred to the cockpit of a real plane than lectures on the same topic from an experienced pilot. When transfer does not occur, the reason is often inert knowledge, knowledge students "know" when completing a multiple-choice test but are unable to apply anywhere else. The failure of efforts to teach skills, concepts, and procedures out of context and in isolation and then expect students automatically to apply this knowledge led researchers at Vanderbilt University to develop constructivist instructional strategies such as anchored instruction:

The major goal of anchored instruction is to overcome the inert knowledge problem. We attempt to do so by creating environments that permit sustained exploration by students and teachers and enable them to understand the kinds of problems and opportunities that experts in various areas encounter and the knowledge that these experts use as tools. We also attempt to help students experience the value of exploring the same setting from multiple perspectives (e.g., as scientist or historian). (Cognition and Technology Group, 1990, p. 3)

Less Threat and Anxiety

Some constructivist instruction permits students to experiment—to try out alternatives they might avoid in other situations. Students tend to view simulations and other forms of constructivist instruction more as play than as learning and respond to them with more enthusiasm and less anxiety.

Encouragement of Socialization and Collaboration

In the 1970s and 1980s, some educators were concerned that putting computers in classrooms would isolate students from each other and reduce the amount of interaction and socialization in the classroom. Constructivist uses of technology actually increase socialization. Many constructivist approaches require intense collaboration between students.

Realism Adjusted for Maximum Learning

Simulations like *SimCity* and anchored instruction like the *Jasper Woodbury* materials are ways of representing aspects of the real world in the classroom. They need not, however, exactly recreate the real world. This is, in fact, often an advantage. In many learning situations, the real event occurs very quickly or very slowly. Fast-paced events may be unsuitable for learning because novices cannot process the information quickly enough to learn what to do. Slow-paced events may waste time because the student spends too much time waiting. Simulations can slow down fast-changing events in the beginning of the simulation and speed them up as the student learns the correct procedures for handling them. Simulations can also condense the essential elements of a slow process, such as the evolving ecology of a tropical island, so that students more effectively use the time available for instruction.

HyperFly simulates multigenerational genetic breeding experiments with flies. Figures 7.7 and 7.8 are screens from *HyperFly*. Such experiments are interesting educational activities, but they would take far too long if actually conducted (and the flies can present their own set of problems in the classroom). *HyperFly* allows students to conduct their simulated experiments quickly and with detailed reports of the results. Figure 7.9 is a screen from *Virtual Flylab, HyperFly*'s counterpart on the World Wide Web.

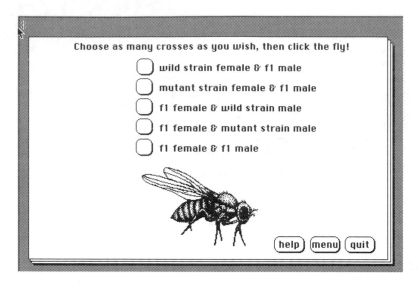

FIGURE 7.7   Students using the *HyperFly* simulation have many choices to make when organizing their studies. This screen lists some of them.

Reprinted by permission from Thomas Thelen.

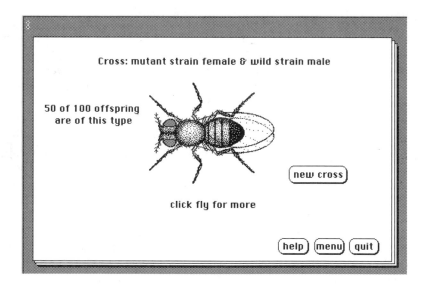

FIGURE 7.8   This screen illustrates one type of feedback students get after a cross-breeding study.

Reprinted by permission from Thomas Thelen.

FIGURE 7.9 *Virtual Flylab* (http://cdl-flylab.sonoma.edu/VirtualFlyLab/Design.html) supports learning the principles of genetic inheritance. This educational simulation is available from Biology Labs On-Line (http://www.biologylab.awlonline.com/)

Reprinted by permission from Addison Wesley Longman.

Simulations may also make better use of learning time when the real environment can provide learning opportunities only under certain (unpredictable) circumstances. For example, simulations of student responses in a program designed to teach administration of an informal reading inventory (Willis & Willis, 1991) can provide teacher-education students with far more effective practice than they might receive in a real, uncontrolled situation.

POTENTIAL PROBLEMS OF CONSTRUCTIVIST APPROACHES

Although constructivist uses of technology may not exhibit all seven advantages discussed in the previous section, virtually all of them share the majority of those benefits. However, they are also subject to the limitations and problems described in this section.

Reality Is More Than the Learning Environment

Students who become experts at working through a simulation or anchored-instruction environment may not realize the substantial differences between the learning environment and the real world. Teachers may need to point out the difference between the learning environment and the real-world processes or procedures they represent.

Time Demands of Constructivist Instruction

Another major problem most educators face when they use constructivist approaches is that most activities do not fit neatly into a standard class period. Restructuring the school day and creating plans that make maximum use of the time available can be difficult.

More Threat and Anxiety

Less threat and anxiety were discussed earlier as an advantage of constructivist activities, but the opposite can also be true. Because these activities call for intensive interaction among participants, and because the results of decisions and suggestions students make are often apparent to their peers, many of these activities may create situations in the classroom in which students feel anxious about making decisions, offering suggestions, or supporting an idea than they would when traditional lecture or demonstration methods are used.

Adoption of the Material but Not the Concept

A few years ago one of the authors observed a teacher in an inner-city school organize her fourth-graders for a unit in the *Jasper Woodbury* series of math experiences. This teacher had all the materials needed: computer and software, laser disk, teacher's manual, and student guides. She had also received some training in the constructivist theory that underlies the *Jasper Woodbury* materials. In essence, students become problem solvers in a sequence of adventures that Jasper Woodbury has. Each adventure can be solved using math procedures the students should be learning in that grade. Teachers sometimes provide direct instruction on basic math skills in this approach, but they generally do that with minilessons or on-the-spot activities that help students puzzle through another Jasper Woodbury problem. This teacher had decided that her students, who were mostly poor, inner-city children, could not be trusted to take that much responsibility for their own learning. She thus began the lesson with a teacher-centered discussion of the math skills they would be learning. Then she handed out ditto sheets with a sequence of numbered steps the children could use to solve the problem.

This teacher began with a constructivist lesson in which children create their own understanding of the problem (and solution) by working through the process themselves. She converted it into a behavioral lesson in which the teacher delivers prepackaged solutions to her students. Constructivists would, of course, argue that students may be able to use the prepackaged solutions to answer questions on a test but that they are not likely to be able to apply that inert knowledge to other situations.

Constructivist approaches call for teachers to take on different roles in the classroom and for students to study and learn in different ways. Adopting the material of a constructivist approach is not enough. A deeper and more fundamental change in the classroom milieu is required before you can say, "This is a constructivist learning environment."

Difficulty in Deciding When to Intervene Directly

Constructivist teaching does involve some direct instruction, such as short lessons to introduce a new concept as well as helping students when they get "stuck." Deciding how much to "preteach" and when to intervene is not easy, however:

> One of the greatest challenges that anchored curricula pose for teachers derives from the need to change their role from a "provider of information" to a coach and often a fellow learner.... In the Sherlock program, different students might choose to explore a variety of issues relevant to the Young Sherlock and Oliver anchors—issues such as the Egyptian culture that is mentioned in the movie, the nature of schooling in Victorian England, and so forth.... In order to encourage and support student generated learning, teachers must be flexible; they cannot follow a fully scripted lesson plan. In addition, teachers cannot be experts in each topic that students choose to pursue, so they must often become learners along with their students. This can be difficult for many teachers, especially when children are accustomed to classroom cultures in which the teacher normally functions as "expert" rather than as "guide" and "learner." (Cognition and Technology Group at Vanderbilt, 1993, p. 54)

Objectives Mismatch

It is an unfortunate fact that many types of educational software, including some constructivist software, do not always accomplish the learning objectives they purport to help students achieve. When determining whether a particular activity is appropriate for your setting, do not rely on the advertising blurb, or the documentation. Work through it yourself and form your own opinion. Talk with other teachers who have used the material and ask them about it.

Another type of mismatch constructivist educators often face is the current national emphasis on knowledge that can be demonstrated on multiple-choice tests. In districts and states that rank schools on the basis of tests of simple facts, it is quite possible that constructivist teaching strategies would not improve student test scores as much as more direct types of instruction such as drill-and-practice and tutorial software. Constructivists, however, would argue that the inert knowledge these approaches teach (and some achievement tests measure) is not as valuable or useful as the type encouraged by constructivist methods. Student accomplishments in constructivist learning experiences are more likely to be evaluated through portfolios, results of the process of solving a problem, or student reports on explorations of a topic. Although these forms of evaluation have many advantages over multiple-choice tests, educators who advocate constructivist teaching and assessment must confront the fact that many parents, legislators, and business leaders think achievement is measured only in terms of grade-level scores on standardized achievement tests.

Competitive Focus

Constructivist approaches to learning emphasize collaboration and cooperative learning skills students need in their social, family, and occupational lives after graduation. However, the reality of some situations is naturally competitive, and many simulations also have an element of competition. Competitive learning environments are not necessarily all bad, but far too many educational simulations require raw competition, and too few require collaboration and cooperation among participants. Moreover, teachers can increase or decrease the competitive nature of some programs depending on how they structure the use of the simulation.

Consider, for example, *Forever Growing Garden,* a CD-based simulation of gardening that allows players to plant and tend a garden in up to three locations: home garden, farm garden, and castle garden. Much of this is realistic. You can plant tomatoes and pumpkins in the farm garden, for example, and, with a little luck and good care, harvest a bumper crop. The program also takes you past the growing phase. Flowers, for example, can be made into arrangements that are sold in the market along with produce. A teacher could divide the class into groups and organize a competition to decide which group grows the best garden. Or the same software could be the center of several collaborative projects in which different groups share expertise and work out collaborative planting schedules that produce both vegetables and flowers throughout most of the growing season.

Forever Growing Garden, we should mention, is supported by excellent color graphics, sound effects, and animation. Like many successful simulations, *Forever Growing Garden,* is not simply a colorful rendering of reality on the computer screen. Different items on each screen react with movement or sound when children explore them. They can grow some plants that cannot be found in the latest Burpee seed catalog. For example, snapdragon seeds produce dragons and fireworks flowers explode when you click on them.

SUMMARY

Once rare, constructivist uses of technology in the classroom are now more common. They are, however, still not commonplace. One reason is that constructivist applications involve much more than assigning students time at the computer. They require considerable planning to ensure that resources students may need are available. However, they cannot be fully preplanned, so teachers may not know what they will be doing at any particular moment. Constructivist teaching calls for flexibility, on-the-spot analysis and decision making, and a comfortable confidence that students can learn and achieve without constant teacher-centered instruction and direction.

QUESTIONS TO CONSIDER

1. What aspects of the subject you plan to teach are well-structured? What aspects are ill-structured? What types of computer-supported instruction could be used to teach well-structured content? What types could be used to teach ill-structured content?

2. Are you comfortable teaching from a constructivist perspective? If not, what types of experiences and information do you need to become more comfortable?

RELATED ACTIVITIES

1. Select a piece of computer-assisted instruction (or a lesson plan using some form of information technology) that is based on a drill or tutorial approach. Then write a brief description of how this content could be taught using a constructivist approach. What types of technology support could you use?
2. Select an educational computer simulation or software to support another constructivist approach to teaching. Create a lesson plan that integrates technology into the learning experiences.
3. Locate at least four papers in the education literature on the use of technology-supported constructivist approaches in the classroom. What reasons do the authors give for using them? Are the reasons similar to the advantages described in this chapter? Were there problems or barriers to be overcome? Are they mentioned in this chapter?

REFERENCES

Andolsek, D. (1995). Virtual reality in education and training. *International Journal of Instructional Media, 22*(2), 145–152.

Balajthy, E. (1984, March). Computer simulations and reading. *Reading Teacher, 38*(3), 590–593.

Berliner, D. (1999). *Telling the stories of educational psychology.* Retrieved March 12, 2000, from the World Wide Web: http://courses.ed.asu.edu/berliner/readings/stories.htm

Boud, D. & Feletti, G. (1998). *The challenge of problem-based learning* (2nd ed.). New York: Kogan Page.

Brown, J. S., Collins, A., & Duguid, S. (1989, January–February). Situated cognition and the culture of learning. *Educational Researcher, 18,*(1), 32–42. Retrieved March 12, 2000, from the World Wide Web: http://www.ilt.columbia.edu/ilt/papers/JohnBrown.html

Bruffee, K. (1993). *Collaborative learning.* Boston: Johns Hopkins University Press.

Cena, M., & Mitchell, J. (1998). Anchored instruction: A model for integrating the language arts through content area study. *Journal of Adolescent & Adult Literacy, 41*(7), 559–561.

Cognition and Technology Group at Vanderbilt. (1990). Anchored instruction and its relationship to situated cognition. *Educational Researcher, 19*(6), 2–10.

Cognition and Technology Group at Vanderbilt. (1993). Anchored instruction and situated cognition revisited. *Educational Technology, 33*(3), 52–70.

Cooper, J. (1990). Cooperative learning and college teaching: Tips from the trenches. *The Teaching Professor, 4*(5), 12–14.

Coston, Y. M. (1994). The effect of a graphics calculator enhanced college algebra curriculum and cooperative learning on mathematics achievement. In L. Lum (Ed.), *Proceedings of the Sixth International Conference on Technology in Collegiate Mathematics* (pp. 460–466). Reading, MA: Addison-Wesley.

Crawford, C. (1983, December). Programmed to play. *Science Digest,* 78–79.

Crews, T., Biswas, G., Goldman, S., and Bransford, J. (1997). Anchored interactive learning environments. *International Journal of Artificial Intelligence in Education, 8,* 142–178.

Dewey, J. (1933). *How we think* (Rev. ed.). Boston: Heath.

Fagen, R. (1983, December). Horseplay and monkeyshine. *Science, 83,* 71–76.

Johnson, R. (1987). *Uses of video technology to facilitate children's learning.* Unpublished doctoral dissertation, Vanderbilt University, Nashville, TN.

Jonassen, D. H. (1994). Thinking technology: Toward a constructivist design model. *Educational Technology, 34*(4), 34–37.

King, A. (1993). From sage on the stage to guide on the side. *College Teaching, 41*(1), 21–23.

Kinzer, C. K., & Risko, V. J. (1988). *Macrocontexts to facilitate learning.* Paper presented at the 33rd Annual Conference of International Reading Association, Toronto, Ontario.

Malone, T. (1980). *What makes things fun to learn? A study of intrinsically motivating computer games.* Unpublished doctoral dissertation, Stanford University, Palo Alto, CA.

Marsh, E., & Kumar, D. (1992). Hypermedia: A conceptual framework for science education and review of recent findings. *Journal of Educational Multimedia and Hypermedia, 1*(1), 25–37.

Martin, A. (1984). Microworld for the classroom. *Interactive Learning International, 1*(1), 7–8.

Millis, B. (1993). *Cooperative learning.* Workshop presented at Dalhousie University, Halifax, Nova Scotia, Canada.

Pearson, M., & Smith, D. (1986). Debriefing in experience-based learning. *Simulations/Games for Learning, 16*(4), 155–171.

Reeves, T. (1998). *The impact of media and technology in schools: A research report prepared for the Bertelsmann Foundation.* Athens: The University of Georgia.

Skinner, B. F. (1968). *The technology of teaching.* New York: Appleton-Century-Crofts.

Spiro, R., & Jehng, J. (1990). Cognitive flexibility and hypertext: Theory and technology for the non-linear and multidimensional traversal of complex subject matter. In D. Nix & R. Spiro (Eds.), *Cognition, education, and multimedia* (pp. 163–206). Hillsdale, NJ: Lawrence Erlbaum.

Squire, L. R. (1987). *Memory and brain.* New York: Oxford University Press.

Steffe, L. (1998). Intersubjectivity in mathematics learning: A challenge to the radical constructivist paradigm? *Cherods: A Journal of Writings Exploring Educational Issues with a Maths Education Tendency, 13.* Available: http://s13a.math.aca.mmu.ac.uk/

Torp, L., & Sage, S. (1998). *Problems as possibilities: Problem-based learning for K–12 education.* Alexandria, VA: Association for Supervision and Curriculum Development.

University of California. (1999). *Teaching assistant's handbook* (Chapter 3). Santa Barbara, CA: Author. Available: http://id-www.ucsb.edu/ic/ta/hdbk/ta3-5.html#CLG

Whitehead, A. N. (1929). *The aims of education.* New York: Macmillan.

Willis, D., & Willis, J. (1991). Development and evaluation of a teacher education simulation for the informal reading inventory. *Computers in the Schools, 8*(1/2/3), 245–248.

Wittgenstein, L. (1953). *Philosophical investigations.* New York: Macmillan.

SOFTWARE DISCUSSED IN THIS CHAPTER

Forever Growing Garden. Available from EduCorp, 7434 Trade Street, San Diego, CA 92121-2410. Phone 800-843-9497.

GAS: Intellimation, P.O. Box 1922. Santa Barbara, CA 93116-1922. Phone 800-346-8355.

HyperFly. Intellimation, Box 1922, Santa Barbara, CA 93116-1922. Phone 800-346-8355.

Modern Physics. Intellimation, P.O. Box 1922, Santa Barbara, CA 93116-1922. Phone 800-346-8355.

The Adventures of Jasper Woodbury. Http://www.peabody.vanderbilt.edu/projects/funded/jasper/Jasperhome.html

Odell Lake. Minnesota Educational Computing Corporation. Phone 800-685-6322.

Sante Fe Trail. Educational Activities, P.O. Box 392, Freeport, NY 11520.

Sell Bicycles (discontinued). Minnesota Educational Computing Corporation. Phone 800-685-6322.

Sell Lemonade (discontinued). Minnesota Educational Computing Corporation. Phone 800-685-6322.

Sim series of simulations including *SimHealth: A Democracy and Society Computer Simulation.* Maxis, 2 Theatre Square, Orinda, CA 94563. These programs are distributed by Broderbund and are widely available in computer and software stores.

Tarski's World. Intellimation, P.O. Box 1922, Santa Barbara, CA 93116-1922. Phone 800-346-8355.

Winnie the Pooh and the Hundred Acre Wood. Available from Educational Resources, 1550 Executive Drive, Elgin, IL 60123. Phone 800-624-2926.

The Would-Be Gentleman. Intellimation, P.O. Box 1922, Santa Barbara, CA 93116-1922. Phone 800-346-8355.

INTEGRATING INFORMATION TECHNOLOGY INTO THE CURRICULUM

This chapter was coauthored by Valentyna Kolomiyets.

Goal: To introduce the idea of technology integration (teaching with technology), to differentiate it from teaching about technology, and to present some examples of how integration can occur.

KEY TERMS

cognitive tools (p. 179)

events of instruction (p. 180)

learning from (p. 179)

learning with (p. 179)

Madeline Hunter (p. 180)

student-centered (p. 183)

teacher-centered (p. 180)

teaching about technology (p. 178)

teaching with technology (p. 179)

Some analyses of computers in schools have lumped all the ways technology can be used in schools into one big category. Questions such as, What impact do computers have on learning? and, Do computers make a positive difference in schools? represent this way of thinking. Such questions cannot be sensibly answered because there is no meaningful way to make a single judgment about computers in schools. Of the many ways computers and other forms of technology can be used in schools, some may be useful and beneficial whereas others may not be. Adding up the negatives and positives cannot lead to a single conclusion. Imagine asking, "What impact do drugs have on human health?" Or, "Do drugs have a positive effect on human health?" What drugs? Insulin? Penicillin? Cocaine? And what type of effect? Reduction of infection? Control of diabetes? It is unproductive to try to answer general questions about whether computers are effective. Like drugs, some uses of information technologies in schools are probably effective, and some are not.

As educators began to think seriously about the educational usefulness of computers and other information technologies, they devised two general categories: teaching *about* information technology and teaching *with* technology. These categories clearly differentiate two ways technology can be put to use in the classroom. The following lists exemplify each type.

TEACHING ABOUT TECHNOLOGY

- Keyboarding lessons for elementary schoolchildren
- A computer literacy class for middle-grade students that covers word processing and other applications programs
- A class in programming for high-school students that teaches languages such as Pascal, C++, or Visual Basic
- A college course in designing web pages using the Java and HTML programming languages
- A certificate program at a community college for students interested in becoming certified computer network managers

TEACHING WITH TECHNOLOGY

- Sixth-grade students create a history of their town and produce a multimedia document that includes text, images, video, and audio interviews.
- Middle-grade students use computer-controlled science probes to take a number of measures of environmental pollution and collaboratively write a "State of the City" brief that identifies regional problems, and use background material they locate on the Web to propose a set of solutions to the most pressing problems.
- High-school students in a social studies class work in small collaborative groups to develop four "histories" of the Vietnam War. One version represents the perspective of the U.S. government. Another represents the view of U.S. protesters. Another represents the North Vietnamese perspective, and a fourth represents the viewpoint of villagers from one of the most hotly contested areas in South Vietnam.
- College students in a chemistry class use virtual reality software to create and "walk through" a molecule as part of an effort to learn about the structure of compounds.

Whether you *teach about* technology or *teach with* technology, students may use technology extensively in the classroom. The difference is in the focus. When you are **teaching about technology,** the primary purpose is for students to learn how to use certain tools of technology: word-processing programs, presentation software such as *PowerPoint*, programming languages such as Visual Basic, or a resource such as the World Wide Web. When you are **teaching with technology**, the focus of learning is on a subject or topic: social studies, mathematics, history, physics, and so on. Technology in this case is used to support teaching and learning in these areas.

Computer literacy courses and courses on other computer-related topics, such as programming, are important but are not the focus of this chapter. This chapter focuses on the use of technology to support teaching and learning in other content domains. Even this focus is too broad to permit any general conclusions about the effectiveness of using computers in the classroom. Again, they are used in so many ways that nothing meaningful can be said about teaching with technology. We still need a way of organizing the thousands of examples of teaching with technology into meaningful categories.

One effort is the Type I and Type II categorical scheme discussed in earlier chapters. A second way was proposed by Reeves (1998): "First, students can learn 'from' media and technology, and second, they can learn 'with' media and technology" (p. 1). Reeves goes on to describe these two categories. **Learning from** involves receiving information from media. He cites two examples of this approach: (1) educational television and (2) integrated learning systems. Most learning-from applications are based on behavioral theories of learning, specifically on the idea that technology can tutor the student. A typical learning-from application involves four steps:

1. exposing students to messages encoded in media and delivered by technology,
2. assuming that students perceive and encode these messages,
3. requiring a response to indicate that messages have been received, and
4. providing feedback as to the adequacy of the response. (Reeves, 1998, p. 2)

Drill-and-practice programs, tutorial software, integrated learning systems, and some simulations based on behavioral theory all follow this basic format. Most educational software produced in the twentieth century used the learning-from model.

Learning-from applications are integrated into the classroom in a relatively straightforward manner. They generally take the role of the teacher, but they often work as individual tutors so that some aspects of the teaching approach can be customized for each individual student. Customization is typically limited to the pace of instruction and the amount of remedial work provided. The goals of instruction are generally the same for all students, and the methods of instruction are usually built into the software.

Reeves's second category, **learning with,** is generally compatible with constructivist theories of learning. Students use computers and other forms of information technology as **cognitive tools.**

Computer-based cognitive tools have been intentionally adapted or developed to function as intellectual partners to enable and facilitate critical thinking and higher order learning. Examples of cognitive tools include: databases, spreadsheets, semantic networks, expert systems, communications software such as teleconferencing programs, on-line collaborative knowledge construction environments, multimedia/hypermedia construction software, and computer programming languages. (Reeves, 1998, p. 3)

Learning-with resources are not integrated into the classroom in a straightforward manner. The cognitive tools are given to students who then use them in ways that are at least partially determined by the students. "Learners themselves function as designers using media and technology as tools for analyzing the world, accessing and interpreting information, and organizing their personal knowledge, and representing what they know to others" (Reeves, 1998, p. 3).

Reeves' learning-from and learning-with metaphors are similar to the Type I and Type II categories presented earlier in this book. This chapter focuses on integration—how technology can play a role in the classroom. This topic has been addressed many times in the literature. Often, the result has been a recipe. Teachers are given a series of steps they are to follow to create a useful lesson. Two popular recipes are the **Madeline Hunter** direct-instruction model, and Gagné's **events of instruction.**

Hunter's approach to direct or **teacher-centered** instruction has seven steps (Kuzlik, 2000):

1. Objectives.   Begin the preparation of a lesson by developing a clear, precise set of objectives. What do you want to accomplish in the lesson?

2. Standards.   Develop standards or expectations for what you want the students to accomplish. Convey those standards to the students and explain how the lesson will be taught. Students thus begin their study with an understanding of what is expected of them and an explanation of how they will be taught. The expectations include knowledge to be acquired and skills to be learned, and students will know precisely how to demonstrate this knowledge and how well.

3. Anticipatory Set.   Prepare students for a lesson in advance. For example, involve the student's attention with a story, an analogy, or a problem, or present a structure or "advance organizer" that will guide the students' thinking.

4. Teaching.   Teaching has three phases: input, modeling, and checking for understanding. First, the teacher delivers information (input). This can take many forms—a lecture, reading assignment, video, field trip, computer program, or visit to a website. Then the teacher models what will be expected of the students. If the lesson is on geometry, the teacher may model how to use a theorem to analyze a figure. In the modeling stage, the teacher explains difficult concepts and helps students understand the facts or skills being taught. Finally, the teacher checks for understanding, often with probing questions, to be sure the students have "got it."

If the check shows students have not understood the concept or skill, it should be retaught.

5. Guided Practice/Monitoring.   Once students understand the concept being taught, give them the opportunity to practice applying the concept with your guidance and support. If students are learning a concept in algebra, for example, present the class with a set of problems to be solved that involve the application of the concept. As students work on the problems, walk around the room and check each student's progress, offering praise, support, and guidance as needed.

6. Closure.   Once students have successfully completed practice under your guidance, bring closure to the activity. Help students realize they have reached a new level of understanding—they have learned something new. At this time, teachers should help students deal with any confusing issues or questions they have and summarize key points in the lesson.

7. Independent Practice.   Students should now be ready to work on their own. They can apply what they have learned to similar and not-so-similar contexts or problems, either in class or at home. The goal is to consolidate learning and reinforce what students know or can do.

Hundreds of thousands of teachers were taught to write lesson plans using the Madeline Hunter method when they were in college. Hunter's approach is best suited to creating lessons of the teaching-from type. Many tutorials and drills have been developed using this model. A great many others have been created using a second direct-instruction model: Robert Gagné's events of instruction (Gagné, 1977; Gagné, Briggs, & Wagner, 1992; Gagné & Driscoll, 1988). According to Gagné, there are nine events of instruction:

1. Gaining Attention.   Alert the student that some important information is about to be received.

2. Inform the Learner of the Objectives.   It is important for students to know the purpose of the lesson. Tell students simply and precisely what they will be able to do after the lesson.

3. Stimulate Recall of Prerequisite Learning.   Most lessons require students to use knowledge and skills they already have to begin learning the new material. Teachers may simply remind students of that knowledge or provide some review of the prerequisites.

4. Present Stimulus Material.   Students are presented with the material they are to learn. This may be done in many different ways, but a typical pattern involves dividing the content into small units and presenting some basic material first, then presenting more complex material, or material that builds on the

material already presented. There is a great deal of research and professional practice knowledge on how to break material down and on what types of support
should be provided as the material is presented to students.

5. Provide Learner Guidance.   The support provided while students learn the
material can take many forms. For example, students may be assisted in creating
a semantic map of the content. Much of what is called *learning* in this theory involves transferring material to be learned from short-term to long-term memory.
Cognitive science research has studied the process of storing material in long-term
memory and has many suggestions for helping students do that. West, Farmer,
and Wolff (1991) have written an excellent and readable book on the learning
aides developed by cognitive scientists titled *Instructional Design: Implications from
Cognitive Science.*

6. Elicit Performance.   Once students have stored the material in long-term
memory, the next step is to have them respond in ways that demonstrate they
have learned the content.

7. Provide Feedback and Assess Performance.   As students perform, the
teacher should provide feedback on how accurate or correct their responses are.
The teacher assesses performance, provides information on any errors, and re-
teaches or provides remediation when necessary.

8. Enhance Retention and Transfer (Generalization).   This final event of
instruction involves working with students to facilitate and encourage both the
retention of what they have learned and the ability to use the information or skills
in different contexts. The teacher may, for example, present new problems that
require students to use the content they have learned to solve them.

   The Events of Instruction have been taught to many teachers and instructional technologists over the past 40 years as a general and relatively universal
model for teaching and learning. Preservice teacher-education students were
often required to use either the Madeline Hunter or events of instruction framework when they developed lesson plans. Neither of these is, however, a general
model. Both work best when the purpose is to create teacher-centered or direct
instruction. As you know from the previous two chapters, direct (or learning-
from) instruction is based primarily on behavioral theories of learning. Another
approach, student-centered instruction, is based on constructivist theories.

STUDENT-CENTERED INTEGRATION
OF TECHNOLOGY IN THE CLASSROOM

Constructivist educators must sometimes envy educators who advocate heavy
reliance on direct instruction. It is relatively easy to present Madeline Hunter's

model or the nine Events of Instruction. These two models are clear and concrete, and many preservice teacher-education students find them comforting because they provide structure and direction for creating decent lesson plans.

In contrast, constructivists trying to explain how to create a **student-centered** learning environment (the constructivist equivalent to a lesson plan) will quickly point out that they can only offer suggestions and that those suggestions will not be followed by all constructivist learning environments. It must sometimes be frustrating to both the professor and the student. But that is, for better or worse, a characteristic of constructivist mentality. Concrete, do-this then-do-this guidelines do not exist for creating CLE. At best, only general principles, like the ones developed by Jonassen (presented in Chapter 7), or illustrative case studies of how someone else did it can be used to create these learning environments.

The remainder of this chapter presents two case studies that demonstrate how some constructivist educators developed and implemented CLEs that use technology to support learning.

Anchored Instruction for a Middle-Grade Language Arts Class

Cena and Mitchell (1998) described a language arts unit they developed for middle-grade students. They wanted to combine language arts skills with study of content in other subjects. To do this they selected an anchor (see Chapters 6 and 7) and developed a learning environment around it. In their description of the unit, they divided the work into eight steps:

Choose a Unit of Study.   Cena and Mitchell selected the unit themselves, but they point out that in many cases teachers do this with the participation of students (or give students most of the responsibility). In this case, they selected life in the Middle Ages as the focus of the unit.

Identify an Anchor.   One purpose of an anchor is to "establish a common core of knowledge for all class members" (p. 559). For their anchor they selected two PBS videos based on a famous book about cathedrals.

Present the Anchor.   Students viewed the videos and worked on a "thinksheet" that helped them organize what they had learned and what interested them about the Middle Ages. With the help of the teacher they identified the following possible topics: (1) technology of medieval building construction, (2) class distinctions of medieval society, (3) the role of religion in everyday life, (4) political and economic forces, and (5) the artistic design of a cathedral. They selected the fourth topic as a focus for their thinksheet.

Discuss the Anchor.   Class discussions covered what had been learned from watching the video. Students used their thinksheets to help them participate in the discussion, and the teacher created a graphic representation of the discussion on a large chart.

Generate Research Questions.   Students formed collaborative groups to review the information on the chart and to consider research questions they wanted to pursue. Cena and Mitchell concluded that these students, who did not have much experience with anchored instruction, could develop research questions but needed more help and support from the teacher than did students who had extensive experience.

> Students may need to know the difference between simple remembering and more thoughtful types of questions. A research question such as "How long did it take to build a cathedral?" may be answered in a short sentence with little research. Conversely, a question such as "Why did people decide to build cathedrals?" will require deep thought and promote greater research. In general, teachers will want to encourage students to develop a variety of types of research questions—some easy and others more thought provoking. (p. 560)

Organize Research Communities.   Once the students created research questions of interest to them, the teacher helped them create research communities—small groups of students who were interested in the same research question. In classes where students have little experience working in collaborative groups, the teacher must provide considerable support and mentoring to help students develop the skills they need to work successfully. This includes learning how to organize the learning community, "planning who will do what part of the research, and establishing individual accountability and positive group interdependency" (p. 560).

Conduct Research.   The collaborative groups have two jobs: learning how to work together and doing the research. Students may need help with both these jobs. If they do not have research skills, the teacher may spend time helping them learn to search efficiently for relevant information on the World Wide Web and to use both traditional and multimedia materials in the school's learning resource center. Sometimes a minilesson, a form of direct instruction that is also called *just-in-time instruction*, may be appropriate. For example, a collaborative group may decide to search the web for good sites but discover they do not have the skills to use the best search engines. The teacher may teach a 10- to 20-minute minilesson on searching to that group.

In this way, students studying a topic in social studies also learn a great deal about several language arts topics: how to find information and write research notes, how to organize research data, and how to create a presentation of the results of the research. At various times the teacher may be involved in encouraging a collaborative group, teaching a minilesson, being taught by a group as they work on their research question, and mentoring a group that is working on a thorny research problem.

Present the Research.   When each group has completed its research and pre-pared a report or presentation, the groups have an opportunity to present their findings to the class. And "after the last group has presented, the teacher and the students select new topics or extensions of the current topic for another anchored instruction unit" (p. 561).

Although Cena and Mitchell divided their unit into eight steps, these steps are more a way of organizing the process of the unit work than a set of guidelines they expect others to follow. This unit presents one form of anchored instruction, but many different forms are possible.

Using a Simulation in a Fifth-Grade Class

Our second case study of constructivist learning illustrates how a social studies simulation might be used in the fifth grade. In this hypothetical study, a fifth-grade teacher named Jan wants to use a simulation that is relevant to several social studies objectives on migration. The process of using a particular simulation might be divided into six phases (Willis, Hovey, & Hovey, 1987).

Selection.   The process begins with the selection of a simulation. Local sources such as the school media center or the district software library may be explored. In addition, a number of websites feature simulations that can be used in classrooms with an Internet connection. When Jan, our hypothetical fifth-grade teacher, searched the Internet using the terms *simulation* and *education,* she had 345 hits. One of them, the Washington Social Studies Site (http://www.learningspace.org/socialstudies/student_projects/sim.html), was linked to several online simula-tions. She did not find what she wanted, however, and continued her search. She looked through software catalogs, teacher magazines that publish reviews and de-scriptions of educational software, education journals, and electronic discussion groups for teachers on the Internet.

Jan also used the CD-ROM version of the ERIC database to search for infor-mation using the search terms *social studies AND elementary AND simulation.* She is taking graduate courses at a university in her area and has access to the database at the university's library. The *AND*s in the search string tell the system to find ar-ticles, papers, and books that deal with all three topics. The search produced sev-eral hits, and Jan looked up articles in four publications: *Learning and Leading with Technology, Electronic Learning, Technology and Learning,* and *Computers in the Schools.* As she read several articles, ideas about how to incorporate simulations into her lessons developed. In addition, she found references to six different simulations that might be appropriate.

After further study, she narrowed her choice of simulations to three. The list was reduced to one after she attended a regional conference on computers in schools. At that conference, she attended a presentation by an elementary social studies teacher in a nearby district who described in detail how she had integrated a program called *The Oregon Trail* into her social studies classes. After talking with that teacher, Jan selected this program for her first simulation. The program is distributed by The Learning Company and is available in several versions. She bought the simulation from her classroom supplies budget and began planning how to introduce it to her students.

Adaptation.   Virtually any simulation you select requires some adaptation to fit local needs and conditions. Issues such as the time available and the resources needed can require teachers to make changes in the way simulations are used. Adaptations may also have to be made depending on whether objectives and a preferred teaching/learning style differ from those of the simulation's developers. *The Oregon Trail* simulates the trek of pioneers on the Oregon Trail in 1847 (Figure 8.1). The trip begins in Independence, Missouri, and ends in Oregon City, Oregon. Players must make many decisions during the 2000-mile trip. The cost of goods and the probabilities of different events are based on books about the period and historical records such as diaries.

The objectives listed in the documentation coincided with several of Jan's, and after looking over the recommended lesson plan in the teacher's manual for the simulation, Jan decided to use most of the suggestions. She did make one major change in line with her emphasis on multicultural issues. At several points in the simulation the players must decide what to do when riders approach. Many students, perhaps because of the emphasis in western movies on the treachery of Native Americans,

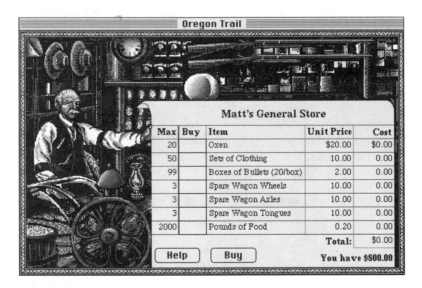

FIGURE 8.1   Before beginning the trip on the Oregon Trail you must decide what, and how much, to buy at Matt's general store.

The Oregon Trail® is a copyright and registered trademark owned by MECC. Used with permission. All rights reserved.

decide to circle the wagons and begin shooting when Native Americans approach. When other riders approach, however, they are assumed to be friendly and students do not try to defend themselves. The historical data indicates, however, that Native Americans were often helpful to people on the Oregon Trail whereas other riders were often bandits bent on robbing the traveling pioneers. Jan modified the lesson plan to help students recognize how prejudice can influence decisions.

Preparation.   The manual for *The Oregon Trail* includes a 5-day lesson plan that begins with a discussion of the westward movement and ends with follow-up activities that include a comparison of the student's results on the simulation with the actual results of wagon trains to Oregon. Much of the lesson described in the manual involves teacher-centered instruction. Students are given information they need to play the simulation successfully, then they play it. One of the assumptions of Jan's constructivist teaching philosophy is that telling students facts is often not as effective as other approaches. She modified the 5-day lesson plan so that groups of students begin playing *The Oregon Trail* without any preparation. Jan predicted most of them would not get to Oregon because they did not have the information needed to make informed decisions. The prediction was accurate. All the teams died on the trail.

After the disaster, she helped students organize into groups to discuss what they needed to know about the westward movement before playing the simulation again. The groups of students then used resources Jan provided, as well as resources in the school library and on the Web, to create briefing reports for settlers planning to make the trip to Oregon. When the students searched the Internet using the term *Oregon Trail*, they found The Oregon Trail website (http://www.isu. edu/~trinmich/Oregontrail.html), which has much valuable information. The site supports a PBS video, *The Oregon Trail*, rather than the simulation, but was still a very useful site for Jan's students.

The briefing reports were prepared with desktop publishing software and the documents were shared with the class. Each report concentrated on a particular type of information the students considered important. One, for example, covered the cost and type of goods needed on the Oregon Trail. Another dealt with relationships between pioneers and others on the trail, and a third explained weather patterns on the trail at different times of the year, as well as the geography of different regions of the trail. In addition, before playing the simulation a second time, each group designated a "senior consultant," who met with other groups to discuss their findings and make recommendations.

Support.   When students play a simulation, the role of the teacher depends on the objectives of the lesson, the type of simulation used, and many other factors. The teacher's role can range from that of a war games–style referee to helper and guide to hardware and software troubleshooter. Most uses of simulations call for the teacher to play many different roles at various points in the process.

Important windows of learning opportunities, or teachable moments, may occur while students are playing a simulation (or while they are planning their play); however, deciding when to take a particular role is probably as important as deciding which role to take. Encouraging a group of students to continue puzzling through and analyzing a problem that has stumped them can be the best approach, even when your inclination is to give students the "answer." On the other hand, letting students struggle with a problem well past the point at which they have exhausted all their problem-solving skills discourages them and wastes time. Intervening with suggestions, guidance, hints, or even direct instruction on a critical concept can be the best approach. There is no recipe for making these decisions, however. They are based on the teacher's interpretation of the situation.

When the lesson began, Jan explained the mechanics of running the simulation to one person from each small group while others read some of the handouts Jan had duplicated from the manual. Then students played the simulation once in groups of four or five. (Jan would prefer groups of three or four but she has 25 students in her class and a cluster of five computers in the back of her classroom.) Decisions were to be made by the group after discussion (Figure 8.2). After each group had run the simulation once, the small groups discussed reasons why their wagon train did not make it to Oregon City. The groups developed lists of subjects for which they needed more information, and Jan helped the class organize the lists developed by each small group into a master list of subjects. Then each group selected topics to research and report on in writing.

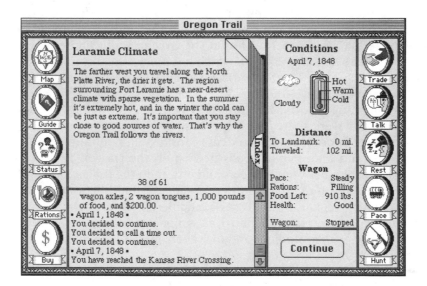

FIGURE 8.2   *The Oregon Trail* requires many decisions. Some of the types of decisions players can make are listed on the left and right sides of this screen. Other parts of the screen provide information on the climate in the region and the current conditions in the wagon train.

After groups distributed their reports and talked to the consultants, each group formulated strategies for second and third (if time permitted) attempts. (Most groups were successful by the third attempt.) As groups ran the simulation, Jan took a supportive but nonintrusive role.

Debriefing.   An important, though often overlooked, aspect of any instructional procedure is the post-activity debriefing, or closure. Debriefing is especially important with simulations. During the debriefing phase, a discussion of the issues students dealt with in the simulation often helps them consolidate the concepts and procedures they learned. Debriefing also helps students identify misconceptions or false assumptions about the simulation and provides an opportunity for students to discuss the differences between the simulation and reality.

Jan's follow-up activities for Oregon Trail differed somewhat from those in the program's manual because Jan's objectives and teaching philosophy differed. Some of the recommended activities were used, such as having a group write a letter to relatives "back East" describing hardships of the trip. Even this activity, however, was chosen by the students rather than selected by the teacher. Most of Jan's other debriefing activities were not in the manual. They included a discussion of the reasons for migration, with applications to more recent migrations to the United States (e.g., from Haiti, Cuba, South Vietnam, Mexico, and Eastern Europe). Jan also spent some time debriefing students on how collaboration helped them succeed and discussing how problems in collaborating and cooperating could be avoided in future activities.

Evaluation.   The final phase in using a simulation activity is evaluation. This does not mean students take a multiple-choice test on the information taught. The evaluation can take many forms and is often a thoughtful reflection on how the lesson progressed and where changes might make it more successful. Jan asked herself several questions: Did the simulation accomplish the desired cognitive and affective objectives? When it is used again, would it be more successful if some adjustments or changes were made? In many cases, students provide excellent suggestions for improving the way a simulation is used.

Most of Jan's methods of evaluation were informal. She examined the reports and analyses of the groups and asked students for suggestions during the debriefing phase. Jan concluded *The Oregon Trail* was a very effective focal activity for the study of migration, particularly during the westward expansion in the 1800s. However, she has planned to make two changes for next year. Students suggested that additional simulations be added to the lesson. Jan plans to find one or two more simulations on related topics. She also plans to use *The Oregon Trail* as part of her instruction on a math topic, probability. *The Oregon Trail* manual includes a list of the probabilities for events such as getting lost in the mountains (10 percent for each 2-week turn) and illness (25 percent if eating poorly, 19 percent if eating moderately, and 13 percent if eating well). After one round, Jan will provide students with the information on probabilities and help groups interpret the probabilities and use them to adjust their decisions to maximize the likelihood of reaching Oregon City. Adding this task to the work with *The Oregon Trail* will take a bit more time, but playing the simulation seems to create a teachable moment when students can learn and apply the concepts of probability—a topic they have had problems with in previous classes.

SUMMARY

There are many different ways to integrate computers into the classroom. Some of them involve teaching about technology and some involve teaching with technology. Information technology can be used in many different ways even when the technology is used to teach other topics. Some use the technology for a tutorial approach, but others use information technologies as cognitive tools.

QUESTIONS TO CONSIDER

1. Consider the different ways technology can be used in the classroom. What aspects of the subject you plan to teach could be effectively taught with technology that tutors the student? Why?

2. What aspects lend themselves to the cognitive tools approach? Why?

RELATED ACTIVITIES

1. Search the Internet for lesson plans on the subject you plan to teach. Analyze them and determine whether they follow the format proposed by Madeline Hunter, Gagné, or constructivist educators. Why?

2. Select an educational simulation or other cognitive tool and develop a lesson plan that integrates that technology into a learning activity.

3. Locate at least four papers on the topic of this chapter, technology integration. Analyze the assumptions the authors make. Do they work from a behaviorist perspective? Do they take into consideration cognitive science research? Is their approach based on constructivist theory?

REFERENCES

Cena, M., & Mitchell, J. (1998). Anchored instruction: A model for integrating the language arts through content area study. *Journal of Adolescent and Adult Literacy, 41*(7), 559–561.

Gagné, R. M. (1977). *The conditions of learning* (rev. ed.). New York: Holt, Rinehart and Winston.

Gagné, R. M., Briggs, L. J., & Wager, W. W. (1992). *Principles of instructional design* (Rev. ed.). New York: Harcourt, Brace, Jovanovich.

Gagné, R. M., Driscoll, M. P. (1988). *Essentials of learning for instruction* (Rev. ed.). Englewood Cliffs, NJ: Prentice Hall.

Kuzlik, R. (2000). *ADPRIMA: It's about education choices.* Retrieved March 14, 2000, from the World Wide Web: http://www.adprima.com/mainmenu.htm

Reeves, T. (1998). *The impact of media and technology in schools: A research report prepared for the Bertelsmann Foundation.* Athens: The University of Georgia.

West, C., Farmer, J., & Wolff, P. (1991). *Instructional design: Implications from cognitive science.* Hillsdale, NJ: Lawrence Erlbaum.

Willis, J., Hovey, L., & Hovey, K. (1987). *Computer simulations: A source book to learning in an electronic environment.* New York: Garland.

CHAPTER NINE

APPLICATIONS SOFTWARE IN THE CLASSROOM
Word Processing, Databases, and Spreadsheets

Goal: To understand the nature of three computer applications, word processing, database management, and electronic spreadsheets, and how these applications can be useful in education.

KEY TERMS

authentic writing (p. 197)

contextualized literacy learning (p. 200)

Corel's *WordPerfect Office* (p. 208)

database template (p. 207)

electronic thesaurus (p. 199)

field (p. 204)

flat file database (p. 203)

grammar checkers (p. 199)

inquiry projects (p. 200)

metacognition (p. 196)

Microsoft Office (p. 208)

process writing (p. 200)

record (p. 203)

relational database (p. 203)

spelling checkers (p. 199)

word wraparound (p. 194)

Chapter 1 pointed out that most computer applications were developed and first used by business, with education adopting them later. This is certainly true when it comes to electronic word processing, databases, and spreadsheets. As computers became available, business adopted them because they offered electronic tools that could make much of the work of business more efficient. They replaced the typewriter with the word processor; they replaced much of their bulky filing systems with electronic databases; and they replaced their ledgers with electronic spreadsheets. As the use of these new tools grew in business, educators began to discover that they had potential as natural teaching and learning tools.

This chapter provides an overview of three of the most useful and popular Type II educational applications for computers: word processing, database management, and spreadsheets. This chapter also explores concepts relating to using these applications as educational tools and examines some of the related software being used in education. We discuss some of the research on using these three applications, and explore techniques for integrating the computer into the curriculum using these relatively traditional educational computing tools.

WORD PROCESSING IN THE CLASSROOM

Prior to the advent of the World Wide Web, many computer users believed that word processing was the most useful of all computer applications. Back in 1989, Lillie, Hannum, and Stuck suggested that if a vote were taken in society at large on the most useful application of microcomputers, word processing would win. By 1995, Geisert and Futrell inferred that computers had revolutionized the business world by providing new ways of producing printed materials with word processors. In 1993, Lewis, commenting on the importance of word processing, asserted that such programs constituted the most popular uses of computers in homes, schools, and businesses.

As with all computer applications, schools have been slower than businesses and homes in adopting word processing, but the conversion is now largely a matter of history. Most middle-school, high-school, and higher-education students turn to word processing when they begin the task of completing written assignments.

WHAT WORD PROCESSING IS
AND HOW IT WORKS

Flake, McClintock, and Turner (1990) define a word processor as "a computer program that allows for writing, inserting, deleting, changing and formatting the written word" (p. 73). Long (1988) defines word processing as "using the computer to enter, store, manipulate, and print text in letters, reports, and books" (p. 92). Roberts and coauthors (1988) suggest that all word processors allow three related activities: "the ability to create and edit text; the ability to format and print text; and the ability to store and retrieve files or works in progress" (p. 4). Mandell and Mandell (1989) say that word processing is "a computer application that enables you to write, edit, format, print, store, and retrieve text" (p. 64). According to Geisert and Futrell (2000), nearly all present-day word processors enable the user to produce text, edit text, save text, retrieve text, and print text. After reading these definitions, it should be clear that word processing is a computer writing tool that replaces traditional writing tools, such as paper and pencil or typewriter.

THE ADVANTAGES OF WORD PROCESSING

The major advantage of word processing over other writing tools is that the word processor imparts to the user great power and ease of revision. This power is so important that moving from typewriting to word processing is even more beneficial than moving from handwriting to typewriting. Although the typewriter is a wonderful writing tool, its major advantage over handwriting is speed. However, typewriting does not make it easier to make revisions. In fact, it could be argued that typewritten text is even more difficult to revise than is handwritten text. After all, text that is handwritten in pencil can be easily erased whereas the same cannot be said for typewritten text. Word processing, on the other hand, brings the advantage of speed, while making even major revisions possible with only a keystroke or two. To give you some idea of what word processing is like, we contrast typewriting versus word processing an essay for an English course.

An Imaginary Typewriting Session

To begin, you roll a piece of typing paper into your typewriter and begin typing. As you approach the end of each line, you listen for a bell. When you hear the bell, you finish the word you are typing (if space permits) and then push a button that causes the typewriter to space down to the next line and move the carriage to the beginning of that line. Minor typing errors can be corrected fairly easily if you catch them as you make them. If not, correction is much more difficult. Many major revisions are impossible without extensive retyping. For example, if you complete your rough draft and then decide that you should have added a paragraph in the middle of page 7, you will have to retype the entire document from that page to the end of the text.

An Imaginary Word-Processing Session

To begin word processing, you turn on your computer and load your word-processing program. As you type, the computer keeps track of how much space is left at the end of each line and automatically moves to the next line when appropriate, taking any partial words to that line. This automatic feature is called **word wraparound.**

Minor typing errors are simple to correct. If you misspell a word, you use the arrow keys to move the cursor (usually a flashing line or block indicating your place in the document) to the word and type the correct word over the incorrect one. You can delete an extra space with a single keystroke. Such corrections can be made as easily at the time errors are made as at any later time.

Most popular word-processing software today provides a feature that automatically checks your spelling as you type. Such spell checker features cue you to any words not found in a huge electronic dictionary by underlining the word in red. You then have several options: ignoring the misspelling cue (as in the case of proper names), choosing a suggested spelling shown on the screen, or editing the word yourself. Most popular word-processing software also provides a grammar checker that catches certain common errors and offers suggestions for revision.

Even major revisions can be made easily. To add a paragraph to the middle of page 7, you simply place the cursor at the point where you wish the paragraph to begin. Then you type the paragraph. As you type, the computer automatically moves to the right all of the following text on that line to make room for the new text. The computer also adjusts the rest of the document all the way to the end of the text, making each page end at a new, appropriate spot without any retyping whatsoever. You can print out any number of clean copies at any time.

When you are finished with the document, you can print out a final draft. You may also decide to save a copy of the document on the hard drive of your computer or to any other type of storage device, such as a floppy disk. The resulting document is an electronic file that can easily be sent anywhere in the world over the Internet. When printing your completed document, you can specify top and bottom as well as right and left margins, order automatic page numbering, place a header or footer on every page, change the size of type, or make other formatting changes.

WORD PROCESSING AS A TYPE II
EDUCATIONAL APPLICATION

It should be obvious that word processing is a good example of a Type II computer application. Like many other Type II applications, word processing begins with a blank screen, or, figuratively speaking, a blank sheet of paper. It is an extremely powerful way to fill that screen, or page, with whatever the user desires. Empowering the user is always a strong clue that an application falls into the category of Type II.

Many teachers sense the potential of word processing in education. Research has demonstrated that word processing is effective in teaching writing (Geisert & Futrell, 2000; MacArthur, 1988). The literature of the past 12 years or so has fully endorsed word processing as a tool for teaching writing. Most of these endorsements are based on (1) logic, (2) personal experiences of an author using word processing to aid professional writing, or (3) personal experiences in teaching writing using word processing.

The literature on word processing as a tool for teaching writing falls into four categories: (1) ease of production and revision, (2) cognitive advantages, (3) social advantages, and (4) attitudinal advantages.

Ease of Production and Revision of Text

Ease of production and revision is the most obvious advantage of word processing, whether it is used by professional writers, teachers, students, or anyone else. Roblyer, Castine, and King (1988) suggested that teachers have found word processing attractive primarily because it takes the drudgery out of composition. Dudley-Marling (1985) suggested that students and teachers favor word processing

> because good writing requires editing and editing requires recopying, which is tedious and may even be viewed as punishment.... Word processing makes editing easy. Text can be inserted, deleted, or moved about with the touch of a key. Once satisfied with what they have written, students can obtain nicely typed, perfectly formatted texts by performing a few additional operations. (p. 390)

Word Processing and Cognitive Advantages

Some educators base their word-processing advocacy on cognitive advantages. Kinzer, Sherwood, and Bransford (1986), for example, suggested that word processing facilitates efficient use of memory and provides more immediate reinforcement:

> The word processor enables student writers to free short-term memory by concentrating on large-scale revision of ideas, while holding concerns with spelling and punctuation for later. In addition, having several neatly revised drafts quickly available allows the writer instant feedback on global revisions without the burden of reading through messy corrections and deletions. Having the capability to receive clean copy immediately after revising provides strong, immediate reinforcement. (p. 239)

Bangert-Drowns (1993) cites two possible cognitive advantages of teaching children to write with word processors. The first is that ease in revising text may change the way children think about written communication. That is, they may correctly begin to perceive it as a dynamic and easily changeable medium that is closely related to thinking and speaking. Second, word processors may enable children to concentrate on more complex writing acts (those that involve increasing clarity, for example) by relieving them of the many burdens of getting their thoughts down on paper and making mechanical revisions.

Other applications that focus on cognition include word processors that are specially designed with an interactive component. The programs contain prompts to stimulate self-questioning and self-instruction. Such programs attempt to make use of metacognitive principles. (**Metacognition** refers to the knowledge we have about our own thought processes, in this case thought processes related to writing.) Bangert-Drowns (1993) describes such programs as follows: "Unlike tools that try to make certain tasks invisible, these tools try to open up cognitive processes to reflection and thus *increase* the user's mental effort by stimulating the kind of inner dialogues that typify self-regulated learners" (p. 71).

Word Processing and Social Advantages

Hill (1992) emphasizes the importance of making writing serve a real purpose in school and avoiding what she calls "kid-work," or writing activities that are artificial, such as multiple-choice or fill-in-the-blank activities. Instead, she emphasizes that writing should be about real subjects that affect students and should address real audiences, such as peers or community members, rather than the writing teacher solely. She adds that computers and word-processing programs are real-world tools that should be used for real-world activities, not kid-work.

MacArthur, Graham, and Schwartz (1993) agree and define a process approach as folllows:

> In our view, process approaches have two key features. First, they emphasize the communicative purpose of writing by establishing a community of writers in the classroom. Students write on meaningful topics and share their work with audiences of peers. Second, they focus on the cognitive and social processes of writing—planning, writing, revising, editing, and publishing—by providing a predictable structure to support these processes. (p. 674)

These authors go on to emphasize the importance of **authentic writing:** "Students' awareness of the goals of writing develops gradually as they engage in tasks that are meaningful to them and that have authentic purposes and audiences" (p. 674). A related social advantage is the opportunity for collaboration (teaming up with others) in writing classes using word processing (Butler & Cox, 1992; Dickinson, 1986; Heap, 1986; Montague & Fonseca, 1994). Collaboration is seen as desirable for its own sake and has been shown to have a beneficial effect on writing.

Word Processing and Attitudinal Advantages

Many educators value word processing because of its potential to change students' attitudes about writing. Flake, McClintock, and Turner (1990) emphasized that word processing can change students' attitudes about revision by helping them to realize that their work is part of a drafting process instead of finished copy. Geisert and Futrell (2000) agree that computers and word processing can be used to improve students' attitudes toward writing. They hypothesize that the improvement in attitude comes about for three reasons. First, even though computers are daily becoming more common in our culture, they are still novel and interesting, especially as tools for use in schools. Second, students may begin to attach more importance to writing when they see that an expensive, prestigious, and scarce tool has been provided for this activity. Third, the computer printout is neat and professional looking, adding even more importance and authenticity to the writing task.

What about Keyboarding Skills?

A variety of questions can be asked about keyboarding. Teachers are sometimes concerned that young children may not be able to master keyboarding well enough to benefit from word processing. As early as 1988, Collis pointed out that most studies have shown that young children can learn to handle the keyboarding required to profit from word processing. MacArthur, Graham, and Schwartz (1993) emphasize that keyboarding skills are important but point out that students need not develop sophisticated touch-typing skills to benefit from word processing: "A reasonable goal for typing skill is for students to use the correct fingering with occasional looks at the keyboard and to type about as fast as they write by hand (usually about eight to ten words per minute in sixth grade)" (p. 676).

Geisert and Futrell (2000) reviewed the literature on keyboarding and keyboarding instruction and concluded that most children enjoy learning to use a keyboard and learn to do so quickly and easily. Furthermore, they suggest that direct instruction in keyboarding is helpful and that keyboarding software is one efficient way to implement such a program. Finally, they suggest that instruction in keyboarding is a controversial curricular issue that should be addressed by an entire school policy rather than by individual teachers.

SUMMARY OF RESEARCH ON WORD PROCESSING IN EDUCATION

Of the research available on word processing (Geisert & Futrell, 2000; Montague, 1990), endorsements for word processing are far more common than empirical studies of effectiveness. Roblyer and Edwards (2000) summarized extensive reviews of the research by stating:

> Generally, studies seem to conclude that students who use word processing in the context of writing instruction programs tend to write more, revise more (at least on a surface level), make fewer errors, and have better attitudes toward their writing than students who do not use word processing. (p. 116)

Also, it is important to point out that the trend toward school-aged children using word processing for writing seems irreversible, regardless of whether research can show that it improves writing. According to a 1998 national report, the percentage of students who used a computer at home or at school to write a story or a paper increased dramatically between 1984 and 1998. For fourth-graders the increase was from 23 percent to 79 percent, for eighth-graders the increase was from 15 percent to 91 percent, and for eleventh-graders the increase was from 20 percent to 96 percent.

OTHER COMPUTER WRITING AIDS

Word processors, idea processors (tools that assist in the organization of ideas), and the newer interactive programs are not the only computer writing aids. Supplementary aids are sometimes added to word processors and sometimes produced as separate tools.

Grammar Checkers

Grammar checkers are not well named because they do not check for all kinds of grammar errors. They can also check nongrammatical errors as well. For example, they can call the writer's attention to commonly misused words such as *affect/effect* and *principal/principle,* and many can check for trite phrases such as *at this point in time,* and *in order to.* Some flag sexist language. Improper punctuation can also be highlighted.

Properly used, grammar checkers can be useful writing aids. Willis (1987) evaluated all term papers written in a university graduate class and concluded that over 70 percent could have been substantially improved had the students used a grammar checker. Users should remember, however, that suggestions are only suggestions, and final judgment concerning changes is the responsibility of the human writer, who is aware of the entire context.

Spelling Checkers

Spelling checkers scan documents to find, in context, any words not contained in a program file that serves as an electronic dictionary. The user then decides whether to correct the spelling or to allow the spelling to remain unchanged. Nearly all word-processing programs today offer the option of having the spell checker operate during writing so that it flags any spelling not in the dictionary file as it is typed. As mentioned earlier, the writer can either modify a misspelled word onscreen or choose an alternate spelling from a list of words to replace the misspelled word. Most spelling checkers permit users to add words to the dictionary, which prevents the spelling checker from identifying and flagging any words—proper names, professional jargon, or other unusual words—that a user decides are acceptable spellings. Once added to the dictionary, these words are not flagged in the future.

Electronic Thesaurus

An **electronic thesaurus** allows the user to view a list of synonyms for any word in a word-processed document. The user may choose one of the suggested words to be substituted in the text or may retain the original word. Again, little research has been conducted on the use of electronic thesauruses. However, their use may result in user vocabulary growth and the production of manuscripts with more varied vocabularies.

Desktop Publishing

A useful variation on word processing is a software category known as *desktop publishing.* Lewis (1993) describes such programs as follows:

Desktop publishing programs provide writers with the tools to "publish" their own stories, books, reports, newsletters, and newspapers. Like word processors, they allow easy manipulation of text. However, their distinguishing characteristic is their capacity for integrating text and graphics in a variety of different page formats, or layouts. With most desktop publishers, students can write text, arrange that text in a single- or multicolumn format, add graphics to illustrate the text, and insert heading and picture captions. Whereas word processors emphasize text, and graphics programs are concerned mainly with manipulating graphics, desktop publishing programs represent a combination of these tools in one integrated program. (pp. 322–323)

Desktop publishing programs can be very helpful in writing curriculums that employ computers in a process approach. Because process approaches to teaching writing emphasize the importance of developing in students a sense of audience, the act of publishing can contribute to developing that awareness. When students realize that they are writing for real communication rather than merely to satisfy a teacher's assignment, learning to write becomes highly motivating.

AN EXAMPLE OF USING WORD PROCESSING IN THE CLASSROOM

Baker (2000), in a case study report, provided an excellent example of how word processing can be integrated into the normal flow of classroom learning activities. Baker describes a fourth-grade technology-rich classroom, where every student had access to a computer with a rich array of information technology devices, including CD-ROM drives, laser disk players, and a modem making possible one Internet connection. These fourth-grade students spent much of their classroom time in **inquiry projects,** which involved **process writing.**

An inquiry project began with the teacher announcing a new inquiry topic. Students read assigned reading materials to identify questions relating to the topic. Students then formed into inquiry teams. Each team searched out information relating to their topic and interests using both print and electronic resources. An inquiry project culminated in each team "teaching" the rest of the class what they learned about their topic. An important part of preparing for this teaching/sharing assignment was to create written materials that organized and summarized findings. The writing process involved brainstorming, drafting, editing, revising, and publishing. Word processing, and related tools such as idea processing, provided the writing medium for this entire process.

Baker discusses **contextualized literacy learning** as an important underpinning to process writing. In this type of learning, students don't just learn a skill, but also learn when and how to use the skill. For example, the use of commas can be explained and students can complete exercises emphasizing comma use, but that doesn't mean they will be able to use commas correctly when they actually sit down to write a story or report. During contextualized literacy learning projects, students write, their writing is critiqued, they revise, they polish, and finally they present their written work as a public document. The key factor in this process is to simulate real-life writing and thus, in the case of comma usage, real-life use of commas.

COMMON SCHOOL-ORIENTED WORD-PROCESSING SYSTEMS

Although word-processing software was purchased as stand-alone packages at one time, today almost all word processors are part of some integrated software package that combines the features of word processing with those of electronic spreadsheets, databases, graphics and charting tools, as well as tools for computer telecommunications. Whereas many schools use high-powered integrated software packages such as *Microsoft Office,* which provides *Microsoft Word* as a word-processing tool, a couple of integrated software packages designed more for school use are still popular. *Microsoft Works* and *AppleWorks* were among the early software packages used in schools during the advent of the microcomputer movement. Both of these packages have undergone numerous iterations and have evolved along with advances in hardware and peripherals. The word-processing tools in each of these software packages provide all the basic word-processing elements and more. Judging by their long history, we expect these two integrated software packages to continue to be used widely in schools for a long time to come.

ELECTRONIC DATABASES IN THE CLASSROOM

The simplest definition of the term *electronic database* is an organized collection of information that is stored electronically. Database management software turns a computer into a machine that can be used to create electronic databases and to manipulate the information stored in such databases.

The term *database* may be used to describe collections of information that range from a simple set of note cards in a shoebox to a large library. Even the library at your school can be thought of as a giant database. When such information is organized and stored electronically, the result is an electronic database. Because modern technology is constantly expanding our ability to store information electronically, information we collect in libraries today will very likely be accessible in electronic databases in the near future.

WHAT DATABASE MANAGEMENT IS AND HOW IT WORKS

Organizing and storing information are natural applications for a computer. As we move further into the information age, more and more information will be organized into, or converted to, some form of electronic media. Small desktop and laptop computers can now store vast amounts of information that just a few years ago could only be stored on the very largest computers.

The filing cabinet used to be a common symbol for describing an electronic database because the first electronic databases were little more than electronic storage bins. Information stored in these electronic databases could be retrieved and examined in much the same way that information in a filing cabinet can be retrieved and examined. Today, however, database management software is available that does much more than just store information. Current software allows for powerful manipulation of data as well.

The power of the computer as a tool resides in two unique qualities. First, it can manipulate symbols much faster than the human brain. Second, it can manipulate symbols much more accurately than the human brain. As advances are made in database software, more of the power of the computer is used. Easy-to-use database management systems are now available that can organize, sort, rearrange, and exchange information in a matter of milliseconds with perfect accuracy.

Most early electronic databases were small, in terms of number of records they could hold, and narrow in focus. In earlier eras, educators tended to think of useful electronic databases in terms of a listing of the items in a school library stored on a computer disk or a roster of all the students that could be used for mailing lists. Two trends in the use of information technology beginning in the early 1990s changed our thinking about the concept of an educational database. These two trends, discussed in more depth elsewhere in this book, are computer telecommunications and hypermedia.

Computer telecommunications (see Chapters 4 and 10) expand the concept of the educational database by providing access to huge amounts of data organized and stored on remote computers around the world. A student with a computer and an Internet connection can, for example, search the Library of Congress card catalog from the classroom and read or download many of the holdings of that vast library and many others.

Hypermedia (see Chapter 11) expanded our idea of databases containing organized text to include databases containing organized text, graphics, video, and sound. An example of such a database is a CD-ROM encyclopedia. A student interested in the inaugural address of President John F. Kennedy may search such an encyclopedia to find information they can read about the event, to view pictures of the Kennedy family, or to view a videoclip complete with audio segments of President Kennedy delivering the address. During the late 1990s we saw the supersonic development of the largest database of all, the World Wide Web, which is a fully functioning hypermedia database.

Although, as you would expect, there are differences in database management software, all packages allow you to do the following five tasks:

1. Create a database.
2. Add information to and delete information from the database.

3. Sort or rearrange the information in the database.
4. Search for specific information in the database.
5. Print out reports containing information selected from the database.

Creating a Database

Creating a database from scratch using database management software is similar to setting up a traditional filing system. As a teacher, to set up a filing system for use in your classroom, you would first gather the physical materials you need, perhaps a filing cabinet, file folders, some indexing materials, or paper or cards on which to record specific information. The database management software you choose to create an electronic database provides you with the electronic equivalents of all these physical materials.

Just as creating a traditional database requires decisions about what information to include as well as how to organize it, so, too, does the creation of an electronic database. Database management software merely provides you with the tools. How you organize the information determines the efficiency of your database and requires careful thought to ensure that it serves you well. One advantage of the electronic database over the traditional database is that the information in an electronic database can be easily reorganized when so desired.

Although the terminology used in database management software differs slightly from one package to another, some terms and procedures are virtually universal. The word *database* usually suggests one or more data files containing related information. For example, a collection of information that students gather on the vegetation in their neighborhood would comprise a database. In some cases, data file and database are used interchangeably because all of the information making up the database is organized into one file.

Larger, more sophisticated databases, however, often consist of more than one data file, and the database program can select and reorganize information from several different data files. These databases are sometimes referred to as **relational databases.** Suppose, for example, that students creating the database on local vegetation create one data file that contains information on the name and typical location of each plant they find and a separate data file containing detailed information, including pictures, on each plant. With a relational database students can search the entire database for specific information without having to worry about which data file contains that information. The database software automatically finds the requested information, even when the data is in several data files.

A database with all the information in one file is often referred to as a **flat file database** in contrast to relational databases, which work with more than one data file. In both types of database, the information is divided into records. A **record** is a set of data for one logical subunit of the file. For example, if students include information on Arizona ash trees in their vegetation database, all the information about Arizona ash trees would constitute one record in the database. Each of the other trees, flowers, and grasses in the database would also have its own record.

The term *field* is usually used to denote the next smaller unit in a file. A **field** is where a specific piece of information is stored. In a student file, for example, the field "Last Name" would contain each student's last name for each record in the database. Figure 9.1 shows an example of a student file that a teacher might use as an electronic filing system. For purposes of illustration, assume that the information presented in Figure 9.1 is a small part of a large, districtwide database that Mrs. Jones selected and retrieved for her class of 20 students.

Adding Information to and Deleting It from a Database

Developing a good database is often an evolutionary process. Once the format of the database has been determined and an initial body of information organized, new information generally needs to be added regularly. Database management software allows you to add and delete a whole record or change the information in one or more fields of a particular record. Most programs enable you to add or delete fields to the database as needed. If you are creating a database on the computer, new information can be automatically inserted into its proper place in the database.

FIGURE 9.1   A database of student information.

Cardon Brent	123 Adams Drive	M	A	C	B	C	A	A	235
Crofford Kathy	27 Water Street	F	A	B	A	B	A	B	234
Gregory Fred	53 Grand Place	M	A	B	B	C	A	A	679
Gregory Jill	53 Quail Drive	F	A	A	A	A	A	A	124
Harlow Mary	84 S. Dunbar St.	F	A	A	A	A	A	B	347
Hartford Sam	19 S. Dunbar St.	M	A	A	A	A	A	B	831
Johnson Mary	12 S. Dunbar St.	F	A	A	A	A	A	A	268
Johnson Matt	12 S. Dunbar St.	M	A	A	A	A	A	A	567
Jones Kelly	83 Quail Drive	F	B	C	B	C	B	A	345
Jones Kenneth	42 Quail Drive	M	B	C	B	C	B	A	654
Kroft Jim	125 Water Street	M	A	B	A	B	A	B	156
Munk Bart	123 Sherman St.	M	A	C	B	C	A	A	734
Parker Jacky	192 Quail Drive	F	B	A	B	A	B	A	908
Parker Jerry	192 Smithridge	M	B	B	B	B	B	A	781
Rodreguez Juanita	923 Quail Drive	F	A	A	B	B	A	A	123
Rodreguez Mark	112 Quail Drive	M	A	B	A	B	B	A	159
Smith Billy	24 N. Sycamore	M	B	B	A	A	A	A	981
Smith Robert	14 N. Sycamore	M	B	B	C	C	A	A	678
Washington LaVon	900 Snow Place	M	B	A	B	A	B	A	789
Washington Sue	24 Grand Place	F	B	A	A	A	A	B	450

Sorting the Information in the Database

When it comes to sorting information in a database, computer power really goes to work. *Sorting* means to rearrange the information. (Some database management software packages use the term *arrange* instead of *sort* to indicate the reorganization of the database contents.)

The most common way to organize a database is alphabetically. When setting up your student database, for example, you would probably organize it alphabetically according to last name. Likewise, when setting up a database of U.S. states, it would be logical to organize the records alphabetically by state name. Either of these databases could then be quickly rearranged by using the sort or arrange feature of your database management software. For example, a student database could be reorganized according to birth date or according to math grade. Figure 9.1 shows Mrs. Jones's 20 students sorted alphabetically by last name. Figure 9.2 shows the same information sorted according to district ID number, in ascending order.

Searching for Specific Information in the Database

The major reason for setting up any kind of database or filing system is to make it possible to find information quickly. Using appropriate commands in a database

FIGURE 9.2   A database sorted according to district ID number.

Rodreguez Juanita	923 Quail Drive	F	A	A	B	B	A	A	123
Gregory Jill	53 Quail Drive	F	A	A	A	A	A	A	124
Kroft Jim	125 Water Street	M	A	B	A	B	A	B	156
Rodreguez Mark	112 Quail Drive	M	A	B	A	B	B	A	159
Crofford Kathy	27 Water Street	F	A	B	A	B	A	B	234
Cardon Brent	123 Adams Drive	M	A	C	B	C	A	A	235
Johnson Mary	12 S. Dunbar St.	F	A	A	A	A	A	A	268
Jones Kelly	83 Quail Drive	F	B	C	B	C	B	A	345
Harlow Mary	84 S. Dunbar St.	F	A	A	A	A	A	B	347
Washington Sue	24 Grand Place	F	B	A	A	A	A	B	450
Johnson Matt	12 S. Dunbar St.	M	A	A	A	A	A	A	567
Jones Kenneth	42 Quail Drive	M	B	C	B	C	B	A	654
Smith Robert	14 N. Sycamore	M	B	B	C	C	A	A	678
Gregory Fred	53 Grand Place	M	A	B	B	C	A	A	679
Munk Bart	123 Sherman St.	M	A	C	B	C	A	A	734
Parker Jerry	192 Smithridge	M	B	B	B	B	B	A	781
Washington LaVon	900 Snow Place	M	B	A	B	A	B	A	789
Hartford Sam	19 S. Dunbar St.	M	A	A	A	A	A	B	831
Parker Jacky	192 Quail Drive	F	B	A	B	A	B	A	908
Smith Billy	24 N. Sycamore	M	B	B	A	A	A	A	981

FIGURE 9.3 A database sorted for students living on Quail Drive.

Gregory Jill	53 Quail Drive	F	A	A	A	A	A	A	124
Jones Kelly	83 Quail Drive	F	B	C	B	C	B	A	345
Jones Kenneth	42 Quail Drive	M	B	C	B	C	B	A	654
Parker Jacky	192 Quail Drive	F	B	A	B	A	B	A	908
Rodreguez Juanita	923 Quail Drive	F	A	A	B	B	A	A	123
Rodreguez Mark	112 Quail Drive	M	A	B	A	B	B	A	159

management system, you could find all the names of children in a student database who have a given ZIP code, were born in a given year, and are also passing math about as quickly as you could find one student's birth date alone.

Printing Database Reports

Having the capability to organize information and print it out in a report format is useful any time you want to have a printed copy of the information you have gleaned from searching the database. It is especially useful when you want to organize the information you have gathered into a handy table or chart. Good database management software allows you to juggle the information to display it just as you want and then turn it into a printed report. For example, the computer could be asked to search for all the students in Mrs. Jones's class who live on Quail Drive and print out a report that includes first name, last name, address, grades, and ID number. Such a report could look like Figure 9.3.

THE ELECTRONIC DATABASE
AS A TYPE II APPLICATION

A database management program that can organize, sort, rearrange, and exchange information at rapid speeds is a Type II computer application (see Chapter 5) because such software enables the computer user to be in control of doing a task that is impossible to do without the computer.

Imagine, for example, that you work in a very large school district where records of 10,000 students are kept. A measles epidemic breaks out in the community, and the school district needs to know which children have been vaccinated for measles within the past 4 years. What do you think a secretary is going to say when told to search through every file in every drawer of every filing cabinet and record the name, address, and phone number of every student who has not been vaccinated in the past 4 years? This task would take one person approximately 20 days. By the time the task was accomplished, its purpose would, of course, be obsolete. If this same school district were using a typical database management system with a typical computer for record-keeping purposes, such a task could be accomplished in seconds.

Imagine further that a new records manager is hired for this school district with 10,000 children. This individual decides that it is more efficient to organize all records according to Social Security number than according to name. How long would it take someone to go through all 10,000 files and reorganize them? Again, such a task could be accomplished in minutes or even seconds with an electronic database.

Many educators who are enthusiastic about the potential of using database management software and ready-to-use databases in the classroom often base their enthusiasm on a belief that effective use of databases in the classroom can lead to enhanced development of metacognitive and problem-solving skills. Geisert and Futrell (1995) summarize this type of thinking in the following statements:

> Cognitive strategies are the skills that a student uses to govern his or her own learning, remembering, and thinking behaviors. They are like a set of behind-the-scenes organizational rules, which direct and govern how a student approaches the solving of a problem. (p. 127)

Hoelscher (1986), an early advocate of using databases in teaching and learning, went right to the heart of the matter when she wrote:

> The process of using the computer as a data workhorse creates more openings for students to peer into the information they have and to play out their strategies for creating and sharing new information. It may now make more sense to look at things in a number of very different ways before deciding upon "the answer." And, once decided upon, the answer may be more fully understood. (p. 25)

Beth Holmes (1998) maintains that electronic database software can be

> a powerful tool for addressing a student's need to make sense out of "collections" of information. In moving from preoperational thought to concrete operations, a developing thinker naturally seeks to make collections of various objects: stamps, butterflies, baseball cards, arrowheads, Barbie dolls, toy airplanes, solders, hats, and so on. Virtually any category of concrete object can be manipulated, classified, and stored for safekeeping. (p. 7)

Three distinct learning activities can be incorporated into using a database in any subject area. The first learning activity involves having students design a database. Database management software does not automatically organize data into a usable format. To design a database, a set of goals relating to what the database is meant to accomplish must be established. Usually an extensive trial-and-error exercise is required to ensure that, once data is entered into the database, it is used to accomplish the purpose for which it was designed. The design process requires extensive thinking about organizational processes and structure. Once a design is complete, it is often referred to as a **database template.** This pattern guides how information is gathered and entered into the database.

The second learning activity involves gathering information. Here, numerous lessons on research strategies can be taught. A useful database contains reliable information gathered from multiple sources and organized according to the database template.

The third learning activity involves searching a database and producing reports. Once students have access to an extensive database, they can begin using it to answer questions. Such questions can be generated either by students or teachers. To answer a well-reasoned question, information usually has to be gathered. Questions relating to specific databases require students to formulate research strategies for obtaining and summarizing the appropriate information from the database. Often, this process includes generating one or more specially formatted reports based on information in a database.

AN EXAMPLE OF USING ELECTRONIC DATABASES IN THE CLASSROOM

A good illustration of using a database as a teaching and learning tool is described in a case study by Matovinovic and Nocente (2000). The database aspect of this case study is only one part of an authentic scientific investigation conducted by a group of tenth-grade science students, but it focuses on essential elements of database power in the classroom. In this project-based approach to studying weather and plant physiology, the students gathered extensive data on eight plant species that leaf out in response to warming temperatures in the spring. The students were involved in the science of phenology, which is the study of the seasonal timing of life cycle events.

Students gathered data relating to the prescribed plants from a variety of resources including Internet sites, particularly one that manages the educational project Plantwatch (http://www.devonian.ualberta.ca/pwatch/). When sufficient information was gathered, the students were able to enter their synthesized data into a class database. The database contained details such as a brief description of the topography of the area where each sample plant was located and the temperature readings at the time of first- and full-bloom dates of each plant. Once the database was complete, students were assigned projects that involved using the scientific method to answer questions, such as, What effects does carbon dioxide have on the first-bloom dates of plants? The scientific method involved forming hypotheses and then searching and sorting the database in an attempt to verify the hypothesis.

COMMON SCHOOL-ORIENTED DATABASE MANAGEMENT SYSTEMS

As with all tool software, the movement has been away from self-contained software packages that serve one purpose toward integrated programs that serve several purposes. Many high-school computer labs use *Microsoft Office* or **Corel's** *WordPerfect Office,* which are integrated software packages they are likely to encounter when they enter the workplace. Other integrated software packages that are simpler and more student-oriented, such as *AppleWorks* and *Microsoft Works*, are still popular with younger children. Database software that is appropriate for school use usually should have three features in common: (1) it should be sophisticated enough to allow for real database power; (2) it should be relatively easy to use; and (3) it should have available ready-to-use educational databases, or templates. Let's look now at some database management systems that are well accepted and well suited for school use.

The first database management program that received wide classroom use was *AppleWorks*. *AppleWorks* was an influential force in increasing the use of computers in classrooms because it turned the old Apple II series computers, which at the time were by far the most popular classroom computer, into very useful classroom tools. Networks of educators began sharing their database designs (sometimes called *instructional templates*) and ready-to-use databases with one another.

One of the first writers to suggest the idea of using instructional templates to turn the computer into a teaching and learning tool was Henry Olds (1986). Olds set the stage for thinking of the computer as a teaching and learning tool when he described his first experience in working with teachers who were using *AppleWorks* database templates. According to Olds:

> They [teachers] had grown tired of primarily using the computer as a means for presenting "canned" drill-and-practice programs or educational games; they wanted to begin to use more widely the many tool programs becoming available in forms appropriate for schools; and they wanted computer use to be closely integrated with normal curricular and instructional practices and be closely related to established educational priorities. In short, they were anxious to apply the power of the computer to achieving sound educational goals. (pp. 7–8)

Despite the fact that the Apple II series computer has long since been left behind, in terms of technological advances, *AppleWorks* remains on the market and is widely used in classrooms across the country. As an integrated software package, *AppleWorks* provides six core capabilities: word processing, spreadsheet, database, presentation, drawing and painting, and communications. Although *AppleWorks* was originally developed for Apple computers, it was later run on the Macintosh platform and is now available for the Windows platform as well.

Another old standby integrated software package is *Microsoft Works*. *Microsoft Works* offers a word processor, a database, a spreadsheet, and a communications program. This integrated software package was the answer to early MS-DOS users who wanted an *AppleWorks*-like program. As with *AppleWorks*, *Microsoft Works* has matured through many revisions and has kept pace with advancing hardware and is now available for both Windows and Macintosh platforms.

Both these classic school-oriented software packages have accumulated educational support groups, third-party sales groups, and fan clubs. Such groups provide templates, user tips, and lesson plans for using the software packages. The Web is a rich resource for discovering these groups. For *AppleWorks*, a couple of websites are http://lowendmac.net/macinschool/991115.html and http://www.

tek-tips.com/glinks.cfm/lev2/3/lev3/18/pid/87. For *Microsoft Works,* two good starting points are http://www.microsoft.com/education/schools/default.htm and http://www.teachers.net/lessons/posts/326.html.

In addition to software publishers, some companies that publish books and curriculum materials also publish ready-made databases. Sunburst Communications, Scholastic, and Minnesota Educational Computing Consortium (MECC) all publish such databases. Databases relating to science, geography, weather and climate, endangered species, history, world geography, and economics are only a few of those available through such companies.

A key factor that makes a ready-to-use database a good educational tool is its size. Early technology was limited by the number of records a database could contain yet still be run on a classroom computer. With the hugely expanded capability in memory and speed of today's computers, very large databases can now be purchased and used in the classroom. The technological innovation that has done most to advance the quality of ready-to-use educational databases is the CD-ROM (see Chapter 3). An advantage that CD-ROMs have for educational database users is that they combine graphics, sound, video, and text to form a multimedia database. In addition to the multimedia advantage of a CD-ROM database, the comprehensiveness of such databases allows students to perform tasks that databases compatible with older technology could not allow. Large-scale databases such as ERIC, *Reader's Guide to Periodic Literature,* and *Books in Print* are now available on CD-ROM.

ELECTRONIC SPREADSHEETS IN THE CLASSROOM

In its simplest form, a spreadsheet is a grid with letters across the top that serve as labels for columns and numbers along the side as labels for rows. When we create a pronounced grid effect by drawing lines to separate the rows and columns, as in Figure 9.4, we can see that an entire page or sheet is divided into many cells. Each cell has a distinct name consisting of a letter and a number. For example, if you count down three rows and across five columns in Figure 9.4, you are at cell E3. If you count down five rows and across three columns, you are at cell C5.

Such grids, bound together to form ledgers, have been used for many years for bookkeeping. In bookkeeping, the columns are usually labeled by time periods, such as days, weeks, months, or years. The rows are usually labeled with designated financial terms, such as income, taxes, and wages. The spreadsheet provides an organized way of keeping track of numbers whose relationship to each other provides important or meaningful information.

WHAT AN ELECTRONIC SPREADSHEET IS AND HOW IT WORKS

A story can be told about how the electronic spreadsheet was first conceived. Dan Bricklin, a Harvard MBA student, was laboring over a set of financial cases using

	A	B	C	D	E	F	G	H	I	J	K	L
1												
2												
3												
4												
5												
6												
7												
8												
9												
10												

FIGURE 9.4   A blank spreadsheet screen with lines.

paper, pencil, and calculator to compute financial projections. As he labored, he began to ask an age-old question: Isn't there an easier way to do this? A logical answer to his question seemed to be to program the computer to do all of the "grunt work" for him.

Bricklin envisioned a program that would resemble an electronic chalkboard. Labels, numbers, and formulas would all be visible, and changing any set of numbers would automatically cause the program to recalculate and adjust all other affected numbers. After Bricklin teamed up with an old friend, Bob Frankston, the idea became a reality. The first commercial spreadsheet software, *VisiCalc*, was born. Needless to say, these two young men became very wealthy (Alsop, 1982).

To glimpse the power the creators of *VisiCalc* saw in the electronic spreadsheet, pretend that you decide to convert your paper-and-pencil personal budget to an electronic spreadsheet. The spreadsheet you see in Figure 9.5 was created using an electronic spreadsheet program. Three types of information can be entered into the spreadsheet cells: (1) numbers, (2) spreadsheet formulas, and (3) text. The formulas in the spreadsheet tell the computer to carry out specified mathematical calculations on the numbers. Text can be used to create labels that explain or identify numbers and formulas.

The spreadsheet you see in Figure 9.5 was set up so that when you type numbers in the Pay Check and Parents' Check rows (rows 6 and 7), the computer automatically adds together these two amounts and inserts the total in the Total Income row. Likewise, all the separate expense items are added, and the total is inserted and displayed in a cell designated Total Expenses. The numbers in the Savings row are automatically inserted by the computer and are the result

	JAN	FEB	MAR	APR	MAY	JUN	TOTAL
INCOME							
PAY CHECK	350	350	350				
PARENTS' CHECK	200	200	200				
TOTAL INCOME	550	550	550				1650
EXPENSES							
CAR PAYMENT	150	150	150				
RENT	100	100	100				
FOOD	100	110	120				
TUITION	20	20	20				
BOOKS	10	10	10				
CLOTHING	30	15	30				
RECREATION	50	60	50				
OTHER	20	15	25				
TOTAL EXPENSES	480	480	505				1485
SAVINGS	70	70	45				185

FIGURE 9.5   An electronic spreadsheet of a simple personal budget.

of subtracting numbers in the Total Expenses row from numbers in the Total Income row.

When using an electronic spreadsheet, the computer becomes a calculator. Any time you change a number in a cell, the computer can automatically recalculate to provide updated totals. This spreadsheet is very flexible. If you decide you need a separate category to keep track of your laundry expenses, you can easily insert a new row labeled Laundry. If you were to insert this category between the Clothing and Recreation rows, the Total Expenses row could be moved down to make room for the new row. When an amount is inserted in the new Laundry row, the computer would include that amount in calculating the Total Expenses row.

ADVANTAGES OF THE ELECTRONIC SPREADSHEET

Four advantages of an electronic spreadsheet turn the computer into an efficient and powerful numbers management tool. First, vast amounts of numerical data can be stored in a tiny space in electronic memory. Second, the spreadsheet can be edited, as in word processing, with rows and columns being inserted, deleted, or revised. Third, the heart of the electronic spreadsheet's power is its ability to perform instant automatic calculations on any or all numbers in its cells. Fourth, data from a spreadsheet can instantly be transformed into one of several different types of charts or graphs.

The instant and automatic recalculating characteristic of the electronic spreadsheet allows the computer user to forecast. *Forecasting* is the process of inserting hypothetical numbers into the spreadsheet to test certain theories or hunches. This has made the electronic spreadsheet an invaluable tool for business. A large company can test the effects on the profit margin of hundreds or thousands of different production costs. Forecasting can be thought of as playing a What If? game. A businessperson might ask, What if we save 5 percent of our labor costs by not working overtime and producing a smaller number of units? The answer to such a question can be obtained almost instantly by simply changing a couple of numbers in the spreadsheet. The entire spreadsheet is then automatically recalculated.

Let's look again at the imaginary personal budget shown in Figure 9.5 to get a clearer picture of how the What If? game works. Let's assume you want to have $500 saved by the end of June so that you can take a vacation. After 3 months of staying on your budget, you only have $185. You don't have to be a student of economics to know that to save $315 during the next 3 months you either have to increase your income or decrease your spending.

To get an idea of how drastically your budget will need to be changed, you can project what will happen if you stay at the same level of income and spending. The spreadsheet program can easily do this. As you can see in Figure 9.6 (page 214), at your present rate you will only save $320 by the end of June.

Your challenge is to find some combination of percentage increase in income and decrease in spending that will result in a savings of $500. The power of the electronic spreadsheet now comes into play. Even with a budget this small, many combinations of changes can be made. For the personal budget spreadsheet to help us play the What If? game, we have added a new column to your spreadsheet as shown in Figure 9.7 (page 215). The new column has been inserted between the March and April columns. This new column is labeled "Pct. raise" (percent raise needed to save $500) at the top of the spreadsheet.

Another new column has been added in the expense section labeled Pct. Less Spent (percent less spent to save $500). In this spreadsheet, the Parents' Check, Car Payment, Rent, Tuition, and Books rows are all fixed amounts. Therefore, the only way to increase your income is to get a pay raise. The only way to decrease your expenditures is to spend less on food, clothing, recreation, and other expenses.

Some formulas have been inserted into the spreadsheet that make it possible for you to use whole numbers to represent the percentage pay raise and

	JAN	FEB	MAR	APR	MAY	JUN	TOTAL
INCOME							
PAY CHECK	350	350	350	350	350	350	
PARENTS' CHECK	200	200	200	200	200	200	
TOTAL INCOME	550	550	550	550	550	550	3300
EXPENSES							
CAR PAYMENT	150	150	150	150	150	150	
RENT	100	100	100	100	100	100	
FOOD	100	110	120	120	120	120	
TUITION	20	20	20	20	20	20	
BOOKS	10	10	10	10	10	10	
CLOTHING	30	15	30	30	30	30	
RECREATION	50	60	50	50	50	50	
OTHER	20	15	25	25	25	25	
TOTAL EXPENSES	480	480	505	505	505	505	2980
SAVINGS	70	70	45	45	45	45	320

FIGURE 9.6   Simple personal budget projected to end of semester.

percentage decrease in spending you want to examine. The spreadsheet then does all the necessary arithmetic on these percentages and balances the spreadsheet so that the total projected savings by the end of June is shown.

Literally hundreds of different combinations of pay raises and decreased expenses could be examined. Suppose you ask yourself, What if I get a 5 percent pay raise, decrease what I spend on food by 7 percent, decrease what I spend on clothing by 10 percent, decrease what I spend on recreation by 7 percent, and decrease my other expenses by 6 percent? If you were sitting in front of a computer with this spreadsheet running, you could type in these hypothetical figures. Just as you typed in the *4* to represent the percentage of decreased spending for the Other row, you would see the Total Savings cell change to $421.70. At this rate, you would be $78.30 short of your goal. At this point, you may try a little larger pay raise and more drastic cuts in spending. Finally, you find a combination of changes that seem realistic to you and result in $500 saved by the end of June. Figure 9.7 shows just one of many combinations that might qualify. A 10 percent raise seems high, but you have worked hard, you feel you deserve it, and you make up your mind to go for it. If only solving the national debt were so easy!

	JAN	FEB	MAR	PCT. RAISE	APR	MAY	JUN	TOTAL
INCOME								
PAY CHECK	350	350	350	10	385	385	385	
PARENTS' CHECK	200	200	200		200	200	200	
TOTAL INCOME	550	550	550		585	585	585	3405
				PCT. LESS SPENT				
EXPENSES								
CAR PAYMENT	150	150	150		150	150	150	
RENT	100	100	100		100	100	100	
FOOD	100	110	120	10	108	108	110	
TUITION	20	20	20		20	20	20	
BOOKS	10	10	10		10	10	10	
CLOTHING	30	15	30	15	25.5	25.5	25.5	
RECREATION	50	60	50	10	45	45	45	
OTHER	20	15	25	15	21.25	21.25	21.25	
TOTAL EXPENSES	480	480	505		505	505	505	2904.30
SAVINGS	70	70	45		45	45	45	500.75

FIGURE 9.7   Simple personal budget used to forecast saving $500.

THE ELECTRONIC SPREADSHEET AS A TYPE II APPLICATION

The electronic spreadsheet would have little place in education if all it could be used for is managing a personal budget. As we suggested earlier, the spreadsheet is beginning to be viewed as an important teaching and learning tool. A report by Wilson (1985) is typical of the enthusiasm some educators show when they begin to appreciate the power of this new educational tool. According to Wilson,

> [the spreadsheet] can be a valuable tool in science, mathematics and social studies by developing and reinforcing skills in problem solving, generalizing, predicting, decision making and hypothesizing. Students can gain practice in setting up mathematical formulas, which can be used to find totals, subtotals, differences, percents, etc.; they can predict what would happen if an entry were changed. Deciding which entry to change and how to change it provides practice with decision making. (p. 30)

John Turner (1988), a professor at the U.S. Naval Academy, sees the electronic spreadsheet as a valuable tool in teaching undergraduate mathematics. He provides his students with enough expertise in one session to start them on their way to using the spreadsheet in solving problems and exploring concepts. For example, Turner encourages his students to test new formulas. They do this by plugging the formula into the spreadsheet and then entering diverse numbers. Thus, they discover how the different variables in the formula affect the final answer.

The way Turner is using the spreadsheet is similar to the way a teacher might use a computer simulation program. Actually, any concept that involves numbers can be simulated with a spreadsheet. An example is the concept of compound interest. After you explain what compound interest is and how it works, you can have your students sit down at the computer with a spreadsheet and experiment with different numbers. They could take out imaginary loans with compound interest. The length of time of the loan and the interest rate can be altered, and students can see how these two variables affect the monthly payment and the total amount of interest paid.

Friedlander (1998) explains how spreadsheets have a natural application in the mathematics curriculum:

> Spreadsheets seem to fit particularly well in the early stages of learning algebra. The fact that students can construct formulas without actually naming a variable makes their transition from number use to symbol use easier. Spreadsheets allow the user to include variables in formulas by physically moving the mouse or the arrow keys to the cell that contains the required quantity and thus to represent and test relationships in ways that are not possible with traditional paper-and-pencil work. (p. 1)

Feicht (1999) went right to the heart of the matter regarding Type II uses of computers by explaining how running a spreadsheet program can contribute to learning in brand-new ways, ways that were not possible before computers became available. Fiecht says that

> modern spreadsheets can make powerful mathematical concepts accessible to students at a younger age than ever before. Contours and three-dimensional graphing are topics that were previously reserved until well into the first year of college calculus. Three-dimensional graphing now can be successfully taught to middle school students with the assistance of a computer spreadsheet. This combination of the computer with hands-on activity exposes students to numerical and graphical representations of data on the same spreadsheet "page" and forces them to make connections between the two forms of data. (p. 166)

One aspect of modern spreadsheets that is very useful in math is the ability to represent relationships and data graphically (Bridges, 1991). Bridges used *Microsoft Excel*, but many spreadsheets have graphical tools today. Other educators have put the graphical tools of spreadsheets to work in teaching about Taylor polynomials (Timmons, 1991) and about creating and interpreting graphs in a high-school general mathematics course (Wood, 1990). In fact, several programs designed specifically for graphically representing mathematical relationships have been developed over the past 10 years. Popular programs include *The Geometric Supposer* and *Mathematica,* but many others are available.

The educational uses of spreadsheets are not, however, limited to math classes. They also can be used in many other subjects. For example, Brown (1987) described how she used spreadsheets and databases in a geography class, and Hannah (1986) described the use of spreadsheets and databases in a junior high–school social studies class to evaluate the "livability" of U.S. cities.

AN EXAMPLE OF USING ELECTRONIC SPREADSHEETS IN THE CLASSROOM

Gallagher (2000) has illustrated an interesting and ingenious use of the electronic spreadsheet with first-grade students. The project started when Mrs. Sheridan's first-grade classroom acquired five student computers, software for each machine, a color printer, Internet access, an LCD projector, and the support of an instructional technology trainer/consultant. Mrs. Sheridan had used a weather project in the past to connect a science and math lesson. She felt that past projects had been weak because they lacked good visual representations of weather patterns. She wanted her first-grade students to be able to see relationships between numbers and color-coded temperatures. Therefore, she decided to put the new computers to work.

With the aid of the technology trainer/consultant, Mrs. Sheridan selected a website and a spreadsheet software package that fit the needs of her class. Both these selections had to fulfill two requirements: they could not assume any reading or keyboarding skills. The website is maintained by Ohio State University and features color-coded temperature maps of each state in the United States. These maps are accessed solely by mouse clicks (http://twister.sbs.ohio-state.edu/text/wximages/us/ustemp.gif). The software Mrs. Sheridan chose was *Graphers* (Sunburst Communications), a program designed to help young students learn about graphs and to allow them to use graphs to solve problems. With this software students can create pictorial data and easily manipulate the data using simple point, click, and drag motions with a mouse.

Each student in Mrs. Sheridan's class was assigned to study the weather in a particular state. They used graph paper and coloring tools to record the temperature of their assigned state each day. At the end of each month, they entered the temperatures into a *Graphers* spreadsheet file and converted the data into a variety of colored graphs. Using these graphs, Mrs. Sheridan involved the students in a host of learning activities. For example, she could ask them which color (temperature) occurred most often or least often during a particular month and which student's assigned state had the most different colors (temperatures) on their graph.

COMMON SCHOOL-ORIENTED SPREADSHEET SOFTWARE

We have already alluded to several integrated software packages or suites that include spreadsheet software. *Microsoft Office* or Corel's *WordPerfect Office* both provide very sophisticated spreadsheets whereas *AppleWorks* and *Microsoft Works* offer spreadsheets that are still powerful but easy to use and popular with younger children.

SUMMARY

As with many computer applications that are now viewed as educational tools, word processing, databases, and spreadsheets were developed and first accepted by business. These applications are general and flexible enough to be effective teaching and learning tools. In this chapter, you have read about word processing, database management, and spreadsheet software. You have been exposed to the necessary terminology for understanding and becoming conversant about these three types of applications software. We explained that the advantages often cited for using word processing in schools fall into one of the following categories: (1) ease of production and revision, (2) cognitive advantages, (3) social advantages, or (4) attitudinal advantages.

Research supporting the use of these three computer applications was discussed. This research strongly suggests that word processing seems to lead to better attitudes toward writing and to longer manuscripts with more surface revisions than does text written using paper and pen. It also suggests that incorporating electronic database and spreadsheet applications into the school curriculum can positively affect teaching and learning. Specific software packages come and go, but some popular application packages were discussed for both Windows and Macintosh platforms.

QUESTIONS TO CONSIDER

1. Is the ability to use spreadsheets and databases an aspect of "literacy" in today's world? Is it a specialized skill that should be taught in specialized courses such as business education?

2. The business community was quick to adopt word processing. Do you think it is easier to assess the success or failure of a business innovation than an educational innovation? Explain.

3. Good research on educational computing in general and on the use of word processing, database management, and spreadsheets in education in particular is scarce. Can you think of any special problems in doing such research?

RELATED ACTIVITIES

1. Locate at least four lesson plans (using ERIC, the Internet, or any other resources available to you) that integrate the use of databases into lessons on subjects you plan to teach. What roles can the teacher play in these lessons? What does the teacher need to know about the software and the computers that would be used?

2. Analyze four lesson plans that involve using spreadsheets in terms of the roles required of the teacher and the hardware and software knowledge and skills needed by the teacher.

3. Locate a public school teacher who uses word processing to help teach children writing skills. (Ask one of your education professors to recommend such a teacher.) Interview that teacher about how he or she uses word processing. If possible, visit the class and observe.

REFERENCES

Alsop, S. (1982, January). Software Arts wrote the first bestseller. *Inc., 4,* 71–74.

Baker, E. (2000). Integrating literacy and tool-based technologies: Examining the successes and challenges. *Computers in the Schools, 16,* 73–90.

Bangert-Drowns, R. L. (1993). The word processor as an instructional tool: A meta-analysis of word processing in writing instruction. *Review of Educational Research, 63*(1), 69–93.

Bridges, R. (1991, November). Graphical spreadsheets. *Mathematics in School, 20*(5), 2–5.

Brown, M. (1987, summer). The computer as a tool for information processing in geography. *History and Social Science Teacher, 22*(4), 197–202.

Butler, S., & Cox, B. (1992). DISKovery: Writing with a computer in grade one: A study in collaboration. *Language Arts, 69,* 633–640.

Collis, B. (1988). *Computers, curriculum, and whole-class instruction: Issues and ideas.* Belmont, CA: Wadsworth.

Dickinson, D. (1986). Cooperation, collaboration, and a computer: Integrating a computer into a first and second grade writing program. *Research in the Teaching of English, 20,* 357–378.

Dudley-Marling, C. C. (1985, January). Microcomputers, reading, and writing: Alternatives to drill and practice. *Reading Teacher, 38,* 388–391.

Feicht, L. (1999). 3-D graphing, contour graphs, topographical maps, and matrices using spreadsheets. *The Mathematics Teacher, 91* (5), 166–174.

Flake, J. L., McClintock, C. E., & Turner, S. (1990). *Fundamentals of computer education.* Belmont, CA: Wadsworth.

Friedlander, A. (1998). An excellent bridge to algebra. *The Mathematics Teacher, 91*(5), 382–383.

Gallagher, S. (2000). Collecting and manipulating weather data: Using technology tools in a first-grade classroom. *Computers in the Schools, 16,* 167–176.

Geisert, P. G., & Futrell, M. K. (1990). *Teachers, computers, and curriculum.* Boston: Allyn & Bacon.

Geisert, P. G., & Futrell, M. K. (1995). *Teachers, computers, and curriculum* (2nd ed.). Boston: Allyn & Bacon.

Geisert, P. G., & Futrell, M. K. (2000). *Teachers, computers, and curriculum* (3rd ed.). Boston: Allyn & Bacon.

Hannah, L. (1985–1986, December–January). Social studies, spreadsheets and the quality of life. *The Computing Teacher, 13*(4), 13–16.

Heap, J. (1986, April). *Collaborative practices during computer writing in a first grade classroom.* Paper presented at the American Educational Research Association, San Francisco, CA.

Hill, M. (1992). Writing to learn: Process writing moves into the curriculum. *Electronic Learning, 12*(3), 20–26.

Hoelscher, K. (1986). Computing and information: Steering student learning. *Computers in the Schools, 3*(1), 23–34.

Holmes, B. (1998, April). The database: America's presidents. *Learning and Leading with Technology, 25,* 6–11.

Kinzer, C. K., Sherwood, R. D., & Bransford, J. D. (1986). *Computer strategies for education: Foundations and content-area applications.* Columbus, OH: Merrill.

Lewis, R. B. (1993). *Special education technology.* Pacific Grove, CA: Brooks/Cole.

Lillie, D. L., Hannum, W. H., & Stuck, G. B. (1989). *Computers and effective instruction: Using computers and software in the classroom.* New York: Longman.

Long, L. (1988). *Introduction to computers and information processing* (2nd ed.). Englewood Cliffs, NJ: Prentice Hall.

MacArthur, C. A. (1988, Winter). Computers and writing instruction. *Teaching Exceptional Children, 20,* 37–39.

MacArthur, C., Graham, S., & Schwartz, S. (1993). Integrating strategy instruction and word processing into a process approach to writing instruction. *School Psychology Review, 22*(4), 671–681.

Mandell, C. J., & Mandell, S. L. (1989). *Computers in education today.* St. Paul, MN: West.

Matovinovic, D., & Nocente, N. (2000). Computer technology in an authentic science project. *Computers in the Schools, 16,* 109–120.

Montague, M. M. (1990). *Computers, cognition, and writing instruction.* New York: State University of New York.

Montague, M., & Fonseca, F. (1994). Using computers to improve story writing. In J. J. Hirschbuhl (Ed.), *Computers in education* (6th ed., pp. 80–83). Guilford, CT: Dushkin Publishing Group.

Olds, H. F. (1986). Information management: A new tool for a new curriculum. *Computers in the Schools, 3*(1), 7–22.

Roberts, N. (1988). *Integrating computers into the elementary and middle school.* Englewood Cliffs, NJ: Prentice Hall.

Roblyer, M. D., Castine, W. H., & King, F. J. (1988). *Assessing the impact of computer-based instruction: A review of recent research.* New York: Haworth.

Roblyer, M. D., & Edwards J. (2000). Integrating educational technology into teaching. Upper Saddle River, NJ: Merrill.

Timmons, T. (1991, March). A numerical and graphical approach to Taylor polynomials using an electronic spreadsheet. *PRIMUS, 1*(1), 95–102.

Turner, J. (1988). The use of spreadsheets in teaching undergraduate mathematics. *Computer Education, 12*(4), 535–538.

Willis, J. (1987). *Educational computing: A guide to practical applications.* Scottsdale, AZ: Gorsuch/Scarisbrich.

Wilson, J. (1985). VisiCalc in the elementary school. *The Computing Teacher, 12*(9), 29–30.

Wood, J. (1990, Spring). Utilizing the spreadsheet and charting capabilities of Microsoft Works in the mathematics classroom. *Journal of Computers in Mathematics and Science Teaching, 9*(3), 65–71.

CHAPTER TEN

■ ■ ■ ■ ■

THE INTERNET AND THE WEB IN THE SCHOOL CURRICULUM

Goal: To understand how the Internet and the World Wide Web can be used to enrich the classroom curriculum.

KEY TERMS

acceptable use policies (AUP) (p. 248)

address book (p. 239)

bookmarks (p. 237)

chat (p. 241)

critical thinking (p. 227)

free-mail (p. 239)

graphical user interface (GUI) (p. 238)

mailing lists (p. 240)

message boards (p. 241)

newsgroups (p. 240)

search engine (p. 236)

web-enhanced learning projects (p. 223)

webquest (p. 246)

Jason, Karen, and Melissa, three students in Mr. Smith's tenth-grade science class, are excited about a research project. Much of the structure for this project is provided by a webquest (discussed later in this chapter). The project is long term and constitutes a major portion of the group's science study for the next several months. The research topic is on the causes and prevention of acid rain. The goals the students have set for the project include learning more about acid rain through scientific investigation, preparing reports and materials to be used in enlightening their classmates, and offering suggestions to leaders in their community on ways to prevent the problem.

These three students comprise one of many student research teams that are participating in a worldwide study of acid rain. The Internet is being used as the medium of communication and data exchange in this international webquest project. The project is carried out through the following steps:

1. Existing information on acid rain will be gathered by searching Internet resources, including special websites where collections of information on acid rain and related topics are maintained.
2. Additional information will be gathered through electronic interviews and discussions with scientists who are studying acid rain.
3. A data-gathering procedure will be established by common consent and will involve teams from around the world taking measurements of acid rain indicators at their individual locations.
4. The information and data gathered will be organized into database files that will be made available on the Internet.
5. The data will be made available to all participants, and each team will be free to analyze the data using whatever method they choose.
6. Each research team will prepare a report based on the database information and on the various data analyses. All reports will be made available on the Internet.
7. Jason, Karen, and Melissa will prepare an instructional module on acid rain for their classmates, make a presentation to interested individuals at a town hall meeting, and write an article that will be submitted to their local newspaper for possible publication.

Hundreds of projects similar to the one just described are taking place today, and educators around the world are excited about the potential of the Internet to change and enhance the nature of education. This chapter provides a basic understanding of how the Internet and World Wide Web (Web) can be used to enhance teaching and learning.

The development of the Internet and the Web has been one of the most interesting stories in history (see Chapter 4). It has affected people's lives around the world. It has had a great effect on the lives of the authors of this text. It has affected the way we teach, the way we learn, and the way we write. An interesting parallel has taken place between the extraordinary growth of the Internet and the contents of this book with regard to computer telecommunications. In the first edition of this book (1992), the topic of computer telecommunications covered six pages. In those six pages, we expressed a rather negative view of what we called "hype" to describe all the fuss being made about computer telecommunications.

In that first edition of this text, we cited a 1984 reference about an electronic field trip. Our reaction to the electronic field trip follows:

> Considering that the above description was written before high-resolution graphics and interactive videodiscs were common, calling a computer telecommunications session a "field trip" was certainly stretching the point. We suggest that realistically naming computer telecommunications applications would help educators develop more realistic impressions of what they actually are. (p. 126)

In the second edition of this text (1997), an entire chapter was devoted to educational telecomputing. This chapter reflected our change in attitude toward computer telecommunications as a teaching and learning tool:

The explosive growth of the Internet and its expanding availability to public schools, together with plummeting costs for modems and other hardware, have eliminated many...problems and have made telecomputing a practical teaching and learning tool in many schools across the country. (p. 152)

If you have read very far into this book, you will have noticed that the Internet and the Web play a prominent role in every chapter of this third edition. We have devoted two full chapters to the Internet and the Web (Chapters 4 and 10) and have lauded these new developments as among the most important technological innovations ever for education. Indeed, we now admit that *electronic field trip* is not only a realistic term, but also a commonly used and effective teaching device.

In the second edition of this text, we suggested classroom activities, some of which involved Internet activities that have since become virtually extinct. For example, one of the key methods of archiving and finding information on the Internet at that time was a program called *Gopher.* At the time, Gopher seemed like an efficient Internet tool. Today, however, it has almost been forgotten. In the words of Conner-Sax and Krol (1999):

Gopher's relation to the Web is rather like that of the Neanderthals to *Homo sapiens:* they evolved at similar times, shared a common ancestry, and even superficially resembled each other. One, however, was much better suited to survival than the other. (p. 430)

At the time we were writing the second edition of this text, the Web was in its infancy. It was just one part of the Internet, the hypermedia part. The Web expanded so rapidly between 1996 and 2000 that it has become almost synonymous with the Internet. Technically, the Web is still just one part of the Internet, but it is by far the largest part, and most interaction on the Internet occurs via the Web. Therefore, the remainder of this chapter refers simply to the Web, except when, for precise clarification, a distinction needs to be made between the Web and other Internet applications.

THE POTENTIAL OF THE WORLD WIDE WEB

As the Web has mushroomed, so has the use of **web-enhanced learning projects** in U.S. classrooms (see Chapter 4). Nearly every school in the United States now has at least one connection to the Web. As access to the Web has increased and as its use has expanded, more questions are being asked regarding how best to use it in the classroom. Johnson and Liu (2000), in an attempt to develop an integration model, analyzed 102 case studies relating to the integration of information technology in teaching and learning situations. The projects covered all curricular areas and included grade levels ranging from preschool to graduate school. The overarching question of the study related to whether the integration project described in the case achieved its stated goals and objectives. The strategy was to try to determine which instructional components contributed to successful learning outcomes.

One of the instructional components in the study was the use of the Web as a general information resource. Interestingly enough, this instructional component had no effect on the perceived success or failure of the case studies. According to the authors of this study,

> the reason the "Use of Web Information Resources" did not achieve significance lies in the fact that there was almost no variance in this instructional component. Almost all of the cases used this resource and therefore it added nothing to the prediction of success. This variable, then, is probably best viewed as a ubiquitous integration resource. (p. 3)

We, like many computer-using educators, saw potential educational benefits in what we first called *computer telecommunications,* but before 1990 that potential remained unrealized and untapped because of a host of practical, financial, and technical problems. The explosive growth of the Internet and its expanding availability to public schools, together with plummeting costs for connectivity and hardware, have eliminated many of these problems and have made using the Web a practical teaching and learning tool in many schools across the country. And although the costs and problems associated with the Internet have decreased, the ways in which it can be used in education have expanded dramatically. Writing about the potential of the Internet in schools, Maddux and colleagues (1995) stated:

> It can empower students and improve problem-solving ability by bringing about a new relationship between children and information. It can expand the horizons of students everywhere, and make quality information equally accessible to students in both rural and urban settings. (p. 581)

The Web represents a new set of tools that brings forth new power and new ways of doing things. The obvious value of these educational tools is similar to that of word processing, but much greater. Although this entire text is laced with a great deal of caution about overselling the potential of technology to "fix" education, it also may contribute to the hype about the Web by students and teachers. Of all the computer applications that have been adapted to educational purposes, the Web holds the greatest potential for revolutionizing the teaching and learning process.

Among the many advantages of the Web in education is its ease of use. Since the beginning of the microcomputer movement, technology enthusiasts have struggled to convince other educators of the potential for integrating technology into the classroom (see Chapter 8). One of the barriers that impeded progress in this area is the personal investment on the part of teachers to learn certain information technology applications, in relation to the functionality of the application. The question many teachers asked was, Does the amount of use I can get out of this application justify the time and effort necessary for me to master it?

Authoring systems, for example, do not enjoy wide use among classroom teachers partly because they require a great deal of personal investment to master and then can only be used in a rather narrow range of situations (see Chapter 2). When it comes to getting teachers excited about using information technology in their classrooms, however, the Web is a good place to start. Both prospective teachers and practicing teachers immediately see the potential of this application to enhance and enrich teaching and learning experiences.

Johnson (1998), in writing about this relationship between the amount of personal investment required by a teacher to prepare a lesson using a given application and the degree to which that lesson is functional in terms of integration, developed the graph shown in Figure 10.1. In this graph, *personal investment* is defined as the time and effort a teacher needs to invest to master the application, develop a lesson, and modify the curriculum to accommodate the lesson. *Functionality* summarizes ease of integration, breadth of situations in which an application can be applied, and natural relationship between the application and the traditional lesson. The graph illustrates that the information technology application with the lowest personal investment and the highest degree of functionality (usefulness) is the Web.

In teaching preservice and in-service teachers to use the Web to enhance learning in their classrooms, we have developed an easy-to-understand and very workable framework for getting started. We have worked with teachers in planning web-enhanced learning projects and begin by having them think of learning as dealing with information. We then break down the idea of dealing with information into steps by which the learner gathers, organizes, assimilates, stores, and represents information. In a typical traditional learning situation, the learner gathers new information in many ways, including reading, listening, and

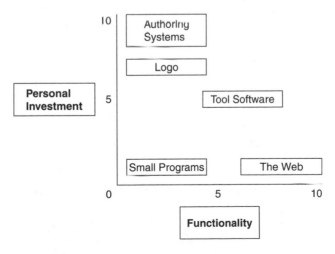

FIGURE 10.1   Graph illustrating the relationship between degree of personal investment and functionality for different types of computer applications.

observing. A good student then organizes this information using note taking, outlining, and filing skills. Although *assimilate* usually refers to a complex cognitive process, it is also used to imply the physical act of carrying organization one step further by fitting new information into a broader scheme of information as, for example, fitting a new file into a filing system or a new note card into a note card system. Once information is gathered, organized, and assimilated, it can be stored. Again, we use the word *store* to mean both the cognitive process of putting information into memory and the physical processes for preserving and storing information. Finally, most learning situations require some type of representation of information, such as tests, themes, and presentations.

Next, we encourage teachers to think of computers and related information technology as information machines. One definition of *machine* is "a system or device, such as a computer, that performs or assists in the performance of a human task" (http://www.dictionary.com). Because learning concerns information, it is natural to think of a computer as an information machine. It is a machine that can enhance learning by facilitating human tasks involving information. The most common use of the Web in schools is gathering information. This is the magic dust aspect of the Web—a world of information at the fingertips of the student. The accuracy and authenticity of information on the Web can be disputed, but the simple fact remains that an Internet connection in a classroom brings to that classroom the world's largest repository of information. So, by teaching teachers and students how to gather information on the Web, they are learning how to use this phenomenal information machine. When used correctly and appropriately, this information machine can expose students to a far wider array of facts and opinions than could be exposed if limited to their textbooks and school library.

The next step in using the information machine in learning is to organize the newly acquired information from the Web. This can be done through such common applications as databases and spreadsheets (see Chapter 9). Although databases and spreadsheets are generally considered software packages for personal computers or for local area networks, opportunities are arising to create and manage databases and spreadsheets on the Web. First, many databases can be accessed on the Web, such as huge databases of government data. An example is the FedWorld website at http://www.fedworld.gov/gpo.htm. This site links you to numerous government reports and databases. An example of a database management system that allows you to create and manage a database as part of your own website is *unicaWeb planner* (http://www.unicamultimedia.com/planner/database.html).

Spreadsheets also can be created, maintained, and manipulated on the Web. An example of such a website is Formula One/Net at http://www.visualcomp.com. When we think of using information technology for assimilation in learning, we think primarily of multiple representations. With the information machine, learners may experience many examples and iterations of a concept, which helps them assimilate or internalize that concept. Using the Web, students can often find many different ways of expressing or representing a concept.

In addition to the great advantages of using the information machine to store information electronically, it can enhance cognitive information storage through multisensory stimulation. More and more information can be presented in text, graphic, audio, and video formats on the Web. At the click of a mouse, learners can receive information through almost every sensory channel.

Often, the most exciting part of any learning situation is when learners get a chance to show what they have learned. Demonstrating what has been learned is often a reward for the hard work involved in learning. Information technology, the information machine, offers a host of new options for representing information in ways that demonstrate learning. Students can summarize their learning in text format and publish it to the class, the community, or the world. Student articles can be laced with impressive graphical images, audioclips, and videoclips. *PowerPoint* presentations can be developed and presented to various audiences and converted to Web presentations. And, of course, students can develop their own web page formats for unique representations of information relating to their learning.

Tying together the idea that learning concerns information and the analogy of the information machine, a simple model can guide teachers in developing Internet-enhanced learning projects for their students. This simple model contains six elements to consider when planning to infuse the Web into a learning activity: (1) critical thinking, (2) problem solving, (3) constructivist learning environment, (4) collaborative learning, (5) integrated curriculum, and (6) reporting.

The importance of **critical thinking** is made quite obvious by the definition put forth by Halpern (1996):

> Critical thinking is the use of those cognitive skills or strategies that increase the probability of a desirable outcome. It is used to describe thinking that is purposeful, reasoned and goal directed—the kind of thinking involved in solving problems, formulating inferences, calculating likelihoods, and making decisions when the thinker is using skills that are thoughtful and effective for the particular context and type of thinking task. Critical thinking also involves evaluating the thinking process—the reasoning that went into the conclusion we've arrived at and the kinds of factors considered in making a decision. Critical thinking is sometimes called directed thinking because it focuses on a desired outcome. (p. xx)

Another important aspect of the critical thinking movement is the emphasis on deep understanding. Simply put, the emphasis is on the importance of bringing learners to a point at which they deeply understand a concept as opposed to just covering many concepts. For more information and background on critical thinking, consult the following websites:

http://Web.kcmetro.cc.mo.us/longview/ctac/definitions.htm
http://Web.yorku.ca/admin/cdc/lsp/read/read4.htm
http://Web.westwords.com/GUFFEY/critical.html

The problem-solving element implies developing problem-based assignments in which there is no one way to solve the problem. Problem-solving assignments should also encourage active participation in learning by all students. For information on creating problem-solving assignments, refer to the following websites:

http://Web.yahoo.com/Education/Programs/Future Problem Solving Program/
http://lonestar.texas.net/~lhutto/index.html

Chapter 7 of this book provides a thorough discussion of the constructivist view of teaching and learning and presents ways to establish constructivist learning environments. For additional information regarding this important element of our model, see the following websites:

http://www.ieev.uma.es/edutec97/edu97 co/goodyear.htm
http://www.ed.psu.edu/insys/who/jonassen/cle/

The curriculum integration element in our model is intended to encourage teachers to incorporate as many aspects of the total school curriculum as possible into each web-enhanced learning project. For specific ideas and suggestions on how to accomplish this, see the following websites:

http://www.mneta.net/~mfinstr1/candi.html
http://www.corona.bell.k12.ca.us/teach/imag/portfo.html
http://www.aea2.k12.ia.us/Curriculum/curriculum.html

SOME EXAMPLES OF WEB-ENHANCED LEARNING PROJECTS

This section presents three sample web-enhanced learning projects based on the concepts and guidelines presented thus far in this chapter. These examples should help you gain a deeper understanding of how to begin incorporating the Web into the classroom.

Case 1

The first web-enhanced learning project we present (Dutt-Doner, Wilmer, Stevens, & Hartman, 2000) was targeted primarily at the middle-school science curriculum but was an interdisciplinary project that integrated science, social studies, and language arts. The problem to be solved in the project concerned global warming. Students were divided into heterogeneous groups that collaborated on various aspects of the overall project. The collaborative groups took on roles as members of various groups that would be testifying before a special congressional subcommittee. The task of the subcommittee was to decide whether to recommend that the U.S. Senate ratify the Kyoto Protocol, an international agreement that outlines varying target levels for reductions in greenhouse gases for industrialized nations. Each group used the Web to research a specified point of view on this topic. The end result was that different groups with different points of view made presentations before the Senate subcommittee, just as in real life.

Many underlying principles guided the work in developing this project. First was the notion of active learning based on a constructivist model. The project designers agreed strongly with research that suggests students learn more and retain more when they are actively engaged in their own learning. They also worked from a belief that participating in real-life simulations not only provides students with an authentic task in which to demonstrate knowledge and skills, but also gives credibility to the task. They defined the teacher's role in the project as one of guiding students to help them develop a deeper understanding of content and skills.

Collaborative group work was an important element in the project because the project designers believe that students are academically stronger when working with others than when working alone. In addition, they believe that by using collaborative groups, the teacher can structure classroom activities in such a way that students support one another, with guidance, to truly learn new information.

The authors of this case study explained that teachers must consider ways to integrate content knowledge in web-enhanced learning situations because of the ever-expanding curriculum and the standards movement. The project developers (Dutt-Doner et al., 2000) stated:

> By implementing an interdisciplinary, technology-based group research project we hoped that students would (a) become more interested and involved in their learning, (b) better understand and practice the use of research skills, (c) be able to retrieve more current information for research projects from the Internet, (d) support one another in their learning (about using technology, about the in-depth content of global warming), and (e) have a better understanding of reliable and unreliable Internet resources. (p. 151)

The specific goals for this project included ensuring that each student would

1. Gain experience exploring resources and learn how to use them to complete a research assignment
2. Gain experience using evidence to construct and present logical supporting arguments for an assigned point of view
3. Learn how economic, as well as societal and scientific, factors influence national and international political decisions
4. Gain insight into how (what appears to be) a given set of scientific and/or economic facts can be used to support differing points of view
5. Gain new background knowledge and insights regarding the greenhouse effect, global warming, and related science and social studies content.

Before starting the Global Warming WebQuest, the teachers provided the students with some background information. The first student homework assignment was to think of three questions they would like to answer about global warming and the greenhouse effect. The questions generated by the students were compiled by topic area into one list that included global warming causes, gases, treatments, and effects; ozone depletion causes and effects; and general effects (related to global warming and the greenhouse effect). The next assignment required the students to list everything they already "knew" about global warming and the greenhouse effect, without any feedback from the teachers. After students had had a chance to study some foundational text and graphic materials relating to their topic, they were given a list of research questions and began their research using a webquest created by the teachers (http://www.scarborough.k12.me.us/middle/quest/resourc.htm).

In order to support the group research project, the class was assigned to the computer labs for as many days as it was available, approximately three to four times per week for 4 weeks. Sometimes only one lab was available; other times, two. One lab had about 15 computers available for student use whereas the other had 10. Students had access to the Internet in the school computer labs and also in the classroom, where they could work individually or in their groups to find and compile information for their presentation.

The students had to pass certain checkpoints to ensure that they were making progress toward their final objective, which was to make an oral presentation with visuals, as if they were addressing a Senate subcommittee, who would then recommend whether the United States should ratify the Kyoto Protocol. Important guidelines to help support the students in their project were provided on the webquest site and included background information for each group.

After all the research was done and the presentations had been made, the teacher who conducted this web-enhanced learning project (Dutt-Doner et al., 2000) concluded the following:

> It was clear to us that students learned more about global warming using the WebQuest approach. Upon reviewing student reflections on the project, it became clearer that the WebQuest not only taught them about the issues surrounding global warming but also encouraged them to understand the real-life implications. (p. 151)

One of the great benefits of this type of project is that the webquest site remains active and is structured so that other teachers can use it for their own web-enhanced learning project.

Case 2

This project demonstrates the tremendous flexibility of the Internet in the classroom. In describing the project, Nancy Yost (2000) begins her narrative as follows:

> When was the last time you had children asking if it was their turn to write? Or children going home upset because they had not gotten to write today? Or a child crying to write one more piece, after having chosen to write for an hour of choice time? I have experienced all of these situations in my kindergarten program. (p. 17)

Yost accomplished these amazing results with the simple activity of having the kindergarten children send electronic expressions, or e-mail messages, back and forth with their family and friends. Yost explained that prior to discovering the value of using e-mail, she felt that her effort to teach creative writing to young children was contrived and teacher-driven. According to Yost:

> A child's creative urges need outlets beyond story writing.... Having children write in a limited number of genres does not create writers. Children need to write through a variety of experiences and processes. Engaging children with e-mail allows them to begin to see that writing is a dynamic communication tool.

Because kindergarten children's literacy levels typically range anywhere from those of a 3-year-old to those of an 8-year-old, Yost used a technique of inviting all the children to do their own typing. When a child refused, the teacher offered to help. Teacher assistance included some independent typing by children, some typing by the teacher, teacher support with spelling, and children typing words written down by the teacher. In some cases none of these options met the needs of the child, so the child simply dictated the e-mail message for the teacher to type.

Early in the school term Yost sends a letter to the parents discussing the e-mail project as a part of the writing program. She asks the parents to provide information on any family members or friends who may enjoy communicating with their child. Some adults become overly enthusiastic and send multiple messages in one day. She notifies adults who are interested in communicating with a child that they should not be disappointed or discouraged when the child does not always write back.

Once a list of adults and their e-mail addresses have been obtained for each child, the teacher uses *Netscape Composer* to compile a classroom e-mail directory page. This page contains the names of each student in the class along with picture clues for nonreaders, and each child's name is linked to an individual e-mail directory page. The individual e-mail directory page contains a list of names and e-mail addresses of people with which the child will be communicating. For example, clicking on John's name in the class directory page leads to a list of names with e-mail addresses of people who want to exchange e-mail with John. Now all John has to do is click on a person's name in his individual e-mail directory page, and an e-mail composition window opens up containing the e-mail address of that person. John can begin his e-mail communication by simply adding a subject line and a message. Yost has found that most children can learn to use these pages and the mail program with a minimum of instruction.

Writing and reading e-mail messages in Yost's classroom is not a stand-alone activity. She integrates technology into subject areas or themes with special projects and activities. For her, integrating technology through e-mail became a core component of her writing program and a daily occurrence no matter what was the topic of discussion for that day. Yost believes that kindergarten children write longer and more in-depth passages using e-mail than when using traditional writing tools because traditional writing tools require children to spend much of their time in the effort to manipulate a pencil to form letters. In Yost's words:

> Children writing e-mail are able to focus on the sound/symbol relationship, writing conventions, and content. These young writers also learn quickly to take advantage of editing features such as deleting, copying, inserting, and moving text. This gives them the same ability to rewrite and revise that older writers have when doing computer compositions. (Yost, 2000)

Yost attests to the value of using the Internet in her kindergarten class with the following statement:

> Using e-mail as a portion of my writing program has gone beyond encouraging and nurturing these writers. This program also:
> 1. Promotes independence and autonomy in the writing process
> 2. Establishes a positive and safe environment for these young writers
> 3. Validates the children as writers, by my trusting that the children can and will write to their families
> 4. Fosters positive relationships between the school and the families of the children
> 5. Establishes authentic and meaningful writing situations for the children (p. 18)

In summarizing her project, Yost expressed the hope that other teachers would come to realize how easily they can incorporate computers as a writing tool in early education classrooms. She believes that teachers of young children can make a smooth transition to using e-mail in a writing program. She also believes that young children are often able to accomplish writing tasks at a more advanced level when they use e-mail as a writing tool than when they use pencils or markers. Finally she states that "as the children begin to explore and see writing as a dynamic communication tool, their electronic expressions become rich, rewarding experiences for all involved—the children, their family and friends, and me."

Case 3

This case is a good example of a Type II technology application. It demonstrates that not only can some tasks be performed better with modern information technology, but that some tasks would be impossible to accomplish without it. In this web-enhanced project (Dove, Fisher, & Smith, 2000), the project developers used what they call *computer-mediated communication* (*CMC*), which is defined as an application that relies on computer technologies that enable individuals to share information while working and learning together. Using the long-established tradition of pen pals as a basic model, the developers of this project attempted to broaden the cultural perspective of their students by establishing a one-to-one

Internet connection among students in a U.S. school and students from two other countries.

The traditional pen pal projects had obvious limitations, the main one being the time delay between communications when sending and receiving letters through the postal service. Dove et al. describe the advantages of using the Internet in this type of learning experience:

> While modern forms of communications like e-mail successfully addressed the delays and costs of traditional mail, these traditional pen-pal type projects were also limited in that they were often undertaken without addressing specific curriculum issues. While a cultural exchange might be a worthy goal in and of itself, such a project offers the opportunity to integrate the curriculum into the pen-pal experience. Cultural exchanges provide knowledge acquisition at a first-hand and personal level. Students learn what life is like for children their own age in different parts of the world. By giving thought to how the standards and goals of the curriculum can be developed through an international and intercultural project, teachers can enrich and enhance goals for student achievement.

In this project, the Internet was used to establish such a learning environment by connecting three groups of students: second-grade students in southern Florida, an English-as-a-second-language class in Finland, and a class of second-graders learning English in Slovenia. The project went far beyond simply using the Internet to provide a medium for cultural exchange; it attempted to integrate specific curriculum standards in geography and language arts and also incorporated a constructivist approach to facilitate this learning. The project was not limited to using e-mail only. The students in the three countries made use of all the resources on the Internet, including its multimedia capabilities and interactive properties. The Web, with its vast multisensory informational resources, played a vital role in the success of the project.

The students in the U.S. classroom were accustomed to working in cooperative learning settings. They had been divided into groups of five or six for a learning project leading up to the project described here. Each week these cooperative learning groups had been required to observe, measure, and write about the seasonal changes occurring in southern Florida. The case study authors believe that a direct link exists between cooperative learning and successful construction of models to demonstrate knowledge. The U.S. students were grouped according to strengths and weaknesses as their various ability levels in writing and reading became apparent. Each student was required to work out his or her role and to make a contribution to the group. Dove and associates believe that the process of learning cooperatively actually improves the acquisition and retention of content and skills throughout the curriculum.

Starting in September, each student in the U.S. school created notebooks called "Our Wonderful World" to store all the data he or she had collected. One item in the notebooks was a map of the world, which students labeled with common geographical terms (*continents, hemispheres, oceans, equator,* etc.). Each student also plotted the locations of the other two participating schools and kept copies of e-mail correspondence.

Although geography and language arts were the main foci of this project, curriculum-wide goals were achieved by informally incorporating math, science, and reading into the learning activities. The standards and goals of each teacher in the classrooms of the three countries were, of course, different and individually based on the needs of the different classrooms.

In integrating language arts standards for writing, the U.S. students used the software program *Kid's Works Deluxe* to create illustrations and write observations for their notebooks. They used this same software to create illustrations to express their understanding of the changes around them, which constituted a representational element of the project. After the students had gathered data through e-mail exchanges and other informational resources, such as the Web, they were taught to analyze their data using higher-order thinking skills, which required them to examine and sort the data. The students learned how to determine what data were valuable and how the data fit into various categories. They were then required to graph, write about, and illustrate the results of their analyses.

This project was intended to be integrated into the total curriculum. It was long term, therefore, attempting to maintain student interest for the full academic year by adding new and different dimensions as the year progressed. As a starting point, students studied the geographical aspects of their world by participating in a web-based project called "Signs of Autumn" (http://home.talkcity.com/academydr/nicknacks/NNabout.html). Gradually the project was expanded to include the other two schools, and finally it evolved into a full-blown, international cooperative educational project in which students from three different schools in three different countries were in constant contact with one another. From this point, they gathered information, organized and analyzed the information, and created unique representations to demonstrate their learning.

The case study authors reported that various obstacles were encountered along the way, but that these obstacles were far outweighed by the positive gains in student knowledge, skill development, and ability to work cooperatively. In a fitting conclusion to the report on this project, the project developers quoted the teacher from Slovenia, who initially was concerned about the ability of her second-graders to cor respond with U.S. students in English. As the project proceeded, however, this teacher "found that the motivational level of her students more than made up for their lack of language skills" (Dove, Fisher, & Smith, 2000, p. 45).

BASIC INTERNET APPLICATIONS AND THEIR USE IN WEB-ENHANCED LEARNING PROJECTS

In this section, we further break down the use of the Internet into specific applications and discuss how these applications can be used individually in planning and implementing web-enhanced learning projects.

Finding Information on the Web

As previously addressed, one of the most direct information technology applications for classroom use, and the one that is easiest to start with, is finding information on the Web. Three basic strategies can be used to find information on the Web, and each has advantages and disadvantages in terms of classroom use.

The first strategy for finding information on the Web is casual browsing. A student sits down to a computer with Internet access and simply explores what is on the Web. It is akin to browsing through books in a library or videos in a video rental store. Students may not know what they are looking for; they just want to see what is there. As items catch their interest, they may follow leads that eventually focus their attention and interest. The Web, of course, is superbly well suited to this type of browsing because of its hyperlinks. The structure of information organized by hyperlinks is suited to just exploring the landscape.

The advantage to casual browsing is that it clearly puts the student in control and fosters creativity. Browsing may not have a goal or objective; it is just browsing. Students may sit down to the computer with no theme or subject in mind and leave excited about a topic because their instincts led them to a web page that sparked their interest, and that page linked them deeper and deeper into a theme or subject.

There are several disadvantages to casual browsing as well. The main disadvantage relates to time. Just casually surfing the Web can be time consuming, and students who have trouble focusing may spend a lot of time on the computer without ever zeroing in on a theme or subject. Putting this strategy to use effectively in the classroom should be carefully thought out ahead of time. Limits and requirements should be specified in most cases, but teachers should not dismiss the magic of allowing students to browse the Web to see what is there.

Entering URLs

A URL (uniform resource locator) can be thought of as simply the Internet address for a website. URLs are everywhere. We see them on TV, in magazines, and on billboards. We hear them on the radio and receive them in our junk mail. A fast and direct way to find information on the Web is to go directly to a specified website by entering a URL. The teacher can provide specific URLs and ask students to go to these web pages to complete specific tasks for an assignment.

The advantages of this strategy are efficiency and control. Students can get in and get out quickly when provided with a specific website to visit. This strategy also allows the teacher to exercise control over which websites students visit. A simple statement that tells students they are not to visit any websites not specified on the teacher's list of URLs (or consequences will follow) provides teachers with a great deal of control.

The greatest disadvantage to this strategy, of course, is that it stifles creativity and greatly diminishes the power of the Web. Teachers should always keep in mind that the Web is a vast resource library organized by hyperlinks, and restricting learners to a few specific locations of information flies in the face of the spirit of the Web. An analogy would be sending students to a large library full of information on every imaginable subject but restricting them to a few pages in a few books. However, sometimes this strategy may be used to best fit into a web-enhanced learning project.

Search Engines and Web Directories

The third strategy is to find information on the Web using a **search engine** or web directory. Both search engines and web directories are simply web pages themselves. These web pages are designed to use a search string (a word or phrase entered by the user) to search a huge database of web pages for pages that relate to the search string. Such a search should then result in producing a list of web pages relating to a theme or topic. Once the search engine or web directory displays a list of sites relating to the students' theme or topic, they can proceed by browsing the links that the search engine or directory has identified, until the desired information is found.

There is a technical difference between a search engine and a web directory. According to Maddux (http://www.unr.edu/educ/captta/mods/):

> A Web directory has in its database only those pages that a human being has viewed and categorized. A search engine, on the other hand, uses a computer program (called a *robot*, or a *spider*) to automatically search all the pages on the Web and to categorize each page in its database. Because of the time involved for humans to look at a page and categorize it, most search engines include many more Web pages than do most directories.

Having said this, we use the term *search engine* generically to mean both web directories and true search engines.

The advantage of using a search engine is quite obvious. It does something that would be quite impossible to do without it: search the entire contents of the Web in a matter of a few seconds. Although students still have work to do, the search engine narrows their search and lists all the links it can find relating to their topic.

Hundreds of search engines are available on the Web. None of them are perfect in terms of being able to find every web page relating to a given theme or topic. Search engines differ in efficiency and in ease of use. In the final analysis, the efficiency of a search engine depends on the quality of the search engine itself and on the student's ability to use it well.

Both teachers and students should select one or two search engines and learn to use them well. This means you should study the various search strategies specific to that search engine and practice using these strategies. Unless you spend a great deal of time using many different search engines, you will find your usage is superficial; when you use one search engine consistently, you are more likely to use its full power and use it well.

Some websites even specialize in keeping track of and evaluating search engines. One such site is Search Engine Watch, at http://www.searchenginewatch.com/. A list of search engines could easily fill the rest of this chapter; therefore, only a few major search engines that have both a long history and reliable reputation are mentioned: AltaVista (http://www.altavista.com/), Excite (http://www.excite.com/), Google (http://www.google.com/), Yahoo! (http://www.yahoo.com/), and Ask Jeeves (http://www.ask.com/index.asp).

Educators, of course, are interested in search engines that are appropriate for children. When a search engine indicates it is appropriate for children, it means some type of filtering device is operating. Again, hundreds of such search engines are available. In the recent past all the major search engines have created subengines specifically designed for children. If you go to any of these search engines, you can find an option that indicates a child, student, home, or family version.

Although we have discussed three different strategies for finding information on the Web, obviously the best approach is to use a combination of these three strategies. Sometimes it is useful to start students with some URLs or let them begin with some they have already discovered from print, radio, or TV. It is also important to teach them to use search engines effectively. Within the parameters of every effective Web-enhanced lesson, however, there should be some opportunity for casual browsing. In the final analysis, the gold nuggets are usually found in the casual browsing realm.

Using Bookmarks

All web browsers provide a feature that allows you to save and organize the URLs (web addresses) you find while searching the Web. Netscape calls this feature **bookmarks** whereas Microsoft Explorer calls it *favorites*. The usefulness of such a feature becomes obvious. Netscape's use of the word *bookmarks* provides a good analogy. Often when we read or browse an information-rich book, we mark various places in the book so that we can quickly and easily return to them without searching through the entire book again. If you think of the Web as a gigantic book, and think of yourself browsing through this book, you can imagine that you would want a convenient way to mark certain pages (locations, sites, etc.) so that you can quickly and easily return to them. Netscape and Explorer provide not only a way to mark websites, but also a way to organize them into a nice filing system.

Organizing the websites you find is important. If you were to mark only a few places in a book, finding the bookmark you are looking for would be easy. If, however, you marked hundreds of places, finding the one bookmark you wanted might take a long time. The same is true for electronic bookmarking. When you create a new bookmark, it can be filed in an appropriate folder at the time you create it, or it can be added to the end of a general list—like tossing a document onto a stack for future filing. Without organizing your bookmarks or favorites list, you end up with a long list of unfiled folders. As such a list gets longer and longer, it becomes more and more difficult to locate the file you want. Teaching students to use this feature of web browsing is important, not only because using it increases the efficiency of using the Web, but also because using it is a great way to learn organizational skills.

Using E-Mail

Next to just finding information on the Web, using e-mail is probably the most straightforward and practical Internet application for the classroom. Many successful web-enhanced learning projects have been carried out using e-mail alone, and most successful projects incorporate some type of e-mail activity. E-mail is a valuable teaching and learning tool because it provides simple and instant communications around the world. This is truly a Type II use of information technology. Although comparisons between traditional mail and e-mail are often made, the similarity between the two forms of communication is slight. E-mail allows teachers and students to incorporate international communications into learning projects in ways that are not possible with traditional mail systems.

Two types of software are used in Internet e-mail. The first type is a **graphical user interface (GUI)** mail program that resides on your computer. Both of the most commonly used web browsers, Netscape and Microsoft Explorer, have GUI mailing programs as part of an Internet user's total package. The Netscape mail program is *Messenger,* and the Microsoft Explorer mail program is *Outlook Express.* This type of mail program is the most commonly used. One of the great advantages of such programs is that it is very easy to send attachments (e.g., along with any e-mail message, you can attach any file, text, or graphics) from your computer. You simply click on an attachment button, which tells your computer that you want to attach a file, and then identify the file you want to attach, and it is sent along with your e-mail message. One of the disadvantages of this type of e-mail program, however, is that each computer you use has to be configured for your personal e-mail account.

To configure a mailing program, you enter essential information that the program needs to communicate with an Internet server and to allow you to send and receive e-mail messages across the Internet. To use your computer for Internet e-mail, it must first be authenticated by an Internet server. This means that you must have a user ID and a password for your messages to pass through the server and out across the Internet. This is not a problem most of the time because you only have to do it once. After you save the configuration, your computer is ready for you to use e-mail at any time.

In some situations, however, configuring a GUI mailing program may be impossible or seriously inconvenient, for example when you are away from your computer and want to check your e-mail quickly or send an important e-mail message. In these cases you can use a text-only mailing program. One of the most common text-only programs is *Pine,* which runs on Unix and Windows platforms. *Pine,* designed at the University of Washington in 1989, enjoys wide use today. To use *Pine,* you do not have to have the software loaded on your computer. The

Pine software can reside on your Internet server, and you can run it remotely as long as you can make contact with your server. This provides an opportunity to mention briefly another handy Internet tool: *Telnet*. *Telnet* is a simple program that is bundled with Microsoft Windows and allows you to connect your computer to nearly any server on the Internet. Using *Telnet* and *Pine* together, you can conduct e-mail activities from anywhere in the world. All you have to do is gain access to an Internet server, use *Telnet* to connect to your server, access *Pine* on your server, and conduct your e-mail business.

A recent development in Internet e-mail is **free-mail.** Free-mail is a mailing program that is web-based. A free-mail program can be either a separate web page or a subpage to a major web page, such as a search engine. AltaVista's e-mail (http://mail.altavista.com/) and Netscape's *WebMail* (http://Webmail.netscape.com) are just two of many free-mail programs. To use these programs you have to register and receive a login ID and a password, and you are in business. Using a free-mail program, you can access your e-mail account anywhere you can gain access to the Web.

An important part of any e-mail program is the **address book** feature. Although this feature may have different names, *address book* is usually part of the name because it is based on the analogous paper-and-pen address book. In using an address book, you may enter names, addresses, phone numbers, and most importantly e-mail addresses. These programs have two features that go beyond a traditional paper-and-pen address book. First, you can click on the name of a single person you want to contact, and that information is automatically inserted in an e-mail message to that person, saving you the trouble of looking up and entering that person's e-mail address. The second feature is really what makes address books worth the time and effort it takes to build and maintain them. Using this feature, you can organize your address book by groups or organizations. For example, you could organize all the teachers in a school in the category *Teachers*, and by entering *Teachers* in the address line of your mail program, a message could then be sent to every address in that list.

E-mail is an important classroom skill to teach. Not only can students use this skill widely in learning projects, but e-mail is so ubiquitous that they will use it extensively at home and as well as when they enter the work place.

Mailing Lists, Newsgroups, and Message Boards

Another category of Internet applications includes mailing lists, newsgroups, and message boards, which provide a valuable addition to the arsenal of tools a teacher can use in creating and implementing web-enhanced learning projects. The basic idea surrounding these three tools is like the old-fashioned bulletin board. In fact, some electronic bulletin boards exist and are very similar to the Internet tools we are discussing here. On a traditional bulletin board, people post messages; other people read those messages and sometimes reply. Discussions may then ensue based on the initial posted message. That's just what happens when we use mailing lists, newsgroups, and message boards. This method of communicating over the Internet is sometimes called *asynchronous communication.* In reality, this type of communication is very much like e-mail. The difference is that e-mail is usually more personal—you send a message to a specific person or group of people. Mailing lists, newsgroups, and message boards provide an opportunity to join into a discussion on some topic usually being carried on by a nebulous group of people.

When you subscribe to a mailing list, you join a group of people who are interested in a certain topic. A **mailing list** is an e-mail address that serves as an alias to many other e-mail addresses. A mailing list works very much like an address book—the e-mail addresses of many people are stored under one name, and, by invoking that name in a mail program, a message can be sent to all of the e-mail addresses. The difference, again, is that a mailing list is usually less personal than regular e-mail.

When you participate in a mailing list, you are usually entering into a discussion with hundreds or thousands of other people, most of whom don't know and will never know each other. The discussion, however, takes place in your regular e-mail account. Once someone in the mailing list has begun a discussion, by posting a message, and other people join in the discussion, that discussion topic is referred to as a *thread.* After you receive a message from the mailing list, you can ignore it, send a reply to the person who posted the message, or send a reply to all the people in the mailing list.

To participate in a mailing list, you have to subscribe to that list by sending an e-mail message to the person or organization that controls the list. When you decide that you no longer want to participate in the list, you have to send another e-mail message to unsubscribe. When you are part of a mailing list, every time someone posts a message to that list, the message is sent to every member of the list. Therefore, you get a copy of every message sent. You can search for mailing lists according to topic by sending e-mail to listserv@listserv.net. Leave the subject line blank, and in the body of the message type: *list global topic.* For an extensive list of mailing lists relating to education, visit http://www.esd105.wednet.edu/edlistservs.html.

Newsgroups are a little more anonymous than mailing lists. Although some news reading programs use the terms *subscribe* and *unsubscribe,* you don't have to make any official declaration regarding participating in the discussion. All you have to do is go to a newsgroup (usually by opening a folder under the name of the newsgroup), and you become part of the newsgroup. Anyone can participate in the discussion. Although newsgroups require a special program called a *newsreader,* which is usually available with your Internet browser, such programs function exactly like e-mail programs. Newsgroups are like magazines you buy at the newsstand only when you want to read a particular issue. You may not purchase every issue.

In contrast, mailing lists are like magazines to which you subscribe. They arrive in your mailbox every month whether you read them or not. We recommend subscribing to lists only when the topic is something so important you don't want to miss a single comment about it. Subscribe to newsgroups when you have an interest in the topic but don't want messages about it clogging up your mailbox everyday. Some lists generate only a few messages a week, but others can forward a hundred messages or more a day. Many lists are "echoed" as newsgroups so that you have the option of subscribing to them as lists or as newsgroups.

A slightly different version of this genre of Internet tools is message boards. **Message boards** are discussion groups that are totally web-based. You don't have to subscribe or use any special program to participate in them. Frequently, when you go to a website, you may notice that one of the menu items for that site is a discussion group. Some websites refer to this option as *forums,* implying an open discussion about a particular topic relating to that website. Some good examples of message boards (forums) can be found at the National Geographic website: http://magma.nationalgeographic.com/2000/intro/forum/index.cfm.

The three discussion group tools just discussed have earned somewhat of a bad reputation among teachers and parents because of the content of some of them. Thousands of mailing lists, newsgroups, and message boards exist on the Internet. They cover every conceivable topic including the good, the bad, and the ugly. However, this genre of Internet application can be very useful in developing web-enhanced learning projects. When used correctly, they can extend a class discussion far beyond a single classroom.

One of the best ways to make use of these Internet applications is to start your own discussion group and limit participation to individuals who are appropriate for the discussion and who are approved. Discussion groups in all three of these applications can be established on a limited basis. You might, for example, plan a project that involves classrooms from three schools around the world. When you plan your project, plan to establish a mailing list, a newsgroup, or a message board, and limit it to teachers, parents, and students at the three schools. You can start your own mailing list at http://www.gweep.bc.ca/~edmonds/usenet/ml-providers.html.

Chat

One other type of Internet commination is **chat.** Chat actually belongs to a group of communications methods referred to as *real-time communications.* Real-time communications are messages that can be seen immediately by another person who is participating in the same communications session. It is analogous to talking on the telephone, except you are talking with your fingers instead of with your voice.

The first form of real-time communications was a UNIX program called *Talk.* This program, which ran on Internet servers, allowed two people to establish a "talk" session by typing messages back and forth. They could even interrupt each other, which occurred when one person started typing before the other person was finished. This little program was widely used before the advent of the Web, and students, especially, loved it. It was exciting for students to go online, contact a stranger in a faraway place, and engage that stranger in a real-time conversation.

Talk, for the most part, has been replaced by chat. Chatting is a popular Internet application. Chat differs from talk in that more than two people can participate in the real-time conversation. At its best, chat is like a group of people in the same room chatting about a certain topic. At its worst, which is frequently the case, chat is like a group of children saying silly things and trying to shock each other with crude language.

A third method of participating in real-time communications on the Internet is called *instant messaging.* Instant messaging is almost identical to e-mail except that the messages fly back and forth between two or more computers instantly; therefore, it resembles chat. Instant messaging differs from chat because it is proprietary—you can only converse with people using the same service. This makes it much more private and closed than chat, in which anyone can usually jump into a conversation. Some websites that offer both chat and instant messaging services are

Netscape AOL Instant Messenger
  (http://www.newaol.com/aim/netscape/adb00.html)
Yahoo! Pager
  (http://messenger.yahoo.com/messenger/help/themes.html)
ICQ   (http://www.icq.com/)

Real-time communications on the Internet has earned a bad reputation among educators. A quick visit to a randomly selected chatroom can often illustrate why this has happened. Don't dismiss this Internet application, however, because it has tremendous potential for web-enhanced learning projects. The vision of a group of sixth-grade students from six different countries engaged in a live conversation about an important topic suggests a powerful learning activity. This is possible with many chat and instant messaging services because you can easily create and manage your own chatroom or instant messaging centers in which the only participants are those invited to enter, and they need a password to do so. There is no reason why these tools cannot be used for very serious discussion among participants in any given learning project. The ICQ website (http://www.icq.com/), for example, offers user-created chatrooms.

FTP

FTP stands for *file transfer protocol,* a process by which you move files from one computer to another. One application of ftp is to find files on a remote computer and download them to your computer. Some important files still exist on the Internet that are not part of the Web. These files are stored at ftp sites rather than at websites and are stored in ftp format rather than http format. An example of an ftp site you might want to visit is ftp.microsoft.com, where hundreds of notes, explanations, and manuals are available relating to Microsoft products. Although ftp sites still contain some valuable information, this information, like all other

Internet information, is gradually being moved to the Web where it can be located with your web browser and search engine.

A more common use of ftp is for personal transfer of files from one computer to another. For example, you are working at home on a document that is not finished. You want to be able to work on the same document at school. One way to transfer the document, of course, is via a storage disk. But this is not always possible. Your home computer and school computer may not be compatible, or, as is the case with some Macintosh computers, you may not have a disk drive. Ftp is a simple and reliable way to transfer the file. You simply ftp the file to your server; then, when you get to school, you ftp it down to your school computer.

A third, and very important, use of ftp is part of the process of creating a web page. Usually all the files that go into a web page (text, graphics, etc.) are created or stored on a personal computer and then uploaded to a web server where they are accessible through the Web. Ftp is the simplest way to transfer such files from the computer where you create and store your web files to your web server.

CLASSROOM APPLICATIONS

Thus far, this chapter has discussed various ways of thinking about the Internet and the Web with respect to integrating their power into the school curriculum. Finally, we ask you to think about the Internet and the Web from the perspective of resources and aids that are geared specifically toward classroom application.

Keypals

Thousands of students each year communicate via e-mail with students in other schools, states, and countries. Stan Smith, a seventh-grade teacher in Missouri, says students like e-mail "because part of what drives the kids' enthusiasm for going online is their desire to communicate with other students. They think that it's great to make a new friend in a distant state or country—especially a friend of the opposite sex" (Crim, 1995). Keypals offers a good way to get students involved in communicating with students in other schools as one aspect of a long-term web-enhanced learning project. A good place to start with keypals is a website called Epals (http://www.epals.com/index_en.html).

Global Classrooms

Many web-enhanced learning projects involve group-to-group interactions. For example, Harris (1994) described how U.S. literature classes at two schools read *The Glass Menagerie* together and discussed the play via e-mail. Telecommunications can take students beyond the classroom walls and make the world their classroom. For details on how one teacher used class-to-class telecommunications see Montoya (1992). A few examples of the type of messages teachers post to establish links between classes follow. (We have not included the teachers' e-mail addresses because these posts were made in early 1995 and may not be active now.)

> I am a teacher/librarian at Wanniasa Hills Primary School in a suburb of Canberra. I am working with grades five and six on the effects of drought on people, the land, and animals. We are applying de Bono's Six Thinking Hats and Gwen Gawaith's Action Learning steps in our investigation. We would like to contact people living in drought areas who would like to assist us in learning about this topic. We welcome drought-related information from anyone.

> I am a sixth-grade teacher in Mendocino, California, seeking to telecommunicate with a class outside the U.S. to arrange an Environmental Box exchange. The purpose is to gain a deeper understanding of each local environment and how it affects and is affected by lifestyles of the people who live there. Students will plan and discuss the exchange by e-mail. Each will contribute at least one item for the box with museum catalog cards telling about the item. Items might include samples of flora and fauna, audio or video tapes, postcards, photos, newspaper articles, and so on. Students will discuss the environment after the exchange. I would like to begin this project the end of October.

> Our fourth graders at Audubon Elementary School, Baton Rouge, LA, would like to correspond with others studying threatened and endangered species. We're also learning to use CD-ROMs, scanners, translation software, and telecommunications. Also, our fifth grade gifted classes are planning a "trip" around the French-speaking world. We'd like to learn about the customs and habits of the countries we might visit. We'd like to hear your ideas for other activities and any information about Francophone countries.

Another favorite middle- and junior high-school global classroom activity is cooperative publishing. An example of an international cooperative writing effort is the following:

> Hi,
>
> We are students of an Italian school (11–14 years old) in Preganziol (Treviso)—North of Italy. We've founded a magazine called *U.G.O.* (UGO FOSCOLO is the poet to whom our school is dedicated.) We are looking for some classes that would like to work for foreign editorial offices. Can you please send us regularly (our magazine is printed every two months) reviews, surveys, articles, or interviews on these subjects:
>
> 1. comics
> 2. video games
> 3. films
> 4. books
> 5. music (rock, jazz, rap,...)
>
> We appreciate contributions both in English and French. Our magazine is edited with *MS-Publisher.* We can read texts in ASCII standard as well as in all other formats accepted by *MS-Publisher.*
>
> In exchange, we'll be glad to give our own contributions to anyone who might need it for their school magazine.

Electronic Appearances

Guest appearances by community leaders, authors, publishers, and other people that students may read about or whose work students may have read are often highlights of a school year. However, the limitations of geography and time mean that most of the people you would like your students to meet are not able to come to your classroom. One alternative is to make contact electronically. Many authors, for example, have electronic mail accounts, and quite a few are willing to correspond with students who are reading their works.

Electronic Mentoring

Sam Houston State University is one of several schools that have created an electronic support network for new teachers. Graduates of SHSU can use their e-mail accounts to communicate with each other and with faculty at SHSU after they begin their teaching careers. Many find this service an excellent way to get advice, help, and support. Lists and newsgroups sponsored by special interest groups are another source of support and advice for teachers.

Electronic mentoring has also been used with students. At the University of Houston, for example, teacher-education students in a reading methods course taught by Dr. Lee Mountain worked with elementary children who were writing papers. The teacher-education students were an audience for the children's writing and helped them edit and enhance their compositions. Telecommunications may provide a way for writers, journalists, scientists, and business people to participate more fully in the education process via mentoring activities supported by e-mail.

Another mentoring project concerns math. *Ask Dr. Math* helps students with math problems and questions. It was developed by Steven Weimar at Swarthmore College, Swarthmore, Pennsylvania. *Ask Dr. Math* can be accessed at dr.math@forum.swarthmore.edu.

Successful web-enhanced learning projects usually involve collaboration between at least two classrooms and have an information-gathering element. Although some information-gathering projects simply exchange information between classes, many involve pooled data analysis, such as comparing the water quality of different regions and the environmental regulations in place. Often a report is produced and electronically published on the Internet. A few collaborative projects have even created databases that other schools can access via the Internet.

One Internet application that seems to appeal to students is using the Internet to conduct surveys. This activity is a natural use of the Internet and provides many interdisciplinary learning opportunities. Students in a given class can devise and distribute a questionnaire and expect to receive responses from around the world in just a few days, or immediately in a chat session. Students can organize, analyze, and summarize their data and share the results with other classes anywhere in the world. Possible lessons in which such an activity could be integrated include sampling techniques as they relate to how predictions on the outcomes of elections are made, the concept of objectivity, the development of report-writing skills, simple statistical concepts, and diversity.

Another way classes use the Internet for information gathering is "tele-fieldtrips." In many parts of the country students can take electronic field trips to local sites, such as a zoo or museum. And, as additional resources become available on the Internet, students can electronically visit locations such as the Louvre, in Paris, or outer space. Telefieldtrips can also involve receiving messages from students who are on real trips. For a list of telefieldtrips, go to http://www.springfield. k12.il.us/resources/Webprojs/fieldtrips.htm.

WebQuests

Webquests are online learning projects that engage students in learning about an authentic topic or problem. Most webquests are cooperative activities in which students assume different roles relative to an authentic problem. The Internet serves as the primary information resource, although other more traditional resources, such as magazines and journals, are sometimes included. The webquest provides the structure for the investigation of the authentic topic and increases the likelihood of students successfully navigating the unstructured nature of the Internet. Students then develop a product that demonstrates their understanding of the problem and its potential solutions. A webquest is an inquiry-oriented activity designed to use the learners' time well, to focus on using information rather than looking for it, and to support learners' thinking at the levels of analysis, synthesis, and evaluation. The model for the webquest was developed in early 1995 at San Diego State University by Bernie Dodge with Tom March.

A good place to get started with a webquest is at the WebQuest page (http://edWeb.sdsu.edu/Webquest/Webquest.html). This site is designed to serve as a resource to those who are using the webquest model to teach with the Web itself. Another good starting point is a website that teaches you how to design your own webquest (http://www.memphis-schools.k12.tn.us/admin/tlapages/wq-write.htm). A third place to go to get started with a webquest is a site that provides an index of webquests (http://www.macomb.k12.mi.us/wq/Webqindx.htm). A good example of a timely webquest is one that deals with the holocaust (http://www.greenepa.net/~wgsd/computerlab/Holocaust/Holocaust.html).

A good way to get involved in any or all these web-based applications is to visit the website of an organization that has made a successful business out of developing resources for using the Internet in K–12 classrooms. Classroom Connect (http://www.classroom.net/home.asp) markets videos, texts, workbooks, and training packages all relating to integrating the Internet into the classroom.

THE QUESTION OF STUDENT ACCESS

There is some debate over the issue of whether students should be allowed to log on and interact with the Web or whether the teacher should control the resource, uploading and downloading information for the students. We take the stand that the power of the Internet lies in its interactive nature. Late-breaking information looses something after the teacher or librarian has downloaded it, printed it out, copied it, and passed it out to the class. Letters from an electronic pal in a foreign country are not as exciting when they are printed out by someone else, 3 days after their arrival. Searching for information interactively on the Internet is far more interesting and productive than passing on requests for information to the teacher.

The issue of student access to the Web lies at the heart of a broader issue relating to the use of technology in education. We believe, as we have mentioned in several other places in this book, that, before technology can have an impact on education, fundamental changes in the way we have come to think of the educational process must occur. George Gilder (1993) strikes at the heart of such change:

> The trouble is, school systems began imitating the structures of the Industrial Revolution at the very time society began moving into the Information Age. Of course, schools should never have assimilated industrial structures in the first place, because education is not an industrial function. Schools are information tools, governed by the rules of information technology, and the prime law of information technology is the distribution of intelligence and power rather than the concentration of it. (p. 9)

Allowing students interactive access to telecomputing services, it seems to us, is consistent with "the distribution of intelligence and power" whereas restricting such access to teachers, administrators, and librarians is consistent with the "concentration" of intelligence and power.

Consider for a moment our discussion throughout this book of Type I and Type II computer applications. Teachers retaining control of telecomputing resources clearly makes it a Type I application. In such a case, the teacher controls the flow of information but does it in a slightly different way. Allowing students to search and explore interactively is a Type II application because they are in control and they are part of a learning environment that previously was not available. The chief advantage of the Internet and other telecomputing services is that they expand the classroom. To observe students interactively engaged in telecomputing is to be reminded that part of the thrill is in the search and exploration itself, not just in the eventual end of the search.

One of the main concerns expressed by educators who think students should have either no access or limited access to information services, such as the Internet, is about "adult" material on the Internet. Themes dealing with sex and violence make up a very small part of the Internet, but once students enter the electronic world, it is difficult to control where they travel. In an informal survey we conducted, we discovered that many teachers who use the Internet in their classrooms believe that students need to have online access to telecomputing services, but that most learning experiences involving telecomputing should have some structure and control, as opposed to free browsing.

To provide you with a peek into cyberspace, where such issues can be explored, we present an opinion expressed by a superintendent of a large metropolitan school district during a live electronic conversation. One of the authors, during the writing of this book, noticed that the superintendent was online and requested a few minutes of her time to ask the following question: "Do you think students should be allowed to work interactively on the Internet, or should it just be a resource for teachers, administrators, and librarians?" The superintendent responded:

> Interactive is great! One morning I was reading my electronic mail and I got a talk message from a student at a local elementary school in one of the poorer sections of the city—what a kick! We had a terrific conversation. She should be able to do that with other students in Australia, or China, or wherever. We do need some controls, probably, about access—but you can only control so much. If kids are determined to get access to something they shouldn't—you can set up the best controls in the world and they may not work. (Author, personal communication, January 23, 1993)

We offer two suggestions that can help in addressing this issue. The first suggestion is to make good use of your school or district's **acceptable use policies (AUP).** If your school or district does not have a formal AUP, you might want to get involved in developing one. The AUP can be a good friend to you. Make sure your students and parents understand it and agree to it. If a student objects to any part of the AUP, then that student should not be allowed to use the Internet at school. When students use the Internet, make it very clear that, when rules and procedures stated in the AUP are broken or violated, the student who commits the offense will lose Internet privileges at school.

One successful way to do this is to use the information super highway analogy and issue each student who agrees to abide by the AUP an Internet driver's license. Then post explicit, clearly stated rules of the road. When a rule is violated, the violator receives a citation. When a student receives two citations, he or she loses the driver's license. The bottom line is that you make the rules clear, specify the penalty for breaking the rules, and, finally, enforce the rules by invoking the penalty. Avoid punishing those students who observe the rules by levying penalties to an entire class when one student violates a rule.

SUMMARY

We began this chapter by illustrating that of all the computer applications available today, the Web may have the most potential because it is easy to learn, easy to use, and is amplifiable to nearly all teaching and learning situations. We presented an analogy that compares a computer connected to the Internet to an information machine. With this machine, the learner can gather information, organize information, assimilate information, store information, and represent information. We proposed a simple model to guide teachers in developing

Internet-enhanced learning projects for their students. This simple model contains six elements to consider when planning to infuse the Web into a learning activity: critical thinking, problem solving, constructivist learning environment, collaborative learning, integrated curriculum, and reporting. Three case studies were presented that illustrate how the model can be applied in the classroom.

Various Internet and web tools and applications were discussed with an emphasis on how they can be used in teaching and learning situations. And finally our views were presented on how to make full use of the Web but at the same time avoiding sensitive issues relating to its use.

QUESTIONS TO CONSIDER

1. How does the analogy of the information machine help you understand how the Internet can be used to enhance teaching and learning?

2. What are some ideas for web-enhanced projects that you have gained from this chapter?

3. How would you approach the problem of students viewing sensitive materials on the Internet?

4. Which of the Internet applications discussed in this chapter would be the easiest to incorporate into a typical classroom?

RELATED ACTIVITIES

1. Visit a classroom where the teacher makes effective use of the Internet. Interview the teacher and then write a summary of one web-enhanced project you identified in the classroom.

2. Choose a grade and a subject and write a web-enhanced project that you think would work well in that situation.

3. Identify a webquest by searching the Web and write a summary of how you would structure activities to allow students to participate in that webquest.

REFERENCES

Conner-Sax, K., & Krol, E. (1999). *The whole Internet: The next generation.* Cambridge, MA: O'Reilly.

Dove, M. K., Fisher, S. C., & Smith, D. L. (2000). Internet learning connections between second graders and university teacher education electronic mentors. *Computers in the Schools, 16,* 45–58.

Dutt-Doner, K. M., Wilmer, M., Stevens, C., & Hartman, L. (2000). Actively engaging learners in interdisciplinary curriculum through the integration of technology. *Computers in the Schools, 16,* 151–166.

Gilder, G. (1993, March) The information revolution. *The Executive Educator, 15*(3), 16–20.

Halpern, D. F. (1996). *Thought and knowledge: An introduction to critical thinking.* Mahwah, NJ: Lawrence Erlbaum.

Johnson, D. L. (1998). Rethinking the teacher as developer model. *Computers in the Schools, 14* (3/4), 1–4.

Johnson, D. L., & Liu, L. (2000). First steps toward a statistically generated information technology integration model. *Computers in the Schools, 16,* 3–12.

Maddux, C. D. (1994). The Internet: Educational prospects—and problems. *Educational Technology, 34*(7), 37–42.

Maddux, C. D., Johnson, D. L., & Willis, J. W. (1992). *Educational computing: Learning with tomorrow's technologies.* Boston: Allyn & Bacon.

Maddux, C. D., Johnson, D. L., & Willis, J. W. (1997). *Educational computing: Learning with tomorrow's technologies* (2nd ed.). Boston: Allyn & Bacon.

Maddux, C. D., Johnson, L., & Harlow, S. (Eds.). (1995). Teacher education and the Internet: Where do we go from here? In *Technology and teacher education annual, 1995* (pp. 581–584). Charlottesville, VA: Association for the Advancement of Computing in Education.

Montoya, I. (1992, December–January). Put a star in your classroom. *The Computing Teacher, 20*(4), 18–19.

Yost, N. (2000). Electronic expressions: Using e-mail to support emergent writing. *Computers in the Schools, 16,* 217–228.

CHAPTER ELEVEN

MULTIMEDIA AND HYPERMEDIA IN EDUCATION

This chapter was coauthored by Valentyna Kolomiyets.

Goal: To introduce the concepts of multimedia and hypermedia and explore the many types of educational material available in these two categories.

KEY TERMS

CD-ROM (p. 253)
cognitive overload (p. 274)
collections of data (p. 261)
electronic books (p. 268)
electronic texts (p. 269)
enhanced books (p. 269)
expanded books (p. 270)
hypermedia (p. 255)
hyperspace (p. 276)
information landscape (p. 275)
interactive fiction (p. 271)

laser disk (p. 259)
linear instruction (p. 256)
linking (p. 255)
multimedia (p. 252)
new media (p. 253)
new media book (p. 272)
new media encyclopedias (p. 263)
nonlinear instruction (p. 256)
replicated books (p. 269)
virtual reality (p. 278)

The field of education always has at least two or three "hot" topics that capture more than their share of attention during conferences, courses, workshops, and in journal articles. Typically, a topic heats up for a few years and then cools down; however, hot topics don't necessarily disappear after their time in the spotlight. Instead, they join the long list of other topics that continue to compete for the attention of educators. Nongraded elementary schools were popular in the 1970s, but by the end of the 1980s they were just another topic competing for attention. Hot topics in the 1990s included site-based management, accountability, back to the basics, collaborative learning groups, problem solving, reflective practice, reading and writing workshops, whole-language instruction, hypermedia, and multimedia. In the first decade of the twenty-first century, the Internet and its impact on society and education is a very hot topic. However, two 90s-era hot topics, multimedia and hypermedia, are still important, and they are the focus of this chapter. Hypermedia and multimedia have now moved into the mainstream of education and into the mainstream of society. You can find articles about this type of computer software in teacher publications, general interest magazines, and even local newspapers. And, you can learn about them on CNN, in several current television programs, and in more than a few recent movies. In this chapter, the basic definitions of these two types of software are discussed, along with expanded meanings of the terms. This chapter also explains how several types of hypermedia and multimedia can be used in education.

TECHNICAL DEFINITIONS AND FUZZY DEFINITIONS

Definitions of *hypermedia* and *multimedia* can be simple and technical or fuzzy and more complex. Both approaches to defining these decidedly slippery concepts are discussed in this chapter.

Multimedia

Technically, the term **multimedia** applies to any piece of consumer software that uses more than one medium of communication. Suppose, for example, that you create a tutorial program that contains only text. Then you add a few black-and-white figures or graphics to the program. Technically, the program is now multimedia because it contains two types of media—text and graphics. Some software developers actually use the term *multimedia* in this sense in their advertisements, but most people expect a bit more of a multimedia program. Fortunately, the great majority of software companies do not describe their programs as hypermedia just because more than one medium is involved.

The more complex, and hazy, concept of multimedia is harder to explain in the medium of text. Tay Vaughn (1994) has, however, made a good effort:

> Multimedia is an eerie wail as two cat's eyes appear on a dark screen. It's the red rose that dissolves into a little girl's face when you press "Valentine's Day." It's a small window of video, showing an old man recalling his dusty journey to meet a rajah, laid onto a map of India. It's a catalog of fancy cars with a guide to help you buy one. It's a real-time video conference with three colleagues in Paris, London, and Hong Kong on your office computer. (p. 4)

Vaughn is trying to create a word picture that conveys some of the excitement and interest generated by information presented in a multimedia format. If you go beyond the text and figures commonly seen in textbooks, magazines, and term papers, you're probably in multimedia territory. In Vaughn's definition, graphic animation ("cat's eyes appear on a dark screen"), sound ("an eerie wail"), morphing (the rose gradually changing to a child's face as you watch), video overlaid onto other types of graphics (the old man talking with a map of India in the background), and regular video (images and voices of distant colleagues in a video conference) all come together to produce this multimedia format. Some people prefer the term *new media* because it emphasizes media that has only recently become available on computers: high-quality sound, video, sophisticated animation, photographs, and high-quality graphics. The term **new media** generally refers to materials that are both multimedia (in the fuzzy sense) and hypermedia (discussed in the next section).

To be considered a legitimate piece of multimedia, a computer program should include text along with at least one of the following: audio or sophisticated sound, music, video, photographs, 3-D graphics, animation, or high-resolution graphics. However, this more detailed, technical definition isn't really the heart of multimedia. There is a different feel to multimedia. Part of the feel of multimedia is created by the quality of the sound and graphics. The backgrounds are sophisticated; the audio is spectacular; the photographs are crisp and clear. Part of the feel is created by the way multimedia materials are used. Most multimedia educational materials lend themselves to Type II rather than Type I uses, particularly when the material is formatted with hypermedia as well as multimedia.

A good example of a multimedia program is *Beethoven's 5th*, a detailed exploration both of the composer and his famous symphony. The opening screen of this program, which is distributed on **CD-ROM** because it is so large, presents four topics that can be explored (see Figure 11.1). (A fifth option takes players to games that test their knowledge, and a sixth allows the user to control the CD drive to play the symphony, in much the same way as you would on a regular CD player.) The topics cover both the symphony and the composer. For example, when you select the "Beethoven's Biography" option, you move to a series of screens about the composer and his family.

Figure 11.2 is the first screen in that series. On the right side of the screen is a drawing of an ancestral home; on the left is text about one of Beethoven's ancestors. The bottom left of this screen displays clickable buttons, a feature you can find in many multimedia packages. When you click the "Quote" button, a box of text appears on the screen that contains a quotation from Beethoven. This text box temporarily covers up the material under it until you click the mouse button again and it disappears. Today hundreds of multimedia packages are available on topics as diverse as Beethoven and NASCAR drag racing. They are usually sold on CD-ROMs and cost between $29 and $129 (most are between $29 and $59).

FIGURE 11.1   The opening menu for a program that combines text, graphics, and CD-quality sound.

Reprinted by permission from Plastronics Interactive Multimedia Ltd.

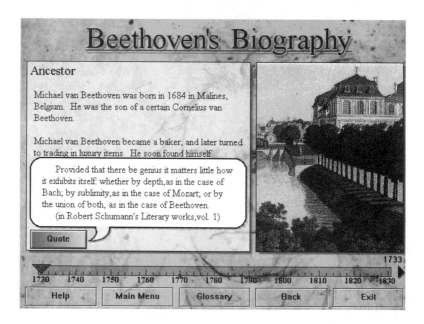

FIGURE 11.2   This program has quite a bit of information about Beethoven's background.

Reprinted by permission from Plastronics Interactive Multimedia Ltd.

Hypermedia

The term *multimedia* is a bit difficult to define, but defining the term *hypermedia* is even more difficult. The simple definition emphasizes the technical aspects: **hypermedia** are media that are linked. Remember how we explained earlier in this chapter that a simple tutorial could become a multimedia tutorial by adding a few graphics? That simple tutorial also can be made into a hypermedia program by replacing each graphic with text such as "Picture 1" and "Picture 2." In a hypermedia program a user can click on such text and see the actual picture pop up on the screen. In a simple sense, the text is "linked" to the picture. You can click text (or an icon that looks like a picture) and jump to another piece of information. This is hypermedia, the heart of which is **linking.** Linking text such as "Picture 1" to a photograph is one type of link, called a *text-to-graphic link.* Another type could link a word to its definition.

Consider the following example of a paragraph constructed using hypermedia:

> *Constructivist instruction* is not really instruction in the traditional sense. It is guidance and mentoring that focus on the child and his or her interests, background, and experience. Constructivist instruction often involves situated or anchored instruction that puts the learner in the role of a problem solver who must collaboratively work with other learners to learn basic skills and to acquire knowledge in order to solve the problem. 🖥 🖥

The italicized words in the preceding paragraph have special meanings in education. They are part of the vocabulary of constructivist approaches to teaching and learning that have emerged as major influences in the 1990s. (These approaches are discussed in Chapters 6 and 7.) In our example of a hypermedia paragraph, the italicized words would be linked to explanations or expanded definitions. If you clicked on the italicized word *Constructivist,* for example, a text window might pop up that contained additional information on the special meaning of that word in education. This is one type of hypermedia linking. If you clicked on the image 🖥 at the end of the paragraph, a short videoclip of children engaged in a constructivist activity in a fifth-grade classroom might appear on the screen. Similarly, clicking on the second image 🖥 might display a video from a middle-grade classroom. Both of these picture links are known as text-to-graphic links as mentioned earlier.

Hypermedia, in this simple example, is useful, but a definition does not really convey the power inherent in true hypermedia. Vaughn's (1994) more complex definitions of multimedia, interactive multimedia, and hypermedia have more punch:

> Multimedia is...woven combinations of text, graphic art, sound, animation, and video elements. When you allow an end user—the viewer of a multimedia project—to control what and when the elements are delivered, it is called *interactive multimedia.* When you provide a structure of linked elements through which the user can navigate, interactive multimedia becomes *hypermedia.* (p. 6)

A good example of interactive multimedia is *Leonardo: The Inventor,* a CD-ROM that traces the life of Leonardo da Vinci. This program combines voice narration, color graphics, animation, and superb background music to create a very interesting story of the life and accomplishments of da Vinci. The initial screen of this program is shown in Figure 11.3. A student can click the "Biography" button and go directly to a piece of information on his life. Click the "Inventions" button, and another screen allows you to select one of Leonardo's interests to explore: flight, water, music, civil engineering, or warfare (see Figure 11.4). The ability to move about in a hypermedia program and choose what next to explore signifies the material is **nonlinear.** Teacher-centered Type I instruction is generally **linear instruction:** the lesson begins at a particular point and proceeds through a set sequence. In contrast, nonlinear instruction, which is generally student-centered Type II instruction, does not have a prescribed sequence. In fact, much of the nonlinear educational material available today might best be described as information rather than instruction because it is designed for exploration rather than direct instruction, allowing students to determine what they want to learn.

Some theorists believe the nonlinear nature of hypermedia is its most important feature (Hartman & Schell, 1991). Others (McLellan, 1992; Riskin, 1990) believe the nonlinear nature of hypermedia requires explanation for students to understand and use effectively. McLellan (1992) studied how fifth-graders responded to nonlinear stories and traditional stories in children's books. She con-

FIGURE 11.3   The main menu screen from *Leonardo: The Inventor.*
Reprinted by permission from Mattel Interactive.

FIGURE 11.4   Selecting "Inventions" on the main menu takes you to this set of options.

Reprinted by permission from Mattel Interactive.

cluded that children who have not been exposed to the nonlinear structure of hypermedia stories can understand them and even create such stories of their own, but they do need guidance and help. Riskin (1990), in his study of multimedia in social studies, concluded that requiring students (in this case college students in a sociology class) to create multimedia modules using film, sound, photographs, text, and video resources helped them to think in a more creative and nonlinear way.

The *Leonardo* CD-ROM is interactive multimedia because the user determines which part of the program is displayed next on the screen. It is also hypermedia because a structure of linked elements allows the user to jump from one segment to another. These links allow you to explore one topic in depth or browse introductory material on many topics with equal ease; however, the lack of a set, prescribed way of progressing through the material means students may need navigation skills that are not necessary when they read magazines or books, which generally have an obvious linear sequence.

THE HARDWARE ISSUE

Early personal computers communicated with their human users through fuzzy text displayed on black-and-white (or green) video monitor screens. With the advent of graphics capabilities, users began to see simple line drawings, charts, and figures on their screens. That was 1978. Since then, progress has been rapid. Today, computers can display a fantastic array of text and graphic images, as well as sound quality that equals that of a CD player, and video that may look better than the videotape you rented last night (see Figure 11.5). We have come a long way in the past 25 years.

All that great sound, video, graphics, and text is possible because of advances in hardware and software. Video monitors, for example, are now capable of displaying color images that approach the quality of a color photograph in a magazine, and color scanners allow students to create electronic versions of images in magazines or books. In addition, sound cards can generate high-quality music, sound effects, and even synthesized voices (see Figure 11.6). (More work is needed, however, before you mistake computer-generated voices for those of your Aunt Marta or Uncle Horace.)

Of course, none of this was possible until computers became fast enough to handle all the data that must be processed each second when a multimedia program is running. Today's computers operate thousands of times faster than the 1970s-era machines, and the amount of memory and hard-disk storage the typi-

FIGURE 11.5   Extremely high-resolution graphics can now be displayed on computer screens.

Reprinted courtesy of ViewSonic.

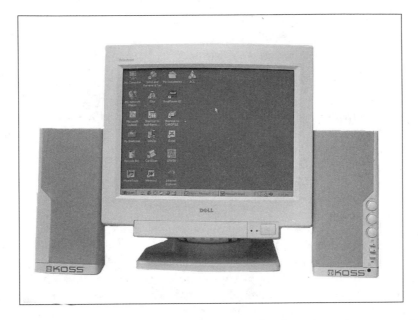

FIGURE 11.6   Now that high-quality sound and music are incorporated into many multimedia programs, several companies are manufacturing speaker systems for computers that attach to the monitor.

KOSS is a registered trademark of Koss Corporation, Milwaukee, WI, USA.

cal computer contains is gargantuan compared to machines only a few years old. In addition, new ways of storing data have expanded the possible uses of computers. When CD-ROM drives became available, all sorts of multimedia materials could be stored on CD. Most multimedia software sold in the 1990s was sold on CD. However, a single CD did not have the capacity to store something like a full-length Hollywood movie. A few years ago, a new type of storage medium, DVD, was developed. DVDs look like ordinary CDs but store four to eight times as much on each disk—the capacity to store a movie and lots of information about the movie, as well as the soundtrack in two or three different languages. CDs and DVDs have largely replaced **laser disks** for storing multimedia programs and movies to be played on computers.

Early video-based educational materials like the *Jasper Woodbury* programs discussed in Chapter 6 came with several videodiscs. The *Voyage of the Mimi*, which was developed by Bank Street College of Education, is another example of materials that used laser disks. The *Mimi* materials involve students as the crew on an ocean voyage of the 72-foot ketch, *Mimi*. The purpose of the voyage is to study whales. To complete the first voyage successfully, students must learn and use navigation principles, map reading, and many other skills. Seven videodiscs support this program, with videoclips that illustrate different phases of the voyage as well as simulated trips to museums, aquariums, and other places where scholars study the behavior of whales and other marine life.

The *Second Voyage of the Mimi,* which involves a voyage to Mexico to study the ancient Mayan civilization, also used laser disks. However, material such as *Jasper Woodbury* and *Voyage of the Mimi* are now being converted to CD-ROM and DVD, and new materials are being published only in CD or DVD formats. In addition, more and more material that would have been published on CD a few years ago are now appearing on the World Wide Web. Many sites contain everything from photographs to videoclips that can be run on a computer with an Internet connection. It is even possible to play complete movies over the Internet though the quality is still not outstanding.

NEW MEDIA IN SCHOOLS

New media, which includes hypermedia and multimedia, has many uses in schools. (Note: although the word *media* is plural, the term *new media,* as used here, denotes one genre of software and is, thus, singular.) All the types of new media discussed in this chapter—presentation support, collections of data, new media encyclopedias, and new media books—can be used for Type I applications. That is, they can support and enhance teaching strategies and methods that have traditionally been used in the classroom. However, they can also support innovative Type II approaches as well, and in many cases they were specifically designed to support Type II applications.

Presentation Packages

Presentation packages were discussed in Chapter 11. With many of these programs teachers as well as students can create presentations that include video from laser disks, audio from CDs or computer files, animation, photographs, and color graphics.

Collections of Data

If you or your students create multimedia presentations, all the sound, video, photos, and illustrations can be created locally if the topic also is local. Digital still cameras, such as the Sony Mavica, and digital videocameras are now affordable for many schools. Students can take a camera with them on field trips or into the lab, and capture images that can be downloaded from the camera to the computer in a matter of seconds. What happens, however, when your students want to produce a multimedia presentation on European geography or the Irish immigration to the United States? Students can create some of the graphics and design the presentation, but they need a source of images (and possibly video) to complete these projects. For class projects, many teachers allow students to scan images from encyclopedias, books, and magazines and then place them in their multimedia compositions. Scanners, when they work well, can capture some excellent images, but many times the result is less than satisfactory. Fortunately, several companies are now producing many collections of clip art, clip video, and clip photos. Clip collections were created specifically for use in building presentations. A few of the collections on CD-ROM from Andromeda Interactive, a British company, appear in the following list:

- *100 Flowering Plants:* Exotic and familiar plants
- *Wilderness Stills:* Three hundred photos of animals and nature
- *Famous Faces:* Digital video of famous people in the twentieth century
- *Space in Motion:* Digital video of Soviet and U.S. space voyages

A sample of the clip art distributed by Andromeda can be viewed at the company website: http://cdroms-dvds.org/publ10061.htm. Andromeda's collections cost around $50 each, and information is provided on each image and videoclip. That is not always the case, however. *Full Bloom* is a CD-ROM produced by Aris of photographs of one hundred different flowers. The photos can be displayed while appropriate music plays in the background, but Aris does not provide any information on the flowers in the photographs, something that might be needed for many educational applications.

A collection of data that does provide relevant support information (and an excellent user interface for searching the database) is *World History: 20th Century.* This $79 CD is a collection of more than one hundred newsreels in digital video format, as well as photos, graphs, and maps that highlight the major events of the twentieth century. If your school or school district acquires a few collections from suppliers such as Andromeda, students and teachers can draw on them for their multimedia productions. EduCorp, Laser Learning Technologies, and Computer CenterLine (addresses provided at the end of the chapter) carry large collections of clip art and digital video on CD-ROM as well as a growing number of DVD disks with videoclips.

Clip collections are not the only type of multimedia **collections of data.** A growing number of companies are producing multimedia materials on specific topics that take the form of tours or explorations (Figure 11.7). The CD-ROM *Leonardo: The Inventor,* for example, is a collection of data about Leonardo da Vinci. *Mammals,* which was produced by the National Geographic Society, is a multimedia database of text, photos, and (very fuzzy) video of mammals. *In the Company of Whales* is a multimedia CD on the ecology of whales (narrated in part by Patrick Stewart, who played Captain Picard on "Star Trek: The Next Generation").

A popular CD on painting is the *Microsoft Art Gallery.* This $80 program presents art from the National Gallery in London. You can visit the gallery through four different tours, with a tour guide who has an appropriately British voice. Each tour emphasizes a different topic: composition and perspective, making paintings, paintings as objects, and beneath the varnish (changes in painting over the ages). In addition, you can select topics such as time periods, everyday life, centers of art such as Florence, or mythological gods and goddesses and then view paintings related to the topic. As you move around the gallery, high-quality images of the paintings are displayed on the screen, and information on

FIGURE 11.7   You can find a number of free multimedia materials in the form of tours or explorations on the World Wide Web. The Franklin Institute Online (http://sln2.fi.edu/biosci/heart.html), for example, has an impressive multimedia database of materials on the heart.
Courtesy of The Franklin Institute Online.

everything from biographies of the artist to details about the creation of the painting is available. The images of the paintings are small, but the CD contains more than 2,000 of them. It also has a number of interesting links between different topics. For example, when you view a painting by Jean-Paul Forian that was owned by Henri Rouart, a hypermedia link can be clicked to take you to a painting by Edgar Degas of Rouart's daughter.

One of the best multimedia CDs on a specialized topic is *Ancient Cities*. It was developed in cooperation with the magazine *Scientific American* and is based on a book by the same name. *Ancient Cities* covers the cultural, military, and commercial history of four different centers: Crete, Petra, the Roman Empire's Pompeii, and the Aztec center of Teotihuacan. The text was written by experts on the archaeology of these sites, but the music that accompanies your tour of these places was created by an Academy Award winner, John Lewis, and the narration is by Rod McKuen. The CD has some of the most beautiful artwork, maps, and photography available on CDs of this type. It can be searched for information on different topics. Text you select, as well as photographs and video, can be exported and used in other programs.

Another popular collection of data is *BodyWorks,* a CD-based database of graphics and video on the human body. This program includes 3-D rotating images of different parts of the body, some digital movies, and high-quality graphics (see Figure 11.8). And for teachers interested in computer literacy topics, *ComputerWorks* is a multimedia CD on the fundamentals of how a computer operates that features animated graphics and a nice review of the history of computing

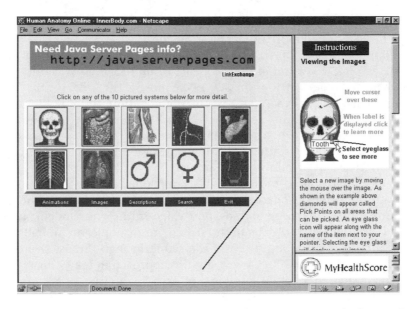

FIGURE 11.8   Human Anatomy Online (http://www.innerbody.com/htm/body.html) is *BodyWorks'* counterpart on the World Wide Web. This interactive reference site has text, graphics, and animations.

Screen shot from Human Anatomy Online (www.innerbody.com) provided by Intellimed International Corporation.

machinery. Many of these multimedia programs can be used as resources by students researching a topic. They also can be used by students or teachers for presentations or to support a presentation.

New Media Encyclopedias

Many forms of new media have been slow to penetrate the schools even after they achieve considerable popularity in homes. However, one genre of new media is already in many schools today, new media encyclopedias. Several companies, including Grolier, Compton's, Encyclopedia Britannica, and Microsoft, offer **new media encyclopedias.** They all are distributed on CD-ROM, and all have a user interface that permits students to search for information and download relevant data to a disk so that it can be used as source material for student compositions and presentations. Several of these encyclopedias are also available online. You can, for example, access Encyclopedia Britannica online at http://www.eb.com. You can try the online version for 14 days, but there is a fee for use after that. However, if you subscribe to America Online, the online version of *Compton's Interactive Encyclopedia* is available free of charge.

Compton's Interactive Encyclopedia is a popular and widely available CD-ROM encyclopedia. Macintosh and Windows versions are available in discount software stores, but we will not quote a price because by the time you read this it will have changed. (Encyclopedia Britannica's CD version originally sold for $995 but soon was selling for under $50 through special offers mailed to potential customers. Also, the CD-ROM version of Encyclopedia Britannica2000 was offered to registered owners of older versions for $20.) Like most of the others, *Compton's Interactive Encyclopedia* relies heavily on text. It contains more than 32,000 articles, but it also has 7,000 images, maps, and graphs, as well as more than 50 minutes of sound, music, and speech. The current version also includes many multimedia sequences that combine sound and either slide presentations or videoclips (which are shown in a small window on the screen).

The manual that comes with this encyclopedia says that "nine different entry paths to the encyclopedia" are provided, but four of them are no more than lists of the articles, pictures, sounds, and video in the encyclopedia. If you click on a "Picture" button at the top of the screen, for example, an alphabetized list of several hundred photos appears. You can scroll through the list and click on the short title of a photograph to view it, but this approach to searching leaves a great deal to be desired. Also of little use is the "Atlas" icon. Click it and a world globe appears on the screen. If you want to see a particular area, say around Houston, Texas, you must click on that area of the globe and then use the "Zoom In" command several times to focus on a smaller and smaller area. The wait, which can be substantial, is not worth it because the detail and information provided are often sparse and not helpful. Only two search alternatives, both based on text, are really useful in Compton's. One is "Topic Outline." You can display a short list of general topics and pick a subject such as "Education." Then another list of topics related to education appears. You could then click a topic such as "Bilingual Education" and begin reading an article on that topic.

The other way to search for information in Compton's is using keywords. This search system is well designed and fast. Enter a phrase such as *Colonial America,* and a list of 15 articles appears on the screen. Click any of them and you can begin reading the article (which may have pictures and video as well as text). The strength of Compton's may be that it has an extensive amount of textual information supported by a decent collection of photographs and illustrations. Its weakness is the user interface.

Microsoft's *Encarta* CD-ROM encyclopedia has a much more sophisticated interface and is competitively priced. It is an enhanced version of the Funk and Wagnalls print encyclopedia but has slightly less information (25,000 topics). However, the interface is far more powerful and usable; it contains more useful multimedia clips (e.g., video, sound and music, speeches); and it includes a functional atlas. You can, for example, click on "Southern Africa," locate Gabon, and get a wide range of information. You can even view the Gabonese flag and hear the country's national anthem. When you're not sure how to pronounce the name of a country, click a button and hear it pronounced. *Encarta* also has excellent support material, such as a quick-start booklet, a well-designed tour with voice support that teaches you how to use many features, and a nice set of guidelines on how to write a research paper. *Encarta*'s timeline is a graphic representation of history that begins in 15,000,000 B.C. and brings you up to the present. It is organized by eras and civilizations. The 1,000-B.C. era, for example, includes timelines for the Kush Kingdom in Africa, the Chou Dynasty in China, the Olmec civilization in Mexico, the Assyrian Empire, and Minoan and Greek civilizations. Icons along the timeline indicate important events that can be clicked on for more information.

Encarta also has a number of ways for searching broad topics and then narrowing down the scope of searches, as needed. Figure 11.9 shows the results of a search for Leadbelly, an African American folksinger whose style influenced many others. Figure 11.9 illustrates the layout of Encarta. Text information is in a window on the top right side of the screen. To the left is a section that tells you which general category this topic is in (Musicians & Composers). In the bottom left of the screen is a set of buttons for copying or printing the material. In Figure 11.9 the small speaker labeled "Leadbelly Sings Goodnight Irene" has been clicked, and a media window has opened on the bottom right. You can listen to this song by clicking the dark triangle pointing to the right. The media window also contains more text about Leadbelly. That text window, and most other windows, can be scrolled or expanded for easier reading.

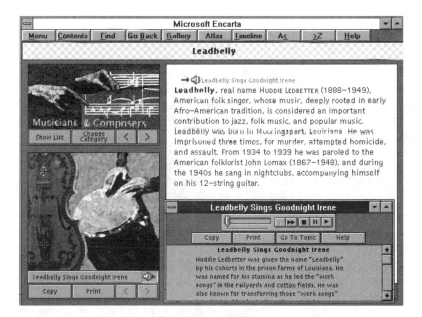

FIGURE 11.9   The speaker icon on this Encarta screen indicates that sound or music related to the topic is available as well as text. Many topics also have photographs, movies, or sound.

Screen shot reprinted with permission from Microsoft Corporation.

Most of the differences between *Encarta* and *Compton's Interactive Encyclopedia* reflect design philosophies. In many ways Compton's is a print encyclopedia that has been put on a CD-ROM so it can be accessed via computer. Microsoft's *Encarta,* on the other hand, is an electronic encyclopedia that uses source material from a printed encyclopedia. This difference in philosophies is evident even in the copyright notices in the user's guides that come with the CD-ROMs. Compton's (1994) notice follows:

> All images reproduced in this product, including photographs, drawings, maps, and video, are protected under international copyright law. No reproduction or reuse of this material may be made in any form without permission in writing from the publisher.

Everyone agrees that students should not write a term paper by copying paragraphs or sentences from a source such as an encyclopedia. They can get the *information* from such sources, but the term paper should be in their own words using their own organization. But what about illustrations, photographs, and videoclips? Many students now have access to programs that facilitate incorporating photographs, drawings, or videoclips into term papers. Compton's copyright notice forbids such use. Now consider *Encarta*'s (1992) message about copyright. After informing you that the "Copy" button should not be used to copy text, pictures, or audio to the Window's clipboard for use in other commercial publications, the manual gives this guideline:

> When writing a research paper, it's absolutely essential to make it clear to your readers which ideas are yours and which came from research material. You do this by acknowledging your source in a citation. A citation for *Encarta* should at least include the copyright information that is automatically included when you copy or print text or pictures. In addition, it will help your readers to know the topic title, and the subheading (if any), in case they want to consult *Encarta* on your subject. (p. 4)

Microsoft *Encarta* thus gives students permission to reuse material *if* it is cited properly. Additional guidelines explain how to handle quoted (versus paraphrased) material. This enlightened approach makes sense for an electronic encyclopedia, which is supposed to be a source of material for students who may be creating multimedia essays or making multimedia presentations. *Encarta* is state of the art in electronic encyclopedias.

Electronic encyclopedias can be used in much the same way as ordinary encyclopedias, with the added benefit of electronic support for organizing, copying, and printing material from them. Using these resources may require some additional instruction, but that is probably justified in view of the trend toward electronic information resources in virtually every profession. Some teachers, and some librarians, may yearn for the heft and feel of "real" (i.e., printed-book) encyclopedias, and they may think that electronic encyclopedias complicate the student's life unnecessarily. Most, however, are enthusiastic about them. Melnick (1991), for example, made these observations:

> Why would children want to use electronic encyclopedias rather than the traditional bound volumes? The most obvious answers are motivation and ease of use. While observing a middle-school librarian instruct a child in the use of the electronic encyclopedia (which took only about 5 minutes), I noticed that several other children gathered to watch the search. When the librarian finished, another child, John, who had been watching, sat down and began a search on mammals. Within minutes, he was able to successfully define his search and skim relevant articles that would have been spread over several bound volumes of the encyclopedia.
>
> Another feature that makes the electronic encyclopedia unique is Hypertext. For instance, John encountered several difficult words in the text.... If these words were highlighted, he was able to have a voice pronounce the word for him and give a brief definition of it. Even if the word was not highlighted, by placing the cursor over the word and clicking the mouse, John was presented with a complete dictionary entry of that word. (p. 433)

Some research even indicates that students can actually get more, and better, information from electronic encyclopedias. Edyburn (1991) found that junior high–school students, both learning-disabled and nondisabled, were more successful when they used menu-driven electronic encyclopedias such as *Encarta* to search for information rather than regular print encyclopedias.

Because electronic encyclopedias are purchased in large numbers by parents and schools, this segment of the multimedia market is volatile as companies compete to capture the attention of customers with new versions and innovations. Recently, for example, a version of the Funk and Wagnalls encyclopedia was put online at http://www.funkandwagnalls.com/. This occurred in spite of the fact that Microsoft's *Encarta* is based on the print version of the Funk and Wagnalls encyclopedia. The online site offers free access and is clearly designed to appeal to students. Advertisements on the site seem to be the source of income for the site owner, but the site has much to offer including access to a dictionary, thesaurus, and world atlas, as well as a general and an animal encyclopedia. *Encarta,* the first electronic "child" of Funk and Wagnalls, has regularly added new features, including links to sites on the Internet. If the information in *Encarta* itself is not adequate, students can click on links that take them to World Wide Web locations where more information is available.

One good source of information about both electronic and print encyclopedias is *Purchasing an Encyclopedia, 12 Points to Consider,* published by the American Library Association. The fifth edition was published in 1996, but by the time you read this book, a more current edition should be available. This short booklet contains general guidelines for selecting an encyclopedia as well as information about current editions of popular encyclopedias. Joyce Valenza's (1997) article "How to Choose an Encyclopedia" is another helpful source. Valenza divides CD-ROM encyclopedias into two categories: mass-market versions for children age 9 and above (*Compton's Interactive, Encarta, Grolier,* and *World Book*) and "academic" encyclopedias for ages 14 and above (*Britannica CD* and *Encyclopedia Americana*).

Electronic Versions of Books

The final type of new media to be discussed in this chapter is **electronic books.** Traditional print books have a long history of use in both elementary and secondary schools, and some teachers are concerned that new electronic forms of books may replace traditional print books, to the detriment of children's learning. Jobe (1984), for example, wondered, "Will books have a place in the computer classroom" (p. 6)? He was concerned that computer-based reading instruction, using traditional drill-and-practice and tutorial approaches, might replace the teacher as the primary means of providing reading instruction. And along with the teacher would go real literature. The result could be a barren classroom where children learn to read with uninteresting and decidedly nonliterary material delivered on the computer screen. Jobe concluded that keeping children's literature in the schools was absolutely essential, and teachers must be ready to fight for it.

Now, almost 20 years after Jobe's paper, the situation seems quite different. The computer has not taken over reading instruction in the elementary grades, and there does not appear to be any chance that it will over the next decade. Computers do support the reading program in many schools, but the emphasis is on support, not replacement (Anderson-Inman & Horney, 1997; McNabb, 1998). With the arrival of new media, however, many classics of literature, as well as the work of several contemporary authors, have been produced in electronic book form. Instead of driving literature from the classroom, which was Jobe's concern, multimedia and hypermedia (new media) allow authors to create a new type of book, thus introducing even more literature into the classroom.

When hand-copied books first became popular to the educated and well-to-do, some Greek philosophers worried that writing down thoughts might lead to a reduction in the memory capacity of readers because people had been required to memorize material before books were available. Then, when Gutenberg invented the printing press, some criticized this mechanical approach because it did not have the grandeur and quality of the manuscripts produced by hand. That did not prevent the new, mechanically printed books from becoming a foundation of civilization for the next several hundred years.

Similar concerns have been expressed as innovations such as desktop publishing and laser printers have revolutionized the creation and production of books. It is not difficult to imagine how people accustomed to books being hand chiseled on stone tablets might predict doom and destruction, pointing out that the newfangled paper books are too fragile and not as permanent as stone. Now some people express negative reactions to electronic books. Some find it anathema even to think of placing a classic children's book (or a current novel) on a computer screen. This section explores some of the issues related to electronic books and describes several types of "e-books."

A number of educators have enthusiastically endorsed the use of e-books (Parham, 1993; Truett, 1993). Several types of e-books exist. Some do not seem to be worth the effort whereas others add many additional features to the traditional printed book. In this section five types of electronic books are discussed: replicated books, electronic texts, expanded books, interactive fiction, and new media books.

Replicated Books.   **Replicated books** are electronic versions of printed books that do no more than replicate or copy the pages of a book onto a computer screen. Electronic books of this type are often called *page turners* because the only involvement you have with them on the computer is turning the pages. Generally, replicated books are not worth the extra cost and inconvenience when compared with traditional books.

Electronic Texts.   For several years, Michael Hart has been the director of the Gutenberg Project at Illinois Benedictine College. This project is an effort to make electronic versions of classic documents, texts, and literature available to everyone who has access to the Internet. Hart and his colleagues have organized and made available thousands of texts. **Electronic texts** are text-only copies of well-known books and documents. They can be downloaded from the Gutenberg Project website (http://www.gutenberg.net/).

Electronic texts might not seem as useful as replicated books because they do not even include illustrations or figures. However, electronic texts are ordinary data files and can be read by word-processing programs and database software. Therefore, any operation you can perform on a standard text file can be performed on an electronic text. For example, in a unit on Shakespeare, students could use textual analysis in a study of Shakespeare's works to identify gender biases prevalent in the Tudor era. Electronic texts are an ideal format for such an analysis because they allow searching for instances of certain words and text patterns necessary for the analysis.

Enhanced Books.   Apple's original laptop computer, the Powerbook, inspired The Voyager Company, a pioneer in educational laser disks, to begin producing a form of enhanced book.

> On June 16 [1989], the day fans of James Joyce celebrate the groundbreaking novel *Ulysses*, The Voyager Company held a conference on a literary experiment of a different sort—the electronic book. The scholars and critics present were of one mind: No one, they said, will ever voluntarily read on screen without significant incentives, most likely in the form of masses of linked text, video and audio clips, or other elements from a multimedia trick bag. The people at Voyager tended to agree—until they saw Apple's Powerbook. (Matazonni, 1992, p. 16)

An **enhanced book** is a book in electronic form that takes advantage of at least some of the capabilities of a computer to add features to the book. Voyager called theirs **expanded books.** The Voyager expanded books are quite different from the Gutenberg e-texts. Expanded books contain all the graphics and illustrations found in the print versions of a book, and they can be searched by keyword just as electronic texts can. You can also mark interesting passages with a black line on the right margin, type your own notes in the margins, "dog-ear" a page by turning down the top edge or putting an "electronic paper clip" on the side, mark passages and name them so you can return to them by selecting the name or retrace your steps through the book after you have been browsing around.

Voyager has tried to keep the feel and appearance of a book while adding some electronic features. As Matazoni notes, "Instead of setting up a screen full of buttons, icons, and scroll bars, the Expanded Books team decided on a display that looks as much as possible like a book. All features remain hidden until you ask for them. You don't scroll text, you turn pages. To mark a page, you turn down a corner or insert a paper clip" (p. 17). All the expanded books have the same, simple format, because, as Voyager project manager Sandra Mueller explains, "We're introducing the basic construct—this is what a book looks like on the screen. We want to keep the design consistent so that the metaphor gets firmly established in readers' minds" (quoted in Matazonni, 1992, p. 19).

Whether Voyager's expanded book format will be successful is still open to question. After the novelty of a book on a computer disk wears off, there may not be enough "value added" in them to be anything more than a novelty. They may become a niche product that meets the needs of certain people. For example, travelers who carry laptop computers anyway could put several expanded books on their hard-disk drive and read them on the trip instead of carrying printed books. Their use in classrooms, however, may be limited. On the other hand, expanded books could become a normal part of literature classes because they offer so many options for personal study and annotation.

We take this same cautious approach to a new generation of specialized computers that are about the size of a hardback book and designed specifically to display "books" on a flat panel display. Softbook and Rocketbook are two of several models that are sometimes called *tablet computers* because they look a little like a traditional writing tablet or legal pad. Owners can purchase and download books, as well as other types of publications, into the memory of the computer and read them as pages are displayed on the flat display. Using a stylus, you can make the electronic equivalent of marginal notes on the book.

Another company that produces expanded books is Discis. Whereas most of the books from Voyager, Softbook, and Rocketbook are for adults, Discis is the best-known developer of expanded books for children. Discis produces enhanced book versions of a wide range of classic and contemporary books for children. Discis' books have color illustrations and many features that allow children to interact with them. Like the Voyager expanded books, they retain much of the feel of a traditional printed book, with enhancements accessible only on a computer. Most enhancements involve support for various types of interaction. They include the following options: having stories read aloud in a variety of voices; changing the appearance of text; using background music and sound effects; a help feature allowing students to identify problem words, to hear them pronounced, and to have meanings explained; and versions of books written in different languages. In contrast to replicated books, which offer little in the way of added value, the Discis books do add value to the traditional print book. It would be interesting to study, for example, the impact of these features, such as selecting a word and hearing it pronounced and defined, on students with reading problems. Might they read more because difficult words do not stop them or make them lose the meaning of a sentence? Might they recognize and understand the words in other contexts? Might they read more printed books?

Interactive Fiction.   Another type of electronic book that has been used in classrooms is **interactive fiction.** Interactive fiction is a form of writing that requires the reader to respond regularly to the situation presented in the text. Often the reader takes the role of one of the characters in the story and makes decisions about that character. The reader's decisions then determine what happens next in the story. Some interactive fiction books have hundreds of decision points in the plot, which means the story can have many different endings.

Several educators have reported that interactive fiction is effective as a way of teaching certain reading and writing skills (Grabe & Dosmann, 1988) as well as problem solving (Desilets, 1989). Although most of the research has been conducted in elementary and middle schools, Finnegan and Sinatra (1991) used interactive fiction to teach basic and advanced literacy skills to adults.

In the elementary and middle grades, Lancy and Hayes (1988) found that reluctant readers spent more time reading when the material was interactive fiction (if students were successful in any quests or problem solving required by the story). The authors started students on interactive fiction that required only limited reading skill and gradually progressed to interactive fiction that required much more reading skill. When the interactive fiction presented problems or puzzles a student could not solve, he or she was given help. Some students, however, became "stuck" at particular points in some interactive fiction programs. This was the only condition that caused them to give up and stop reading. The authors concluded that interactive fiction can be one way of encouraging students to read independently.

Plot decision points that require solving a puzzle can be frustrating, particularly when a difficult or poorly designed mystery must be figured out. This is one design problem frequently encountered in interactive fiction. In his review of interactive fiction, Packard (1987) also found wide variations in the quality of the writing style, subject matter, ethical content, and appeal of choices at plot branches. Teachers considering the use of interactive fiction in their classes should evaluate each interactive fiction book carefully for appropriateness, appeal, and usability. They should also keep in mind that some interactive fiction is designed for adults and may have a strong sexual theme.

Even considering the precautions that should be taken when thinking about interactive fiction, this form of electronic book has considerable potential for engaging sustained attention and for improving reading and study skills (Grabe &

Dosmann, 1988). It can also be an expressive medium. Newman (1988) described work with Australian fifth-graders that included creating interactive fiction using a program called *Story Tree*. In the 1990s extensive work was done to develop lessons that involve the use of interactive fiction for many different subject areas. Desilets (1999) developed and maintains a website about the many ways interactive fiction can be used in the classroom. The site (http://k12s.phast.umass.edu/ ~desilets/fun.html) includes information on many interactive fiction programs, descriptions of ways teachers have used the programs, and lesson plans as well as advice on how best to integrate interactive fiction into your teaching.

New Media Books.   The final type of electronic book to be discussed is the **new media book.** New media books (often referred to as *multimedia books,* although the term *hypermedia books* is more appropriate) take full advantage of the multimedia and hypermedia capabilities of computers. They are nonlinear; they use graphics, animation, and video; and they support many types of interaction. Several new media books have already been discussed in this chapter. *Leonardo: The Inventor,* for example, is a new media book as well as a collection of data. It is considered a collection of data because it contains many types of information about a particular topic. It is considered a book because it is a systematic, organized presentation on a particular topic. If it had been created 25 years ago, it would have been a standard printed book. Today it combines animation, text, narration, a musical soundtrack, photographs, and outstanding color illustrations. Not all collections of data are books, however. *World History: 20th Century* and the *20th Century Video Almanac* are just collections of data. You can find and select material from the collection, but no organizing structure makes it into a book. *Beethoven's 5th,* on the other hand, is another new media book, as are *BodyWorks* and *Ancient Cities.* Hundreds of new media books are already available, and thousands soon will be.

New media books have been particularly successful as children's books. New media children's books have sold more than any other type of e-book. The best-known of this genre is the *Living Books* series from Broderbund. Many are based on the printed books of well-known children's book authors, and quite a few are original creations, by established authors, in the new media book format. Perhaps the best-known thus far in this genre is Mercer Mayer's *Just Grandma and Me,* a CD-ROM storybook about a child's trip to the beach with his grandmother (Figure 11.10). This new media book can be read in much the same way as a printed version. Detailed illustrations appear on each page, with some text at the bottom of the page. There are, however, much more interactive ways of using books such as *Just Grandma and Me.*

For example, a reader can select to have the story read in English, Spanish, or Japanese. As you might expect, there are options for moving from page to page in the story. These features are not, however, why children are so attracted to them. While writing this chapter on a Sunday afternoon, I (JW) found it necessary to make a trip to a software store to pick up one or two examples of the Voyager expanded books. In the store I heard the unmistakable sound effects and music of *Just Grandma and Me*. Two young children were playing on a demonstration computer while their mother and father shopped for other types of educational software. The rich drawings on each screen of *Just Grandma and Me* contain many "hot spots"—objects that react when they are clicked with the mouse cursor. For example, when you click on the knothole in a tree while the grandmother and child are waiting for the bus to take them to the beach, a squirrel peeks out and then runs around the tree trunk. When you click the mailbox, it pops open. None of these objects are marked *active* or *clickable*. Part of the appeal is finding those that are.

Some objects actually add additional material to the story. Click on a balloon at the beach, and grandma buys one. When she hands it to the child, it flies into the air taking the child with it, complete with appropriate sound effects and comments. The rich, creative interactivity of the *Living Books* is why the kids at the software store sought out their parents and insisted they see the program. On any page 10 to 20 objects react when clicked. Most reactions are animations; most include sound and music; and some react differently when clicked a second or third time. All add appeal to the program.

Other popular new media books in this series include *The Tortoise and the Hare* and *Arthur's Teacher Troubles*. All use the same format of a lushly illustrated storybook that can be read by children or to children in any of several languages.

FIGURE 11.10   A screen from *Just Grandma and Me*. Many of the objects on this screen respond when clicked.

Copyright © 1992 Living Books.

Each illustration has active objects for the child to explore. Today, children's entertainment is dominated by television, a passive medium in which most popular programs do not ask much of the viewer. New media books such as *Just Grandma and Me* offer some of the action and color of television with the benefit of being interactive rather than passive. New media books may encourage reading, which today must compete with television (a few rungs higher on many children's priority list) for a child's attention. The genre is too new to predict how these books will be used in education, but a bright future should await interactive books such as *Just Grandma and Me*.

THE PROBLEMS AND PROMISES OF NEW MEDIA

The promise of new media is apparent when you use a program. Instead of reading about the D-Day invasion, a CD on the event allows you to hear broadcasts from the front, see photographs and video of different theaters of battle, and travel from one battle area to another by clicking on a map displayed on your computer screen. New media brings you closer to an event, process, or concept than most other forms of information. It can be, as an ad says, "the next best thing to being there."

Cognitive Overload

For all their promise, however, there are a number of problems with new media. Perhaps foremost is the problem of **cognitive overload.** Textbooks have built-in limits to the way they are organized and the amount of information that can be delivered. Publishers limit the size of textbooks. If your contract calls for a 200-page book and you submit a manuscript that will produce a 600-page book, the editor is not going to be happy. A chapter is typically about 15 to 25 pages, and the amount of text you can include is reduced by each figure, photograph, and table you add. In addition, a textbook is inherently linear. You begin with Chapter 1, proceed through that chapter, and then move on to Chapter 2. The limitations of a textbook do not apply, however, to a multimedia instructional package that is delivered on CD-ROM. All the text, figures, and black-and-white illustrations in a typical 250-page textbook could be stored electronically in about 90 meg of space on your computer's hard drive. A CD-ROM, which costs about 90 cents to manufacture, can store more than 500 meg of data. Teachers who can proudly announce that their students "cover the entire textbook" each year without skipping any of the chapters will have a hard time saying the same thing when a CD replaces the text. There is just too much information to cover, and electronic resources do not lend themselves to traditional teaching strategies in which students study an assignment and then are tested on the material. They are better suited to other forms of instruction, such as problem solving and cooperative learning projects, in which the information resources available are used selectively by students as they work toward a common goal, such as solving a problem.

Ineffective Information Landscapes

The amount of information, and the ability to arrange the information in nonlinear ways, puts considerable pressure on the user interface. When it is difficult, or confusing, to locate relevant information in a multimedia resource, the problem generally lies in the user interface. One of the authors of this book ordered a CD of educational software from an ad recently and found that it was organized into about 25 different subdirectories (or folders) with names such as 001WD, 234KL, and so on. The only way to use any of the software on the CD was to open each subdirectory (folder), read the names of the files (which had equally nonfunctional names, such as SpotRD and Baloon2), select a piece of software, and run it. There was virtually no user interface, only a collection of about 500 programs on a CD. Multimedia resources need outstanding user interfaces because it is easy to get lost or confused when you are working with huge amounts of information.

As you evaluate multimedia, an important feature to consider is the user interface or **information landscape.** The term *information landscape* refers to the way information is organized, as well as to the interface by which the user accesses information. Florin (1990) highlights the critical importance of the information landscape in new media materials:

> How do people present knowledge so that others can understand it? The traditional method is a linear, narrative, unfolding of sequential information...for example, lectures and textbooks. Other methods rely on a nonlinear, spatial layout of information...for example, diagrams and maps.... I have begun to think of our HyperCard environments as information landscapes which can be thought of as virtual towns or intellectual amusement parks....
>
> As you visit an information landscape, you can merely walk along pathways and look at roadside attractions, or you can choose from many different options. Some of the options take you on linear trails, which you experience passively from start to finish, as you would a ride in a bus. Other activities give you local control similar to driving a car. Maps can show you a bird's eye view of the territory; and guides can take you on tours or give you more conversational assistance.
>
> The terrain on which the information landscape is built is the raw database, rich with various materials, from which the "visitor" can create new documents or exhibits. However, the information structure is what gives the landscape its distinctive features. (pp. 29–31)

Before computers and other information technology were widely available, finding information was often a critical task. Today, following the computer and information revolutions, the problem is not so much finding information as it is sifting through the huge amount that is readily available and locating the particular pieces that are of most interest at the moment. The quality of the *user interfaces* (the old term), or *information landscapes* (the new term), has a great deal to do with whether a new media program is easy to use and helpful or frustrating and irritating. There is much to be learned about the design of information landscapes, but it is clear that most new media products require graphical interfaces.

Often graphical information landscapes apply traditional landscape elements such as a table of contents, an index, chapters, and headings. A graphical information landscape may also serve as the main interface, with options that are text-based. For example, *The Animals,* a CD-ROM collection of data from the San Diego Zoo, has a colorful graphic map of the entire zoo that can be displayed onscreen. If you are interested in particular types of animals, such as those that live on the savannas of Africa, you can click on that area of the graphic map and move directly to the material about the animals of that region. The data on *The Animals* CD-ROM can also be searched by keyword. If you would like to go to the section on meerkats, for example, you can enter that word, press the "Return" key, and move immediately to the section that has text, photos, and a short movie about these interesting animals.

Often information landscapes are designed around a metaphor. *The Animals,* for example, uses the metaphor of a zoo. *Life Story,* a program discussed in more detail in the next chapter, is about the discovery of DNA (Florin, 1990). The information landscape for this program is the double helix structure of DNA. The story revolves around the work of two British research teams, one in Cambridge and one in London, who were working on the same problem. In this new media program, students see a double strand of DNA on the computer screen. Each strand represents the work of one of the teams. Click along the "London" strand and you get information (video, text, audio) on the work of that research team. The user interface, or information landscape, of *Life Story* facilitates exploration of the information. The quality and "fit" of a program's information landscape determines, in part, how useful the program is.

If you would like to view samples of interesting information landscapes, visit the Atlas of Cyberspaces website to view a number of examples. This website is the work of Martin Dodge (2000) at University College London and is devoted to the study of visual representations of cyberspace—the electronic space occupied by information stored on computers. One part of the site is devoted to information landscapes (http://www.cybergeography.org/atlas/info_landscapes.html). You can go directly to this page and view several information landscapes, but other parts of the site also discuss and illustrate information landscapes (Figure 11.11).

Lost in Hyperspace

Is it easy to use? Can students comfortably move about the information landscape of the resource? Can they browse through the information to get a feel for both how much there is and how it is organized? In very large databases, can they specify search criteria and go directly to the relevant information? Is there a way of placing bookmarks to make it easier to find their way back to that spot? Does the interface "remember" past excursions and allow students to retrace their steps? All these features help a person keep track of where they are in the information space, sometimes called **hyperspace** or *cyberspace*. With huge amounts of information and a poorly structured information landscape, it is easy for students, and teachers, to get lost in hyperspace.

Does the visual organization of the user interface help the user understand the structure of the information? Information landscapes need not be as inti-

FIGURE 11.11   A screen from The Atlas of Cyberspaces (http://www.cybergeography. org/atlas/info_landscapes.html).
Courtesy of Keith Andrews, Graz University of Technology, Austria.

mately tied to the topic as in *Life Story,* but they all should be easy to understand and use and should help students quickly develop an understanding of the depth and breadth of the information resource. Many of the information landscapes used today do not meet these criteria.

Appropriate Links

Another area of concern is the way different pieces of information are linked. Are the links appropriate for your purposes? Are there too few links? Too many? Are the links understandable: do students know where they're going when they use a link? In hypermedia packages, are the links between different pieces of information fixed or can students create their own links? The links in most of the hypermedia materials on the market today are fixed. They cannot be changed, and new links cannot be added. For some applications, however, it is desirable for students to be able to create their own links or pathways through the information.

SUMMARY

Multimedia, hypermedia, and *new media* are all terms associated with a hot topic in education today, the merging of computer technology with media such as animation, sound and music, video, photographs, and high-quality graphics. The power of new media in education is only just being realized; however, several types of educational software, including presentation programs, multimedia collections of data, electronic encyclopedias, and electronic books are already on the market. Teachers are already exploring how they can be used in the classroom, but these initial explorations of the new media frontier will likely lead to teaching strategies and approaches that are only vaguely realized today. The problems of new media—cognitive overload, information landscapes that do not effectively convey the structure and extent of the information hyperspace, and the tendency to get "lost in hyperspace"—all have to be addressed and solved.

New media may even give way to **virtual reality,** an emerging technology that creates a complete electronic environment in which the player experiences activities as if they were real. For example, *Beethoven's 5th,* a program discussed in this chapter, uses animation, CD-quality music, voice narration, and excellent graphics. In a few years, perhaps a virtual reality program will allow a student to walk into an empty room and, by asking different questions, have the experience of watching Beethoven work on the symphony or of walking down the streets where Beethoven grew up (as they were when he was alive), or of sitting in a front-row seat as the symphony plays.

QUESTIONS TO CONSIDER

1. Think of the worst and best class you had in elementary school (or middle school or high school). If new media resources had been used in that class, how would it have been different? If you were teaching that class today, how would you be able to use new media?

2. If new media materials become a major source of information, will it be necessary to rethink what it means to be "literate"? Will the ability to navigate complex information landscapes be important?

RELATED ACTIVITIES

1. Explore at least three pieces of new media instructional materials on topics of interest to you. Decide what type of new media they are (e.g., replicated book, electronic encyclopedia), then evaluate the design and structure of the products in relation to a particular use (such as an optional reading for a group of middle-grade students in a remedial reading program). Is the breadth and depth of content suitable? Is the interface (information landscape) appropriate?

2. Locate a lesson plan that does not use new media resources and modify it to include the use of new media materials available to you.

3. Visit a local software store that carries educational products (or the preview center of the university or a local school district). Make a list of new media materials (at least 5 items but no more than 15) that would be particularly useful in teaching a topic that interests you.

REFERENCES

American Library Association. (1996). *Purchasing an encyclopedia: 12 points to consider.* New York: Booklist Publications.

Anderson-Inman, L., & Horney, M. (1997). Electronic books for secondary students. *Journal of Adolescent and Adult Literacy, 40*(6), 486–491.

Desilets, B. (1999). Fun and learning with interactive fiction. Retrieved April 16, 2000, from the World Wide Web: http://k12s.phast. umass.edu/~desilets/fun.html

Desilets, B. (1989). Reading, thinking, and interactive fiction (instructional materials). *English Journal, 78*(3), 75–77.

Dodge, M. (2000). The atlas of cyberspaces. Retrieved April 16, 2000, from the World Wide Web: http://www.geog.ucl.ac.uk/casa/martin/atlas/ atlas.html

Edyburn, D. (1991, fall). Fact retrieval by students with and without learning handicaps using print and electronic encyclopedias. *Journal of Special Education Technology, 11*(2), 75–90.

Finnegan, R., & Sinatra, R. (1991, October). Interactive computer-assisted instruction with adults. *Journal of Reading, 35*(2),108–119.

Florin, E. (1990). Information landscapes. In S. Ambron & K. Rooper (Eds.), *Learning with interactive multimedia.* Redmond, WA: Microsoft.

Grabe, M., & Dosmann, M. (1988, September). The potential of adventure games for the development of reading and study skills. *Journal of Computer-Based Instruction, 15*(2), 72–77.

Hartman, D., & Schell, J. (1991, winter). Using hypertext to enhance advanced learning, thinking, and application. *Journal of Studies in Technical Careers, 13*(9), 47–59.

Jobe, R. (1984). *Explore the future: Will books have a place in the computer classroom?* British Columbia, Canada (ERIC Document Reproduction Service No. ED 243 102).

Lancy, D., & Hayes, B. (1988, November). Interactive fiction and the reluctant reader. *English Journal, 77*(7), 12–16.

Matazzoni, J. (1992, October). Books in a new light. *Publish, 7*(10), 16–21.

McLellan, H. (1992). Narrative and episodic story structure in interactive stories. In *Proceedings of Selected Research and Development Presentations at the Convention of the Association for Educational Communications and Technology* (pp. 124–133). (ERIC Document Reproduction Service No. ED 348 012).

McNabb, M. (1998). Using electronic books to enhance the reading comprehension of struggling readers. *National Reading Conference Yearbook, 47*, 405–414.

Melnick, S. (1991, February). Electronic encyclopedias on compact disk (reading technology). *Reading Teacher, 44*(6),432–434.

Newman, J. (1988, March). Write your own adventure. *Language Arts, 65*(3),329–337.

Packard, E. (1987, October). Interactive fiction for children: Boon or bane? *School Library Journal, 34*(2),40–41.

Parham, C. (1993). CD ROM storybooks: New ways to enjoy children's literature. *Technology & Learning, 13*(4), 34–41.

Riskin, S. (1990). *Teaching through interactive multi media programming. A new philosophy of the social sciences and a new epistemology of creativity.* (ERIC Document Reproduction Service No. ED 327 133).

Truett, C. (1993, August–September). CD ROM storybooks bring children's literature to life. *The Computing Teacher, 21*(1), 20–21.

Valenza, J. (1997, May–June). How to choose an encyclopedia. *Electronic Learning, 16*(6), 50–53.

Vaughn, T. (1994). *Multimedia: Making it work.* Berkeley, CA: Osborne McGraw-Hill.

SOFTWARE DISCUSSED IN THIS CHAPTER

The Adventures of Jasper Woodbury. Available from Optical Data Corporation. The company's web page is at http://www.opticaldata.com/

Ancient Cities. Sumeria, 329 Bryant Street, Suite 3D, San Francisco, CA 94107. Phone 415-904-0800.

Andromeda clip collections are available from Andromeda Interactive, 11 15 The Vineyard, Abingdon, Oxfordshire OX143PX. Phone 44-0235-529595.

The Animals. The Software Toolworks, 60 Leveroni Court, Novato, CA 94949. Phone 415-883-3000.

Arthur's Teacher Trouble. Mattel Interactive. http://www.mattelinteractive.com

Beethoven's 5th: A Multimedia Symphony. Interactive Publishing Corporation, 300 Airport Executive Park, Spring Valley, NY 10977.

BodyWorks. Software Marketing Corporation, 9830 South 51st Street, Bldg. A, 131, Phoenix, AZ 85044. Phone 602-893-3377.

Encyclopedia Brittanica. http://www.brittanica.com.

CD Storytime. Interactive Publishing Corporation, 300 Airport Executive Park, Spring Valley, NY 10977.

Compton's Interactive Encyclopedia. Compton's New-Media, 2320 Camino vida Roble, Carlsbad, CA 92009.

ComputerWorks. Software Marketing Corporation, 9830 South 51st Street, Bldg. A, 131, Phoenix, AZ 85044. Phone 602-893-3377.

Discis Books. Discis Knowledge Research, P.O. Box 66, Buffalo, NY 14233-0066. Phone 800-567-4321.

Encyclopedia Americana. Grolier Educational Publisher. http://www.publishing.grolier.com

Full Bloom. Produced by Aris, available from Edu-Corp, 7434 Trade Street, San Diego, CA 92121-2410. Phone 800-843-9497.

Grolier Multimedia Encyclopedia. See the World Wide Web home page at http://www.grolier.com

Gutenberg Project CD-ROM. Walnut Creek CD-ROM, 4041 Pike Lane, Suite D353, Concord, CA 94520. Phone 800-786-9907.

In the Company of Whales, Discovery Communications. Phone 301-986-1999.

Just Grandma and Me. Mattel Interactive. http://www.mattelinteractive.com

Leonardo the Inventor. Produced by Interactive Electronic Publishing, 300 Airport Executive Park, Spring Valley, NY 10977. Phone 914-426-0400.

Life Story. Scholastic Press. http://www.scholastic.com

Living Books (Just Grandma and Me, The Tortoise and the Hare, Arthur's Teacher Trouble). http://www.mattelinteractive.com

Mammals. Produced by the National Geographic Society, this program is available from many sources including ComputeCenterline, 1500 Broad Street, Greensburg, PA 15601. Phone 800-852-5802.

Microsoft Art Gallery. Microsoft Corporation, P.O. Box 3018, Bothell, WA 98041-3018. Phone 800-426-9400.

Encarta. Microsoft Corporation, P.O. Box 3018, Bothell, WA 98041-3018. Phone 800-426-9400.

Story Tree. Scholastic Press. http://www.scholastic.com

20th Century Video Almanac. Produced by Mindscape. See the web page at http://www.mindscape.com

Voyage of the Mimi. Sunburst, 101 Castleton Street, P.O. Box 100, Pleasantville, NY 10570-0100.

Voyager electronic books. See the Voyager Company World Wide Web home page at http://www.voyager.com

World History: 20th Century. MultiEducator, 244 North Avenue, New Rochelle, NY 10801. Phone 800-866-6434.

TYPES OF CLIP ART AND DIGITAL VIDEO

Computer CenterLine, 1500 Broad Street, Greensburg, PA 15601. Phone 800-852-5802.

EduCorp, 7434 Trade Street, San Diego, CA 92121-2410. Phone 800-843-9497.

Laser Learning Technologies, 120 Lakeside Avenue, Suite 240, Seattle, WA 98122-6552. Phone 800-722-3505.

CHAPTER TWELVE

PROBLEM-SOLVING SOFTWARE

Goal: To become aware of the various approaches to teaching problem solving and to explore some of the issues and controversies that surround this important topic.

KEY TERMS

affective domain (p. 289)

affective variables (p. 293)

analysis (p. 289)

application (p. 289)

Bloom's taxonomy (p. 283)

cognitive domain (p. 289)

comprehension (p. 289)

concrete thinking (p. 289)

domain-specific software (p. 291)

evaluation (p. 289)

executive skills (p. 286)

factual knowledge (p. 289)

formal operational thinking (p. 284)

higher-order thinking skills (HOTS) (p. 286)

IDEAL (p. 286)

idea processors (p. 292)

lower-order thinking skills (p. 289)

metacognitive (p. 286)

non-domain-specific software (p. 292)

psychomotor domain (p. 289)

synthesis (p. 289)

transfer (p. 287)

In Chapter 7 the constructivist approach to using technology in schools was presented. As even a casual scanning of recent educational literature will reveal, *constructivism* has become a popular term in education. Indeed, a recent AltaVista (http://www.altavista.com/) web search using the search string *"contructivism"* (with quotation marks) produced more than 25,000 pages dealing with this topic. Further restricting the search by adding *"education"* to the search string (type +*"constructivism"* +*"education"*) still produced almost 15,000 hits.

We are ambivalent about the popularity of this new term. On the one hand, we believe there is much of value to be found in many of the educational ideas and strategies recommended by various advocates of constructivism. For example, some constructivists take the position that effective learning generally occurs within a context that is meaningful to the learner. Many language experience approaches use the child's own spoken language and stories about things familiar to the child to begin teaching reading. Often, in fact, some of the first things children read are stories they have related orally. Software such as Microsoft's *Creative Writer*, or any of a number of children's writing and publishing programs, can help transform the oral story into an attractive, illustrated printed story. Another important part of the curriculum as advocated by some constructivists is problem-based learning. We find these ideas to have merit.

On the other hand, the current constructivist movement is a little disturbing. The problem is not with most of the specific, methodological recommendations such as the examples in the preceding paragraph, but with the widespread lack of understanding by many advocates of the underlying theoretical tenets of constructivism. Advocacy without understanding amounts to nothing more than blind devotion to fad and fashion, a problem that has plagued education in general and information technology in education in particular.

One indication of this problem is the fact that there is no widely accepted definition of constructivism, or even agreement on the general nature of what the term represents. It has been variously described in educational literature as a philosophical explanation (Airasian & Walsh, 1997), a theory (Jaramillo, 1996), a category into which many theories can be placed (Slavin, 1997), a "prominent element of many cognitive learning theories" (Ormrod, 1998, p. 206), and a teaching approach (Kindsvatter, Wilen, & Ishler, 1996). We have also seen it described as an attitude, a model, an epistemology, and a framework, to name only a few other descriptors. However, theory seems to be the most common descriptor among educators.

This is a problem, because constructivism is not itself a theory. It is at best a general term or concept that is loosely and often haphazardly derived from a variety of theories in developmental psychology. As long as constructivism is a poorly understood and variously defined concept among educators, it will remain impossible to apply it in schools or to use it as the basis for educational research (Maddux & Cummings, 1999).

Because there is so much confusion about the definition of the term and about its basic tenets, we have chosen to include a complete chapter (Chapter 7) in this book dealing with it. This is necessary, we think, so that the reader can know what we are referring to when we use the term *constructivism*.

One point on which we agree with advocates of constructivism and many other educators is the importance of problem-based learning, in which students are given a problem, and it becomes the focus that engages them in many different learning experiences. Problem-based learning is important because it encourages learning of all sorts—from remembering the chief products of South Dakota to selecting procedures for reducing pollution in industrial parks.

For educators who believe in problem-based learning, there is a critical issue—whether problem solving should be treated as a separate topic that can be taught independently of other types of content. Such a stance can lead to teaching problem-solving skills in the belief that such skills can then transfer to specific content areas such as science or social studies. If such general, transferable problem-solving skills are believed not to exist, then we would be better advised to pose problems in specific content areas with no expectation that skills learned can transfer to other areas. To state it as simply as possible, the question is whether problem solving can be taught separately, as a topic in itself, or whether it can be taught only as it applies to specific content areas.

This chapter discusses current and future attempts to use the computer for teaching problem solving. We begin by discussing some of the accepted definitions of problem solving and then move on to a review of research on teaching problem solving. We then present a section on **Bloom's taxonomy** of educational objectives and discuss how his categories can help us to develop a problem-solving curriculum across grade levels. We provide a review of different types of commercial problem-solving software, and we conclude with some recommendations about computers and teaching problem-solving skills.

THE NATIONAL CONCERN ABOUT PROBLEM SOLVING

Recently, education has been the target of intense criticism from diverse sources. This criticism has frequently concentrated on the perceived lack of success by schools in teaching effective problem-solving skills to children. Many educational observers have deplored the overemphasis on facts and rote learning in the curriculum and the underemphasis on critical thinking and problem solving. A report of the National Assessment of Educational Progress (NAEP) points out the following:

> One of the consequences of students learning mathematical skills by rote is that they cannot apply the skills they have learned to solve problems. In general, NAEP results showed that the majority of students at all age levels had difficulty with any non routine problem that required some analysis or thinking. It appears that students have not learned basic problem-solving skills. (Corbitt, 1981, p. 146)

The most recent report of NAEP results in mathematics was from assessments made in 1996. It is encouraging that a great deal of improvement was found over the results discussed in the previous paragraph. It is also interesting that publicity about this improvement has been almost nonexistent whereas publication of the less encouraging results in the previous paragraph was widespread. The following are some of the results from the Executive Summary of the NAEP report (Reese, Miller, Mazzeo, & Dossey, 1997):

> National data from the NAEP 1996 mathematics assessment showed progress in the mathematics performance by students on a broad front, compared with both the 1990 and 1992 assessments.
>
> ■ Students' scores on the NAEP mathematics scale increased for all three grades.
> ■ Scores were higher in 1996 than in 1992 for all three grades, and higher in 1992 than in 1990. The national average scale score for fourth graders in 1996

was 224, an increase of 11 points over the national average for 1990; the average for eighth graders in 1996 was 272, an increase of 9 points; and the average score for twelfth graders was 304, also an increase of 10 points.

- Student performance also increased as measured by the three mathematics achievement levels set by NAGB. The percentage of students at or above the *Basic* level increased for all three grades. The percentage of fourth-grade students at or above the *Proficient* level increased from 1990 to 1992, and from 1992 to 1996, while the percentage of eighth- and twelfth-grade students at or above the *Proficient* level increased over the period 1990 to 1996. However, only eighth-grade students showed an increase in the percentage at the *Advanced* level, and this increase was for the period 1990 to 1996.
- For fourth-grade students, the percentage performing at or above the *Basic* level was 64 percent in 1996, as compared to 50 percent in 1990; for eighth-grade students, 62 percent as compared to 52 percent; and for twelfth-grade students, 69 percent as compared to 58 percent. (p. ii)

Sprinthall and Sprinthall (1990) have pointed out that many science teachers and writers of science textbooks wrongly assume that most high school students are capable of advanced problem solving, even though studies have shown that only between 18 and 33 percent of students in grades 9 through 12 are able to apply **formal operational thinking** (advanced conceptual thinking needed for problem solving) to scientific problem solving. They go on to suggest that research shows that "the great majority of pupils have difficulty in understanding the basic assumptions of the science curricula in secondary schools" (p. 121).

Sprinthall and Sprinthall suggest that the picture in the humanities is no more encouraging. The Project Talent study, for example, determined that only 8 percent of a random sample of more than 500,000 teenagers could understand passages from Jane Austen, and only 33 percent could understand passages from Stevenson's *Treasure Island* (Flanagan, 1973).

These findings in science and humanities are not surprising in light of the fact that many studies have shown not even all college students are capable of formal operational thinking. Sprinthall, Sprinthall, and Oja (1998) point out that estimates run as high as 50 percent of college students who are still functioning at a concrete level in some subjects. They conclude as follows: "For teachers, the most important result of all these studies is the implication that children are not adults and should not be treated like miniature adults in the classroom" (p. 142).

Problems such as these have recently been highlighted in a number of commission reports that conclude there are major problems in U.S. schools. These reports have been given wide coverage in the media and are a source of concern to politicians, educators, and the general public.

WHERE SHOULD A DISCUSSION OF PROBLEM SOLVING BEGIN?

Deciding where to begin a discussion of problem solving is difficult in the extreme. After all, in a general sense, skill in problem solving is the ultimate goal of education at all levels. It is possible to argue that problem solving is the principal activity of human beings and the single ability that most clearly distinguishes our activities from those of other animals. Entire books have been written on the topic.

Adding to the dilemma is the fact that the subject is controversial. There is little agreement about what constitutes problem solving, whether or how it should be taught, and whether problem-solving skills learned in one domain can be transferred to problems encountered in another context.

Thus, writing this chapter is a bit intimidating (and also a bit presumptuous, given the scope and complexity of the topic). Nevertheless, even though we recognize many problems, we are excited about the potential of computing as an aid to teaching problem-solving skills. Therefore, we will begin the formidable task of writing a chapter on problem solving in computing by considering the definition of *problem solving* itself.

WHAT IS PROBLEM SOLVING?

Defining *problem solving* is not as easy as it seems. Some experts attempt to define *problem solving* itself whereas others elect to discuss characteristics of problems or of problem solvers.

Jonassen (2000) defines *problem solving* as follows: "*Problem solving* involves systematically pursuing a goal, which is usually the solution of a problem that a situation presents" (p. 30). He adds that problem solving is perhaps the most common complex thinking skill, and he identifies the following steps:

1. Sensing the problem
2. Researching the problem
3. Formulating the problem
4. Finding alternatives
5. Choosing the solution
6. Building acceptance

Flake, McClintock, and Turner (1990) describe problem solving as follows:

Problem solving involves intellectual curiosity. It is wanting to find out: to find answers to questions, to find ways to overcome difficulties, to find solutions to puzzles, and to find ways of accomplishing goals.... This problem-solving attitude is a part of the person's personality pattern. (p. 97)

Polya (1957), a writer and researcher who has concentrated on problem solving, describes it as a goal-directed activity involving a sequence of stages. (Although not all authorities on problem solving agree on what constitutes the stages of problem solving, most have described stages or sequences in the solution of problems.) Polya (1957) suggests that problem solving involves (1) understanding the problem, (2) formulating a plan, (3) carrying out the plan, and (4) looking back, or evaluating the results.

Similarly, Kinzer, Sherwood, and Bransford (1986) describe a five-stage process making use of the mnemonic aid **IDEAL.** (The five stages can be remembered by recalling each letter in IDEAL.) These stages are (1) identifying the problem, (2) defining the problem with precision, (3) exploring some possible strategies, (4) acting on these strategies, and (5) looking at the results.

Gore (1988) prefers "skills in critical thinking and/or logic," a general definition applicable to a wide range of disciplines. She goes on to define what constitutes a problem by endorsing a nontechnical definition by Moursund (1985), who suggests that a problem has three parts:

1. How something actually is (initial state)
2. How you would like the thing to be (goal state)
3. What you can do about the situation (allowable types of actions to move from the initial state to the goal state) (p. 3)

Moursund (1985) goes on to suggest that (1) problem solvers must be motivated to solve the problem, (2) they must have an extensive foundation of knowledge and experience, (3) they must possess a feeling of power and a repertoire of possible actions, and (4) they must have the ability to act and to evaluate their actions.

Vockell and van Deusen (1989), who wrote an entire book on using computers to teach **higher-order thinking skills (HOTS),** suggest that such skills "may be arranged into several overlapping sets of categories" (p. 3). These categories include (1) **metacognitive** or **executive skills** (awareness of our own thinking and the ability to use that awareness to improve performance); (2) critical and creative thinking; (3) thinking processes including problem solving, concept formation, principle formation, comprehension, decision making, research, composition, and oral discourse; and (4) core thinking skills. (These writers suggest that the distinction between core thinking skills and thinking processes is fuzzy, but that the former "can often be taught much more directly than the more global thinking processes" [p. 10]).

Singh and Zwirner (1996) take a Piagetian approach and define problem solving as "the employment of action schemes or operators to manipulate the components of the problem" (p. 70).

It should be evident from this short discussion that problem solving means various things to various people and that no hard and fast definition exists.

THE RESEARCH ON PROBLEM SOLVING

We briefly discussed research on problem solving in an earlier chapter. As we mentioned at that time, there is considerable controversy about whether a set of generic problem-solving skills exists that can be taught. If such skills exist, then constructing a problem-solving curriculum makes sense. Activities promoting such skills could be identified, and children would spend a portion of each day engaging in such activities. When these skills were learned, children would be able to apply the skills to problems encountered in any subject in everyday life, in a job, and so on.

This controversy actually raises the question of whether problem-solving skills can be generalized. If a child learns skills that help to solve problems in one area (domain), will these skills generalize, or **transfer,** to another area (domain) and improve the problem-solving ability of the individual in the new area? For example, will learning to be a better problem solver in math automatically improve one's problem-solving ability in social studies?

As you may suspect, this question troubled educators and researchers long before computers began to find their way into schools. (Readers who are interested in this research, especially as it applies to computing, will be interested in reviews by Berson, [1996]; Burton and Magliaro [1988]; Dugdale, LeGare, Matthews, and Ju [1998]; Linn [1985]; McCoy [1996]; Perkins and Salomon [1987]; Singh and Zwirner [1996]; Tetenbaum and Mulkeen [1984]; and Weller [1996].) Although there is no universal agreement about the transferability of problem-solving skills, most knowledgeable observers agree that problem-solving skills have been shown to be relatively domain specific (Frederiksen, 1984; Krasnor & Mitterer, 1984; Woronov, 1994). In other words, skills learned in one domain probably do not automatically or easily transfer to other domains.

Frederiksen (1984) concluded: "There appears to be little if any transfer from one domain to another" whereas Ginther and Williamson (1985) observed that "decades of research on problem solving, with both animal and human subjects, has shown that transfer of general problem-solving skills is difficult to achieve" (p. 76). Judah Schwartz, codirector of Harvard's federally funded Educational Technology Center (ETC), took a similar position when he was interviewed for an article in *Computers in the Schools*. He said, "I, for one, fall very much on the side of domain specificity.... To talk about problem solving in a kind of undifferentiated way and then look for transfer and domain generality seems to me to be much too hard a task" (Johnson, Maddux, & O'Hair, 1988, p. 14).

Cyert (1980) suggests that teachers have traditionally hoped to develop higher-order cognitive processes in children, but have been largely unsuccessful. Tetenbaum and Mulkeen (1984) agree and point out that computer educators hope the computer can succeed where other methods and materials have failed in developing problem-solving skills, even though there is very little evidence to support this idea.

As we have shown, most authorities do not believe in the automatic transfer of problem-solving skills. However, the most important word in the previous sentence may be *automatic*. Even the most optimistic of writers and researchers emphasize that, if transfer is possible, it must be nurtured through proper teaching strategies.

Jonassen (2000) takes the position that problem-solving skills can be taught, and that most technology-based innovations have failed because they were not properly implemented. He suggests that teachers must first master the use of computer applications called *Mindtools*. These include semantic organization tools such as databases; dynamic modeling tools such as spreadsheets, expert systems, and *MicroWorlds;* interpretation tools such as search engines; knowledge construction tools such as hypermedia; and conversion tools such as e-mail, chat-rooms, and other software for Internet communication. Then, teachers will have to change their teaching styles from "purveyor of knowledge to instigator, promoter, coach, helper, model, and guide of knowledge construction" (p. 276). Specifically, he suggests:

> Rather than telling students what you know and hoping they will understand it as you do, you need to allow them to represent what they know and then "perturb" their understanding. Try to avoid telling students that the models that they construct are wrong (that is, they do not agree with yours). Rather, ask if their model has considered this, or represented that. Does the students' model accommodate another idea? Or what if something else happened? Viability of knowledge is assessed in terms of community standards. For example, to argue that human traits are in no way hereditary is not viable. The scientific community has too much evidence to support the claim. So if a students' model of human development ignored hereditary influences, you would merely need to ask students to explain their model in light of that evidence, that is perturb their model. It is the model that you are questioning, not the student. (p. 276)

Vockell and van Deusen (1989), in their book on the teaching of HOTS, suggest that such skills can be taught if specific teaching steps are taken. Glover, Ronning, and Bruning (1990), in discussing programs for teaching general problem-solving skills, provide a cautious endorsement, given proper use:

> Intuitively, it seems that teachers using such programs must carefully show their students how skills learned from the programs can be used to help acquire new domain-specific information.... Of course, confidence that these programs will enhance problem solving in domain-specific areas of problem solving awaits further research. (p. 180)

Similarly, Burton and Magliaro (1988), although generally pessimistic concerning automatic transfer, conclude:

> One area of research that offers some hope to this transfer dilemma is the explicit instruction of strategic knowledge within the domain.... While this hypothesis needs further study, the general idea of teaching explicitly how to analyze, for example, the relevant features of problem domains and identify those features seems to be a promising avenue. (p. 68)

Thomas and Upah (1996) suggest that negative findings regarding transferability are due to flawed research carried out when the field was in its infancy and the use of research methodology that was "too narrow in scope" (p. 97). These authors suggest that focusing on metacognitive skills (skill in thinking about one's own thought processes) while teaching programming, for example, is necessary in order to facilitate generalizability of problem-solving skills in students.

We will give some suggestions for maximizing transfer at the end of this chapter.

BLOOM'S TAXONOMY AND ITS RELEVANCE
TO PROBLEM SOLVING

If this discussion has led you to conclude that there is a bewildering array of ways to think about problem solving and that teaching methods will vary greatly according to which of these ways is selected, you are correct. In addition, research on the topic is in its infancy and has provided few definitive answers.

Although there is much of interest and value in all the conceptualizations of problem solving discussed so far, we find the observations of Benjamin Bloom (1956) to be particularly appropriate and useful.

Bloom felt that a major educational problem was the lack of consensus among educators concerning the goals of schooling. To help resolve the problem of selecting educational goals and then defining how these goals will be achieved and evaluated, he developed a taxonomy for educational goals and objectives in the **cognitive** (intellectual), **affective** (attitudinal), and **psychomotor** domains. These taxonomies consist of a hierarchy of objectives. (A hierarchy is a listing in order of rank, grade, or the like. Bloom's taxonomy is ordered from simple to complex, from concrete to abstract.)

In the cognitive domain (the domain of most relevance to problem solving), Bloom's taxonomy includes (1) **factual knowledge,** (2) **comprehension** (understanding), (3) **application** (applying skills), (4) **analysis** (reduction of a solution into component parts), (5) **synthesis** (arriving at a solution by combining component parts), and (6) **evaluation** (judging). The first three of these categories are sometimes referred to as **lower-order thinking skills;** the last three are said to be higher-order thinking skills, (Church & Bender, 1989). These are the skills that are usually thought of when problem solving is discussed.

Sprinthall, Sprinthall, and Oja (1998) point out that, although Bloom has never equated his taxonomy with developmental stages, the first three of his categories are consistent with, and can be accomplished through, Piagetian **concrete thinking** (nonabstract thinking available to children of elementary school age), whereas the final three require formal operational thinking (abstract thinking available to secondary and adult ages).

This is an interesting observation for several reasons. First, it suggests that elementary schools should emphasize the objectives of basic knowledge, comprehension, and application (lower-order thinking skills), and middle schools and secondary schools should emphasize analysis, synthesis, and evaluation (higher-order thinking skills). Additionally, it suggests a continuum of skills in any specific content area, with the lower-order skills being, to some extent, prerequisite to the higher-order skills.

Following this line of thinking, it would be unrealistic to expect students to become expert at evaluation, the most advanced, abstract goal in the hierarchy, if they have not mastered the lower-level objectives, including (1) acquisition of basic knowledge and facts, (2) understanding of those facts, and (3) application of their knowledge to real situations. Furthermore, acceptance of these ideas suggests that effective teaching of problem solving must involve attention to goals from all six levels of the taxonomy and that neglect of any of these six levels could render ineffective any attempts to teach problem-solving skills.

Unfortunately, many advocates of school reform do not seem to understand this point, and their suggestions often assume that any child of any age can learn any skill, regardless of the developmental level of the child. One of the authors of this textbook pointed this out in a recent article:

> Furthermore, the teaching strategies proposed by many of the modern experts who claim to be constructivists fail to differentiate among methods that are appropriate for children at different developmental levels. A common error, for example, is to propose methods that presuppose abstract conceptual thinking abilities in elementary age children. In fact, many of these proposals about methodology do not even mention grade or age level of students and imply that suggestions are appropriate for all children regardless of age, grade level, or development (Maddux & Cummings, 1999).

DETERMINING WHAT TO TEACH

Bloom's taxonomy is useful in helping us to classify goals for children and in reminding us not to neglect any of these categories of goals. Furthermore, even superficial general knowledge of the sequence of stages hypothesized in Piagetian developmental psychology gives clues about when to emphasize each goal. Such superficial knowledge, however, does little to simplify the task of deciding exactly what and how to teach.

Unfortunately, we cannot provide a simple formula to solve this ubiquitous teaching problem. As you have seen, there are simply too many different ideas about the nature of problem solving, and research is too mixed on the transferability question to permit hard-and-fast prescriptions.

The best advice we can give is to invest a great deal of time and energy in becoming familiar with a number of the theoretical approaches to problem solving. We recommend that you look back over the part of this chapter where we reviewed some of the definitions of problem solving. Perhaps one or more of these approaches (or some other approach we have not mentioned) appeals to you as being particularly compatible with your own knowledge, attitudes, and skills. As you study a specific approach, you will find that the theory provides a path that leads you to try a specific method with specific content. The more you learn about the theory, the more sophisticated these methods are likely to become, and the more likely they are to be successful. (This process of intensive study of theory, which leads to generation and refinement of method, is the essence of professionalism and the mark of the master teacher.)

However, teachers must often make teaching decisions before they have the time or energy to invest in such intensive study. Therefore, at the end of this chapter we provide some recommendations, with the understanding that they are tentative and are intended only as a temporary solution to a problem that is best solved uniquely by each teacher over a long period of time.

COMMERCIAL PROBLEM-SOLVING PROGRAMS

Problem-solving software is appearing in ever-increasing quantity (Burton & Magliaro, 1988; Jonassen, 2000; Lockard, Abrams, & Many, 1987). Several different types of computer software are often advertised as problem-solving software:

1. Computer programming languages: We have discussed this kind of software and its potential to teach problem solving in another chapter.

2. Domain-specific problem-solving software: **Domain-specific software** is intended to make better problem solvers within a specific subject, such as science or math. Examples of software advertised as domain specific include that offered by Sunburst Communications, a Houghton Mifflin Company (Sunburst Communications, 101 Castleton Street, Pleasantville, NY 10570, USA, 1-800-321-7511 or 1-914-747-3310). For example, Sunburst advertises a number of math and science programs intended to teach problem solving within those subject areas for students grades K–8. Details and prices can be found on their web page at http://sunburstdirect.sunburst.com/.

A caution is in order concerning such software. Sunburst classifies a software program called *The Incredible Laboratory* as science software. Their website suggests that the software presents problem-solving activities, because the skills emphasized in the program are skills that are often identified as important in science (trial-and-error processes, manipulating notes, and studying the data collected). However, we do not agree that this software should be listed as science software because it makes use of no actual science content.

In *The Incredible Laboratory,* users are presented with a list of imaginary chemicals that can be added to a beaker. Each ingredient produces a specific feature in a monster that is supposedly created by the chemical mixing. Because there is no actual science content, *The Incredible Laboratory* should be classed as non-domain-specific problem-solving software. The authors apparently believe that skills learned while using this software to construct imaginary monsters from imaginary chemicals automatically transfer to real science problem solving. As we have already pointed out, this is an unsubstantiated assumption. Although children enjoy *The Incredible Laboratory,* we would prefer software that makes use of actual science content.

Domain-specific problem-solving software also includes tool software such as Judah Schwartz's *Geometric SuperSupposer* and the *Function Supposer: Symbols and*

Graphs, both marketed by Sunburst Software. These programs are designed as an aid to students while they work on problems in their textbook or from elsewhere. The *Geometric superSupposer* can be used as a modeling environment for the making of geometric models in fields such as physics, industry, economics, and accounting. We find software such as these to be truly domain specific and highly promising.

Also included in this category are various tool programs to aid writing. These include **idea processors** designed to allow writers to make use of an outline and the various tutorial programs designed to aid writers by asking critical questions at strategic points in the writing process. Again, many of these programs are exemplary, because they do a good job of helping students learn domain-specific problem-solving skills.

3. Non-domain-specific, general problem-solving programs: **Non-domain-specific software** is based on the premise that general problem-solving skills can be taught and that, once learned, such skills can be applied to problems in other domains.

Some Recommendations Concerning Problem-Solving Software

There is much more to be said about problem solving than we have included in this short chapter, and there is much more to be learned. Programs for teaching problem solving, with or without computers, are still in the experimental stage. We agree with the following assessment by Hyde and Bizar (1989):

> We have carefully reviewed the many programs and have concluded that they are each valuable but incomplete. Each seems to stake out only a section of the territory on what might be considered key intellectual processes. In promoting his program, each author exaggerated the importance of the kind of thinking encouraged by his program, as if that is all there is or should be to thinking. A few programs attempt to be more complete or comprehensive, to encompass the many varied kinds of thinking. However, these seem to be like a smorgasbord of processes, without a clearly defined theoretical model that shows teachers how they fit together. (pp. 15–16)

Levinger (2000) has done an excellent job of summarizing the research to date:

> Increasingly, the field of cognitive science is shedding important insights on how knowledge transfer occurs and the conditions that facilitate it. Essentially, the more varied the kinds of problems learners confront, and the more they have to think to solve them, the greater the chances are that when new real-life problems are encountered, transfer of skills or knowledge to the new situation will occur.

Although the state of the art of teaching problem solving is in its infancy, we believe there is presently enough evidence available to permit some useful conclusions. With the above qualification in mind, we recommend the following:

1. *Although problem solving is an important goal at all levels, elementary schools should think of problem solving within a context that does not exclude or minimize lower-order thinking skills.* For example, problem-based learning emphasizes problem-solving activities that frequently require students to acquire many lower-order thinking skills in the process. It could be argued, of course, that this approach is just as appropriate in secondary schools. We tend to agree, but if non-domain-specific problem solving should be taught at some level, it is probably secondary school. Teachers at all levels should remember that effective teaching of problem solving must involve attention to goals from all six levels of the taxonomy because lower-order skills seem to be prerequisites for higher-order skills.

2. *Computer programming should not be taught exclusively with the hope of teaching generalizable problem-solving skills because research as to its potential to accomplish this goal remains unclear.* We believe that there are other good reasons to teach programming, and these are discussed in another chapter. That chapter also presents recommendations generated from research and from experience that we think will maximize the likelihood of transfer of skills learned. Furthermore, we believe that the Logo computer language is the most appropriate for use with children. Unfortunately, teaching of Logo has recently been abandoned by many U.S. teachers, although Logo is often taught in schools in other countries, such as Australia.

3. *Domain-specific problem-solving software should be chosen over non-domain-specific software.* Bransford and Stein (1984), in their book on problem solving, assert that knowledge is a necessary tool in problem solving and that good problem solving requires the development of the ability to acquire new knowledge. Kinzcr, Sherwood, and Bransford (1986) echo this assertion:

> We argued earlier that it is difficult to significantly improve problem solving by emphasizing only general strategies such as trying to identify potential problems, defining problems carefully, and so forth. The ability to solve problems requires specific knowledge that can function as a conceptual tool. If we want to solve problems about population control, for example, we need information about biology, and if we want to make informed decisions about a journey (e.g., along the Oregon Trail), we need information about resources and potential hazards. (p. 175)

Therefore, we believe that exemplary problem-solving software is domain specific and knowledge intensive.

4. *Non-domain-specific software should be used only if the goal is to influence attitudes toward problem solving or if the specific skills taught are valuable in and of themselves, rather than as a vehicle to teach transferable problem-solving skills.* If you look back over the beginning section of this chapter, in which we presented various definitions related to problem solving, you may note that many authorities refer to the importance of **affective variables** such as intellectual curiosity, wanting to find out, problem-solving attitudes, motivation, belief in one's potential to solve problems, and a feeling of power. We also believe in the importance of these affective variables. Therefore, we can endorse the use of non-domain-specific software such as *The Incredible Laboratory* if they are chosen because they are interesting and enjoyable and because the teacher wants to foster affective attributes such as those listed previously. Once such attributes are established, however, we suggest emphasizing domain-specific problem-solving software. (Non-domain-specific software might also be chosen to teach specific knowledge or skills. For example, the Carmen Sandiego software series, including *Where in the World Is Carmen Sandiego? Where in Time Is Carmen Sandiego? Where in the USA Is Carmen Sandiego?* and others, teaches the use of the World Almanac and certain concepts and skills in geography and history. If such knowledge and skills are considered important, we see no reason why such software should not be used.)

5. *Teachers should keep an open mind concerning the issue of teaching transferable problem-solving skills and should watch for research reports that may shed light on this cloudy issue. In addition, whether domain-specific or non-domain-specific problem-solving software or computer programming is chosen, teachers should use those teaching techniques that have shown promise of maximizing the chances of transfer.* For example, Krasnor and Mitterer (1984) attempt to convert research findings into specific recommendations. They suggest that teachers keep in mind that research shows that (1) transfer requires that some of the knowledge or skills be identical across domains, (2) the learner should be helped to recognize how the new problem is similar to the old one, (3) transfer may depend heavily on the completeness of the original learning, and (4) it is probably important for the child to be exposed to many situations in which the specific skill is useful in more than one domain.

With regard to programming as a vehicle to teach transferable problem solving, McCoy (1989–1990, 1996) suggests that success has been limited because programming is often poorly taught. She recommends: "in order to promote problem solving, there are three essential components that must be taught in computer programming classes: metacognition, planning, and debugging" (p. 46).

SUMMARY

U.S. schools have lately been criticized for emphasizing rote learning and neglecting to teach higher-order thinking skills such as problem solving. One problem in addressing this criticism is that the subject is controversial and research results are mixed. It is, for example, unclear whether general problem-solving skills can be taught, although most authorities believe that problem solving is relatively domain specific and will not automatically transfer to other subjects.

There is preliminary evidence that transfer may be accomplished through proper teaching strategies. One promising technique is for teachers to carefully point out to students how skills learned in one domain can be used to solve problems in other domains.

Bloom's taxonomy of educational objectives can be helpful in providing clues about the teaching of problem solving. Lower-order objectives should be emphasized in the elementary schools, whereas higher-order objectives should be emphasized in middle schools and secondary schools.

Commercial problem-solving software includes (1) computer programming languages, (2) domain-specific packages, and (3) non-domain-specific programs. Recommendations for use of such software include (1) making use of the elementary–secondary dichotomy of the goals explained above, (2) teaching of computer programming to achieve goals other than those related to problem solving, (3) choosing domain-specific over non-domain-specific problem-solving software, (4) using non-domain-specific software only to achieve affective goals or because the specific skills taught are considered important for their own sake, (5) keeping an open mind and staying up-to-date on the latest research on teaching problem solving, and (6) regardless of the type of problem-solving software chosen, using techniques that have shown promise of promoting transfer.

QUESTIONS TO CONSIDER

1. The chapter presents several ways of thinking about problem solving, problems, and problem solvers. Which of these ways do you find the most personally meaningful? Why?

2. Kinzer, Sherwood, and Bransford (1986) describe a five-stage problem-solving process symbolized by the mnemonic IDEAL. Describe a lesson in a specific subject using these stages. Be sure the lesson is domain specific and knowledge intensive.

3. Choose one of Bloom's six categories of goals in the cognitive domain. Write a goal for a short lesson in some specific subject. Be sure the goal will fit in the category you choose. Then outline a brief lesson aimed at that goal using the Kinzer, Sherwood, and Bransford stages (IDEAL).

4. Suppose a software company advertised a piece of math problem-solving software in which children listened to melodies with missing notes and then supplied the notes necessary to complete the tune. If the software company advertised that this taught an important math skill, namely, identifying patterns, would you agree that (1) it is domain-specific software and that (2) such software is highly useful? Explain your answers fully.

5. Can you imagine any circumstances in which the software in question 4 could be useful?

6. Identify activities you might use to convince your students that they have the power to solve problems.

RELATED ACTIVITIES

1. Obtain a copy of *Taxonomy of Educational Objectives* (Bloom, 1956) and read more about the cognitive domain. Then select one teaching topic related to computing (such as learning to move text around in a word-processing document). Prepare a one-paragraph summary of each of six lessons on that topic. Each lesson should be aimed at one of the six cognitive domain goals identified by Bloom. For each paragraph, include a brief statement explaining why you think the lesson could achieve that goal.

2. In Bloom's text (1956), read about educational goals in the affective domain. Then prepare a brief (two- to three-page) paper in which you explain whether you think these affective goals could be useful in computer education and why.

3. Locate a commercial educational software catalog. (Visit your college of education

computer lab or a retail store that sells software.) Determine whether the catalog advertises software intended to teach problem solving. If so, select one program and tell whether it appears to be domain-specific or non-domain-specific problem-solving software. Tell why. If possible, locate the software and run it on a computer to help you decide.

REFERENCES

Airasian, P. W., & Walsh, M. E. (1997). Constructivist cautions. *Phi Delta Kappan, 78,* 444–450.

Berson, M. J. (1996). Effectiveness of computer technology in the social studies: A review of the literature. *Journal of Research on Computing in Education, 28,* 486–499.

Bloom, B. (Ed.). (1956). *Taxonomy of educational objectives, Handbook 1: Cognitive domain.* New York: McKay.

Bransford, J. D., & Stein, B. S. (1984). *The IDEAL problem solver.* San Francisco: W. H. Freeman.

Burton, J. K., & Magliaro, S. (1988). Computer programming and generalized problem-solving skills: In search of direction. *Computers in the Schools, 4*(3/4), 63–90.

Church, G., & Bender, M. (1989). *Teaching with computers.* Boston: College-Hill.

Corbitt, M. K. (1981). *Results from the second mathematics assessment of the National Assessment of Educational Progress.* Reston, VA: National Council of Teachers of Mathematics.

Cyert, R. M. (1980). Problem solving and education policy. In D. T. Tuma & F. Reif (Eds.), *Problem solving and education: Issues in teaching and research* (pp. 3–8). Hillsdale, NJ: Lawrence Erlbaum.

Dugdale, S., LeGare, O., Matthews, J. I., & Ju, M. (1998). Mathematical problem solving and computers: A study of learner-initiated application of technology in a general problem-solving context. *Journal of Research on Computing in Education, 30,* 239–253.

Flake, J. L., McClintock, C. E., & Turner, S. (1990). *Fundamentals of computer education.* Belmont, CA: Wadsworth.

Flanagan, J. (1973). Education: How and for what? *American Psychologist, 28*(7), 551–556.

Frederiksen, N. (1984). Implications of cognitive theory for instruction in problem solving. *Review of Educational Research, 54*(3), 363–407.

Ginther, D. W., & Williamson, J. D. (1985). Learning Logo: What is really learned? *Computers in the Schools, 2*(2/3), 73–78.

Glover, J. A., Ronning, R. R., & Bruning, R. H. (1990). *Cognitive psychology for teachers.* New York: Macmillan.

Gore, K. (1988). Problem-solving software to implement curriculum goals. In W. M. Reed & J. K. Burton (Eds.), *Educational computing and problem solving* (pp. 171–178). New York: Haworth.

Hyde, A. A., & Bizar, M. (1989). *Thinking in context: Teaching cognitive processes across the elementary school curriculum.* White Plains, NY: Longman.

Jaramillo, J. A. (1996). Vygotsky's sociocultural theory and contributions to the development of constructivist curricula. *Education, 117*(1), 133–141.

Johnson, D. L., Maddux, C. D., & O'Hair, M. M. (1988). Are we making progress? [Interview with Judah L. Schwartz of ETC]. *Computers in the Schools, 5*(1/2), 5–21.

Jonassen, D. H. (2000). *Computers as mind tools for schools: Engaging critical thinking.* Upper Saddle River, NJ: Merrill.

Kindsvatter, R., Wilen, W., & Ishler, M. (1996). *Dynamics of effective teaching* (3rd. ed.). White Plains, NY: Longman.

Kinzer, C. K., Sherwood, R. D., & Bransford, J. D. (1986). *Computer strategies for education: Foundations and content-area applications.* Columbus, OH: Merrill.

Krasnor, L. R., & Mitterer, J. O. (1984). Logo and the development of general problem-solving skills. *Alberta Journal of Educational Research, 30*(2), 133–144.

Levinger, B. (2000). *Learning in a new era.* Boston: Education Development Center. Retrieved April 15, 2000, from the World Wide Web: http://www.edc.org/INT/HCD/chp2.html.

Linn, M. C. (1985, May). The cognitive consequences of programming instruction in classrooms. *Educational Researcher, 14,* 14–16, 25–29.

Lockard, J., Abrams, P. D., & Many, W. A. (1987). *Microcomputers for educators.* Boston: Little, Brown.

Maddux, C. D., & Cummings, R. (1999). Constructivism: Has the term outlived its usefulness? *Computers in the Schools, 15*(3/4), 5–20.

McCoy, L. P. (1989–1990). Computer programming can develop problem-solving skills. *Computing Teacher, 17*(4), 46–49.

McCoy, L. P. (1996). Computer-based mathematics learning. *Journal of Research on Computing in Education, 28,* 438–460.

Moursund, D. (1985). Problem solving: A computer educator's perspective. *Computing Teacher, 12*(5), 2–5.

Ormrod, J. E. (1998). *Educational psychology: Developing learners.* Upper Saddle River, NJ: Prentice Hall.

Perkins, D. N., & Salomon, G. (1987). Transfer and teaching thinking. In D. N. Perkins, J. D. Lockhead, & J. C. Bishop (Eds.), *Comprehension instruction: Perspectives and suggestions.* White Plains, NY: Longman.

Polya, G. (1957). *How to solve it.* Garden City, NY: Doubleday.

Reese, C. M., Miller, K. E., Mazzeo, J., and Dossey, J. A. (1997). *NAEP 1996 mathematics report card for the nation and the states.* Washington, DC: National Center for Education Statistics.

Renner, J., Stafford, A., Lawson, J., McKimmon, J., Friot, F., & Kellogg, D. (1976). *Research, teaching, and learning with the Piaget model.* Norman: University of Oklahoma Press.

Singh, J. K. & Zwirner, W. (1996). Toward a theoretical framework of problem solving within Logo programming environments. *Journal of Research on Computing in Education, 29,* 68–95.

Slavin, R. E. (1997). *Educational psychology* (5th ed.). Boston: Allyn & Bacon.

Sprinthall, N. A., & Sprinthall, R. C. (1990). *Educational psychology* (5th ed.). New York: McGraw-Hill.

Sprinthall, R. C., Sprinthall, N. A., and Oja, S. N. (1998). *Educational psychology: A developmental approach* (7th ed.). New York: McGraw-Hill.

Tetenbaum, T. J., & Mulkeen, T. A. (1984, November). LOGO and the teaching of problem solving: A call for a moratorium. *Educational Technology, 24*(11), 16–19.

Thomas, R. A., & Upah, S. C. (1996). Give programming instruction a chance. *Journal of Research on Computing in Education, 29,* 96–108.

Vockell, E., & van Deusen, R. M. (1989). *The computer and higher-order thinking skills.* Watsonville, CA: Mitchell.

Weller, H. G. (1996). Assessing the impact of computer-based learning in science. *Journal of Research on Computing in Education, 28,* 461–485.

Woronov, T. (1994). Six myths (and five promising truths) about the uses of educational technology. *The Harvard Education Letter, X*(5), 1–3.

CHAPTER THIRTEEN

EVALUATING EDUCATIONAL SOFTWARE AND WEBSITES

Goal: To be able to discuss the process of evaluating educational software and websites and making sound decisions about software purchases and website use.

KEY TERMS

documentation (p. 312)
ease of use (p. 301)
Educational Products Information
   Exchange (EPIE) (p. 300)
linking mechanisms (p. 308)

mode of instruction (p. 312)
multimedia (p. 307)
The Educational Software Selector
   (TESS) (p. 300)

One major problem in educational computing is the difficulty in finding good software and good educational websites. The problem of software quality has been acknowledged for years in numerous articles and books dealing with educational computing issues and problems (Kinzer, Sherwood, & Bransford, 1986; Lillie, Hannum, & Stuck, 1989; Morrison, Lowther, & DeMeulle, 1999; Roblyer & Edwards, 2000; Schwartz & Beichner, 1999). Recently, the President's Committee of Advisors on Science and Technology (2000) published the report of their Panel on Educational Technology. In that report, they included the following observation:

> There is widespread agreement that one of the principal factors now limiting the extensive and effective use of technology within American schools is the relative dearth of high-quality computer software and digital content designed specifically for that purpose. While this problem is encountered by educators at all K–12 levels, it would appear to be particularly severe within our nation's secondary schools, which typically demand a broader diversity of instructional content. (http://www.whitehouse.gov/WH/EOP/OSTP/NSTC/PCAST/k-12ed.htm1#4.s)

The Panel on Educational Technology (President's Committee of Advisors on Science and Technology, 2000) went on to suggest that excellent software has the potential to support educational changes that would result in the following improvements in U.S. schools:

- Greater attention is given to the acquisition of higher-order thinking and problem-solving skills, with less emphasis on the assimilation of a large body of isolated facts.
- Basic skills are learned not in isolation, but in the course of undertaking (often on a collaborative basis) higher-level real-world tasks whose execution requires the integration of a number of such skills.
- Information resources are made available to be accessed by the student at that point in time when they actually become useful in executing the particular task at hand.
- Fewer topics may be covered than is the case within the typical traditional curriculum, but these topics are often explored in greater depth.
- The student assumes a central role as the active architect of his or her own knowledge and skills, rather than passively absorbing information proffered by the teacher.

Although quality is a problem, high-quality software and excellent educational websites are available to those who know how to identify them. Therefore, this chapter will be devoted to the topic of software evaluation. Many of the characteristics of good software are also applicable to website evaluation. However, in order to simplify our discussion, we will deal separately with website evaluation, which we will address after our discussion of software evaluation. Our discussion of this topic will be brief, however, since it was covered in depth in an earlier chapter of this book.

We begin by establishing the need for good evaluation procedures, with an emphasis on the quality of current educational software. We go on to consider some reasons much educational software has not been of the highest quality. The chapter then presents short- and long-term solutions to this problem. Because most of these solutions involve formal software evaluation, the chapter presents information on how to find and interpret evaluations written by others. We then move on to the topic of performing your own evaluations. A sample software evaluation form is presented, although we suggest that users should modify such forms to fit their own needs. Finally, we discuss the topic of website evaluation.

THE GROWING BODY
OF EDUCATIONAL SOFTWARE

The need for developing methods of evaluating educational software (sometimes called *courseware*) can be appreciated in light of the fact that there are currently more than 20,000 educational computer programs available and an estimated

2,000 new titles appear each year. The overall quality of educational software has improved in recent years, yet quality still lags far behind quantity. We suggest that the practice of ordering software sight unseen, with catalog descriptions accepted at face value, would be poor practice indeed.

This is especially true because the complexity of educational software has increased enormously in the past few years. The continuous increase in the capability of computers to handle sophisticated graphics, along with the trend by educators to incorporate multimedia and networking into classrooms and computer labs, makes careful and thoughtful software selection ever more imperative.

THE QUALITY OF EDUCATIONAL SOFTWARE

Although software is improving rapidly, quality has been a problem since the beginning of the educational computer movement in the late 1970s. In 1983, the authors of this textbook wrote a series of computer-related mass-market books in paperback for Signet Press. Each book dealt with a different popular brand of personal computer. Because virtually nothing can be done with any computer without software, these books were actually about software.

The book publisher provided us with offices, computers, and a staff of three assistants to telephone software distributors and request programs for review. As we began to review the extensive library of software they provided, we were dismayed at the poor quality of most of it, particularly the educational software. We were especially surprised to find that a significant percentage of this software (about 20 to 30 percent) was technically flawed and would not run properly. A few of the remaining programs were excellent, but the majority of the software we reviewed was so ill-conceived and poorly executed that we agreed we could not recommend it for purchase.

Although our experience was informal, similar conclusions were reached as a result of more formal projects. That same year (1983) the **Educational Products Information Exchange (EPIE)** reviewed and rated most of the educational software then available. They reported that they were able to identify only 5 percent of the programs as "highly recommended" (Komoski, 1984).

Today, EPIE maintains a website (http://www.epie.org/) where users who pay a small subscription fee can preview EPIE's service, **The Educational Software Selector (TESS)** (http://www.epie.org/epie_tess.htm), which can be used to search their database of reviews of over 19,000 educational software titles produced by over 1,300 companies. We describe TESS more fully later in this chapter.

Fortunately, educational software has been improving rapidly since the early 1980s (Roblyer & Edwards, 2000). Currently, many excellent educational programs are on the market. There are a number of reasons software has improved. First, the problem has been widely acknowledged, with hundreds of articles over the last 15 years lamenting educational software quality. Because of wide acknowledgment, software houses have responded by improving the quality of their offerings. Although they still have a long way to go, they are making progress. Second, the field has matured, and there has been time for software developers to learn about schools, curricula, and how children think and learn. This knowledge is beginning to find its way into newer educational software, which is, consequently, much improved over earlier efforts. Third, the educational software market is now firmly established and, with the rapid increase in the number of school and home computers, is seen as an expanding market.

Conversely, educators have begun to learn more about computers and their capabilities and to think about how these capabilities can be used in education. These educators talk to software developers and are beginning to use their influence to improve software developers' efforts. Researchers have begun to investigate the potential of computing, and reviewers have had time to survey past research, draw conclusions and generalizations, and make these reviews available to educators and software developers. Finally, educators have had time to outgrow their initial uncritical infatuation with computers and are becoming more discriminating about educational computing applications. By purchasing better software and declining to purchase poorer software they exert a positive influence on software development.

One area of recent great improvement has been in the technical reliability of software and in its **ease of use.** Most software today can be counted on to run reliably, and improved operating systems have considerably reduced ease of operation problems.

Even though software is improving, poor quality is still a problem. Neill and Neill (1989) and, currently, the Association for Supervision and Curriculum Development (1999) publish an extensive review of educational software entitled *Only the Best: The Annual Guide to the Highest-Rated Educational Software and Multimedia.* In the 1990 edition, 11,000 programs were reviewed. The authors found large numbers of poor programs and identified only 7 percent as excellent. The 1999–2000 edition (Association for Supervision and Curriculum Development, 1999) features 93 new programs and 16 classics categorized as excellent.

Why Is Much Educational Software of Poor Quality?

It is ironic that software quality was often seen as the major educational computing problem during the 1980s. The irony is that only modest progress has been made in improving software quality while hardware quality improved at a breathtaking pace.

There are many reasons this is so. Lockard, Abrams, and Many (1994) identify a number of contributing causes, including (1) the lack of a theoretical base for most courseware, (2) overemphasis on technical concerns such as graphics and sound and underemphasis on educational concerns, (3) the application of old methods to the new computer medium (resulting in many programs that merely duplicate printed educational materials on the computer screen), and (4) the initial scarcity of educational programs and the desperation felt by educators who have consequently failed to demand high-quality programs.

Jonassen (2000) points out that many surveys from the 1970s to the present have shown that at least 85 percent of available educational software is either drill-and-practice or tutorial software. Thus, software houses that modeled their educational catalog on this historical base, if they used any theory at all to guide development, tended to design software based on behaviorist beliefs about the importance of attention to reinforcement of stimulus–response associations. Jonassen asserts that

> Unfortunately, the behaviorist principles underlying drill and practice are unable to account for, let alone foster, the complex thinking required for meaningful learning required to solve problems, transfer skills to novel situations, construct original ideas, and so on. (p. 5)

Mandell and Mandell (1989) cite three causes: (1) the pressure educators felt to rush into computer education, resulting in frantic purchasing without a clear-cut plan, (2) scarcity of personnel with the expertise to select high-quality courseware, and (3) the initial scarcity of high-quality educational computing software resulting from a rush by manufacturers to be the first to place a product on the market. This latter situation meant that educators were "left with little choice but to purchase inadequate software or let their computers sit idle" (p. 200).

Jonassen (2000) agrees with this assessment, adding that simple drill-and-practice programs were easy for developers to produce and were seized on by schools to satisfy demands from administrators that teachers begin to use computers.

Another cause for the quality gap is that, when computers first appeared, educational software was often authored by teacher-hobbyists who had good intentions but were novice programmers. Thus, much of the early software was simplistic or downright flawed. Other early software authors were programming experts who knew little or nothing about schools, curriculum, or how children think and learn. Much of the software produced by these computer experts was technically slick but had little educational relevance (Flake, McClintock, & Turner, 1990). Roblyer and Edwards (2000) point out that some of the early software produced by both of these groups was not designed to handle all possible answers a student might give or could not cope with every conceivable path a student might take through a sequence of instruction. Therefore, when such unanticipated events occurred, the software often crashed or locked up.

Although many software developers today realize the importance of consulting experts in both education and computer science, some software is still developed without consideration of both technical and educational factors (Geisert & Futrell, 1999).

Another cause for poor-quality educational software is the high cost of developing a program versus the low potential profit. There is simply more potential profit in a piece of business software than in a piece of educational software. The Office of Technology Assessment (1988), in discussing capital limitations in educational software development, concluded, "The demand for software is too low to allow most publishers to recoup their development and marketing costs" (p. 143). This report goes on to state, "It is clear that software publishers face a severely fragmented demand that can seldom justify the level of investment necessary to create products" (p. 143). The report also suggests that software piracy contributes to the economic woes of software developers.

Despite all the reasons for the poor quality of educational software just stated, the growing educational software market is beginning to decrease the impact of the poorly qualified developer and problems due to the limited size of the market. As school-based computers continue to be acquired and updated at rapid rates, educational software is becoming more profitable, and as it has done so, competition has led to improved quality. This trend is likely to continue.

What Can Be Done about the Problem of Software Quality?

We believe there are related short- and long-term answers to the problem of software quality.

Short-Term Solution.   In the short term, educators should communicate directly with educational software producers. As Kinzer, Sherwood, and Bransford (1986) suggest, teachers have a responsibility to speak out, and software developers have a responsibility to listen and respond. They suggest teachers find or design a good evaluation form, use this form to evaluate software they use, and send the completed evaluations to software producers.

As more schools have gained access to the Internet and the Web, teachers and policy makers have discovered there a huge, readily available critical literature about educational software. Morrison, Lowther, and DeMeulle (1999) list a number of excellent software review sites including, among others:

1. *AskERIC InfoGuide.*
   http://ericir.syr.edu/cgi-bin/markup_infoguides/Alphabetical_List_of_ InfoGuides/Education_Software-5.96
2. *Get There from Here (Teachers' Resources).*
   http://www.schoolpc.acp.com.au/sites/teachers.htm
3. *Excellent Education References and Tutorials.*
   http://kaleidoscapes.com/1educate.html
4. *SuperKids Educational Software Review.*
   http://www.superkids.com/aweb/pages/reviews/reviews.shtml
5. *World Village Software Reviews.*
   http://www.worldvillage.com/

There are hundreds of other excellent websites that provide reviews of educational software. However, listing the URLs for these serves little purpose because web addresses change frequently, and they can be found easily with a good search engine.

To illustrate the abundance of educational software review sites, we used the popular AltaVista search engine at http://www.altavista.com/ and used the search string +*"educational software review"*, including the plus sign and the quotation marks. This search produced nearly 2,000 sites providing such reviews. Teachers should make it a practice to locate and read reviews from trusted sources before purchasing any educational software.

We have one other strategy to recommend. We suggest that teachers approach software selection more broadly. That is, they should attempt to find the best instructional material to accomplish their educational objectives. Sometimes, this material will involve computers and sometimes it will not.

Long-Term Solution.   In the long term, educators need only decline to purchase poor-quality software and refuse to recommend it for purchase. When software producers are convinced that they can realize a profit only if they produce high-quality, educationally relevant software, they will decline to produce any other kind. The rest of this chapter will concentrate on the long-term solution by presenting a rationale and a method for software evaluation.

Both the short- and the long-term solutions offered previously require that software be expertly evaluated. Teachers can profit from software evaluation in two ways. First, they can find and read evaluations conducted by other educators. Second, they can conduct their own software evaluations. In many ways, most of this book is aimed at helping you to begin to develop the general ability to recognize excellent software when you see it. More specifically, many educators have found a formal evaluation form can be helpful when evaluating software.

In the next section, we discuss how to find software evaluations written by others. We then discuss the use of formal evaluation forms to help you perform your own evaluations.

Finding Software Evaluations Written by Others.   In the early stages of the educational computing movement, a number of state and regional organizations published software reviews. These organizations have gradually discontinued such printed reviews largely because magazines, journals, and more recently, the Internet and the World Wide Web have put them out of business.

One organization that does still publish reviews is the Educational Products Information Exchange (EPIE) (EPIE Institute 103 Montauk Highway, Hampton Bays, NY, 11946). EPIE produces *The Educational Software Selector* (TESS), which is published biennially and is available on CD-ROM (IBM and Mac compatible) and, for members of the State Consortium for Improving Software Selection (SCISS), on a password-accessible website.

TESS was initially developed with support from the Ford, Dodge, and McArthur Foundations and the Carnegie Corporation of New York. Today, TESS is supported by SCISS and by individual sales to parents and schools. As of 2000, TESS included reviews of over 19,000 educational software programs produced by over

1,300 different software publishers. Software reviewed includes all levels from preschool through college. Subject areas covered and the numbers of programs reviewed are as follows (Educational Products Information Exchange, 2000):

Science	3957
Mathematics	3049
Reading	2372
Language Arts	2463
Special Education	2659
Social Studies	2477
Foreign Language	1028
Health	740
Computer Education	584
Music and Arts	764
ESL	316

Each review includes information such as title, subject areas covered, type of software, grade level, distributor, and hardware requirements. The reviews also list published reviews of the program and EPIE's own rating. Individual site licenses are $79.95 and $29.95 for semi-annual updates. Those interested in joining SCISS, or in purchasing school or home licenses to TESS, should contact

P. Kenneth Komoski
Executive Director
EPIE Institute
E-Mail: info@EPIE
Phone: (516)728-9100
Web URL: http://www.epie.org/epie_tess.htm

When there were only a hundred or so programs in a given subject area such as middle-grades math, printed volumes of software reviews such as TESS were useful. Today, when thousands of programs are often available for a particular subject area, unwieldy printed volumes of software reviews are not so useful. Therefore, TESS has been made available as an electronic database, both on CD-ROM and on a web page.

The advantage of having the reviews available on these alternatives to traditional print is that the entire database can be searched quickly and efficiently. TESS, for example, is searchable by computer platform, subject, grade level, learning/teaching approach, curriculum role, and price, and can also be searched by key words chosen by users. For example, a search for "Elementary AND Science AND Estuaries," might generate a number of hits of software that can be used in an elementary science class studying estuaries.

A number of states have joined SCISS and thus have site licenses for TESS. This ensures that any teacher in the state can use it.

Another valuable resource is the SuperKids Educational Software Review site at http://www.superkids.com/. This site, maintained by Educational Software Institute (4213 South 94th Street, Omaha, NE, 68127, 800-955-5570) has links to various categories of reviews including new reviews, a subject index, an alphabetical title index, SuperKids award winners (best of the year, by category), and a search engine for customized searches of the database.

SuperKids' reviews are written by teams made up of parents, teachers, and children, who follow a standard review process. Samples of their review criteria can be found at http://www.superkids.com/aweb/pages/reviews/criteria.shtml. This is a very popular site, with 150,000 visitors a month generating over five million hits per quarter. (SuperKids is a commercial site, and sells advertising.)

Another excellent web resource has been developed by the California Instructional Technology Clearinghouse (http://clearinghouse.k12.ca.us/), which is funded by the California Department of Education. There is a large database of reviews, all written by California educators. Although many programs are reviewed, all programs listed have been rated as either *exemplary* or *desirable*, with approximately 10 percent of all programs evaluated earning the *exemplary* rating and 30 to 40 percent the *desirable* rating. For more information, visit the website, or contact California Instructional Technology Clearinghouse, 801 County Center III Court, Modesto, CA 95355-4490, (209) 525-4979, info@clearinghouse.k12.ca.us.

The Children's Software Finder (http://www.childrenssoftware.com/Tango3.acgi$/softsearch.taf?function=form) provides a way to search their database of over 4,200 reviews of educational software. The site (http://www.childrenssoftware.com/aboutcsr.html) is maintained by the publishers of the *Children's Software Revue*, a traditional print magazine featuring 100 to 200 software reviews in each issue. Reviews are written by employees of the magazine and by test families using a standard evaluation form. After each review is published in the print magazine, it is placed on the website. Each program reviewed receives a rating from 1 to 5, with 5 being the best possible rating. The standard evaluation instrument can be viewed at http://www.childrenssoftware.com/rating.html.

A slightly different approach has been taken on another highly useful web page maintained by Resources for Parents, Educators, and Publishers (PEP). This website (http://www.microweb.com/pepsite/index.html) has a link to the PEP Registry, which is a listing of 2,202 educational software companies, with direct links to their websites. These companies include descriptions of their software on their company pages. Of course, users must bear in mind that these are promotional descriptions that are certainly not objective in any way.

There are many other excellent sources of educational software reviews on the Web. The sources just described are simply examples of sites we have found to be useful. As we mentioned earlier, a search of the Web using AltaVista and the search string +*"educational software review"* produced nearly 2,000 hits. Teachers and others seeking reviews should perform such a web search so that they can locate new software review sites as they become available.

In addition, many of the Internet lists, forums, and newsgroups for educators regularly discuss software (Simonson & Thompson, 1997). On many of these resources it is acceptable to post a message asking for comments on a particular piece of software. Many electronic services for educators have special areas where educators can exchange comments on educational software.

Software reviews are also available from many traditional print magazines and scholarly journals, and these sources can be helpful to teachers. In fact, one of the advantages of looking to periodical literature for software reviews is that you can often find reviews relevant to special interests and needs. For example, *Arithmetic Teacher* publishes reviews on mathematics software that are written for math teachers by math teachers; likewise, the *Journal of Learning Disabilities* sometimes prints reviews of programs intended for use by learning-disabled individuals. Some of the computer-oriented educational publications that include software reviews are *T.H.E. Journal, Electronic Learning, Learning and Leading with Technology, Classroom Computer Learning, Technology and Learning, Educational Technology, Computers in the Schools, Journal of Special Education Technology,* and *Journal of Research on Computing in Education.*

Special Considerations for Multimedia Software

A growing trend in computer use in general, and in educational software in particular, is **multimedia.** Multimedia can be defined as "A computer-based interactive communications process that incorporates text, graphics, sound, animation, and video" (Shuman, 1998, p. 5). *Multimedia* and *hypermedia* were discussed in an earlier chapter in this book.

Although the continuing appearance of new media materials does raise the bar in terms of what we expect to see in educational materials, the process of software selection still comes down to reliability and validity. It is still important to ask: Does this software run reliably and without difficulty? Does this software help students accomplish important instructional goals? Other standard questions are also still relevant: Is it appropriate for the grade level I teach? Can it be effectively incorporated into my curriculum?

Advances in computer technology, however, have made possible and will continue to make possible new types of software that will require new software selection considerations. It must be remembered that new media programs are often based on different theories of teaching and learning than were the drill-and-practice and tutorial software widely available in the 1980s.

The theoretical aspects of educational computing were discussed earlier in this book but deserve additional emphasis here. The reliability of educational software is a relatively universal concept, but validity is much more complex. It is quite possible for two teachers, one a behaviorist and one a constructivist, to evaluate several pieces of software and come to opposite conclusions about how good the programs are. That is because the teachers will, at least to some extent, base their judgments of value on their theoretical perspectives. This aspect of software evaluation is important and must be considered when you read evaluations written by others or conduct your own evaluations. Theoretical issues aside, two additional aspects of cutting-edge software warrant special attention: hardware requirements and linking mechanisms.

HARDWARE CONSIDERATIONS FOR MULTIMEDIA AND OTHER CUTTING-EDGE SOFTWARE

One of the great frustrations of the information age is the rapid change in computers and computer peripherals. We all like to see the new models, and even though the rapid progress in terms of what computers can do is exciting, there is always a certain amount of disappointment when we see the potential of new computer software if we find that we cannot run such software with our existing hardware. It is especially disappointing when software is actually purchased only to find out that, in order to run it, a new circuit board or new peripheral must be purchased and added to existing computers. New media materials are particularly prone to this problem because much of the better new media software has been designed to take advantage of super-high-quality graphics and stereo sound capabilities of multimedia Macintosh and Windows computers.

At a time when some schools are still using very old computers, there are often great gulfs between what is available in educational software and what a school's computer equipment can handle. When considering multimedia and other cutting-edge software, you need to make sure you have the appropriate hardware and peripherals to run the software. If the software you are planning to purchase is expensive, we recommend that before making the final purchase you insist on gaining access to such software on a trial basis to make sure it is compatible with your hardware.

Linking Mechanisms

Video, graphics, and sound are the first things that catch our eye when we see new media programs, but it is the ability to access information in a nonlinear manner that truly sets much of the new media software apart from other types. The key to nonlinear access is **linking mechanisms.** Linking mechanisms determine how the various bits and pieces of information, including, text, video, graphics, and sound, are linked. The development of linking mechanisms is a complex process and, like any other aspect of software development, can be done carefully or carelessly. The quality of multimedia and other cutting-edge software depends greatly on how carefully and thoughtfully linking mechanisms are constructed. Again, it will be difficult to know for sure about the quality of linking mechanisms without actually trying out the software. Whenever possible, try to evaluate software yourself before making final purchasing decisions.

PROBLEMS IN INTERPRETING SOFTWARE EVALUATIONS WRITTEN BY OTHERS

Reviews written by others can be helpful. Published reviews frequently provide essential information about hardware requirements, thus helping to reduce the number of programs a teacher needs to consider. Such useful information (although not always accurate) can usually be obtained from published reviews.

We think some cautions are in order. In the first place, commercial magazines and websites are supported by advertising. They are, therefore, sometimes hesitant to publish negative reviews, especially if producers of reviewed software are major advertisers.

Another important consideration is who has written the reviews. Reviews by staff writers are often superficial, primarily because such writers are pressed for time, are working under stringent deadlines, have many writing assignments besides the review, and base their evaluation on a cursory examination that may consist only of hurriedly booting the software and tinkering with it for 10 to 15 minutes. Reader submissions may suffer from the same superficial approach.

Reviews in scholarly journals or on websites maintained by professional organizations or state departments of education are sometimes of higher quality than those found in slick magazines. Many such reviews are written by faculty members at colleges and universities. Unfortunately, however, administrators in higher education generally do not place much value on such reviews when it comes time for decisions about merit pay, tenure, or promotion, so faculty members are not always highly motivated to write such reviews or, when they do, to invest a great deal of time or effort in them.

Geisert and Futrell (1995) sum up some of the problems in interpreting published reviews:

> First, the review is generally an opinion article—it is one person's view of the product. (Any reader of film or book reviews will know that one critic can pan what another will hail.) Second, there is nothing that guarantees you that a reviewer has ever used the program with its targeted user group (e.g., students) or is even minimally informed about such use. More likely, the reviewer simply looked at the program. Third, reviewers often can get caught up in the "bells and whistles" of a program (for example, startling graphics presentation) and overlook the question of how well the program would be likely to work with students. (p. 191)

We conclude this section with the following recommendation: Published reviews are useful, should be consulted when available, but should never be the sole basis for purchase decisions.

PERFORMING YOUR OWN SOFTWARE EVALUATIONS

Much has been written about how to evaluate software. Nearly every educational computing book on the market has a chapter devoted to this topic, and there are hundreds of web pages dealing with it. Evaluation of software can be thought of as consisting of two parts: (1) engaging in the evaluation process and (2) producing a product, usually a completed evaluation form.

The Evaluation Process

Unfortunately, no hard-and-fast rules have proved to lead to effective software evaluation procedures (Church & Bender, 1989). Little research has been done on this topic. Bitter and Wighton (1987) describe one of the few efforts, in which 28 educational software evaluation agencies were surveyed and asked to rank a list of 22 criteria. Results were mixed, but there was a strong preference for emphasizing content-related criteria and deemphasizing technical features such as graphics, animation, sound, and screen design.

Such a study is relevant because one of the first steps in setting up an evaluation process is deciding what criteria are going to be considered important and desirable. After this decision is made, the criteria can be incorporated into an evaluation form.

As you might expect, there are many different ideas about what criteria should be used. Morrison, Lowther, and DeMeulle (1999) surveyed the literature and suggest that there are four general categories of criteria that are generally used:

1. Accuracy
2. Effective instructional strategies, including learner control of various program features (sound, pace, sequence, etc.)
3. Meets instructional objectives
4. Ease of use, including technical quality and precise and consistent directions (p. 341)

One important consideration in selecting criteria to use in evaluating software is the learning philosophy underlying the instruction. Schwartz and Beichner (1999) take this approach, and they identify criteria that they believe should be used in programs making use of a constructivist philosophy of teaching. They begin by asserting that software should permit the student to take charge and explore questions and issues of specific interest to that student. As a general rule, Schwartz and Beichner (1999) suggest that such software is not intended as stand-alone software, would frustrate students using it without teacher direction due to its relative lack of structure, and will be of value only in the hands of an experienced and skillful constructivist teacher. They suggest that such software would permit the teacher to use the software as follows:

1. Allow the student to engage in a little free exploration.
2. Have the student pose a problem or define a question to be pursued.
3. Guide the student in finding the resources to answer the question or solve the problem.
4. Help the student create a multimedia presentation to be used for sharing about the problem with others.
5. Provide a forum for students to share the multimedia presentations. (p. 18)

Jonassen, Peck, and Wilson (1999) agree with the idea that the learning philosophy must be taken into consideration to properly identify criteria for software selection. These writers are also constructivists, and they suggest that learning results if the software engages learners in:

1. Knowledge construction, not reproduction
2. Conversation, not reception
3. Articulation, not repetition
4. Collaboration, not competition
5. Reflection, not prescription (p. 16)

Calvert (1999) suggests that the criteria for effective computer programs (and for effective educational television) must include the following:

1. Age-appropriate content
2. Gender- and ethnic-appropriate content
3. Perceptually salient production techniques including action, sound effects, and visual special effects
4. Comprehensible language
5. Repetition
6. Interactivity
7. Familiar host and cast
8. Familiar setting
9. Specific theme
10. Experience of learning as fun
11. Multimedia materials

Simonson and Thompson (1997) suggest that criteria should be selected that will not be made quickly obsolete by advances in hardware. They suggest at least three areas that should be evaluated, including content, use, and administration. They go on to suggest that (1) content evaluation can be further broken down into objectives, content accuracy, and methodology of instruction; (2) use deals with the quality of students' interaction with the software and includes ease of use and "crash-proofness"; and (3) administration variables include cost, hardware compatibility, ability to make backups, and availability of site licenses.

Lockard, Abrams, and Many (1994) suggest that software should be evaluated against (1) intended use, (2) learning theory, and (3) specific criteria.

Evaluating against intended use requires that the teacher clearly define the learning objectives of the lesson in which the software might be used, then make a judgment as to whether the particular software can help achieve these objectives. Thus, this assessment is highly individualistic. This part of the evaluation can be facilitated if the software producers have done a good job of articulating the goals and objectives they had in mind when the software was produced; though it is possible that a teacher would elect to use the software for some other important purposes.

Evaluation against learning theory requires that the evaluator understand such theory or theories. An example might be the evaluation of problem-solving software intended by the producers to teach skills that Piagetian developmental theory would characterize as formal operational thinking. Such software probably would not be reasonable for use in a second-grade classroom because children of that age probably are not capable of such abstract thinking.

Lockard, Abrams, and Many (1994) suggest that evaluation against specific criteria might include consideration of variables in four major categories: (1) mechanical factors, (2) general criteria, (3) CAI-specific criteria, and (4) usability factors.

There are many other ways to categorize important criteria. Church and Bender (1989) suggest that the following be evaluated: (1) instructional content, (2) utilization of computer capabilities, (3) goals and objectives, (4) software presentation variables (pacing, ability levels, etc.), (5) product information, and (6) **documentation.** Lillie, Hannum, and Stuck (1989) recommend that attention be given to (1) instructional content, (2) instructional procedures, and (3) instructional management.

We prefer to base evaluation on six criteria: (1) content (2) **mode of instruction**, (3) management, (4) technical presentation, (5) documentation, and (6) ease of use.

FORMAL EVALUATION FORMS

Most authors suggest that a formal evaluation form be used, and examples of such forms abound (Bitter, 1999). Holznagel (1987) has pointed out that most forms overlap considerably. We feel strongly that schools or school districts should adopt their own form. However, it is handy to have a form as an example or to use until a unique form can be adopted. Therefore, we have included a copy of our own software evaluation form in Figure 13.1. This form makes use of the six criteria listed at the end of the previous section.

Many other forms are available, and interested readers should consult any good computer education text for other examples. In addition, the World Wide Web is a rich source for sample evaluation forms. There are literally hundreds of such forms available on the Web. They can be located by using a search engine such as AltaVista (http://www.altavista.com/) and using the search string +*"software evaluation form"*. A recent search using this key phrase produced 635 hits. A few representative forms can be found at the following websites:

1. *California Instructional Technology Clearinghouse.*
   http://www.stan-co.k12.ca.us/sc0173/forms/Software_Report.pdf
2. *Children's Software Review Form.*
   http://www.microweb.com/pepsite/Revue/evaluation.html
3. *Nova Scotia Department of Education Software Evaluation Form.*
   http://www.ednet.ns.ca/educ/program/lrt/eval/evalform.htm
4. *Southern Illinois University Form.*
   http://leader.soed.siue.edu/Evaluations/EvalForm.html

Software Evaluation Form

Name of Evaluator _____   Date _____

Title of Program _____

Title of Package _____

Publisher _____

Address _____

Price _____   Subject area _____

Age/Grade _____

Goal(s) _____
_____
_____

Objectives _____
_____
_____
_____

Prerequisite Skills _____
_____

Instructional Purpose and Design

Type I _____   Type II _____

Operating System ____ _____

Category (Circle one or more)

Drill and practice	Word Processing	Tutorial
Authoring	Simulation	Management
Problem solving	Assessment	Administrative
Computer language	Other _____	

COMMENTS: _____
_____
_____

Recommended for purchase?   YES   NO

FIGURE 13.1   Software evaluation form.   *(continued)*

FIGURE 13.1   *(Continued)*

Rate the software using the following system:

1 - very strongly disagree	4 - agree
2 - strongly disagree	5 - strongly agree
3 - disagree	6 - very strongly agree
NA - not applicable	

Content	disagree					agree	
1. Accurate/factual.							
2. Content is interesting for students.	1	2	3	4	5	6	NA
3. Content is educationally important.	1	2	3	4	5	6	NA
4. Content is appropriate for level of intended users.	1	2	3	4	5	6	NA
5. Prerequisite skills needed are realistic for intended users.	1	2	3	4	5	6	NA
6. Free of stereotypes/biases.	1	2	3	4	5	6	NA
7. Free of errors in grammar, spelling, etc.	1	2	3	4	5	6	NA

Section Average (sum of ratings divided by number, excluding NAs) _____

Mode of Instruction							
1. New *vocabulary* is presented appropriately.	1	2	3	4	5	6	NA
2. New *concepts* are presented appropriately.	1	2	3	4	5	6	NA
3. Students can control pace.	1	2	3	4	5	6	NA
4. Students can control sequence.	1	2	3	4	5	6	NA
5. Program accommodates wide range of ability.	1	2	3	4	5	6	NA
6. Feedback is useful/appropriately stated.	1	2	3	4	5	6	NA
7. Program reflects knowledge of learning theory.	1	2	3	4	5	6	NA

Section Average (sum of ratings divided by number, excluding NAs) _____

Management							
1. Students records can be stored on a diskette.	1	2	3	4	5	6	NA
2. Stored records are useful and complete.	1	2	3	4	5	6	NA
3. Stored information is secure from unauthorized access.	1	2	3	4	5	6	NA

Section Average (sum of ratings divided by number, excluding NAs) _____

Technical Presentation							
1. Graphics and sound (if used) are appropriate.	1	2	3	4	5	6	NA
2. Displays are uncluttered.	1	2	3	4	5	6	NA
3. Program is free of programming bugs.	1	2	3	4	5	6	NA
4. Menu items are understandable and descriptive.	1	2	3	4	5	6	NA
5. Program is appropriate in responses accepted as correct/incorrect.	1	2	3	4	5	6	NA
6. Directions make clear what type of response is solicited.	1	2	3	4	5	6	NA
7. Reading level is appropriate for intended users.	1	2	3	4	5	6	NA

Section Average (sum of ratings divided by number, excluding NAs) _____

FIGURE 13.1   *(Continued)*

Documentation	disagree					agree	
1. Hardware requirements are clear and complete.	1	2	3	4	5	6	NA
2. Program installation procedure is clear and complete.	1	2	3	4	5	6	NA
3. Goals and/or objectives are clearly stated.	1	2	3	4	5	6	NA
4. Prerequisite skills are clearly identified.	1	2	3	4	5	6	NA
5. Grade/age of intended users is clearly identified.	1	2	3	4	5	6	NA
6. Off-computer activities (if used) are appropriate.	1	2	3	4	5	6	NA
7. Documentation for students uses correct reading level.	1	2	3	4	5	6	NA

Section Average (sum of ratings divided by number, excluding NAs) _____

Ease of Use

	disagree					agree	
1. Students can use program with minimal teacher help.	1	2	3	4	5	6	NA
2. On-screen directions are clear.	1	2	3	4	5	6	NA
3. Directions can be skipped at option of user.	1	2	3	4	5	6	NA
4. Directions can be reviewed at any time.	1	2	3	4	5	6	NA
5. Students can review previous screens without restarting program.	1	2	3	4	5	6	NA
6. Students can exit the program at any time.	1	2	3	4	5	6	NA
7. Students can restart program where they stopped.	1	2	3	4	5	6	NA

Section Average (sum of ratings divided by number, excluding NAs _____

Optional Overall Average (Average of section averages) _____

(All calculations of section averages and overall average should be carried out to two decimal places.)

5. *SuperKids Teacher Evaluation Form.*
   http://www.superkids.com/aweb/pages/reviews/teacher.html
6. *Virginia Community College Software Evaluation Checklist.*
   http://www.so.cc.va.us/vccsit/softchek.htm

Buckleitner (1999) sees many problems with the state of the art in software evaluation and suggests that practices are outdated, unreliable, biased by commercial interests, and rarely supported by research. He adds that what is needed is research on software evaluation and evaluation forms such as that done by Escobedo and Evans (1997). These researchers compared ratings from a published evaluation form with the selections of actual students who were videotaped while choosing from among 13 programs. Results showed that children sometimes chose software identified with the instrument as developmentally inappropriate, thus calling into question the accuracy of the form. The most interesting finding was that children tended to choose the software that provided the most potential for user interaction.

Advantages and Disadvantages of Forms

Evaluation forms have advantages and disadvantages. The advantage is that such forms provide a standard that many evaluators can use, thus making it easier to compare reviews by different people. A form is essential for computer education beginners to provide needed structure and to ensure that important considerations are not ignored.

One disadvantage is the amount of time it takes to do a good job filling out a form. Lockard, Abrams, and Many (1994) emphasize the time problem, especially in light of their excellent recommendation that evaluators should run the program at least three times: first as a better student might, then as a weaker student might, and finally as a test of how the program responds to completely inappropriate input. They further recommend that the form not be filled out until the evaluator has field-tested the software with students.

Another disadvantage is that a single form is not likely to be the best form for every type of software or for all subjects at all grade levels. For example, the form we presented in Figure 13.1 is not as good for evaluating tool software such as word processing programs or spreadsheets as it is for drill-and-practice software or simulations. A final disadvantage is the tendency for forms to become institutionalized and viewed as the final word.

Adapting Software Evaluation Forms

We believe that educators should take a flexible approach to the use of forms. In the first place, we think each school or school district should develop its own form that meets the needs of the particular settings in which software is used. Therefore, we think that individuals or committees charged with developing forms should take a look at a large number of forms and then modify them for their own purposes.

Holznagel (1987) lists a number of factors that may indicate that an existing form needs revision. He mentions differences in (1) the audience, (2) time constraints, (3) subject matter focus, and (4) emergence of new categories of software.

Obtaining Software for Evaluation

The suggestions discussed to this point require that teachers obtain software for evaluation prior to making a decision about purchasing. There are several ways to do this besides the ones already mentioned. Many software producers or distributors will provide software on a 30-day approval basis, and many make samples available for downloading on their sites on the World Wide Web. We suggest that educators not buy programs that cannot either be examined before purchase or, if found unsatisfactory, returned after purchase.

Geisert and Futrell (1999) suggest that teachers write, rather than telephone, to request software for preview. They also recommend (1) using a school letterhead, (2) requesting only one or two titles at a time, (3) stating specific instructional goals for the software, (4) stating that you will be personally responsible for ensuring that the software is not illegally copied, (5) ensuring timely return after preview, and (6) guaranteeing that you will supply a brief explanation if you decide not to purchase the software.

There are other ways to obtain software for preview. Sometimes libraries acquire software that can be checked out or used on the premises. This is especially true of libraries or instructional materials centers located in colleges of education. Computer laboratories in colleges of education also frequently maintain educational software libraries that can be useful. Sometimes local software retailers will loan educational software or allow it to be previewed by teachers on premises. Another possibility is that district administrators may arrange for school or school district software fairs in which distributors set up booths and demonstrate their wares. More and more software producers are making sample versions of their programs available on the Web.

EVALUATION OF WEBSITES

A comprehensive treatment of website evaluation is far beyond the space requirements of this book. Many complete books and thousands of articles and web pages deal exclusively with the topic of how the Web can be used in schools (e.g., Abbey, 2000; Ackermann & Hartman, 2000; Heide & Stilborne, 1999; Khan, 1997; Provenzo, 1999; Ryder & Hughes, 1998). Properly evaluating a web page is quite dependent on the educational purpose to which it is applied.

There are, however, certain general guidelines about web pages that apply to just about every page and every purpose. As with software, two main categories should be considered: technical qualities and educational usefulness.

Although the Web abounds with excellent pages, many pages are extremely poor quality. It is not difficult to understand why this is so. The Web's amazing and unprecedented growth did not permit the slow evolution of standards for quality publications that took place over centuries in traditional print publishing. The Web began its meteoric rise in 1993 after the Mosaic Web browser became widely available:

> Within a few months it was being used by millions of people. One can easily imagine that the first books might have been somewhat less useful than are typical modern volumes if the invention of the printing press had also included an "instant solution" to book distribution and affordability problems. (Maddux, 1998, p. 24)

The following is a short list of the more common and obvious problems found in web pages. Teachers should avoid recommending pages that demonstrate these problems.

1. Pages that lack proper identification of the page sponsor
2. Pages that lack links back to the main page
3. Pages that lack a clear, brief purpose statement near the top of the main page
4. Pages that are not up-to-date
5. Pages that contain "under construction" notices

6. Pages that take longer than 10 to 20 seconds to load
7. Pages with links that do not work
8. Pages with graphics that are distorted or missing
9. Pages with backgrounds that are so "busy" they are difficult to read
10. Pages that lack proper identification of the page author and an e-mail link to that person's e-mail
11. Pages that contain inappropriate language
12. Pages that make use of improper mechanics such as grammar, spelling, and so forth

Ackermann and Hartman (2000) make the point that it is important to think critically about information on the Web because some web authors who want "to sell a product or disseminate propaganda can make material appear to be part of a well-researched report" (p. 359). They suggest that a good way to start evaluating a website is to ask the following questions:

1. Who is the author or institution?
2. How current is the information?
3. Who is the audience?
4. Is the content accurate and objective?
5. What is the purpose of the information? (p. 373)

A more complete treatment of this topic can be found in Maddux, 1998; Maddux and Cummings, 2000; and Maddux and Johnson, 1997. In addition, many excellent web pages deal with evaluation of websites and individual pages. These can be found by using a search engine such as AltaVista (http://www.altavista.com/) and the search string +"*evaluating web pages*". A recent search with this search string produced 1,184 hits. The is a list of a few sites that we have found helpful:

1. *Evaluation of Information Sources.*
   http://www.vuw.ac.nz/~agsmith/evaln/evaln.htm
   This page contains dozens of links to various sites dealing with evaluation of websites. It was developed and is maintained by the World Wide Web Virtual Library. The Virtual Library is the oldest catalog of the Web, started by Tim Berners-Lee, the creator of the Web itself.
2. *Evaluating Quality on the Net.*
   http://www.tiac.net/users/hope/findqual.html
   This page is by Hope N. Tillman, Director of Libraries, Babson College, Babson Park, Massachusetts.
3. *Evaluating Web Resources.*
   http://www2.widener.edu/Wolfgram-Memorial-Library/webeval.htm
   This is an article by Jan Alexander and Marsha Ann Tate, of the Wolfgram Memorial Library at Widener University. These authors also have an excellent new book on the topic called *Web Wisdom: How to Evaluate and Create Information Quality on the Web* (Alexander & Tate, 1999).

4. *The Librarian's Guide to Cyberspace for Parents and Kids: What Makes a Great Website.*
   http://www.ala.org/parentspage/greatsites/select.html
   This page contains the selection guidelines from the American Library Association's *700+ Great Sites for Children,* which can be found on the Web at http://www.ala.org/parentspage/greatsites/.

5. *The Good, The Bad & The Ugly: or, Why It's a Good Idea to Evaluate Web Sources.*
   http://lib.nmsu.edu/instruction/evalcrit.html
   This page by Susan Beck from the New Mexico State University Library gives tips for using the following criteria: accuracy, authority, objectivity, currency, and coverage.

6. *Internet Source Validation Project.*
   http://www.stemnet.nf.ca/~dfurey/validate/
   This page, maintained by the faculty of education at Memorial University of Newfoundland, was started to develop a set of guidelines for students and teachers who want to use the Internet as a source of information for research papers.

7. *ICYouSee: T is for Thinking.*
   http://www.ithaca.edu/library/Training/hott.html
   This page, by John R. Henderson of the Ithaca College Library, presents five suggestions when examining web pages.

8. *Internet Detective.*
   http://sosig.ac.uk/desirc/internet-detective.html
   This page is an interactive tutorial on evaluating the quality of Internet resources. It includes interactive quizzes, examples, and practical hints and tips. There is also a link to an offline version that can be downloaded.

9. *Thinking Critically about World Wide Web Resources.*
   http://www.library.ucla.edu/libraries/college/instruct/web/critical.htm
   This page, by Esther Grassian of the UCLA College Library, lists extensive questions to ask about a site and provides links to other sites dealing with evaluation.

10. *Lexington Public Schools Guidelines for Evaluating Web Pages.*
   http://lps.lexingtonma.org/Libdept/edeval.html
   An excellent brief page of guidelines used by the Lexington, Kentucky, public schools.

Instruments for Web Evaluation

There are also many published evaluation instruments that can be used for evaluation of websites and individual web pages. The Web itself contains hundreds of these. A series of forms that we especially like is by Kathy Schrock, whose website is called Kathy Schrock's Guide for Educators (http://school.discovery.com/schrockguide/index.html). This well-known site is excellent in many ways and is well worth a visit for many different purposes. One of the pages at the site is entitled Critical Evaluation Information (http://school.discovery.com/schrockguide/eval.html). This site contains dozens of links to other sites containing evaluation information, and links to Kathy Schrock's four checklists for evaluating websites. The checklists can be found at the following locations:

1. *Critical Evaluation Survey: Elementary School Level* (PDF version).
   http://school.discovery.com/schrockguide/evalelem.html
2. *Critical Evaluation Survey: Middle School Level* (PDF version).
   http://school.discovery.com/schrockguide/evalmidd.html
3. *Critical Evaluation Survey: Secondary School Level* (PDF version).
   http://school.discovery.com/schrockguide/evalhigh.html
4. *Critical Evaluation Survey: Virtual Tours* (PDF version).
   http://school.discovery.com/schrockguide/evaltour.html

In addition, Kathy Schrock's page includes an interactive, online critical evaluation survey and database (http://forms.flashbase.com/forms/web_page_eval). This page displays a website evaluation form, which can be filled out for any site on the Web and submitted by anyone. Each completed form is then added to a large database of reviews that have been submitted by visitors to the page. This database can be viewed at http://forms.flashbase.com/view/web_page_eval/.

Some other excellent examples of instruments for evaluating websites follow:

1. *Northeastern University Web Evaluation Form.*
   http://www.neoucom.edu/library/WomensHealth/evalform.html
2. *Kent State University Website Evaluation Form.*
   http://www.library.kent.edu/subjects/nursing/webevalform.html
3. *Iona College (New York) Comprehensive Evaluation Form.*
   http://www.iona.edu/library/resins/cmpeval3.htm
4. *Aldert Root Elementary School (Raleigh, NC) Web Evaluation Form.*
   http://schools.wcpss.net/Root/evalform1.html
5. *Wolfgram Memorial Library (Widener University) Checklists for Various Types of Sites.*
   http://www2.widener.edu/Wolfgram-Memorial-Library/webeval.htm
   a. *Checklist for Advocacy Web Pages.*
      http://www2.widener.edu/Wolfgram-Memorial-Library/advoc.htm
   b. *Checklist for Business/Marketing Web Pages.*
      http://www2.widener.edu/Wolfgram-Memorial-Library/busmark.htm
   c. *Checklist for Informational Web Pages.*
      http://www2.widener.edu/Wolfgram-Memorial-Library/inform.htm
   d. *Checklist for News Web Pages.*
      http://www2.widener.edu/Wolfgram-Memorial-Library/news.htm
   e. *Checklist for Personal Web Pages.*
      http://www2.widener.edu/Wolfgram-Memorial-Library/perspg.htm
6. *Montgomery County Public Schools Web Evaluation Form.*
   http://www.mcps.k12.md.us/departments/isa/elit/mid/websiteevalform.htm
7. *How to Tell If You Are Looking at a Great Web Site* (by the Children and Technology Committee of the Association for Library Service to Children, a division of the American Library Association).
   http://www.ala.org/parentspage/greatsites/criteria.html

8. *Evaluating Internet-Based Information: A Goals-Based Approach* (Article and form by David Warlick that appeared originally in *Meridian*, a middle school technology journal).
   http://www.media-awareness.ca/eng/med/class/teamed2/warlick.htm

9. *Loogootee (Indiana) Community Schools Evaluation Rubrics for Websites* (Three evaluation instruments for use by students at three different educational levels).
   http://www.siec.k12.in.us/~west/online/eval.htm
   a. *Web Evaluation for Primary Grades.*
      http://www.siec.k12.in.us/~west/edu/rubric1.htm
   b. *Web Evaluation for Intermediate Grades.*
      http://www.siec.k12.in.us/~west/edu/rubric2.htm
   c. *Web Evaluation for Secondary Grades.*
      http://www.siec.k12.in.us/~west/edu/rubric3.htm

10. *Evaluation Form by N. Everhart, St. John's University Division of Library and Information Science.*
    http://www.duke.edu/~de1/evaluate.html

We think that teachers should custom design their own web evaluation forms tailored for each specific grade level, subject, and so on. However, the sample forms found at the above sites can serve as excellent models.

SUMMARY

Educational software quality is improving, and there is a substantial body of excellent educational software that is available. However, software quality continues to be a problem. Solutions to this problem include the need for teachers to communicate with software developers and to refuse to purchase software that lacks educational relevance.

It is possible to find published software evaluations. There are a number of national sources for such reviews, including magazines, journals, and the World Wide Web. Problems with such reviews include superficial treatments, differing philosophies, the time lag between appearance of the software and availability of reviews, and a lack of field testing with students.

Although published reviews are useful, expensive software should always be personally reviewed before it is purchased. Such reviews are often carried out with the aid of a standard evaluation form. Many such forms are available. Educators should develop their own forms, using a variety of published forms as examples. An example of a form is provided, along with suggestions for when revision of a form is appropriate.

Firsthand software evaluation requires that teachers obtain software and evaluate it. More and more software houses have websites featuring samples of their products that can be downloaded and tried out. Additionally, most software developers and distributors provide software on approval or permit return of software if it is unsatisfactory. Other sources of software for preview include libraries, conferences, and colleges of education.

Websites also need to be evaluated. The quality of pages on the Web varies greatly, probably due to the speed with which the Web has evolved. Many sites on the Web present useful information about evaluation of websites. Many published web evaluation forms can be downloaded and used as models for teachers to develop their own evaluation instruments.

QUESTIONS TO CONSIDER

1. What could the federal government do that might improve software quality?
2. What could individual school districts do that might improve software quality?
3. What categories of criteria would you incorporate in a software evaluation form of your own design? Why did you choose those categories?
4. What are some of your favorite websites, and what is it about these sites that you find to be both good and bad?

RELATED ACTIVITIES

1. Call, write, or visit the websites of at least three commercial software companies and determine their preview and return policies for educators.
2. Use the sample software evaluation form to evaluate at least two pieces of educational software. You may find such software in your college of education computer lab, the main college library, the local school district, or local software retail stores.
3. Produce your own software evaluation form, emphasizing areas that you feel are most important.
4. Visit some of the sites listed in the chapter that provide web evaluation forms. Select one that you feel is excellent and use it to evaluate a website of your choice.

REFERENCES

Abbey, B. (Ed.). (2000). *Instructional and cognitive impacts of web-based education.* Hershey, PA: Idea Group.

Ackermann, E., & Hartman, K. (2000). *Searching and researching on the Internet and the World Wide Web* (2nd. ed.). Wilsonville, OR: Franklin Beedle & Associates.

Alexander, J. E., & Tate, M. A. (1999). *Web wisdom: How to evaluate and create information quality on the web.* Mahwah, NJ: Lawrence Erlbaum.

Association for Supervision and Curriculum Development. (1999). *Only the best: The annual guide to the highest-rated educational software and multimedia.* Alexandria, VA: Author.

Bitter, G. (1999). *Using technology in the classroom.* Boston: Allyn & Bacon.

Bitter, G., & Wighton, D. (1987). The most important criteria used by the education software evaluation consortium. *The Computing Teacher, 14*(6), 7–9.

Buckleitner, W. (1999). The state of children's software evaluation: Yesterday, today and in the 21st century. *Information Technology in Childhood Education,* 211–220.

Calvert, S. (1999). *Children's journeys through the information age.* Boston: McGraw-Hill.

Church, G., & Bender, M. (1989). *Teaching with computers: A curriculum for special educators.* Boston: College-Hill Press.

Educational Products Information Exchange. (2000). *EPIE Institute: TESS list of subjects and categories.* Retrieved May 7, 2000, from the World Wide Web: http://www.epie.org/tesscatg.htm.

Escobedo, T. H., & Evans, S. (1997, March). *A comparison of child-tested early childhood education soft-*

ware with professional ratings. Paper presented at the annual meeting of the American Education Research Association, Chicago, IL.

Flake, J. L., McClintock, C. E., & Turner, S. (1990). *Fundamentals of computer education.* Belmont, CA: Wadsworth.

Geisert, G. G., & Futrell, M. K. (1999). *Teachers, computers, and curriculum* (3rd ed.). Boston: Allyn & Bacon.

Geisert, G. G., & Futrell, M. K. (1995). *Teachers, computers, and curriculum* (2nd ed.). Boston: Allyn & Bacon.

Heide, A., & Stilborne, L. (1999). The teacher's complete and easy guide to the Internet. Toronto: Trifolium Books.

Holznagle, D. C. (1987). Selecting software. In R. E. Bennett (Ed.), *Planning and evaluating computer education programs* (pp. 25–42). Columbus, OH: Merrill.

Jonassen, D. H. (2000). *Computers as mindtools for schools: Engaging critical thinking.* Upper Saddle River, NJ: Merrill.

Jonassen, D. H., Peck, K. L., & Wilson, B. G. (1999). *Learning with technology: A constructivist perspective.* Upper Saddle River, NJ: Merrill.

Khan, B. H. (Ed.). (1997). *Web-based instruction.* Englewood Cliffs, NJ: Educational Technology.

Kinzer, C. K., Sherwood, R. D., & Bransford, J. D. (1986). *Computer strategies for education: Foundations and content-area applications.* Columbus, OH: Merrill.

Komoski, P. K. (1984, December). Educational computing: The burden of insuring quality. *Phi Delta Kappan, 53,* 244–248.

Lillie, D. L., Hannum, W. H., & Stuck, G. B. (1989). *Computers and effective instruction.* New York: Longman.

Lockard, J., Abrams, P. D., & Many, W. A. (1994). *Microcomputers for twenty-first century educators.* New York: Harper Collins College.

Maddux, C. D. (1998). The World Wide Web: Some simple solutions to common design problems. *Educational Technology, 38*(5), 24–28.

Maddux, C. D., & Cummings, R. (2000). Developing web pages as supplements to tradi-

tional courses. In B. Abbey (Ed.), *Instructional and cognitive impacts of Web-based education* (pp. 147–155). Hershey, PA: Idea Group.

Maddux, C., & Johnson, D. L. (1997). The World Wide Web: History, cultural context, and a manual for developers of educational information-based websites. *Educational Technology, 37*(5), 5–12.

Mandell, C. J., & Mandell, S. L. (1989). *Computers in education today.* St. Paul, MN: West.

Morrison, G. R., Lowther, D. L., & DeMeulle, L. (1999). *Integrating computer technology into the classroom.* Upper Saddle River, NJ: Merrill.

Neill, S. B., & Neill, G. W. (1989). *Only the best: The annual guide to the highest-rated educational software for preschool–grade 12* (1990 ed.). New York: R. R. Bowker.

Office of Technology Assessment. (1988). *Power on! New tools for teaching and learning* (Publication No. 052-003-01125-5). Washington, DC: U.S. Government Printing Office.

President's Committee of Advisors on Science and Technology, Panel on Educational Technology. (2000). *Report to the President on the use of technology to strengthen K–12 education in the United States.* Retrieved May 5, 2000, from the World Wide Web: http://www.whitehouse.gov/WH/EOP/OSTP/NSTC/PCAST/k-12ed.html#4.s

Provenzo, E. F. (1999). *The Internet and the World Wide Web for preservice teachers.* Boston: Allyn & Bacon.

Roblyer, M. D., & Edwards, J. (2000). *Integrating educational technology into teaching* (2nd ed.). Upper Saddle River, NJ: Merrill.

Ryder, R. J., & Hughes, T. (1998). *Internet for educators* (2nd ed.). Upper Saddle River, NJ: Merrill.

Schwartz, J. E., & Beichner, R. J. (1999). *Essentials of educational technology.* Boston: Allyn & Bacon.

Shuman, J. E. (1998). *Multimedia in action.* Belmont, CA: Integrated Media Group.

Simonson, M. R., & Thompson, A. (1997). *Educational computing foundations.* Upper Saddle River, NJ: Prentice Hall.

CHAPTER FOURTEEN

LOOKING TO THE FUTURE

Goal: To become aware of some of the possible future directions in information technology in education.

KEY TERMS

accreditation (p. 326)	pedagogical issues (p. 328)
assistive devices (p. 330)	platform barriers (p. 328)
commercialization (p. 327)	quality control (p. 326)
dedicated devices (p. 329)	virtual universities (p. 326)
distance education (p. 326)	wireless Internet access (p. 328)

Predicting the future is a hazardous activity for those who dislike being proved wrong. As George F. Will said, "The future has a way of arriving unannounced." This has been made painfully clear to a host of so-called futurists in the field of information technology, whose predictions have been notoriously unreliable. It is indicative of the almost unbelievable speed and magnitude of change over the last decade or so that most of these futurists erred, not by promising too much, but by predicting changes that were far less sweeping and far less startling than what actually came to pass.

Perhaps the best example is that no one predicted either the speed with which the Internet and the World Wide Web would pervade cultures around the world or the magnitude of their effect on the global economic and social fabric. When Clinton took office, the World Wide Web contained only about 50 pages of text. No one predicted that the Internet and the Web would evolve, in fewer than 10 years, from that clumsy, esoteric network for a few scholars to the presently ubiquitous phenomenon used by at least 275 million people worldwide. No one predicted that the Web would grow from 50 pages in 1992 to its present size, which is in the neighborhood of one billion pages containing 6 trillion characters

(Lawrence & Giles, 1999), as well as huge masses of graphics, music, and other information of all kinds. Indeed, no one predicted that the Web would contain so much information that there would be scores of search engines and directories to help users find exactly what they were looking for, that these search engines and directories would be used to perform at least 95 million searches each day, or that research would show, for one 3-month period, that more time was spent surfing the Web by citizens in the U.S. and Canada than the combined playback time of all videos in those two countries (The Madison Avenue Group, 2000).

Because predicting future events in areas related to information technology is so difficult, we usually refrain from this egocentric and somewhat arrogant indulgence. Furthermore, we suspect the future will again prove to be even more revolutionary and more exciting than anyone can presently imagine. We tend to agree with Albert Einstein, who said, "I never think of the future—it comes soon enough."

Nevertheless, there are some very general future developments that seem likely to take place, and it may be beneficial to keep these things in mind when planning for the future uses of information technology in education.

THE FUTURE ROLE OF THE INTERNET AND THE WEB

It seems safe to predict that the Internet and the World Wide Web will continue to grow in size, popularity, and influence, and that teachers and students in the future will continue to make increasing use of them as teaching and learning aids. Therefore, computers with Internet connections will continue to find their way into schools, and the ratio of students to computers will continue to shrink.

Exactly what form the Internet and the Web will assume, or precisely what applications will be possible, is anybody's guess. However, it certainly seems likely that multimedia on the Internet and the Web will continue to grow in type and sophistication and that educational simulations will therefore continue to be more and more similar to the real environments and events on which they are based.

THE FUTURE ROLE OF INDIVIDUAL LEARNING

For many years, educators have paid lip service to individualizing instruction. This goal has been elusive, at best, and most authorities would agree that true individualized instruction has not been achieved in typical classrooms around the country. However, we think that technology in the future will contribute positively to this end and that schools of tomorrow are likely to feature much more individualized instruction and individual learning than do schools of the present. On the other hand, the social element of traditional schooling is one of its strongest and most prized assets. Therefore, we do not believe that educators, policy makers, or the public will support a future in which children plug in to a computer or a computer network and spend their day in a virtual world without person-to-person interaction. A more moderate outcome is likely—one in which the interpersonal element of schooling is preserved, but individualization of instruction and individual learning becomes more common.

THE FUTURE ROLE OF DISTANCE EDUCATION

We think that **distance education** will continue to grow in popularity and that students and teachers in the future will have many more educational options than are now available to them. This trend is already beginning to transform higher education and has stimulated a lively controversy about the future of traditional brick-and-mortar colleges and universities in a future that will certainly include many online options such as **virtual universities.**

In a report released in December of 2000, the National Center for Education Statistics (Lewis, Farris, Snow, & Levin, 2000) reported on a large study of 5,010 postsecondary institutions in the United States. Of these, 1,680 (34 percent) reported offering distance education courses in 1997–1998, and an additional one-fifth said they planned on offering such courses within 3 years. It seems likely that in the future, the trend toward more online educational options will intensify and will extend downward into secondary education and perhaps even into elementary education.

Quality control of online education is currently a burning issue on college and university campuses, and some public and private institutions and commercial entities are already offering entire courses and even complete undergraduate and graduate degrees on the Web. These same concerns about quality will become increasingly important as distance education continues to attract more and more of their clientele away from traditional private and public schools at all levels. **Accreditation** agencies and organizations will be forced to respond (Carlson, 2000), and it is likely that political pressure will continue to force them to offer accreditation to various online education providers, whether accreditation officials consider such a move professionally justifiable. (One quite likely ironic possibility is that traditional schools may become their own competitors by responding to student flight by creating often inferior, online programs and pressuring their own accreditation agencies for recognition of these programs.)

How the trend toward online education will play out is an open question. We think the movement is so strong that it is already unstoppable, even if we decided to try to bring it to an end. Unfortunately, it is hard not to be pessimistic about the overall effect on the quality of education that distance education will likely have in the future. We think it is likely to erode future financial support that will be available for traditional schools, especially postsecondary schools. Schools are already financially strapped, and distance education will intensify that problem. As more and more students are drawn to online options, support for traditional education will continue to decline. This will cause quality in traditional schools to suffer, in turn causing even more students to elect nontraditional options. We have no idea how far such a vicious cycle will go.

However, we do not believe it likely that traditional brick-and-mortar schools will disappear at any level. We do think that such schools of the future will be even more embattled than they are presently and that increasingly difficult financial times lie ahead for schools at all levels, particularly for schools of higher education.

We think that as this scenario works itself out, traditional schools may become ever more customer oriented than they are today. This trend, already well established on higher education campuses across the country, will probably result in further erosion of quality as schools strive to make their customers happier by starting their own, often inferior, online courses and programs, and by making both online and traditional courses and degree programs shorter, cheaper, easier, and more entertaining.

Distance education will intensify the current trend for colleges and universities, and even some public schools, to rely increasingly on solicitation of donations and other external fund-raising to secure financial resources that state and local governments are unwilling or unable to provide. Donations and grants will thus become even more important than they already are, and school administrators in the future will probably find themselves devoting even more time and effort than they presently devote to these activities.

Another related current trend that is likely to increase as a result of competition from distance education is the **commercialization** of secondary and higher education. Schools will increase their efforts to sell advertising and franchise rights to various business interests. (Readers interested in an in-depth analysis of this trend to date should see the excellent book by Anne Matthews [1997] entitled *Bright College Years*.)

Although there are many disadvantages to the current online educational trend, there are also advantages:

- Students in rural areas, as well as others who, for various reasons, cannot travel to urban campuses or who cannot leave their jobs, will have access to courses and programs that were previously unavailable to them.
- The increased competition for students will cause schools to examine outdated policies that have gone unquestioned for years.
- Course proliferation has unnecessarily extended some secondary, college, and university programs, and the belt-tightening that will go with increased competition for student dollars may result in much-needed streamlining of such programs.
- The cost of secondary and college programs may go down, particularly for those who do not live near large urban areas.
- Property taxes and other taxes currently used to support traditional education may decrease (or, at least fail to increase rapidly) as the private sector acquires more and more of the educational market share.
- Traditional programs may be made more convenient and more accessible as online technology is used to supplement traditional courses and programs.

- Distance education will further the goal of lifelong learning as it makes courses and programs available to elderly students and others who are unable or unwilling to leave their homes to travel to traditional campuses.

THE FUTURE ROLE OF HARDWARE

One of the most difficult areas in which to make informed predictions is the future role of hardware. However, we will venture at least a few modest predictions. First, we suggest that in the future, technological advances, especially the continuing evolution of the Internet and the Web, will continue to break down **platform barriers.** (These are the barriers caused by the use of differing standards in hardware and software and are best exemplified in recent years by lack of compatibility between computers using the Apple operating system and those running the Microsoft family of Windows operating systems.) Because of the Internet and the Web, where the type of platform does not matter (the type of platform is transparent) and because of computer programs to translate offline applications from one operating system to another, this problem is much less acute now than it was only a few years ago and will likely disappear completely in the near future.

Second, it appears certain that computers will continue to become more powerful, smaller, and less expensive. There is obviously a limit to all three of these trends. Only so much circuitry can be crammed into a small space, and computers will probably never be cost free. Nevertheless, we believe the near future will continue the trend toward more power in computers that are smaller and less expensive.

A third trend is that some form of inexpensive, very fast, **wireless Internet access** will probably become available to schools. This development, if it takes place, will have the effect of greatly increasing the number of classrooms with Internet access and the number of computers with such access in each of those classrooms. To date, wiring problems in aging schools have been a significant barrier to Internet access. Although fast, wireless Internet connections will not solve the problem of inadequate electrical wiring, it will certainly eliminate the problems involved in running coaxial cable, fiber-optic cable, or telephone lines to classrooms.

THE FUTURE ROLE OF INFORMATION TECHNOLOGY PRESERVICE AND IN-SERVICE EDUCATION

Every indication is that there will be an increasing role for preservice and in-service education in information technology in education. These programs will need to have two main thrusts—one to teach the operation of the hardware and software, the other to address **pedagogical issues** (how technology can assist in the teaching and learning of specific subject matter).

There was a time in the early 1980s when many experts believed that personal computers would someday be like electric motors. That is, we are surrounded by electric motors in our washing machines, refrigerators, and many other common devices, yet we can use these labor-saving machines without understanding anything about how electric motors work, or even how to operate them beyond simple operation of on/off switches. However, it is clear that this is another prediction that is unlikely to be true in the foreseeable future. The difference is that electric motors, as marvelous and useful as they are, are really not analogous to personal computers.

Most electric motors in common devices such as pencil sharpeners, washing machines, or refrigerators perform one limited and narrow motor act—usually rotary movement. Furthermore, they are components of **dedicated devices**—that is, the device does only one specific task such as wash clothes, sharpen pencils, or compress a refrigerant gas. Personal computers, on the other hand, are versatile tools that assist in both motor and cognitive tasks that vary from publishing a newsletter, to balancing an accounting spreadsheet, to serving as an electronic filing system, to providing a means to search and view any of the nearly one billion pages on the World Wide Web.

Some computers are analogous to electric motors, but these are comparatively simple, embedded computer chips such as the ones in watches or microwave ovens. Like users of washing machines who need know nothing about electric motors, users of watches and microwave ovens need know nothing about computing to use these devices to tell time or heat a meal.

However, the same cannot be said of personal computers, because their uses are far more diverse and far more complex than are those of electric motors. Those who predicted that personal computers would be like electric motors envisioned a day when computers would program and operate themselves. Such a scenario is not unimaginable. However, such futurists neglected to consider that the labor-saving devices employing electric motors are useful because they are designed to operate without the need for human input after they are switched on. Personal computers, on the other hand, are designed to interact continuously with human users and to assist us in complex cognitive, rather than simple motor, behavior.

The futurists believed computers would become increasingly easier to operate, until there would be no need for any kind of human intervention. They were right with regard to computer chips embedded in washing machines, microwave ovens, and other dedicated devices. However, it is interesting to consider whether personal computers are easier to operate today than they were in the 1980s. We believe the opposite is true. If anything, personal computers are today more difficult to operate than they were at the beginning of the small-computer revolution because as hardware improves, users demand that computers assist us with human cognitive acts that are more and more diverse and complex. Thus, hardware and software continually become more complex and, because computers can assist in so many more complex activities, users need to learn much more in order to use them effectively. This trend is likely to continue and will ensure that computer users of the future will need more, not less, expertise to use the more complex and useful hardware and software that will continue to become available.

THE FUTURE ROLE OF INFORMATION TECHNOLOGY SPECIALISTS IN SCHOOLS

We suspect that there will be great increases in the number of information technology specialists who are employed in public schools. These specialists will need to have both purely technological expertise to assist in the acquisition and maintenance of hardware and software and expertise in the use of information technology as a tool for teaching and learning. Such specialists will also need to be comfortable conducting in-service workshops for teachers and other employees.

We expect there will be a need for two different types of specialists. One type will consist of those whose expertise is purely technical. These specialists will be in charge of local- and wide-area school networks and will deal with hardware and software issues such as maintenance and repair of hardware and configuration of software. The other type will consist of those whose expertise is in the educational uses of information technology. As schools acquire much more equipment, and as that equipment becomes more complex, the former type of specialist will be forced to spend a growing amount of time on hardware and software problems that are purely technical in nature. The latter type of educational specialist will be needed to locate useful educational websites, prepare hardware and software documentation for teachers and students, and conduct in-service workshops on the use of information technology in education.

THE FUTURE ROLE OF TECHNOLOGY FOR PEOPLE WITH DISABILITIES

We think this area of technology will continue to develop in positive directions. More and better **assistive devices** will be available to help people with disabilities. However, a problem that will continue to provide barriers in this area is cost. Assistive devices tend to be expensive, and the cost comes down very little over time because not enough demand permits mass production or stimulates competition.

A related problem is determining who should pay for these devices. Many people with disabilities do not have the financial resources to make such purchases on their own, and there is as yet no clear consensus about who should provide funding for assistive devices. Nevertheless, we believe that in the future, more people with disabilities will acquire this technology, which will continue to improve markedly.

A FINAL WORD ABOUT THE FUTURE

Although educators will certainly face a number of problems in the future, we are generally optimistic about the role that information technology will play in tomorrow's schools. The authors of this textbook hope they have played a small part in helping to determine how technology was used in education in the past.

However, as readers of this book move into leadership positions in education, they will be the ones who determine the future role of information technology in education. That is a weighty but exciting responsibility.

Eric Hoffer once said, "In a time of drastic change it is the learners who inherit the future. The learned usually find themselves equipped to live in a world that no longer exists." We are confident that tomorrow's educators and tomorrow's information technology will help equip us for tomorrow's world.

SUMMARY

In a time of rapid technological change, predicting the future is difficult. In the past, most futurists were far too conservative in their predictions. For example, no one predicted that the Internet and the World Wide Web would become as important as they are today.

This trend will likely continue, and teachers in the future will probably make increasing use of the Internet and the Web, which will continue to increase in size and importance. The increasingly more sophisticated multimedia content on the Internet will make more and better simulations available there.

Distance education will likely continue to grow. More and more postsecondary institutions will offer courses and programs online, and this trend is likely to extend downward into secondary schools, and perhaps even to elementary schools. There will probably be both advantages and disadvantages with this trend. Courses and programs will be more accessible and less expensive for students, but increased online competition may erode resources and have a negative effect on quality in traditional programs. Increased commercialization will take place on traditional higher-education campuses, and programs may be forced to become shorter, easier, and more entertaining.

Hardware will continue to become cheaper, more powerful, and smaller. The platform barrier will lessen and may disappear completely as the Internet and the Web become more important. Inexpensive, fast wireless Internet connections will become common and will speed the movement of computers with Internet capability into classrooms.

Preservice and in-service education in information technology will continue to increase in importance. Such programs may have two different emphases—one that focuses on purely technical problems and solutions, another that focuses on pedagogical (teaching) issues.

Schools of the future will probably employ increasing numbers of technology specialists. Some of these will devote their time to purely technical problems whereas others will need to focus on pedagogical issues and the conducting of in-service educational programs for teachers and others.

Assistive devices for people with disabilities will continue to evolve and will become better and more common. They will probably remain relatively expensive, however, and a problem that will need to be resolved is how to pay for these devices so that they can be placed in the hands of those who need them.

QUESTIONS TO CONSIDER

1. Do you think the growth of the Internet and the Web could have any future impact on relations among nations of the world? Do you think that impact is likely to be positive or negative?
2. If traditional brick-and-mortar schools at the secondary and postsecondary levels were to disappear in the future and all courses and programs were online, what would be the advantages and disadvantages to students, parents, teachers, and society at large?
3. What college and secondary courses or programs do you think are most and least suitable for online delivery?
4. Of the two types of technology specialists identified in the chapter, which would you prefer to be?

RELATED ACTIVITIES

1. Go to a popular search engine on the Web, such as AltaVista (http://www.altavista.com/), and search for *emerging technologies*. Visit some of these sites and make a list of some of the technology described that you think has promise for use in education.
2. Interview a college professor about his or her attitude toward a future in which distance education plays an increasingly important role.
3. Interview someone in your local school district who has administrative authority related to information technology as an instructional tool. Find out what the district is doing currently at the district level and what is planned for the future. Also, find out what has been done about in-service education in information technology.

REFERENCES

Carlson, R. (2000). Assessing your students: Testing in the online course. *Syllabus, 13*(7), 16–18.

Lawrence, S., & Giles, L. (1999). Accessibility and distribution of information on the web. *Nature, 400,* 107–109.

Lewis L., Farris, E., Snow, K., & Levin, D. (2000). *Distance education at postsecondary education institutions: 1997–98.* Washington, DC: National Center for Education Statistics.

The Madison Avenue Group. (2000). *The CommerceNet/ Nielsen Internet Demographics Survey: Executive summary.* Retrieved March 21, 2000, from the World Wide Web: http://www.madisononline.com/resources/internet.html

Matthews, A. (1997). *Bright college years.* New York: Simon and Schuster.

INDEX